Teaching in American Schools

Robert J. Stevens, Editor

Pennsylvania State University

Merrill
an imprint of Prentice Hall
Upper Saddle River, New Jersey   *Columbus, Ohio*

Library of Congress Cataloging-in-Publication Data
Teaching in American Schools / [edited by] Robert J. Stevens.
　　　p. cm.
　　ISBN 0-13-234071-2
　　1. Teaching—United States.　I. Stevens, Robert J.
　LB1025.3.T33　1999
　371.102'0973—dc21　　　　　　　　　　　　　　98-30978
　　　　　　　　　　　　　　　　　　　　　　　　　　CIP

Cover art: © Stephen R. Schildbach
Editor: Kevin M. Davis
Production Editor: Julie Peters
Design Coordinator: Diane C. Lorenzo
Text Designer: STELLARViSIONs
Cover Designer: Susan Unger
Production Manager: Laura Messerly
Electronic Text Management: Marilyn Wilson Phelps, Karen L. Bretz, Tracey B. Ward
Director of Marketing: Kevin Flanagan
Marketing Manager: Suzanne Stanton
Advertising/Marketing Coordinator: Krista Groshong

This book was set in ITC Century by Prentice Hall, Inc. and was printed and bound by R.R. Donnelley & Sons Company. The cover was printed by Phoenix Color Corp.

 ©1999 by Prentice-Hall, Inc.
Simon & Schuster/A Viacom Company
Upper Saddle River, New Jersey 07458

Printed in the United States of America

10 9 8 7 6 5 4 3 2 1

ISBN: 0-13-234071-2

Prentice-Hall International (UK) Limited, *London*
Prentice-Hall of Australia Pty. Limited, *Sydney*
Prentice-Hall of Canada, Inc., *Toronto*
Prentice-Hall Hispanoamericana, S. A., *Mexico*
Prentice-Hall of India Private Limited, *New Dehli*
Prentice-Hall of Japan, Inc., *Tokyo*
Simon & Schuster Asia Pte. Ltd., *Singapore*
Editora Prentice-Hall do Brasil, Ltda., *Rio de Janeiro*

Preface

Our goals in putting together this volume are twofold: to honor the career of Barak Rosenshine and to provide an advanced look at the psychology of classroom instruction and research on it. The book is focused toward graduate students and faculty in education. The book has two main themes, the overall process of teaching in schools and effective teaching in specific content areas. The chapters create a discussion of current issues in classroom instruction and the related research.

In the first section of the book, "Teaching in American Schools," the chapters discuss systemic issues that cross domains of teaching, learning to be a teacher, accommodating diversity and at-risk students, and peer collaboration and peer relations. Each chapter presents topics of general concern to all educators and, specifically, to teachers. Chapter 1, written by Jane Stallings, provides an interesting, personalized view of the changing forces in our society and the impact they have on teacher preparation programs as they attempt to prepare students to work in one of our society's most important institutions. This is followed by a chapter by Carolyn Evertson and Margaret Smithey discussing early teacher experiences working in educational institutions and how we can better prepare teachers through mentoring. The authors emphasize the need for new teachers to apprentice in their early years under the guidance of master teachers who can help them negotiate the pitfalls of being a novice teacher. In Chapter 3, David Berliner offers an impassioned call to bring new teachers' attention to the role of the educational system as an institution to promote social justice. He promotes the goal of education to serve diverse populations and help all students achieve the opportunities an education provides. N.L. Gage's Chapter 4 takes an overarching look at the research on the teaching paradigm that has provided much of the knowledge about effective teaching presented here.

Chapters 5 and 6 look at issues related to educating students at risk of educational failure in our increasingly diverse society. Russell Gersten, Robert Taylor, and Anne Graves look at effective instruction for language minority children based on their research and that of others working in urban schools. This is complemented nicely by Robert Slavin's chapter that looks at early childhood education as a way to potentially prevent failure and promote success for minority and diverse students who come from disadvantaged environments.

Chapters 7 and 8 take two different looks at peer relationships in the school setting. Chapter 7 by Allison King discusses peer-mediated learning and how students working in small groups can become a valuable instructional resource in the classroom. She describes the research on the effectiveness of peer collaboration and constructs related to effective use of small-group instruction. Wendy Troop and Steven Asher in Chapter 8 look at how students develop positive peer relations in schools, a social outcome of peer interaction. They describe the importance of social outcomes of schooling and how teachers can promote positive peer relations and the development of friends in school, and how that in turn will promote student success.

The second section, "Teaching in Content Areas," is a look at research on teaching in specific subject areas. Chapters 9, 10, and 11 provide different views of effective reading and literacy instruction. In Chapter 9, Bonnie Armbruster and Jean Osborn weave together thirty years of research in reading to provide a rich theoretical view with solid grounding in instructional practice. Chapter 10, by Charles Fisher and Elfrieda Hebert, follows with a microanalysis of classroom literacy tasks and the kinds of learning that result. Chapter 11, by Robert Stevens, Lynne Hammann, and Timothy Balliett, looks at integrated reading and writing literacy instruction in middle schools and how middle school instruction can be restructured to promote student learning and motivation.

In Chapter 12, Marcy Stein and Doug Carnine review three decades of research in effective mathematics instruction. The chapter provides detailed instructional theory with specific classroom instruction examples to portray how effective instruction occurs in mathematics. Chapter 13, by Jere Brophy and Janet Alleman, provides a fresh look at instruction in social studies and how we can restructure social studies curricula in ways that approach history more conceptually rather than just linearly or chronologically.

I would like to acknowledge the following reviewers of the manuscript for this book for their helpful comments: Margaret Anderson, SUNY, Cortland; David Bergin, University of Toledo; Robert L. Hohne, University of Kansas; Victoria Manion, Miami University; and Michael Meloth, University of Colorado.

Our hope in compiling this collection of readings is to provide the readers with a broad look at the field of instruction and learning to teach. The authors provide wide expertise applied to educational issues of our time in an attempt to stimulate thought about what role education serves and how we can best prepare our children as we teach in American schools.

Robert J. Stevens

Dedication

In Honor of Barak Rosenshine: His Career, His Insight, His Passion

We, the authors of the chapters in this book, wish to honor the career of our dear friend and colleague, Barak Rosenshine. His work in the field of effective instruction has been profound and has left a mark on education and, specifically, on our work. Barak has served a unique role in educational research—not that of theoretician or critic, nor that of researcher or innovator. Barak's impact was as a synthesizer of the wealth of research and innovation that has occurred in the past three decades in instructional research. In short, he made sense of what was going on in this field. And we are all thankful to him for that, for it was a complex task that our field often desperately needed. Through his life and work, Barak has affected each of us in ways too numerous to mention.

After graduating from the University of Chicago with a bachelor's degree in history, Barak started his career in education in the army, as a troop information and education specialist stationed in Heidelberg, Germany, where he assisted in GED programs.

Following his return from the army, Barak took a position teaching social studies at Hyde Park High School near the University of Chicago. He taught students of all ability levels, teaching reading to remedial students and U.S. history to students at upper levels. Perhaps it was then that Barak first became interested in effective instruction as he implemented some of the inquiry methods he had learned in his advanced classes at the university. Yet he grew restless after six years, and began to look for other challenges and a different climate.

For graduate school, Barak looked to California, hoping to be accepted at Berkeley and eventually secure a college teaching position in northern California. Berkeley was not impressed by Barak's undergraduate grades, but he got an interview at Stanford and was later accepted. At Stanford, Barak was initially influenced by Fred MacDonald and his classroom research. During his early semesters at Stanford, two important things happened that greatly affected Barak's career. First, in the bookstore, he found the *Handbook of Research on Teaching*, edited by N. L. Gage. Second, he became active as a supervisor of teaching interns in the Stanford Teacher Education Program.

As Barak tells it, he "fell in love" with the *Handbook* and often spent late-night hours reading the chapters. At the time, he had no idea N. L. Gage was at Stanford, but he soon was reading everything he could find that Gage wrote. And Gage, too, had his eye on Barak, listening and watching him in the discussions that were part of the Teacher Education Program. Later, when Stanford's education research center was funded, Nate Gage hired Barak as his research assistant. That relationship galvanized Barak's development and career. The mentoring of a graduate student by an adviser lasts a lifetime, as I know well, and such is the relationship between Barak Rosenshine and Nate Gage. The impact of one on the other has been varied and deep, as you can see in Gage's chapter in this book. The mentoring continues as Nate still gives Barak feedback and corrects his spelling.

While at Stanford, Barak took on a project that began his career as a synthesizer of classroom research. Under the direction of Nate Gage, Barak began pulling all the process-product research together into what became a monograph, entitled *Teaching Behaviors and Student Achievement*, which was eventually published in 1971. This became the first comprehensive review of teacher effectiveness research.

Just as Barak was greatly influenced by the faculty at Stanford, so, too, was he influenced by his relationships with his fellow classmates, such as David Berliner, Tom Romberg, and Jim Guthrie. Perhaps his closest friend, and a frequent coauthor, was David Berliner. Together, in the 1980s, Rosenshine and Berliner helped turn education's attention to engaged learning as critical for student achievement. And although they worked separately, they worked together to promote effective instruction.

Upon graduating from Stanford in 1966, Barak accepted a position at Temple University in Philadelphia, and another pair of fortunate experiences happened. While driving across the country, Barak picked up a hitchhiker who had an undergraduate degree in engineering, but perhaps not the passion to pursue the career. As the two traveled, the hitchhiker became fascinated by Barak's passionate descriptions of his work and his interest in effective instruction. Somewhere along that journey, Charles Fisher became hooked, "swept up in Barak's passion." Charlie later attended graduate school at the Ontario Institute for Studies in Education at the University of Toronto.

At Temple, Barak quickly developed a professional bond and deep friendship with Norma Furst, who also taught there. The two collaborated on a number of chapters and journal articles related to effective teaching. It was also at this time that Barak wrote a chapter on observation in the study of teaching in the *Handbook of Research on Teaching,* second edition (1973), edited by Robert Travers. In his own words, he was "thrilled" to be part of the next edition of the project that had so profoundly affected him years before. The chapter was based in part on the synthesis of process-product research he had started while at Stanford.

The chapter in the *Handbook* gave him notoriety in the field, and opportunity soon came to Barak. In the fall of 1970, Barak was offered a position in the Bureau of Educational Research at the University of Illinois. This was a prestigious offer, for the bureau had at one point been home to Lee Cronbach, David Ausubel, and Nate Gage, among others. It gave him the opportunity to be a full-time researcher with a graduate assistant.

At about this time, Jane Stallings was working on a large study of instructional interventions implemented in elementary classrooms across the country, the Planned Variation Follow Through study. The study was huge in the number of sites used, the number of classrooms involved, and the quantity of observational data collected. As Jane struggled to make sense of it, someone suggested she talk to Barak and get his input. They did talk—and began a fertile and long-lasting friend-

Barak Rosenshine

Education

B.A.   University of Chicago
M.A.   University of Chicago
Ph.D. Stanford University

Professional Experiences

1993 – present   Professor Emeritus of Educational Psychology, University of Illinois
1973 – 1993   Professor of Educational Psychology, University of Illinois
1970 – 1973   Associate Professor of Educational Psychology, University of Illinois
1966 – 1970   Assistant Professor of Educational Psychology, Temple University
1963 – 1966   Research Assistant, Stanford Center for Research and Development in Education, and the Stanford Teacher Education Program, Stanford University
1957 – 1963   High School Social Studies Teacher, Chicago Public Schools, Chicago, IL
1955 – 1957   Education and Information Specialist, U.S. Army

Awards

1992   Senior Scholar, University of Illinois
1984   Interpretive Scholarship Award, American Educational Research Association

Selected Publications

Berliner, D. & Rosenshine, B. (1987). *Talks with teachers: Essays in honor of N.L. Gage.* New York: Random House.

Rosenshine, B. & Meister, C. (1997). Cognitive strategy research in reading. In S. Stahl & D. Hayes (Eds.), *Instructional models in reading* (pp. 85–107). Mahwah, NJ: Lawrence Erlbaum Associates.

Rosenshine, B. (1997). Advances in research on instruction. In J. Lloyd, E. Kameenui, & D. Chard, *Issues in educating students with disabilities* (pp. 197–221). Mahwah, NJ: Lawrence Erlbaum Associates.

Rosenshine, B., Meister, C., & Chapman, S. (1996). Teaching students to generate questions: A review of the intervention studies. *Review of Educational Research, 66,* 181–221.

Rosenshine, B. & Meister, C. (1995). Scaffolds for teaching higher-order cognitive strategies. In A. Ornstein (Ed.), *Teaching: Theory into practice.* Boston: Allyn & Bacon.

Rosenshine, B. & Meister, C. (1994). Reciprocal teaching: A review of the research. *Review of Educational Research, 64,* 479–530.

Rosenshine, B. & Stevens, R. (1986). Teaching functions. In M.C. Wittrock (Ed.), *Handbook of research on teaching* (3rd ed.) (pp. 376–391). New York: Macmillan.

Rosenshine, B. & Stevens, R. (1984). Classroom instruction in reading. In P. D. Pearson (Ed.), *Handbook of reading research* (pp. 745–798). New York: Longman.

Rosenshine, B. (1983). Teaching functions in instructional programs. *Elementary School Journal, 83,* 335–351.

Stevens, R. & Rosenshine, B. (1981). Advances in research on teaching. *Exceptional Education Quarterly, 2,* 1–9.

Rosenshine, B. (1980). How time is spent in elementary classrooms. In C. Denham & A. Lieberman (Eds.), *Time to learn.* Washington, DC: National Institute of Education.

Rosenshine, B. (1980). Skill hierarchies in reading comprehension. In R. Spiro, B. Bruce, & W. Brewer (Eds.), *Theoretical issues in reading comprehension* (pp. 535–554). Hillsdale, NJ: Lawrence Erlbaum Associates.

Rosenshine, B. (1979). Content, time, and direct instruction. In P. Peterson & H. Walberg (Eds.), *Research on teaching.* Berkeley, CA: McCutchen Publishing.

Rosenshine, B. & Berliner, D. (1978). Academic engaged time. *British Journal of Teacher Education, 4,* 3–16.

Rosenshine, B. (1976). Classroom instruction. In N.L. Gage (Ed.), *The psychology of teaching methods: Seventy-fifth yearbook of the national society for the study of education* (pp. 335–371). Chicago, IL: University of Chicago Press.

Rosenshine, B. (1973). The use of direct observation to study teaching. In R. Travers (Ed.), *Handbook of research on teaching* (2nd ed.) (pp. 122–183). New York: Rand McNally.

Rosenshine, B. (1973). Teacher behavior and student attitudes revisited. *Journal of Educational Psychology, 65,* 177–180.

Rosenshine, B. & Furst, N. (1971). Research on teacher performance criteria. In B.O. Smith (Ed.), *Research in teacher education: A symposium* (pp. 37–68). Upper Saddle River, NJ: Prentice Hall.

Rosenshine, B. (1970). Evaluation of classroom instruction. *Review of Educational Research, 40,* 279–301.

Rosenshine, B. (1970). Enthusiastic teaching: A research review. *The School Review, 78,* 499–514.

ship. Barak gave Jane some ideas about the rich data she had collected, and Barak and his graduate students spent years looking through the many tables of the report, which became a significant source in his later writing.

The University of Illinois was an excellent environment for Barak because it was in many ways the birthplace of direct instruction. The process-product research Barak was studying and the instructional curricula developed by Siegfried Engelmann (later with coauthor Doug Carnine) were a natural fit, and the ideas commingled. Barak continued his writing on teacher effectiveness, synthesizing the research of a field that was very active in the 1970s and 1980s. He wrote chapters for *The Psychology of Teaching Methods,* as well as numerous journal articles and reviews. During this time, in 1976, I met Barak and became his research assistant.

During the mid-1970s and early 1980s, Barak and I spent our time reviewing the research of the many classroom researchers around the country. The research included studies such as the Planned Variation Follow Through Study, comprehensive classroom experimental studies, smaller classroom observational studies, and program evaluations. The goal of our work was, in Barak's words, to "make sense" of this varied research, which used different designs, different terms, and different observational measures. The wealth of data was both a blessing and a curse as we looked for patterns of effective teaching behaviors within and across studies. In that time before desktop word processing, we typed teacher behaviors on strips of paper and spread them across the floor in Barak's living room. The piles were arranged and rearranged many times. We called researchers on the phone to ask very specific questions about how behavior was categorized in observation schemes or how it was operationalized in teacher's manuals for experimental conditions. Eventually, a pattern started to evolve, what we called direct instruction.

David Berliner was then serving on the editorial board for the *Handbook of Research on Teaching,* third edition (1986), edited by Merle Wittrock. David asked Barak to write a chapter on teaching functions—those necessary teacher behaviors that led to effective classroom instruction. And so began what became a chapter entitled simply "Teaching Functions," which Barak and I coauthored for that *Handbook.* We also wrote a related chapter on reading instruction titled

"Classroom Instruction in Reading" for the *Handbook of Reading Research* (1984). These two works were the culmination of our work synthesizing a rich decade's worth of research in teaching effectiveness and classroom instruction, and they solidified Barak's unique role in and contributions to educational research.

In the 1980s and 1990s, as the field moved forward into cognitive psychology and into research in teaching reading comprehension, so did Barak in his mission to "make sense" of classroom research. His path led to strategy instruction in reading and to determining what the many experimental studies that taught reading comprehension strategies meant for effective classroom instruction. Barak collaborated with Carla Meister on numerous chapters and articles on the use of cognitive scaffolds in the teaching of less structured skills in reading comprehension. The two also collaborated on a review of reciprocal teaching. In his syntheses and through others' research, Barak saw conceptualizations converge in a model of instruction that he called *scaffolded instruction,* in which the teacher guides students in learning skills to become better readers.

In 1993 Barak officially retired with the rank of Emeritus Professor of Educational Psychology, having spent more than 20 years at the University of Illinois. Effectively, all this meant was that he stopped his formal teaching and filling out all the reports and forms required of faculty. He has continued his writing and his synthesis of research in scaffolded instruction and effective instruction. Currently, he is attempting to identify schools having at-risk students who read at or above grade level. Once the effective schools are identified, he studies their instructional characteristics in an attempt to identify commonalities that may promote student achievement.

Through the evolution of his work, Barak has seen effective classroom instruction as partly teacher-directed and partly teacher-guided, and always teacher-structured. In many ways Barak's career is dedicated to teachers and to their students, so we dedicate our work to the man who helped each of us in important yet different ways. He has been a colleague, a critic, and a friend who shared with each of us a passion for trying to make schools better.

Robert J. Stevens

Brief Contents

Contents

5 Direct Instruction and Diversity 81

Russell Gersten, Eugene Research Institute/University of Oregon
Robert Taylor, Memphis City Schools
Anne Graves, San Diego State University

6 Educating Young Students at Risk of School Failure: Research, Practice, and Policy 103

Robert E. Slavin, Center for Research on the Education
    of Students Placed at Risk, Johns Hopkins University

7 Teaching Effective Discourse Patterns for Small-Group Learning   121

Alison King, California State University, San Marcos

8   Teaching Peer Relationship Competence in Schools   141

Wendy Troop and Steven Asher, University of Illinois at Urbana-Champaign

9   Reading Instruction in American Classrooms: Practice and Research   173

Bonnie Armbruster and Jean Osborn, University of Illinois at Urbana-Champaign

10 The Architecture of Literacy Activities: Patterns in Classrooms and Potentials for Learning   195

Charles Fisher and Elfrieda H. Hiebert, University of Michigan

11 Middle School Literacy Instruction   221

Robert J. Stevens, Lyyne A. Hammann, and Timothy R. Balliett, Pennsylvania State University

12   Designing and Delivering Effective Mathematics Instruction   245

Marcy Stein, University of Washington, Tacoma
Douglas Carnine, University of Oregon

13 Teaching Social Studies for Understanding, Appreciation, and Life Application   271

Jere Brophy and Janet Alleman, **Michigan State University**

Preparing Teachers to Serve a Diverse and Changing Society

Jane Stallings

Texas A & M University

T his chapter is organized by decade to examine social/political trends and teacher preparation from 1950 to the present.

The 1950s

I was trained as a teacher in Muncie, Indiana, in the early 1950s, soon after the Second World War. It was a time when families and communities were coming back together to build a new society. Undergirding teacher preparation was the philosophy and practice of John Dewey (1933): "We should use that method of experimental action called natural science to a disposition which puts a supreme faith in the experimental use of intelligence in all situations of life" (p. 46). Teaching was to take an integrative approach that allowed children to learn by engaging in meaningful activities in the classroom. We were trained to use science and social studies units as the center for reading, language arts, music, art, mathematics, history, geography, and games. Because we were serving the baby boomers, classes were very large. We were trained to organize and manage work with children in small groups. In the absence of research, reasoned pedagogy guided teacher preparation programs. During this decade, the National Council for Accreditation of Teacher Education (NCATE) was formed (1954). Then, as now, NCATE developed standards and criteria for accrediting colleges of education across the nation. Initially the standards did not address issues of diversity in the accreditation process. (Today NCATE criteria requiring multicultural programs and faculty are of primary importance.)

My first class in Long Beach, California, included 45 fourth graders, 7 of whom had been born in Japanese internment camps. There was 1 Caucasian boy, and the rest of the children were African-American. The families lived in army barracks converted to public housing. The area was hemmed in by railroad tracks and warehouses. There were very few streets leading into the area, and many of the children had never been beyond the area's borders of railroad tracks and freeway structures. One Sunday afternoon, I took my children for their first glimpse of the great long beach for which their city was named. Some of the sunbathers looked askance at my children of color.

To meet the needs of the families and children, our principal spent her days helping the many new teachers on her staff make home visits and learn the culture of the community. I was allowed to develop my social science unit around Japan rather than China, since our class included Japanese-American students. It didn't occur to us that 45 was too many children; it simply was the job to be done. Cooperative small-group learning was the mode for organizing classrooms long before the very useful cooperative-learning research and writings of Robert Slavin (1983) and the Johnson brothers, Roger and David (1987). Learning for all of us was interdependent.

The educational diet was not meager. The children wrote publishable poems, learned of perspective from the telephone lines crossing their playground, and probed the mysteries of bulbs, batteries, bells, and wires. When I got married, I invited all the children to the wedding, and many came to the ceremony, asking the usher for their Miss Smith. They came into the dressing room to see the veil being placed on my head. It was a time in society when we could easily experience love, and not fear, with each other.

The 1960s

The advent of Russia's *Sputnik* in 1958 had an impact on the science and mathematics curriculum for schoolchildren and on the preparation of teachers in these fields throughout the 1960s. The federal government funded curriculum development programs that promised to improve our science education, with the expectation of returning us to international leadership in scientific discovery. Several well-funded programs focused on elementary curricula. They ranged from Robert Gagné's (1965) highly structured Science: A Process Approach program, based on the hierarchy of learning tasks, to David Hawkins's (1965) loosely structured Elementary Science Study (ESS). The ESS program required an abundance of activities within each unit and variation of those activities to allow for the differences in children's interests and backgrounds. It was important for children to work on their own, messing about in science to discover relationships. Computer Assisted Instruction (CAI) was initiated in the elementary school mathematics program.

Suppes (1966) defined three levels of CAI: dialogue, tutoring, and drill and practice. These programs did influence the science and mathematics preparation of teachers, to an extent that depended on the existing philosophical approach of their college of education.

A further effort to improve teacher preparation in the 1960s came from the Ford Foundation through its funding of a massive experiment in 43 colleges, known as Break Through Programs in teacher education. To qualify, programs had to include the following components:

First, they had to be designed to prepare teachers, not for the self-contained classrooms of the past, but for the classrooms in which teachers were most likely to be teaching from 1963 or 1964 to the year 2000, with ungraded classes, teaching machines, educational television, and team teaching, with its flexible use of time, space, and personnel.

Second, they were to be planned jointly by university departments of education, representatives of academic departments in the university, and public school teachers and administrators.

Third, they were expected to incorporate changes in the elementary and secondary schools as well as in the colleges.

Fourth, a considerable amount of the responsibility for teacher recruitment, teacher education, and the introduction of the teacher to the profession was to be accepted by the public school itself.

Fifth, they were to represent an effort (1) to place teacher education in the mainstream of higher education by bringing academic professors and professors of education together for joint planning and (2) to create a better articulation for the curricula for elementary, secondary, and higher education through the cooperation of college faculty members with teachers and administrators from the public schools (Stone, 1968, p. 16). (*Note:* These were forerunners of the university and school collaboratives known as professional development schools [PDS] in the late 1980s and 1990s.)

The Break Through Programs took many forms. Some were like the one at Michigan State University, where interns who had earned 75 percent or more of the course credit for a baccalaureate degree could apply for internships in teaching. They were then hired by school districts for 75 percent of a beginning teacher's salary. Interns took coursework in pedagogy and taught under the guidance of veteran teachers functioning as intern consultants. To ensure that the interns received the necessary mentoring, the consulting teachers were released from other responsibilities and received the other 25 percent of the interns' beginning salaries. J. Stone's book *Breakthrough in Teacher Education* (1968) reported the models in detail and assessed the effectiveness of the internship programs. Stone's concluding statements would be appropriate for the 1990s:

> Shall we continue to attempt to change the present agencies or create new ones? Which strategy will more likely lead to genuine reform in the education of America's teachers? We are shadow-boxing with the real problem unless we are willing to develop new structures for bringing together the groups necessary for the education of our

teachers—the schools, the colleges, and the communities in which the schools are located. Both the quality of American education and its quantity are involved in any decision we make at this time. At stake is the development of America's greatest natural resource, our children and youth. (p. 190)

By the mid-1960s, when I entered graduate school, the country was trying to respond to the challenges of the Civil Rights movement and the anger generated by the war in Vietnam. Trust among people was at a low ebb. It had become clear that public education was failing to improve the chances of a better life for economically disadvantaged children. Desegregation, though the law of the land, proceeded at a snail's pace. Very few teacher education programs, outside of the historically black colleges, were preparing teachers to serve a diverse population. Unfortunately, the Civil Rights movement had little immediate impact on the preparation of teachers.

In an effort to change this bleak picture, the federal government initiated several massive intervention programs: Head Start for preschoolers and entitlement programs for low-income, bilingual, and special-needs children. These programs were funded through school districts, churches, day care centers, and research laboratories. Few were associated with colleges of education. However, it became an exciting time for education researchers. Not only did Congress fund the large-scale intervention programs, it also funded national evaluations to examine the effectiveness of the programs, offering opportunities to explore hunches, test hypotheses, and muck around in mountains of data.

The 1970s

The first national evaluation I was involved in required me to develop an observation instrument for evaluating Planned Variation Head Start and Follow-Through. The government funded 22 educational models, all claiming they would improve the life chances of economically deprived children. Interestingly, most of these models were developed, not by colleges of education, but by research and development labs or school systems. The models ranged from highly structured models, such as the University of Kansas token-economy behavior analysis and the University of Oregon's direct instruction, through High Scope's Piagetian-based program, to the open-education smorgasbord approach of Education Development Corporation. Curiously, although some of the Planned Variation Follow-Through sponsors were located on university campuses in laboratories, none came from or were related to the preparation of educators within colleges of education.

The Planned Variation Follow-Through programs had to develop their curriculum materials, instructional strategies, interaction patterns, classroom environments, parent action committees, and a delivery system. Of critical importance was the development of training procedures to ensure that the classroom teachers and classroom aides would reliably implement the models in diverse urban and rural settings. To accomplish this training, sponsors of models often provided their trainers with living quarters at the sites. They worked daily in the classrooms to provide the teachers and aides with an accurate model and corrective feedback while the lessons were being delivered. The progress of the children toward the goals of the model was carefully monitored.

The task of the Stanford Research Institute (SRI) team of which I was a member was to develop a valid and reliable observation system (see Stallings and Gieson, 1977) that could measure whether models were being implemented as specified at multiple sites. Were the teachers and aides doing what they were supposed to do? At the end of our three-year evaluation, there was ample evidence (through discriminant function analysis) that the programs we studied in depth (at five sites each) were successful in training teachers and aides to consistently deliver the essential components of their models. That is, the teachers and aides within a model provided materials, activities, and interactions similar to each other and different from comparison classes and other models (Stallings, 1975, p. 33).

Certainly, finding that the models were being reliably replicated was good news. That is the question we were hired to answer. But, as a researcher, I was interested in possible relationships between instructional strategies and the growth and development of children. Now for the mucking around. What would you do if you had pre- and postinstruction achievement scores, scores from Raven's Colored Progressive Matrices and the Intellectual Responsibility Scale, and absence rates for a national sample of more than 108 first-grade and 50 third-grade classrooms? And what if you had the percentages of occurrence of 48 observation variables for each classroom? Our research team chose to include all of the treatment and classroom comparison data and hold pretest scores constant. We then did a stepwise regression to learn if there were significant relationships between classroom observation variables and student outcomes. Observation variables associated with direct instruction and time spent on academic subjects were found to explain 50–80 percent of test score variance in reading and mathematics achievement for first- and third-grade classrooms.

Raven's Colored Progressive Matrices (Raven, 1965) is a nonverbal problem-solving test thought to be culture-free (i.e., free from influences in the environment). To our surprise, 40 percent of the score variance for Raven's test was explained by the classroom process observation variables associated with whole-child models (e.g., teachers and students asked thought-provoking questions, students used manipulative materials, students engaged in a wide range of activities). Our evidence indicated that Raven's scores were related to what occurred in the classrooms.

The SRI findings indicated that teachers across the nation could be taught to deliver a specific educational model. The analysis relating classroom processes and student outcomes contributed significantly to the understanding of the importance of *what* and *how* teachers teach. The educational diet teachers provided in classrooms contributed fundamentally to what children learned in those classrooms. The result was counter to the reports of Coleman, Campbell, Hobson, McPartland, Mood, Weinfeld, and York (1966) and Jencks (1972), which declared that the compensatory education programs being funded by the federal government were making no difference in the achievement of students in schools. One difference was that the SRI study of classroom processes and student outcomes used classrooms as the unit of analysis, while the Coleman study, based on mailed written surveys, used schools as the unit of analysis. This is an important distinction because within schools there are both effective and ineffective teachers and we know that effective teachers can have a great positive impact. However, the relative effects of good and poor teachers on students' educational achievement and attainment are canceled out when you look only at the school level.

The news regarding the positive relationships between direct instruction and achievement scores was quickly embraced by school systems and state departments of education. Massive in-service training programs were developed to help teachers learn to use the direct-instruction methods. Yet the transformation of college-of-education teacher preparation programs lagged behind the in-service programs being offered by state and local agencies. Few colleges of education noticed or cared that the nonverbal problem-solving skills measured by Raven's Colored Progressive Matrices were positively related to a very different set of instructional processes. It took a decade to understand that drill and practice for short-term memory and right answers did not ensure that students would be able to use the acquired facts to solve problems.

Throughout the 1970s, many educational researchers studied relationships between teaching and learning, arriving at similar conclusions regarding the positive value of excellent classroom management and student time spent on academic tasks. A body of knowledge was developing, and many curricular interventions were adopted based on this process-product paradigm. (See Brophy & Good, 1986, pp. 328–375.)

Throughout the decade, competency-based teacher education programs dominated the field. As many as 50 discrete competencies were defined by colleges of education. Teacher candidates had to teach toward those objectives and demonstrate the competencies defined. By the end of the decade, many college-of-education programs were training new teachers to use direct-instruction methodology and programmed workbooks, and to individualize the pace of children's progress through the lessons.

The 1980s

By the mid-1980s, it became clear that these direct-instruction interventions were not delivering the promised academic achievement or that the achievement was not sustained. Harsh criticism of the public K–12 system and the colleges preparing teachers came from several assessments of our nation's education system commissioned by Congress and private foundations. Of these criticisms, the most dramatic was the opening statement from *A Nation at Risk,* by the National Commission on Excellence in Education (1983). It proclaimed, "If an unfriendly foreign power had attempted to impose on America the mediocre educational performance that exists today, we might well have viewed it as an act of war" (p. 5). In John Goodlad's book *A Place Called School* (1984), the first sentence reads, "American schools are in trouble." In *High School: A Report on Secondary Education in America,* Ernest

Boyer (1983) added his voice to the battle cry for educational change. The effect of these reports was to propel stakeholders in education to a frenzied examination of the goals and conditions of schools in their own locales. The subsequent education reform movement in the 1980s created state and local commissions of excellence that have recommended legislation and mandated change in school curricula, graduation standards, teacher certification, and teacher assessment.

After the first wave of responses to the challenge for excellence, a more in-depth analysis identified education goals that were much broader than gains in achievement test scores. The leaders of business and industry declared a need for employees who had basic skills but were flexible learners and could transfer knowledge from one task to another. They needed employees who were responsible, who had high work standards, and who had the social skills necessary for cooperative tasks. With rapidly exploding information and technology, workers are likely to change occupations three or four times during their lives. Given the expected changes, employees will need learning-to-learn skills. Such outcomes of schooling require a different structure and a different curriculum for schools and colleges of education. To develop the type of citizenry required for the 21st century, schools must be different, principals must be different, teachers must be different, and colleges of education must be different. From the time those demands were first put forward, colleges of education have been under siege.

Throughout the late 1980s and early 1990s, colleges of education (COE) were struggling with relevancy. Several COE were abolished, as at the University of Oregon and the University of Chicago, and several downsized, as at Virginia Polytechnic Institute. Many COE received crippling budget cuts. Universities and state departments of education were seriously challenging the efficacy of colleges of education. They were asking, "What is the purpose of colleges of education? Are they preparing students to serve a diverse population in a technologically driven society? Are the graduates prepared with up-to-date content-area knowledge sufficient to teach the children they will serve? To what extent do COE faculty contribute to the knowledge base of teaching and learning and to social problem solving?" Their accusation was that many COE continued to deliver the status quo, preparing students for the schools of 20 years ago.

This criticism must be taken seriously, given that the national and regional populations were (and still are) rapidly changing. As a result of the Vietnam War and rebellions in South American countries, new waves of immigrants were arriving from the Pacific rim and South America. The new immigrants brought their hopes and dreams, as had the European immigrants when they came to this promised land. To serve this population, professors and classroom teachers needed a broad multicultural knowledge base extending beyond the Eurocentrism of the textbooks then found in curricula and libraries. However, this across-the-curriculum multicultural knowledge base is still sorely lacking for professional educators at all levels. Selections from such books as Ronald Takaki's *A Different Mirror* (1939), Lisa Delpit's *Other People's Children* (1995), Gloria Ladson-Billings's *The Dreamkeepers* (1947), and G. Y. Okihiro's *Margins and Mainstreams: Asians in American History and Culture* (1994) should be required reading for the professorate preparing educators.

Three major reports drove the reconceptualization of teacher education toward models of professional school partnerships linking colleges of education and schools. They were the reports of the Carnegie Forum, the Holmes Group, and RAND.

The Carnegie Forum on Education and the Economy (1986) recommended the development of a National Board for Professional Teaching Standards. This board would create a set of assessments of teachers' subject matter knowledge, pedagogical understanding, and application of this knowledge in simulated classrooms. Specifying a high standard of professionalism in teaching would enhance the prestige of the occupation and would enable the recruitment of more academically able candidates. To prepare teachers to meet these standards, the Carnegie Forum recommended a two-year graduate course, the first year spent in coursework and internship, the second in residency, working under supervision in a *clinical school*. The clinical school was seen as analogous to a teaching hospital. Clinical schools would link faculties in elementary and secondary schools, colleges of education, and colleges of arts and science to provide the best possible learning environment for teacher preparation. The forum's design called for teachers in outstanding public schools to work closely with colleges of education. *Lead teachers* in the clinical school would hold adjunct appointments at the university. They would serve on the instructional staff of the Master's in Teaching degree program. Participants in this partnership would have opportunities to reflect on teaching and learning within the clinical school environment. "The clinical schools should exemplify the collegial, performance-oriented environment that newly certified teachers should be prepared to establish" (Carnegie Forum on Education and the Economy, 1986, p. 77).

The Holmes Group report (1986) described professional development schools (PDS) as institutions that would connect colleges of education with schools in a manner similar to that described in the Carnegie Forum report. Professional development schools were also to be analogous to teaching hospitals. The partnership of practicing teachers, administrators, and university faculty would be based on the following principles: (a) reciprocity, or mutual exchange and benefit, between research and practice; (b) experimentation, or willingness to try new forms of practice and structure; (c) systematic inquiry, or the requirement that new ideas be subject to careful study and validation; and (d) student diversity, or commitment to the development of teaching strategies for a broad range of children with different backgrounds, abilities, and learning styles. These PDS were expected to serve as settings where teaching professionals could implement and evaluate different instructional arrangements for novice teachers, where researchers could work under the guidance of gifted practitioners, where university faculty and practitioners could exchange professional knowledge, and where new structures could be designed around the demands of a new profession (Holmes Group, 1986, p. 67).

Another model of a professional development school was used by Wise et al. (1987) in the RAND study. They called it an *induction school*. Although Wise et al. believed that universities should provide a sound knowledge base, they also believed that a teacher can become fully prepared only through extensive, supervised classroom experience. In the induction school, new teachers would be observed frequently and advised by expert teachers. Recognizing the difficulty of recruiting and keeping good teachers in inner-city schools, the RAND study recommended that the induction school be located in an inner-city neighborhood. The rationale for this proposal was that senior, tenured teachers would be more likely to stay in such schools if offered the chance to advance by serving as expert teacher trainers. Heavy staffing to allow frequent supervision of the novice teachers would be a key feature of this program. Expected benefits included (a) supervision for beginning teachers, with eased entry to teaching, better preparation for teaching, and reduced attrition; (b) an attractive assignment for senior teachers, one that recognized and used their talent and experience; (c) a setting where first-year teachers could be efficiently and effectively evaluated; and (d) more resources and more stable teaching for disadvantaged children (Wise et al., 1987, p. 96).

Although differing somewhat in conceptualization, the professional development schools described were remarkably similar in goals to the Ford Foundation's Break Through Programs of the 1960s. All emphasized partnerships joining teachers, administrators, and college faculties in an effort to restructure the preparation of teachers and their induction into the teaching profession. The goal of those collaborative efforts was to develop schools and colleges where participants would acquire essential (a) subject-area knowledge, (b) reflective, analytic, problem-solving skills, and (c) social skills, to meet the educational needs of society now and in the 21st century. The resultant structure of such consortiums would be schools where administrators, teachers, student teachers, and college faculty could grow professionally.

Although the 1980s were rife with criticism of the public schools' inability to provide an excellent education, very little research was conducted to discover what programs were working and for whom. Very little was mentioned regarding the preparation of teachers for diversity. C. A. Grant and W. G. Secada, writing for the *Handbook of Research on Teacher Education* (1990), say:

> There is much that we do not know about how to prepare teachers to teach an increasingly diverse student population. We think that new responses are called for in teacher recruitment, preservice education, and inservice education. Given the paucity of empirical research that we have found in this area, we believe that a major research effort is called for. More than scattered studies, more than studies that seek to document and to correlate deficiencies, we need programs of research that acknowledge what is lacking but that also provide a vision and hope for what might be done. It is a challenge that must be met. (p. 406)

The 1990s

Although the reports cited in the preceding section proposed specific types of professional development schools, which would require extensive restructuring of schools and colleges, such schools were slow to materialize. For instance, by fall 1994, fewer than one-half of the colleges of education holding membership in the

Holmes organization actually had professional development schools in which they were preparing students to teach.

A primary source for significant change in colleges of education has come from John Goodlad's Center for Educational Renewal. His National Network for Educational Renewal (NNER) includes 16 settings in 14 states, comprising 33 colleges or universities, more than 100 school districts, and more than 500 partner schools. The members of the network are actively committed to implementing the 19 postulates outlined by Goodlad for guiding the preparation of educators. The postulates, which were validated in the 1985–1990 Education of Educators study, were published in *Teachers for Our Nation's Schools* (Goodlad, 1990). Essential to Goodlad's model is collaboration of colleges of education with colleges of liberal arts and science and with school districts. Initially, the grants from the Seattle National Center for Educational Renewal provided funds for meetings with deans of colleges of education, and representatives from colleges of science and liberal arts, and school personnel, where they could share problems and solutions for developing relevant teachers. The 16 NNER centers were attracting funding from state and local sources. In Goodlad's book *Educational Renewal* (1994), he describes this change process, the successes, and the challenges for colleges of education.

Another thrust for change in the preparation of educators has come in the form of interprofessional training for health care workers, social workers, and educators. The need for such interprofessional training derives from the need for comprehensive school services to serve children and families living at or below the poverty level. That need has become more and more apparent. Children need to come to school ready to learn, and far too many children come to school lacking medical or dental care, food, clothing, shelter, or family support.

Six years ago, I was observing a student teacher in a third-grade classroom of the inner-city Houston Teaching Academy (HTA). A child came into the classroom with silent tears sliding down his cheeks. After a few questions and a look into his mouth, the teacher realized that the boy had a painfully abscessed tooth. The child's distress captured everyone's attention. Instruction stopped! Many of the children from this poor and crime-ridden neighborhood do not come to school ready to learn. Admonitions or slogans telling teachers to "Put learning first" cannot be executed under these conditions. Unfortunately, for the children in this Houston school, social services and health services are a bus trip away. What is more, the parents in this particular case could not be located. It is not unusual for teachers in this school to have parent permission slips on hand so that they may take children to their own dentists for emergency treatment. In the absence of services linked to the school, even though it is not in their job description, dedicated teachers become social workers or health care workers. The teachers, the principal, and parents work many hours to provide the best possible instruction for the children.

Over a three-year period, 75 student teachers from the University of Houston graduated from the HTA, under a National Diffusion Network program called Learning to Teach in Inner-City Schools. A three-year follow-up study found 85 percent of those graduates at work in inner-city or multiethnic environments. In comparison with other first-year teachers their principals had hired, those principals gave them high ratings for working with children from diverse backgrounds and their families. Three years after the project began, an examination of the achievement of the children in the HTA on the Texas Education Assessment of Minimal Skills indicated that at all three levels—third, fifth, and seventh grades—the results were better than in any previous years (Stallings & Quinn, 1991).

In addition to the changing multicultural balance in our population, the increasing legions of poor children and families lacking adequate health care, housing, and education challenge even the most committed educators. In retrospect, there can be little wonder why educational interventions based on the body of teaching and learning research from the 1970s and 1980s have had so little lasting effect for children in these situations. The answer has taken a long time to emerge, but it is unequivocal: We were not considering the multitude of intervening variables. For example, although we knew that parents were crucial to child learning and that some children depended for physical sustenance on the food they received at school, we rarely included these variables as we assessed school success or school failure.

Cheri Hays, Executive Director of the Finance Project, writing in the October 1993 *Prospectus*, says, "despite annual public expenditure approaching $350 billion, nearly a quarter of U.S. children are poor and live in families and communities that are unable to meet their basic needs" (p. 4). Child poverty is increasing in the United States, and it is significantly higher than in other developed nations. Rates of academic failure, dropping out of school, chronic unemployment, substance abuse, violence, delinquency, and unmarried teenage parenthood are disturbingly high and, in some sectors, rising. In the early 1990s, there was a broad consensus about national educational goals, and there were strong indications of public eagerness for a renewed emphasis on domestic social policy and fundamental reforms of the nation's education, health, welfare, public housing, and social service systems. Nevertheless, innovative changes have been slow to materialize.

In our efforts to improve education for those most at risk of being failed by the educational system, we have not asked in a systematic way, "What is required for a child to come to school ready to learn so that teaching strategies have an optimal chance of success?" Intervening factors prevent the best teachers from teaching:

- Nearly 13 million children live in poverty, more than 2 million more than a decade ago.
- At least 1 of 6 children has no health care at all.
- At least 100,000 children are homeless in America on any given night.
- Every year there are more than 1 million runaway and homeless young people.
- Approximately 500,000 young people drop out of school each year.
- Overall, the percentage of students graduating from high school decreased from 1985 to 1990 for whites, African-Americans, and Hispanics.
- Dropouts are 3.5 times more likely than high school graduates to be arrested, and 6 times more likely to become unmarried parents.

- Every year approximately 1 million teenage girls become pregnant. The percentage of all births represented by births to single teens increased 16 percent from 1986 to 1991.
- The violent-crime arrest rate for juveniles tripled from 1960 to 1988.
- Every day 135,000 American students bring guns to school.
- Drinking and driving remains the number one killer of adolescents.
- Suicide, now the second leading cause of death among adolescents, has almost tripled since the 1960s.
- Homicide is the leading cause of death among 15- to 19-year-old minority youth.
- The number of reported child abuse cases increased 48 percent from 1986 to 1991.

The educational enterprise is huge and diverse, and for the mainstream population it functions very well, but far too many of our children are at risk of failing or dropping out and never realizing their potential or their dreams.

Multiple perspectives are needed to solve these immense social and educational problems. In many parts of the country, anxious but enlightened communities are forming partnerships of health, welfare, juvenile justice, and education systems to pool insights and resources. Leadership and funding are coming from individual school districts and from several foundations, such as the Children's Aid Society and the Annie Casey, Danforth, Hogg, Stuart, and Ford Foundations. Many pilot projects of comprehensive school-linked services are under way, and others are being planned. The DeWitt Wallace–Reader's Digest Foundation (1996) has funded four colleges of education to develop collaborative professional preparation programs that bring together the professions of nursing, social work, and education.

The colleges leading in these innovations of the 1990s are bright lights leading toward new models for the preparation of educators. All teachers now being prepared to serve the 21st-century student population must have knowledge and experience working with people of color and with multiservice professionals. Such changes are difficult to accomplish and more difficult to sustain. Faculties usually have deep investments in systems and programs they have created during the past decades. It takes great courage and persuasion on the part of deans and faculty leaders to accomplish the revolution needed in the preparation of educators. As Lucretia Mott, an abolitionist and leader for women's suffrage, said more than a century ago, "Any great change must expect opposition because it shakes the very foundation of privilege" (quoted in Bacon, 1985, p. 95).

The Future

The jury is still out on whether colleges of education offer the best preparation for teachers. To be well prepared, graduates of our colleges must be competent to

- teach in several subject areas
- use multimedia technology in delivering lessons
- integrate multicultural materials across the curriculum
- speak the language of the children they serve
- work collaboratively with administrators, teachers, counselors, special educators, parents, health care workers, and social workers
- understand the educational needs of all the children they serve

They must also be committed to meeting those needs.

School districts across the country are considering whether they might be able to prepare teachers as well as colleges of education do. Alternative routes to teacher certification have been developed to bypass baccalaureate degrees in education. For example, Wendy Kopp's Teach for America (TFA) program enlists students with a baccalaureate in any field and provides five weeks of summer classes to prepare these recruits for the teaching profession. To participate in the program, students must agree to teach for at least two years. As in the internship programs supported by the Ford Foundation in the 1960s, participants in TFA receive a beginning teacher's salary, and each is assigned to a mentor teacher. However, there may be little incentive or systematic training for the mentor teachers to support the new recruits. Since its inception in 1989, Kopp reports that more than 3000 recruits have been placed as teachers in 13 geographic regions across the country. "After their two year commitment, 65% of those completing their course remained in the field of education" (Kopp, 1995, p. 1). These self-reports by Kopp are disputed by some state attrition reports and TFA graduates. For example, Jonathan Schorr (1993), a TFA corps member, says that of the 489 original corps members in his class who entered classrooms in 1990, only 206, or 42 percent remained in teaching after two years (pp. 315–318). In 1992 the Brown University *Daily Herald* ran a piece entitled "Graduates Criticize Teach for America," which noted that inadequate training led to confusion, self-doubt, and frustration once the graduates found themselves in the classroom. Of the Brown graduates who started in 1990, 58 percent had left by the third year, an attrition rate more than twice the national average for new teachers. The Maryland Department of Education reports that of 72 TFA corps members who started in Baltimore in 1992, fully 62 percent had left by the fall of 1994. In fact, collaboration among peer facilitators, support directors and on-site cooperating teachers with regard to student teachers' progress was virtually non-existent" (p. 18). Further, the team reported an apparent failure to help student teachers acquire developmentally appropriate techniques and strategies to use in the delivery of instruction. The success of alternate certification programs may depend in large part on the incentives and systematic training provided for the mentor teacher to support the new recruit.

Linda Darling-Hammond (1994) reports on the danger of the poor preparation of teachers for the multicultural and diverse populations of our inner cities and rural areas. "With its inadequate training of recruits, many of whom will teach in urban schools, and its disregard for the knowledge base on teaching and learning, 'Teach for America' continues a long-standing tradition of devaluating urban students and deprofessionalizing teaching" (p. 21).

Longitudinal research is needed to determine how graduates of colleges of education are performing in the variety of tasks required of teachers today. Are the students of our graduates of teacher education programs thriving? Are graduates from colleges of education staying in the education field longer than are graduates of institutions offering alternative routes to certification? How do principals, teachers, parents, and students rate graduates from colleges of education in regard to their knowledge, respect, sensitivity, and appreciation for the diversity among the children they serve? Such research validating the success of college-of-education programs is sorely missing from past decades. Let that not be true for this decade.

It is imperative that those of us reading and writing this book take responsibility for contributing to the body of knowledge regarding the preparation of educators. What programs are effective in preparing students to participate in and contribute to the 21st century, in what contexts are they effective, and how can we improve them? Without such research, colleges of education cannot respond convincingly to critics. We may find ourselves, like dinosaurs, unable to adapt to a changing environment.

References

Bacon, M. H. (1985). *The quiet rebels*. Philadelphia: New Society.

Boyer, E. L. (1983). *High school: A report on secondary education in America* (lst ed.). New York: Harper and Row.

Brophy, J., & Good, T. L. (1986). Teacher behavior and student achievement. In. M. C. Wittrock (Ed.), *Handbook for research on teaching* (pp. 328–375). New York: Macmillan.

Carnegie Forum on Education and the Economy, Task Force on Teaching as a Profession. (1986) *A nation prepared: Teachers for the 21st century*. New York: Author.

Coleman, J. S., Campbell, E. Q., Hobson, C. J., McPartland, J., Mood, A. M., Weinfeld, E. D., & York, R. L. (1966). *Equality of educational opportunity*. Washington, DC: U.S. Government Printing Office.

Darling-Hammond, L. (1994, September). Who will speak for the children? *Phi Delta Kappan, 76*(1), pp. 21–34.

Delpit, L. (1995). *Other people's children: Cultural conflict in the classroom*. New York: New Press.

Dewey, J. (1933). *How we think: A restatement of the relation of reflective thinking to the educative process*. Boston: D. C. Heath and Company.

DeWitt Wallace–Reader's Digest Foundation. (1996). *Comprehensive teacher education national demonstration project handbook*. Washington, DC: American Association of Colleges for Teacher Education.

Gagné, R. M. (1965). *From the conditions of learning*. New York: Holt, Rinehart & Winston, CBS College Publishing.

Goodlad, J. (1984). *A place called school: Prospects for the future*. New York: McGraw-Hill.

Goodlad, J. (1990). *Teachers for our nation's schools*. San Francisco: Jossey-Bass.

Goodlad, J. (1994). *Educational Renewal*. San Francisco: Jossey-Bass.

Grant, C. A., & Secada, W. G. (1990). Preparing teachers for diversity. In W. R. Houston (Ed.), *Handbook of research on teacher education* (pp. 403–422). New York: Macmillan.

Hawkins, D. (1965). Messing about in science. *Science and Children, 2*, 2–5.

Hayes, C. (1993, October). *Prospectus*. Washington, DC: The Finance Project.

Holmes Group. (1986). *Tomorrow's teachers*. East Lansing, MI: Author.

Jencks, C. (1972). *Inequality: A reassessment of the effect of family and schooling in America*. New York: Basic Books.

Johnson, D. W., & Johnson, R. T. (1987). *Learning together and alone: Cooperative, competitive, and individualistic learning*. Upper Saddle River, NJ: Prentice Hall.

Kopp, W. (1995). *Corps member handbook: Teach for America summer institute*. New York: Teach for America.

Ladson-Billings, G. (1947/1994). *The dreamkeepers: Successful teachers of African American children*. San Francisco: Jossey-Bass.

National Commission on Excellence in Education. (1983). *A nation at risk: The imperative for educational reform*. Washington, DC: U.S. Government Printing Office.

Okihiro, G. Y. (1994). *Margins and mainstreams: Asians in American history and culture*. Seattle: University of Washington Press.

Raven, J. C. (1965). *Guide to using the colored progressive matrices*. London: H. K. Lewis.

Schorr, J. (1993, December). Class action: What Clinton's National Service Program could learn from "Teach for America." *Phi Delta Kappan,* pp. 315–318.

Slavin, R. (1983). *Cooperative learning*. New York: Longman.

Stallings, J. (1975). Implementations and child effects of teaching practices in follow-through classrooms. *Monographs of the Society for Research in Child Development, 40*(7–8, Serial No. 163).

Stallings, J., & Geison, P. A. (1977). The study of reliability in observational data. *Phi Delta Kappa Occasional Paper 19.* Center for Evaluation Development and Research, Bloomington, IN.

Stallings, J., & Quinn, L. F. (1991). Learning how to teach in the inner-city. *Educational Leadership, 49*(3), 25–27.

Stone, J. C. (1968). *Breakthrough in teacher education*. San Francisco: Jossey-Bass.

Suppes, P. (1966). The uses of computers in education. *Scientific American, 215*(3), 206–220.

Takaki, R. T. (1939/1993). *A different mirror: A history of multicultural America.* Boston: Little, Brown.

Texas Education Agency. (1993). *Texas educators: Visiting team report.* Austin, TX: Author.

Wise, A. E., Darling-Hammond, L., Berry, B., Berliner, D., Haller, E., Praskac, A., & Schlechty, P. (1987). *Effective teacher selection: From recruitment to retention* (R-3462-NIE/CSTP). Santa Monica, CA: RAND.

Supporting Novice Teachers

Negotiating Successful Mentoring Relationships

Carolyn M. Evertson
Vanderbilt University

Margaret W. Smithey
Vanderbilt University

The past 20 years have been a time of reflection and reform in American schooling. Much has been written about the importance of developing community partnerships, focusing on student learning, developing alternative assessments, and implementing standards in an effort to improve educational opportunities for all children. Those writings have resulted in significant movements for change in American schools.

There is general agreement that effective teachers are a key element in creating the kinds of schools that provide quality education for our children. Each year, a large number of new teachers enters the profession with the potential to be effective teachers and leaders in their schools. However, in many cases they are left to "sink or swim" with little guidance to support their early teaching efforts (Feiman-

We would like to thank Catherine Randolph for her comments on an earlier version of this chapter and for many discussions and editorial suggestions on this and earlier drafts. However, all errors or omissions are solely the responsibility of the authors.

Nemser, 1983; Huling-Austin, 1990b; Lortie, 1975). For the past 15 years, surveys (Schlechty & Vance, 1983; Varah, Theune, & Parker, 1986) have reported that 40–60 percent of new teachers leave during the first five years of their teaching careers (Gold, 1996; Marlow, Inman & Betancourt-Smith, 1997). For teachers in inner-city or urban classrooms, the rate is 50 percent attrition in the first three years (Summers, 1987). Huling-Austin (1990b) argues that this alarmingly high attrition rate for new teachers is due to feelings of isolation and frustration, lack of support, and lack of practical classroom knowledge. There is some evidence that those who do survive must overcome negative initial experiences and may never reach their full potential as teachers (Huling-Austin, 1986; Romatowski, Dorminey, & Voorhees, 1989). The loss of so many new teachers clearly robs the profession of many potentially effective teachers.

In response to this problem, mentoring programs, sometimes called induction programs, have been created. In such programs, experienced teachers nurture new teachers by providing a supportive and collegial relationship. Induction programs are "preplanned, structured, and short-term assistance programs offered in schools for beginning teachers" (Lawson, 1992, p. 163) that function "both as logical extensions of the preservice program and as entry pieces in a larger career-long professional development program" (Huling-Austin, 1990b, p. 535). Common goals of induction programs are (1) to improve teaching performance, (2) to increase the retention of beginning teachers during the induction years, (3) to promote the personal and professional well-being of beginning teachers, (4) to satisfy state and local requirements related to induction and certification, and (5) to transmit the culture of the system to beginning teachers or to socialize new teachers to the school culture (DeBolt, 1992; Huling-Austin, 1988; Romatowski et al., 1989). Researchers studying a variety of induction programs have found that such programs contribute to the educational system by improving retention of teachers, increasing positive attitudes toward teaching, and enhancing teaching performance (Feiman-Nemser & Parker, 1992; Huling-Austin, 1990b; Klug & Salzman, 1991; Odell, 1987; Smithey & Evertson, 1995; Yosha, 1991). Studies of the programs have examined mentor characteristics; the roles, responsibilities, and activities of mentors; styles of mentoring; pitfalls and obstacles of mentoring; payoffs for mentors and protégés; and levels or phases of the mentoring process. Key studies in each area will be summarized here.

Many researchers have investigated the characteristics of effective mentor teachers (Ackley & Gall, 1992; Anderson & Shannon, 1988; Bas-Isaac, 1989; Enz, 1992; Gray & Gray, 1985; Hardcastle, 1988; Head, Reiman, & Thies-Sprinthall, 1992; Kay, 1990; Kay & Sabatini, 1988; Mele & Rossiter, 1989; Odell, 1990; Parkay, 1988; Schmoll, 1983). Roberson (1997) reviewed the literature on mentoring and categorized mentor characteristics as either professional or personal. Professional characteristics include previous experience interacting with adult learners, teaching ability, sufficient time and emotional energy for mentoring, and commitment to being a seminal contributor to the profession. Personal characteristics of mentors include being a good listener, having high integrity, and being consistently friendly, cheerful, outgoing, sincere, patient, confident, flexible, sensitive, secure, tolerant of ambiguity, wise, caring, humorous, nurturing, open, empathic, unselfish, and cooperative.

Researchers have studied the roles, responsibilities, and activities of participants in mentoring programs and have reported many dimensions found within the
interactions and relationships of the mentoring process (Bey & Holmes, 1990;
1992; Gray & Gray, 1985; Hawkey, 1997; Huling-Austin, 1990b; Huling-Austin, Putnam, & Galvez-Hjornevik, 1986; McIntyre & Hagger, 1993; Odell, 1986; Smithey &
Evertson, 1994). Mentors simultaneously assume many roles and initiate varying
activities and interactions with their protégés. Some of these roles may include
trusted colleague, counselor, confidant, friend, door opener, sponsor, protector, and
symbol of expertise (Ackley & Gall, 1992; Anderson & Shannon, 1988; Christensen,
1991; Conlin, 1989; Gray & Gray, 1985; Head et al., 1992; Odell, 1990; Pigge &
Marso, 1990; Wright, 1992). These overlapping roles were identified by researchers
as essential for successful support of new teachers. The many responsibilities and
activities inherent in mentoring include providing resources (Odell, 1990), explaining policies and procedures (Wright, 1992), modeling and demonstrating effective
teaching, coaching, observing, energizing, motivating, providing a scaffold for planning, and giving feedback, assurance, and remediation if needed (Abell, Dillon,
Hopkins, McInerney, & O'Brien, 1995; Cohen, 1995; Roberson, 1997; Sullivan,
1992). Clearly, these roles and responsibilities create a picture of mentoring as a
complex process, deserving of close study.

Huling-Austin (1990a) defines three kinds of mentors, each with a different
style: the "responder," who encourages the beginning teacher to ask for help; the
"colleague," who frequently initiates informal visits to learn of concerns or problems the new teacher may have; and the "initiator," who believes it is his or her
responsibility to foster the professional growth of the beginning teacher to the
greatest degree possible. Roberson (1997) states that "mentoring is an extremely
individualistic role. Even though we can look for patterns in data and propose generalizations, every mentor has a unique style; however, looking for patterns helps
us study extremely complex phenomena and construct substantive knowledge,
which provides a foundation upon which to build theory" (p. 47).

Inherent in the mentoring process are pitfalls and obstacles, as well as benefits
and positive outcomes (Gratch, 1998). Heller and Sindelar (1991) found three pitfalls that mentors need to avoid. First, they must watch for inordinate dependency
by the protégé; second, they should recognize when to "let go" of the protégé; and
third, they should resist accepting an assessment role when asked to assist a new
teacher. Smithey and Evertson (1995) interviewed new teachers after their induction year and found that some mentors did not give sufficient feedback and some
did not sustain support throughout the initial weeks and months of teaching. One
obstacle cited by J. Shulman (1986) is animosity from peers who have not been
chosen as mentors. Lemberger (1992) reported that in some settings, the protégés
saw the mentors as threats rather than advocates.

Even though there are pitfalls and obstacles in the mentoring process, there
are many possible benefits to protégés and mentors (Connor, 1984; Huling-Austin
& Murphy, 1987). For example, new teachers surveyed by Bova and Phillips (1984)
reported that they learned from their mentors' risk-taking behaviors, communication skills, survival skills, respect for people, high standards and refusal to compro-

mise them, good listening skills, ability to get along with all kinds of people, leadership qualities, and understanding of what it means to be a professional. Mentors also experience benefits from mentoring, such as professional growth, revitalization, increased feelings of satisfaction and worth, experience-enhancing roles, collegiality, enhanced enjoyment of teaching, pride in the mentor role, more awareness of their own development as teachers, and mentor training, which is often identified as having value beyond the mentor role (Abell et al., 1995; Ackley & Gall, 1992; Blank & Sindelar, 1992; Killion, 1990; Odell, 1990; Reiman & Edelfelt, 1990; Stevens, 1995; Yosha, 1991).

Healy and Welchert (1990, p. 17) define mentoring as a "dynamic, reciprocal relationship in a work environment between an advanced career incumbent and a beginner aimed at promoting the career development of both. For the protégé, the object of mentoring is the achievement of an identity transformation, a movement from the status of understudy to that of self-directing colleague. For the mentor, the relationship is a vehicle for achieving midlife generativity." According to Healy and Welchert, the possibility of professional growth and redefinition is present for both the intern and the mentor.

The studies summarized thus far have focused on the individuals involved in induction programs. Another helpful group of studies takes a closer look at the evolving relationships between mentors and protégés over time, seeking to understand the mentoring process more fully. In those studies, researchers have described levels or phases in the mentoring relationship (Cohen, 1995; Galvez-Hjornevik, 1986; Gray & Gray, 1985; Head et al., 1992; Krupp, 1987; Odell, 1990; Smithey, Wade, & Evertson, 1993; Smithey & Evertson, 1995; Vickers, 1989). Almost all of the theories about phases of mentoring involve a progression from a dependent protégé in the beginning of the relationship to an autonomous, self-reliant teacher as the novice develops and becomes a colleague and peer. Smithey and Evertson found that "mentoring is a process that changes complexion as it develops across time . . . in a professional relationship where one [the expert] is carefully constructing the climate of the relationship to create a learning environment for the other [the novice]" (1995, p. 35).

Recognizing the benefits of mentoring for experienced teachers and the contributions mentors make in the lives of new teachers challenges us to understand the process better. This chapter takes a close look at what we have found in eight years of observing and monitoring the learning that occurs in mentor-protégé relationships. We have found that there are roles within the mentoring process that must be learned and executed with varying intensity over time. The mentoring role is neither static nor linear but is dynamic and recursive. For the mentoring process to be an effective one, a great deal of effort and insight is required to move through the many phases and challenges of the mentoring process, and this process has only recently been examined critically. What is revealed here is a close look at the complex process that evolves during the mentoring experience.

This chapter describes a three-part process occurring during the mentoring year: (1) the mentor is learning a new professional leadership role, (2) the intern is learning a new role as peer and teacher, and (3) these new identities are forged within an emerging, complex mentor-protégé relationship. Our documentation of the progress of this relationship from the perspective of both mentor and protégé highlights some critical negotiations of roles and relationships that must be accomplished in order for growth in all three of these areas to occur.

Data Collection and Analysis

The findings presented here are part of a much larger data set of interviews, multiple pencil-and-paper assessments, multiple observations of the novices' teaching knowledge, and conferencing assessments of 255 mentors and 189 new teachers. Some new teachers in the study were in their own classrooms for the first time, and others were sharing a classroom with their mentors for a full year. From the larger study, several critical points emerged that mentors and interns must both interpret and reconcile to keep the mentoring process alive. During the years of data collection, we observed that some mentor-protégé pairs had a growing and productive relationship, but others were critically sidetracked at varying points in the relationship. We also noticed that although all mentor-protégé relationships began similarly, they stalled at different points.

This chapter presents a description of the mentoring process experienced by 16 mentor-intern pairs from two universities in the southeastern United States. Each of the 16 interns participating in the study had a minimum of two semester-long placements in classrooms with mentor teachers. The principals were asked by the universities to recommend teachers who were effective classroom teachers and, in the principals' opinions, had the potential to be effective mentors.

During the internship year, data were collected from (1) weekly observations of each protégé's teaching, (2) formal feedback conferences after every observation, (3) two formal group meetings per semester with the mentors for debriefing, (4) informal conversations biweekly with individual mentors regarding their mentoring experiences, (5) two informal group meetings per semester with the interns for purposes of problem solving and debriefing, (6) weekly seminars with the interns, and (7) individual exit interviews with the mentors and interns at the end of the school year.

The interns were college graduates without education degrees who had decided to become certified teachers. While they were completing a masters degree in education, they spent a full school year working with veteran mentor teachers in those teachers' classrooms. The interns had completed only two or three education courses prior to the internship year, making the classroom the central arena in which they learned to teach. Thus, the impact of the field-based experience was heightened.

Exit interviews with 16 mentor-intern pairs were conducted and audiotaped by an individual who was not a participant in the mentoring programs of either the universities or the public schools represented in the study. Audiotapes of the interviews with the 16 interns and mentors were transcribed and were then analyzed by methods of qualitative data analysis (Miles & Huberman, 1984). The researchers first read the transcriptions for a global overview; second, they logged reoccurring statements; and third, they labeled emerging themes. The process continued until all the data had been considered. The themes from the reflective statements the interns had given in the audiotaped interviews were compared with the continuum of the larger study to check for validation of the key junctures that had been identified. From this comparison, we proposed specific grounded theory based on the themes that consistently emerged from the data. Both the themes and the emerging theories were cross-checked by other members of the research team. The grounded theory emerging from the data paralleled the themes found in the larger data set.

The Mentor-Intern Relationship: A Year-Long Process

The study we will describe is of the sample of 16 intern teachers who shared their mentor teachers' classrooms during a full school year. Our data show that within the beginning phases of a mentoring experience, the mentor's role is affirmed and interpreted, and both the mentor and intern are validated as viable participants in the process. Next comes the most visible portion of the mentoring process, when the mentors model teaching and collaboration and the protégés gradually assume those same teacher roles. During the ending phase of mentoring, the mentors and interns reflect on their new identities and consider the meaning of having been in a mentoring relationship.

In the sections that follow, we will provide examples from mentor and intern perspectives that illuminate the relationship and its impact on the mentor's and intern's redefinition of their roles and identities—from classroom teacher to teacher of another adult (colleague) and from intern to classroom teacher and colleague.

Affirming the Mentor and Intern

The first in a series of mentoring events is affirmation, a preliminary phase in which the mentor is selected by the university or district, agrees to participate in the mentoring process, and is accepted by the protégé as mentor. This inaugural event occurs both formally and informally. In this study, teachers were formally affirmed as mentors when the appointment passed through two levels: (1) the school administrator's recommendation and (2) university approval. They were informally affirmed when they accepted the role and, at least minimally, committed themselves to it and when the interns demonstrated a commitment to learn from them.

Our data suggest that the interns, likewise, were both formally and informally affirmed. They were formally affirmed when they (1) were admitted by the university to the intern program and (2) were assigned to the schools by the administrators and university personnel. They were informally affirmed when they met their mentors for the first time. It appeared that the interns felt genuine affirmation when the mentors initially met them and shared information about their new workplace and about the people who worked and studied there. That interns felt affirmed in the beginning as members of the school community was indicated by their reports of such thoughts as, "It is going to be great to be a teacher in *my school*," "I couldn't wait to meet *the rest of* the faculty," and "I remember *feeling like a teacher* from the beginning" [italics added]. The data contained no examples of interns who did not feel affirmed at this initial point.

Interpreting the Mentor Role

In our study, the next step occurred when the mentors moved into interpreting the mentoring role. The mentors who successfully navigated this phase seemed to clarify their understanding of the meaning of mentoring and their expectations of themselves and the other participants in the mentoring process. Dialogue with other mentors and with university personnel often assisted the mentors at this phase, but it was the individual mentor's understanding of the meaning and responsibilities of mentoring that enabled him or her to interpret the role and act on that interpretation.

The mentors in this study attended a workshop that was designed as an inquiry-based experience (IBE) in which they could begin to understand how their roles would change over time, to develop new skills in active listening and the giving of feedback, and to develop their own questions. Mentors who attended the IBE stated that it helped them interpret and begin to make sense of their new role. Further, some mentors commented that the IBE served as a springboard for inquiry that continued throughout the mentoring process.

The importance of mentors' sense of affirmation and role interpretation became clear as they began working with interns. The interns reflected that some mentors seemed to be confident in what they were supposed to do and mentored them from their first meeting, before school began. One intern described how the mentor brought him a picture album in which he could put pictures she would later send him of the students he would be meeting in his second-semester placement with her. He said that this led him to believe that she saw herself as the bridge between him and the students and that she was secure in herself and confident in her role as connector. He said,

> When I arrived second semester, she seemed to have a mental picture of all I needed to know about the new school setting and about where the children were in their studies. She quickly phased me in to teaching and smoothly turned loose of the students, just as I thought she would. She seemed to anticipate my needs and be a step ahead of them all the time. . . . I could put all of my effort into learning to teach; the mentor was preparing the way for me and thinking of how I could become a real teacher of her class.

An intern who did not consider that she had been mentored from the beginning reported,

> My mentor was a very nice lady, but I didn't learn very much from her. I believe she wanted to help a new teacher, but she didn't seem to know how. She just didn't seem to

have the picture of what mentoring was all about. I think she thought if she would just 'mother' me, everything would be OK. What I did learn that semester I learned from other teachers around her, but not from her. She just never made the connection.

Another intern said of a nonmentoring experience,

It was shaky from the beginning. Ms. Jones did not understand what an intern was and thus didn't understand what a mentor was. I think she had been told; I know she had, but it just didn't click with her. Like I said, ours was shaky from the beginning. [All names are pseudonyms.]

As these examples show, interns perceived mentors who did not have clear interpretations of mentoring to be less than helpful and found it necessary to turn to other teachers who were more able to facilitate their growth.

Validating the Mentor and the Intern

The next phase, validating the mentor and the intern, occurred in the school setting at both public and personal levels. The affirmation of the mentors and the interns had been accomplished through systematized channels established by the university and the schools, but validation occurred or did not occur according to the orchestration of this phase by the mentors in their individual school settings. For both the mentors and the interns, the public validation occurred when the mentors genuinely welcomed the interns as insiders in their workplace. The optimal opportunity for this professional validation occurred when the interns first entered the school setting and the mentors introduced or presented the interns as valid members.

When the mentors welcomed the interns as viable members of their specific school culture and introduced them as such, both the public validation and the interpersonal validation of intern by mentor and mentor by intern occurred. At this point, interns recognized and accepted the mentors as door openers in the public school setting, and at the same time, the mentors acknowledged the interns personally as welcome and equal partners in the school community. It is at this point that mentors and interns became more securely bonded in the mentoring process. They seemed to sense more of the reality of the partnership to which they had committed.

For mentoring to be successful, the mentor and intern roles had to be validated, not only with the teachers in the schools, but also with the students in the classrooms and with their parents. Two mentors gave us important insights into those validations. "Interns benefit the entire school," Ms. Edwards reported. She described the interns as part of the school team, saying, "We had seven teachers instead of four. They observed many classes and helped other teachers both on the team and in the school." The entire school culture, according to Ms. Edwards, was positively affected by the presence of interns.

Ms. Caldwell explained in elaborate detail how the validation process worked for her. She met Debbie, her intern, as part of the summer IBE, even though Debbie would not be in her classroom until the spring semester. Here is her account of that first meeting:

The thing that enthralled me with Debbie the first day I met her was the enthusiasm. I realized that this was something Debbie truly wanted to do. She was truly interested and this was going to be "for life" with her, and I began to get, I guess, a little nervous myself as I thought about it over the summer. I guess realizing that made me recognize what a responsibility, as well as opportunity, I had committed to.

At the fall parents' meeting, Ms. Caldwell prepared the parents of her students for Debbie's role in the classroom. She said that the class would have two teachers second semester because, as she stated, "I wanted them [the parents] to have the confidence in her that I felt she deserved." Likewise, she prepared the students in several significant ways. Ms. Caldwell brought a camera to class and took a picture of each student. She described their preparations as follows:

> We have Santa's workshop, and we had all painted Christmas T-shirts. So they wore their Christmas T-shirts one day (no small feat for first graders!), and we took their pictures and they made her a special Christmas book instead of sending her a Christmas card. It was a book of their pictures with their names so she could begin to associate their names and faces.

The class made a banner to welcome Debbie on her first day. Ms. Caldwell appeared to have put much thought and effort into validating this intern.

Another intern said, "My mentor treated me like one of the members of the teaching team from our first meeting. She introduced me to everyone and then helped to include me even in the first planning meeting before school actually began." An intern who lamented her introduction to the school setting reported, "My mentor never really introduced me to more than one or two teachers. I felt real hesitant. I felt like a student teacher or an outsider for a long while."

It appears that the mentoring process is greatly inhibited from this point on when the interns do not feel like genuine members of the faculty, fully accepted as equal participants by their mentors. Without this validation, it seems there is less in-depth sharing of the essence of teaching by the mentor and a lack of enthusiastic receiving by the intern, in contrast to what happens in mentoring relationships in which the validation occurs. When the validation occurs, there seems to be increased enthusiasm and openness, which begins to establish the collegiality important for moving on in the relationship.

Integrating the Novice Into the Teaching Role

Having introduced the intern to the school, the students, and their parents, the mentor now began to assist the intern in classroom practices. As mentoring continued, the mentors (1) modeled teaching techniques; (2) shared the intricacies of their management systems, lesson plans, and curricula; and (3) encouraged the interns to observe other effective teachers teaching.

The mentors described various ways in which they began to integrate their interns into the classroom. They generally gave their interns time to observe in the classroom and to begin to work with students in small groups or to teach one subject at a time.

Ms. Gregory explained how her intern learned to teach. At the beginning of the semester, the intern gradually became an active participant in the classroom. She was often at the front of the room with the mentor and was always very visible to the students. She distributed and collected materials and began her teaching experience by conducting 10-minute lesson segments. When the class engaged in group work, the intern circulated to monitor and assist. Ms. Gregory also asked her to grade some papers, but as she explained,

> I let her grade papers, but I did not use her as a paper grader. I tried to help her understand what grades mean, but it was a loose thing. Maybe one day she would do second period's papers, and I would do all of the other classes.

Ms. Gregory said that every time she did lesson plans, she would include her intern. She commented,

> Everything I did, she did with me. I mean, she was my shadow. . . . In a way it was the most frustrating experience, you know, just constantly having a shadow, but that's the way she learned. I think they learn probably more from just watching than anything else.

The intern's descriptions corroborated Ms. Gregory's sense of the importance of observation, but also indicated that interaction beyond simple observation was also essential.

As the interns reflected on watching their mentors teach and learning from the mentors' explanations of the rationale behind their management systems, lesson plans, and curricula, one intern said,

> I wanted to absorb everything she was doing. I was like a sponge. I took voluminous notes on everything she did. We would talk about what she had done at lunch and again at the end of the day. She would explain why she did certain things and would let me ask questions. I really was learning a lot.

Other grateful interns talked about their mentors' showing them how they developed unit plans and individual lesson plans within the unit. They talked of the mentors' describing the reasons behind their rules and procedures and the way they methodically taught them to their students. In contrast, some frustrated interns reported that they sat for days just watching their mentors teach, with very little dialogue about the whys and wherefores of what the mentors were doing. Another reported, "I just watched him teach for several weeks; I was afraid to ask any questions about what he was doing. I was afraid he would think I was questioning what he was doing."

The interns who perceived that they had truly been mentored reported that their mentors encouraged them to observe other teachers teaching in addition to watching the mentors. An intern reported:

> When my mentor at my second-semester assignment realized I did not get to observe anyone teaching other than my mentor first semester, she told me I could observe other teachers for a month if I wanted to. She really cared about me. She wanted me to be the best I could be.

A disappointed intern stated,

> My mentor never suggested that I observe any other teacher teaching. I think he thought he was the best and that if I got to observe him every day, I was lucky. He was a good teacher, but there were other good ones in the school too. When I would ask him about how he came up with so many creative ways to teach third graders, he would say, "Oh, it just comes natural for some of us."

Interns who saw only their mentors teach believed they were missing out on additional learning experiences. Those interns lamented their "wasted opportunities," and "missing a once-in-a-lifetime chance to see other teachers teach." Interns who were effectively integrated into the teaching process believed they were viable members of the teaching team and were grateful for the opportunities their mentors gave them to better understand the roles and responsibilities of teaching.

Sharing Teaching Responsibilities

After the integration phase, the interns began to assume more responsibility for teaching. At this point, the mentors often became silent observers, coplanners, and givers of feedback. During this phase, interns expanded their definitions of themselves as classroom teachers.

Interns who reflected on their positive experience at this phase of mentoring talked of how their mentors would tell them what curricula were to be covered but left the actual planning to them. Others expressed appreciation for being allowed to design the lessons themselves and for being trusted to choose appropriate teaching strategies and resources for the lessons. One intern chuckled as she described the closet of supplies her mentor made available to her:

> I felt like a kid in a toy store. There were resources, manipulatives I had never seen before that she had collected over 15 years, but she was letting me make the decisions about what to use and how to use them. She just opened the door to the closet and said, "Go for it." She seemed to really want me to learn by doing.

This provision for ownership seems to have been critical both for the interns' sense of development and for the continuing development of the mentor-intern relationship. Some interns felt the mentors inappropriately told them exactly how they wanted them to teach the lessons, what materials they wanted them to use, and how much time they should spend on each segment.

The interns who were allowed to plan their own lessons and to use activities they had created seemed infused with enthusiasm even when the mentors critiqued the activities as needing improvement. The interns spoke positively of the mentors' helping them to see ways to improve their lessons, as long as the mentors had allowed them some free rein in planning how the lessons would be taught. The interns whose mentors wanted to continue the planning and to keep tight control over the interns' choices of teaching strategies seemed to feel deprived of valuable teaching experiences. The interns expressed regret at not getting to try their ideas and receive feedback from their mentors. Failure by the mentors to allow this opportunity for growth discouraged some interns and made them feel not trusted. One intern who felt particularly trapped within his mentor's planning and directions said, "I'll just do what she wants me to do until I get out of this program. I guess I shouldn't have thoughts of my own."

In addition to freedom to plan, the two areas about which the interns spoke most often regarded the mentors' abilities to be (1) silent observers and (2) adequate givers of feedback. When the mentors could not be silent observers while the interns were teaching a lesson, the interns reported feelings of frustration, of not being trusted, or of being thought of as poor teachers. Those interns gave examples of mentors' interjecting ideas into the lesson while the interns were teaching, correcting students' behavior instead of allowing the intern to handle the situation, and giving permission for students to leave the room after the intern had refused permission.

In contrast, one intern reported how her mentor successfully negotiated distance with the students while still observing the intern's teaching:

> My mentor told our students that while I was teaching, she was invisible. That meant they were not supposed to talk to her or ask her any questions while I was teaching. They were to pretend that she was not there, invisible. It worked. They related to only me, even when she stayed in the room to observe my teaching.

It appears from what interns reported that the single most important factor in their development of a sense of themselves as teachers was the amount and quality of feedback they received from their mentors. Feedback was the issue mentioned most often in intern interviews, and the interns often linked feedback to their emerging sense of themselves as teachers.

One intern compared the feedback she received in her two semester experiences:

> Second semester, my mentor gave me feedback all of the time. Corrective as well as positive. I never got any feedback first semester. *I had no idea if I was the worst or the best intern ever* [italics added]. I had no idea. It was so nice to hear my second mentor say, "I like this. . . . What could you try differently here? Let's think about what might work better." She was fabulous. I can't imagine anyone better. I really knew how to grow when I heard her feedback. *I didn't have a clue* [italics added] how to change first semester.

As the interns began their first teaching experiences, they were dependent on mentor feedback to know how they were doing. Even as they became more able to identify their own strengths and weaknesses, interns still felt the need for guidance. As one intern complained, "With the first mentor I just didn't get any feedback unless I asked a specific question, and often I did not know what questions to ask."

Another intern was well aware of her lack of experience:

> Feedback—I really, really wanted it. I wanted someone to tell me: "Why don't you try this?" I was groping. *I knew I needed to improve, but I didn't know where* [italics added]. I needed someone to show me, to hold up the mirror for me.

A lack of feedback, besides hindering interns' ability to develop a view of themselves as teachers, also clearly led to a breakdown in the mentor-intern relationship. One intern described such a breakdown:

> She never gave me feedback. I got the feeling I was there so she wouldn't have to be. I was dumped on in every sense. We never had a discussion, never talked about trying this or trying that. I never felt she was in it for me. I never felt like it was a learning process for me. She was rarely in the room with me. And that was sad because I didn't feel like she cared about the kids either, or she would have been in there to see what they were getting from me. I never was mentored; I was just left in that room with no feedback from her. In the beginning I would mention, "I think I am going to try this." In the beginning I really wanted to talk to her about my ideas, but it went downhill. It dawned on me that it didn't matter to her what I did.

This intern's comments suggest how the perception of not getting feedback brought the mentoring process to a halt. As the intern concluded that he did not matter to the teacher, he stopped seeking help; in his words, "it went downhill."

A challenge for the mentors was to give feedback in a way that did not threaten an intern's growing sense of autonomy and efficacy. Interns spoke highly of mentors who encouraged reflection, rather than simply giving answers.

> After a lesson, I would ask my mentor, "What do you think?" My mentor would say, "What do *you* think?" If she had started by saying, "I think this," or, "I think that," I would not have really learned anything. I would have just thought about what she was thinking about the lesson and not had any thoughts of my own. If she had told me I should do A, B, C, I would have been caught in her own boundaries and not discovered knowledge about teaching that is now really my own.

This claiming of knowledge about teaching that is "my own" appears to us to be a critical part of the growth from intern to professional.

Redefining Self as Teacher of Adults

The mentors' biggest challenge in defining their new roles seems to have come as the interns took on full-time teaching responsibilities in the mentors' classrooms. Ultimately, the mentors themselves had to be willing to accept a new role and to work through that role as it unfolded. The mentors had to give themselves permission to assist only the adult learner—the intern—and to relinquish their students to the intern. This was clearly seen in the transfer of authority within the classroom from the classroom teacher to the intern. This transfer, which Wade (1993) has called the "affirmation shift," was a critical juncture in the mentoring process.

All the mentor interviews revealed this most difficult dilemma and struggle—that of transferring the mentor's source of affirmation from the students in the classroom to the adult learner, the intern. The mentors had to redefine their teaching role from one of teaching only their assigned students to one that included assisting the interns in the process of learning to teach their students. Some mentors were successful and some were not. Further, the grade level in which the shift took place seemed to be a critical factor. Elementary school mentors had more difficulty negotiating the shift than did mentors in middle school and high school.

Whether it was accomplished by leaving the classroom immediately or by slowly transferring teaching responsibilities, negotiating the shift was a complex and pivotal element of the entire mentoring process. It called for a redefinition of the teacher's role from the teacher of students to the teacher of a preservice teacher of students. It called for a true understanding of the process of mentoring and a belief in that process. As one mentor stated, "I had to let go and let her try her wings because you can't tell her everything." That major step—letting go and shifting the focus of affirmation—was a significant area of growth for mentors.

From our observations and interview data, it appeared that effective mentors kept the mentoring process alive and well by relinquishing the classroom, the students, and management of the classroom to the interns. They consciously determined to remove themselves physically from the classroom; they acknowledged that for a time predetermined by the intern and the mentor, the students and the classroom were to belong to the intern. Giving up the teaching and the daily relationship with the students communicated formally to the students, the faculty, and the mentor and the intern themselves, that the novice was no longer perceived as an intern teacher but as a teacher ready to assume all of the responsibilities of a classroom, at least for specified periods of time.

For the interns as well, the mentors' affirmation shift and willingness to let go was a crucial step toward growth. One intern spoke of a mentor who never left the room: "She never gave me the authority to be the teacher, and the students knew that. *I was never the real teacher in that classroom*" [italics added]. Contrast this statement with a description from an intern whose mentor did successfully share authority:

> She used centers and rotated the kids through them. I did that with her for a few weeks, but when I was going to do my solo teaching I wanted to try some whole-group instruction. I felt comfortable talking to her about doing it a different way. She allowed me to change the seating and the instructional format. She allowed me to be the full-time teacher. She let the kids know I was the full-time teacher. You have to have someone who will step back, let you make changes to fit your teaching style, and leave the teaching to you.

This intern spoke with the authority of one who had developed and now owned a "teaching style"—a person well on her way to identifying herself as a teacher and colleague rather than an intern.

Revising the Supporting Role

Even as the mentors shared authority and teaching responsibilities with the interns, and usually removed themselves physically from their classrooms, they had to find ways of continuing the mentor-intern relationship by supporting the intern. The mentors interviewed varied in their support of the intern. Some spoke of letting their interns go it alone without any assistance, while others said that they checked in daily with their interns to "see how things were going." One mentor said that she "sat in on one regular and one honors class each day just to be sure that my objectives were being carried out."

One mentor set up another office in the teacher workroom and proceeded to make reference materials for the intern to use the next year. She said, "I wanted her to take some things with her because it is so hard to start out with nothing." That same mentor would meet with the intern three times each day. The mentor and intern would discuss lessons, the needs of individual children, and plans for the next day. She told her intern, "I want you to use me as an educational assistant. I'll be happy to pull out and work individually with any child you think needs it."

Another mentor, upon leaving the classroom, was given administrative responsibilities by the school principal. She stated that she would let the intern know that she was there but would involve herself in other, schoolwide activities. This same mentor, however, gave her intern time away from the classroom to go to the local teacher center and make materials for the next year, and she let the intern take old bulletin board materials she no longer used.

Thus, there were varying degrees of behind-the-scenes support for the interns. The support given seemed to depend on the mentor's interpretation of support and on the amount of support the intern needed. The mentors viewed their roles in various ways and acted accordingly. The interns described the support they received, or the lack thereof, as ranging from abandonment to assistance.

Interns interpreted behind-the-scenes support as indications that mentors still cared about them and were cognizant of ways to help them. One mentor told her intern: "I want you to think of me as your assistant while I am out of the room and you are the full-time teacher." Her intern reported feeling very supported, even though the mentor rarely came into the room between the first bell in the morning and the closing bell in the afternoon:

> She even offered to grade papers for me, but I thought that was my responsibility. I never asked her for much help, but she was busy most of the days she was out of the room, preparing supplies for me. She made a huge file for each month of the year.

Other mentors whom interns characterized as supportive prepared bulletin boards, laminated materials for the interns to place in their teaching files, went to the library to find newspaper articles appropriate for a lesson they knew the intern was going to teach in a few days, and laminated manipulatives the intern had created. Another intern commented:

> I seldom saw my mentor during the day, and that was fine because we talked before and after school every day about what I was doing. He was my sounding board. I learned so much during that time. I was the teacher, but he was there for me.

Interestingly, the interns all expressed a sincere need to have the classroom to themselves, but if the mentors withdrew support completely during the time when they were totally out of the room, the interns often perceived that they were "being used." Some interns reported that their mentors spent the time preparing their own lessons for next semester or next year, visited all day in the lounge, or went to a local restaurant for a lengthy lunch. An intern commented:

> My mentor just disappeared. She said, "If things aren't going well, I will hear from my students and from the parents." She was just sitting around, and I was carrying all the responsibility. I never saw her after I took over the teaching.

Interns reported needing behind-the-scenes support even though they wanted the full responsibility of the classroom. The supportive mentors' actions communicated confidence in the interns' futures as teachers. In preparing materials and so on, the mentors were tacitly acknowledging that the interns were becoming teachers.

When mentors successfully negotiated the affirmation shift and appropriate levels of support and feedback, there was a transformation in the mentoring relationship from mentor to peer. The relationship during this phase evolved from intern-mentor to teacher-teacher.

Ending the Relationship: Reflecting on Identities as Intern and Mentor

As the school year and the mentor-intern relationship concluded, mentors and interns reviewed the changes they had undergone. At this point, the interns pinpointed and summarized their experiences and assessed their readiness to teach. Out of this came a redefinition of their knowledge, their roles, and themselves. Interns remarked that they had created new knowledge about themselves and about teaching, had understood the need to assume a different role than when they entered the internship, and now saw themselves as different persons, in varying degrees, from the persons who had entered the process 11 months earlier. One intern said,

> I learned how to translate the theory we studied into classroom reality; I learned so much about teaching, and the biggest thing I learned was how to reach out for collegiality and support from other teachers. I have found I like to use other teachers as resources, to talk with them. I can't think of a better way to start off in a new teaching assignment.

Mentors likewise reported having reassessed their roles and beliefs and being revitalized. An extended example from one mentor, a high school teacher nearing retirement, illustrates the impact of her redefinition of herself as a teacher and as a mentor. Ms. Gregory viewed mentoring an intern as the best experience of her teaching career. She had reached a point, three years earlier, where she felt herself becoming "stale." She stated that the inquiry-based workshop and the subsequent mentoring of two interns brought a "freshness" back to her teaching. She was, in her word, "recharged," as the interns brought to her an enthusiasm that was contagious.

As a result of being constantly observed by these teachers-to-be, Ms. Gregory felt a "little sharper." Moreover, she voiced her belief that the experience of mentoring made her reexamine her teaching. She explained,

Both of them were questioners, and I think that's another reason that they were so good. Everything I did I had to justify. . . . It got awfully frustrating, and sometimes I just wanted to say, "I just do it!" . . . but at the same time they were trying to learn. So I took time and I told them why I did something; and sometimes in telling them, I thought, "Why do I do this? Maybe there's a better way. Maybe I am doing it because I have always done it that way and maybe I need to look at it." And so I changed some things because of the questioning and the back-and-forth discussions.

Ms. Gregory stated that as a result of mentoring, she had reconceptualized teaching and learning. She now "goes more for concepts than for facts" and looks at what is, in her view, really important—not little facts, but big ideas. Her view of the classroom changed, as well. She stated her newfound belief that the purpose of classroom management was not to discipline, but to get students involved in the learning process.

Of her career accomplishments, Ms. Gregory placed mentoring at the top. She said that, knowing she was retiring, what meant the most to her was that she had helped others learn to teach. "I have to admit it's a wonderful feeling to think that there are two people out there that I think are going to be great teachers, and that I might have helped."

Ms. Gregory's understanding about teaching shifted significantly during her year as a mentor. Her last interview responses adhered most closely to the thinking Belenky, Clinchy, Goldberger, and Tarule (1986) describe as "constructed knowledge." Like the constructivists in the study by Belenky et al., she aspired "to work that contribute[d] to the empowerment and improvement in the quality of life of others . . . [and felt] a part of the effort to address with others the burning issues of the day" (p. 152).

This change in knowing was not just an event for Ms. Gregory. Her responses indicated that it was the result of a long process, in which she searched for and found her own voice, growing out of what Belenky et al. (1986) have called a *procedural knowledge base,* developed from previous experience with other novice teachers.

Ms. Gregory spoke of the experience of mentoring an intern as one of integrating her voices and developing a new knowledge framework. She viewed mentoring as a slow, evolutionary process. She was willing to endure major confrontations with her interns and was determined to work through them. As she described the relationship, "It took some crying, some talking, some writing."

Ms. Gregory expressed an ability to tolerate the ambiguity that a developmental viewpoint creates. She believed that the interns learned best by watching, asking, and doing. She was willing to let that happen and endure the frustrations inherent in the process.

Questioning, by both the interns and herself, was key to her realization of self and her new knowledge. She was made to question herself and through that questioning to reconceptualize teaching and learning. Her responses indicated that mentoring was an evolutionary process; as a result, she is now able to see the complexity of the mentoring experience. She voiced an ability to see ambiguity and conflict as the norm, not the exception. Most important, Ms. Gregory reported being able to embrace a new knowledge framework for teaching and learning—one in which students are actively involved in the process.

Mentoring an intern was a significant professional experience for many of the mentors interviewed. Out of it, they reported gaining a sense of pride from helping someone learn to teach. In the larger sense, mentoring an intern was like leaving a legacy—a part of the mentor went with each intern as he or she entered teaching.

The rejuvenation that came as a result of mentoring was a major source of change for many mentors. "It's neat to work with someone who has that instinct and to help them learn to sharpen their skills. It kind of juices us back up when we start to get tired and worn out," said one veteran mentor. From another mentor came a very personal account of a change from "staleness to freshness. . . . The enthusiasm that the interns bring is contagious."

Clearly, the mentors' stories are full of struggle. They had to deal with the affirmation shift to enable their interns to grow and learn. Yet, they reported being fulfilled as well. Mentors were proud of preparing their interns to enter teaching, and through mentoring they were made to reexamine beliefs and methodologies. They learned from the interns and were renewed by their enthusiasm. Their stories chronicled growth-and-change patterns—patterns that are significant for the continuance and viability of mentoring programs.

Conclusions and Implications

Our data suggest that interns and mentors face a series of important junctures in the mentoring process, at which both mentors and interns must confront, redefine, and reassess their roles. The mentors and interns in our study highlighted the importance, at the beginning of the mentoring process, of affirmation and interpretation of the mentor's role, and validation of both the mentor and the intern in the school context. They revealed multiple opportunities for mentors and interns to reassess and redefine their roles between the time the mentors began to model teaching and the time the interns completed their teaching responsibilities. As the mentoring relationship entered the last phases, many of the participants recalled the mentoring process and the change in the way they defined themselves—from who they were at the beginning of the mentoring experience to who they were at the end.

When an experienced teacher and a novice teacher moved successfully through the many phases of a mentoring relationship, both gained knowledge about teaching and could, at the end, redefine their roles and identities. Interns who reported learning in a supportive relationship talked about what it meant to be a professional, a colleague, and a teacher, and the mentors reported learning what it meant to be a reflective professional leading another adult to learn to teach.

The data discussed here represent an attempt to understand more about the process of learning to teach and being mentored as well as the process of learning to mentor. We have also tried to build on and extend the work of others who have contributed important insights about the development of the roles and responsibilities in this process (Elliott & Calderhead, 1993; Feiman-Nemser, Parker, & Zeichner, 1993; Furlong & Maynard, 1995; Gehrke & Kay, 1984; Gray & Gray, 1985; Huling-Austin, 1990a, 1990b; Kelly, Beck, & Thomas, 1992; Maynard & Furlong, 1993; Schon, 1987; Wildman, Magliaro, Niles, & Niles, 1992).

If mentors and interns experience the mentoring relationship as part of a continual process of growth and redefinition, we expect that they will be more likely to collaborate, to accept feedback, and to examine and improve their own teaching. We also believe that they will be more likely to pursue collegiality in their professional careers. The potential for this growth seems to lie within the boundaries of the mentoring relationship. Mentoring can apparently be a vital process that renews experienced teachers and initiates competent and confident new teachers. However, renewal does not happen by accident. Experiencing the professional growth that is possible takes effort, intentional inquiry, willingness to risk, and perseverance.

Our study details the mentoring process as seen through the eyes of 16 mentor-intern pairs and highlights the phases through which the mentor-intern relationship moves. Other researchers, as well, are examining more closely the intricacies of these relationships (Gratch, 1998). If our children are our most cherished treasures and our hope for the future, and if teachers are the persons with whom our children will spend the greatest amount of time in their school years, careful attention must be given to ways that teachers can nourish each other's growth and to ways of creating classrooms that nurture our children's growth.

Summary

Recently, there have been reports that education has moved to the top of most Americans' list of concerns, passing crime and violence. The citizens of the United States are finally articulating, in chorus, the reality that what occurs in the classroom ultimately determines our country's future, and they are uniting in a call for improvement in the quality of our schools and classrooms.

Given the call, from American citizens and legislators, for our nation to make education the number one priority, and given that teachers make crucial decisions that influence the learning opportunities of the students in their classrooms, is it not clear that we should give special attention to the induction of new teachers, the people who are going to run our schools for the next 25 to 30 years? To leave new teachers to their own inventions for survival is unconscionable when we know that the induction years can be navigated with much less stress and anxiety and at the same time be a meaningful learning opportunity when one has an effective mentor.

Another way to state the question is to ask, "Can we improve American schools and classrooms and, at the same time, improve the rueful statistic of only 50 percent retention of new teachers?" Sandra Odell (1990) found that the four-year attrition rates for beginning teachers who had participated in the mentoring program she studied were substantially below both nation and state attrition rates and that

88 percent of the teachers who participated expected to remain in teaching or administration over the next five years.

Our suggestion is that we concentrate on how to keep more of our new teachers in our profession by better equipping them with the coping and teaching tools gained in an effective mentoring program. It seems apparent that retaining a larger percentage of new teachers in our profession can best be accomplished by having effective and informed mentors for all novices. The operative words here are *effective* and *informed.* Our research has shown us that effective mentoring is most likely to occur when mentors are aware of the responsibilities and challenges inherent in the mentoring role and when they understand how their opportunities for and obligations in effective mentoring evolve throughout the mentoring process. Our final plea is that more attention be given to the conditions of the work life of new teachers, and we call for wholesale implementation of what researchers already know about effective mentoring. We picture a time in education when "for the future of our teachers" will frequently be heard along with "for the future of our children."

References

Abell, S. K., Dillon, D. R., Hopkins, C. J., McInerney, W. D., & O'Brien, D. G. (1995). "Somebody to count on": Mentor/intern relationships in a beginning teacher internship program. *Teaching and Teacher Education, 11*(2), 173–188.

Ackley, B., & Gall, M. D. (1992, April). *Skills, strategies, and outcomes of successful mentor teachers.* Paper presented at the annual meeting of the American Educational Research Association, San Francisco.

Anderson, E. M., & Shannon, S. L. (1988). Toward a conceptualization of mentoring. *Journal of Teacher Education, 39*(1), 38–42.

Bas-Isaac, E. (1989, November). *Mentoring: A life preserver for the beginning teacher.* Paper presented at the annual conference of the National Council of States on Inservice Education, San Antonio, TX.

Belenky, M. F., Clinchy, B. V., Goldberger, N. R., & Tarule, J. M. (1986). *Women's ways of knowing: The development of self, voice, and mind.* USA: Basic Books.

Bey, T., & Holmes, C. (Eds.) (1990). *Mentoring: Developing successful new teachers.* Reston, VA: Association of Teacher Educators.

Blank, M. A., & Sindelar, N. (1992). Mentoring as professional development: From theory to practice. *The Clearing House, 66*(1), 22–26.

Bova, B. R., & Phillips, R. R. (1984). Mentoring as a learning experience for adults. *Journal of Teacher Education, 35*(3), 16–20.

Christensen, L. M. (1991). *Empowerment of preservice educators through effective mentoring.* Tuscaloosa: University of Alabama Press. (ERIC Document Reproduction Service No. ED 338 614)

Cohen, N. H. (1995). *Mentoring adult learners: A guide for educators and trainers.* Malabar, FL: Krieger.

Conlin, J. (1989). Role of the mentor in teaching. In *A casebook on school-based mentoring* (pp. 16–19). Amherst: Massachusetts University, School of Education.

Connor, E. L. (1984). *Evaluation of the 1983–1984 beginning teacher program.* Miami, FL: Dade County Public Schools, Office of Educational Accountability. (ERIC Document Reproduction Service No. 257 853)

DeBolt, G. (Ed.) (1992). *Teacher induction and mentoring, school-based collaborative programs.* New York: State University of New York Press.

Elliott, B., & Calderhead, J. (1993). Mentoring for teacher development: Possibilities and caveats. In D. McIntyre, H. Hagger, & M. Wilkin (Eds.), *Mentoring: Perspectives on school-based teacher education* (pp. 166–189). London: Kogan.

Enz, B. J. (1992). Guidelines for selecting mentors and creating an environment for mentoring. In T. M. Bey & C. T. Holmes (Eds.), *Mentoring: Contemporary principles and issues* (pp. 65–75). Reston, VA: Association of Teacher Educators.

Feiman-Nemser, S. (1983). Learning to teach. In L. S. Shulman & G. Sykes (Eds.), *Handbook of teaching and policy* (pp. 27–40). New York: Longman.

Feiman-Nemser, S., & Parker, M. B. (1992). *Mentoring in context: A comparison of two U.S. programs for beginning teachers* (Special Report, spring). East Lansing, MI: National Center for Research on Teacher Learning.

Feiman-Nemser, S., Parker, M., & Zeichner, K. (1993). Are mentor teachers teacher educators? In D. McIntyre, H. Hagger, & M. Wilkin (Eds.), *Mentoring: Perspectives on school-based teacher education* (pp. 147–165). London: Kogan.

Furlong, J., & Maynard, T. (1995). *Mentoring student teachers: The growth of professional knowledge.* New York: Routledge.

Galvez-Hjornevik, C. (1986). Mentoring among teachers: A review of the literature. *Journal of Teacher Education, 37*(1), 6–11.

Gehrke, N., & Kay, R. S. (1984). The socialization of beginning teachers through mentor-protégé relationships. *Journal of Teacher Education, 35*(3), 21–24.

Gold, Y. (1996). Beginning teacher support: Attrition, mentoring, and induction. In J. Sikula, T. J. Buttery, & E. Guyton (Eds.). *Handbook of research on teacher education* (2nd ed., pp. 548–594). New York: Macmillan.

Gratch, A. (1998). Beginning teacher and mentor relationships. *Journal of Teacher Education, 49*(3), 220–227.

Gray, W. A., & Gray, M. M. (1985). Synthesis of research on mentoring beginning teachers. *Educational Leadership, 43*(3), 37–43.

Healy, C., & Welchert, A. (1990). Mentoring relations: A definition to advance research and practice. *Educational Researcher, 19*(9), 17–21.

Hardcastle, B. (1988). Spiritual connections: Protégés' reflections on significant mentorship. *Theory Into Practice, 27*(3), 201–208.

Hawkey, K. (1997). Roles, responsibilities, and relationships in mentoring: A literature review and agenda for research. *Journal of Teacher Education, 48*(5), 325–335.

Head, G. A., Reiman, A. J., & Thies-Sprinthall, L. (1992). The reality of mentoring: Complexity in its process and function. In T. M. Bey & C. T. Holmes (Eds.), *Mentoring: Contemporary principles and issues* (pp. 24–40). Reston, VA: Association of Teacher Educators.

Heller, M. P., & Sindelar, N. W. (1991). *Developing an effective teacher mentor program.* Bloomington, IN: Phi Delta Kappa Educational Foundation.

Huling-Austin, L. (1986). What can and cannot reasonably be expected from teacher induction programs. *Journal of Teacher Education, 37*(1), 2–5.

Huling-Austin, L. (1988, April). *A synthesis of research on teacher induction programs and practices.* Paper presented at the annual meeting of the American Educational Research Association, New Orleans.

Huling-Austin, L. (1990a). Mentoring is a squishy business. In T. Bey & C. Holmes (Eds.), *Mentoring: Developing successful new teachers.* Reston, VA: Association of Teacher Educators.

Huling-Austin, L. (1990b). Teacher induction programs and internships. In W. R. Houston (Ed.), *Handbook of research on teacher education* (pp. 535–548). New York: Macmillan.

Huling-Austin, L., & Murphy, S. C. (1987, April). *Assessing the impact of teacher induction programs: Implications for program development.* Paper presented of the annual meeting of the American Educational Research Association, Washington, DC.

Huling-Austin, L., Putnam, S., & Galvez-Hjornevik, C. (1986). *Model teacher induction project findings* (Report No. 7212). Austin: University of Texas, Research and Development Center for Teacher Education.

Kay, R. S. (1990). A definition of developing self-reliance. In T. M. Bey & C. T. Holmes (Eds.), *Mentoring: Developing successful new teachers* (pp. 25–38). Reston, VA: Association of Teacher Educators.

Kay, R. S., & Sabatini, A. (1988). *A research based internship for emergency credentialed teachers* (Report No. NIE-R-85-0012). New York: City University of New York, Baruch College. (ERIC Document Reproduction Service No. ED 307 238)

Kelly, M., Beck, T., & Thomas, J. (1992). Mentoring as a staff development activity. In M. Wilkin (Ed.), *Mentoring in schools* (pp. 173–180). London: Kogan.

Killion, J. P. (1990). The benefits of an induction program for experienced teachers. *Journal of Staff Development, 11*(4), 32–36.

Klug, B. J., & Salzman, S. A. (1991). Formal induction vs. informal mentoring: Comparative effects and outcomes. *Teaching and Teacher Education, 7,* 241–251.

Krupp, J. A. (1987). Mentoring: A means by which teachers become staff developers. *Journal of Staff Development, 8*(1), 12–15.

Lawson, H. A. (1992). Beyond the new conception of teacher induction. *Journal of Teacher Education, 43*(3), 163–172.

Lemberger, D. (1992, April). *The mantle of a mentor: The mentor's perspective.* Paper presented at the annual meeting of the American Educational Research Association, San Francisco.

Lortie, D. (1975). *School teacher: A sociological study.* Chicago: University of Chicago Press.

Marlow, L., Inman, D., & Betancourt-Smith, M. (1997). Beginning teachers: Are they still leaving the profession? *The Clearing House, 70*(4), 211–214.

Maynard, T., & Furlong, J. (1993). Learning to teach and models of mentoring. In D. McIntyre, H. Hagger, & M. Wilkin (Eds.), *Mentoring: Perspectives on school-based teacher education* (pp. 69-85). London: Kogan.

McIntyre, D., & Hagger, H. (1993). Teachers' expertise and models of mentoring. In D. McIntyre, H. Hagger, & M. Wilkin (Eds.), *Mentoring: Perspectives on school-based teacher education* (pp. 86–102). London: Kogan.

Mele, J., and Rossiter, M. (1989). Selection of mentors and interns. In J. Conlin (Ed.), *A casebook on school-based mentoring* (pp. 32–36). Amherst: University of Massachusetts, School of Education.

Miles, M. B., & Huberman, A. M. (1984). *Qualitative data analysis.* Newbury Park, CA: Sage.

Odell, S. J. (1986). Induction support of new teachers: A functional approach. *Journal of Teacher Education, 37*(1), 26–29.

Odell, S. J. (1987). Teacher induction: Rationale and issues. In D. Brooks (Ed.), *Teacher induction: A new beginning* (pp. 69–80). Reston, VA: Association of Teacher Educators.

Odell, S. J. (1990). Support for new teachers. In T. M. Bey & C. T. Holmes (Eds.), *Mentoring: Developing successful new teachers* (pp. 3–24). Reston, VA: Association of Teacher Educators.

Pigge, F. L., & Marso, R. N. (1990, April). *Teacher mentor induction programs: An assessment by first-year teachers.* Paper presented at the annual meeting of the Association of Teacher Educators, Las Vegas, NV.

Parkay, F. W. (1988). Reflections of a protégé. *Theory into practice, 27*(3), 195–236.

Reiman, A. J., & Edelfelt, R. (1990). *School-based mentoring programs: Untangling the tensions between theory and research* (Research Report No. 90-7). Raleigh: North Carolina State University, Department of Curriculum and Instruction.

Roberson, L. J. (1997). *A semester-long study of a mentor and intern teachers' relationship: Roles, dilemmas, and professional change.* Unpublished doctoral dissertation, Vanderbilt University, Nashville, TN.

Romatowski, J. A., Dorminey, J. J., & Voorhees, B. V. (1989). *Teacher induction programs: A report.* (ERIC Document Reproduction Service No. 302 468)

Schlechty, P., & Vance, V. (1983). Recruitment, selection, and retention: The shape of the teaching force. *The Elementary School Journal, 83*(4), 469–87.

Schmoll, B. J. (1983, May). *The making of a mentor-mentee relationship.* Paper presented at the Annual Midwest Research-to-Practice Conference in Adult and Continuing Education, DeKalb, IL.

Schon, D. A. (1987). *Educating the reflective practitioner: Toward a new design for teaching and learning in the professions.* San Francisco: Jossey-Bass.

Shulman, J. (1986, March). *Opportunities of a mentorship: The implementation of the California mentor teacher program.* Paper presented at the annual meeting of the American Educational Research Association, San Francisco.

Smithey, M. W., & Evertson, C. M. (1994, April). *Learning to teach in a year-long internship: Mentors' and interns' perspectives.* Paper presented at the annual meeting of the American Educational Research Association, New Orleans.

Smithey, M. W., and Evertson, C. M. (1995). Tracking the mentoring process: A multimethod approach. *Journal of Personnel Evaluation in Education, 9,* 33–53.

Smithey, M. W., Wade, M. W., and Evertson, C. M. (1993, April). *Collegiality and learning to teach: Interns' responses to the mentoring process.* Paper presented at the annual meeting of the American Educational Research Association, Atlanta.

Stevens, N. H. (1995). R and R for mentors: Renewal and reaffirmation for mentors as benefits from the mentoring experience. *Educational Horizons, 73*(3), 130–37.

Sullivan, C. G. (1992). *How to mentor in the midst of change.* Alexandria, VA: Association for Supervision and Curriculum Development.

Summers, J. A. (1987). *Summative evaluation report: Project CREDIT.* Terre Haute, IN: Indiana State University, School of Education.

Varah, L. J., Theune, W. S., and Parker, L. (1986). Beginning teachers: Sink or swim? *Journal of Teacher Education, 37*(1), 30–34.

Vickers, E. (1989). Stages in the mentor/student teacher relationship. In *A casebook on school-based mentoring* (pp. 23–26). Amherst: University of Massachusetts, School of Education.

Wade, M. W. (1993). *Voices of mentor teachers: Reflections on the mentoring experience.* Unpublished doctoral dissertation, Vanderbilt University, Nashville, TN.

Wildman, T., Magliaro, S., Niles, R. A., & Niles, J. A. (1992). Teacher mentoring: An analysis of roles, activities, and conditions. *Journal of Teacher Education, 43*(3), 205–213.

Wright, K. S. (1992). From the Odyssey to the university: What is this thing called mentoring? *ACA Bulletin, 79,* 45–53.

Yosha, P. (1991, April). *The benefits of an induction program: What do mentors and novices say?* Paper presented at the annual meeting of the American Educational Research Association, Chicago.

Developing a Commitment to Social Justice in Teacher Education

David C. Berliner
Arizona State University

There is currently a heightened demand for classroom teachers throughout the nation. We have gone from about 45 million students at the start of the 1990s to about 52 million in 1996, and a few million more students will be coming soon after the turn of the century. In addition, teacher retirement rates will soar because the mean age of the teaching force is very high, with large numbers of teachers well over the age of 50. So, in the immediate future, there is likely to be a strong demand for persons to staff the classrooms of the nation. But what will those persons be like?

If the 1990s were like the 1950s, then the answer to the question, What should teachers be like? might be that new teachers, fundamentally, should be like the ones they replace, though perhaps better trained in this way or that. But for many families and children, life is meaner now, and continuity of vision simply will not do. Given the times we live in, new conceptions of the role of the teacher, and therefore the role of the teacher educator, may be more appropriate than the conception that was useful in the recent past.

A version of this paper was originally given as an invited address at the meetings of the Association for Teacher Education in Saint Louis, Missouri, in 1995. Another version was given as an invited address at the MOFET Conference on Teacher Education in Netanya, Israel, in June 1996. The author thanks both organizations for the opportunity to explore the ideas contained in this paper.

In the recent past, I, like others, sought an understanding of the skills and processes associated with effective teaching. In that endeavor, I have been fortunate enough to work with the scholar we honor in this volume (Berliner & Rosenshine, 1977, 1987). With him and others, I successfully uncovered many of the characteristics of effective teachers, discovered the origins of successful instructional programs and schools, and thereby developed a knowledge base for making teacher education more rational, technical, and craftlike. But while we were studying and validating craft knowledge that could improve teaching, the plight of poor children in our nation was becoming worse. The United States, by a wide margin, now leads the industrialized democracies in the percentage and the number of children in poverty (Rainwater & Smeedling, 1995). Moreover, the real incomes and life chances of poor people in the United States have declined rapidly in comparison with those of the rich (Berliner & Biddle, 1995). Under these circumstances, it is time to remember that teaching is, after all, a *moral* craft. At this time, it appears to me that the moral dimension of the profession needs to be addressed in teacher education more than the technical or craft dimension.

Teaching has become more difficult in many parts of the nation because we have raised the standards by which we judge the success of schooling, while many more communities must cope with the pernicious effects of poverty on the lives of their inhabitants. Although the problems of educating the poor to high standards of achievement are visible daily in the classrooms of our nation, the origins of those problems are clearly located outside the schoolhouse doors.

An American Dilemma

To make clear that many contemporary educational problems have their origin outside our schools, we can accompany Jonathan Kozol (1995) to the Mott Haven section of the South Bronx, an area my mother grew up in and one I know well from my childhood. Kozol points out that it takes only 18 minutes to ride the New York City subway from the seventh richest congressional district in the United States to the poorest. Mott Haven, one of the most racially isolated sections of the nation, contains the poorest of New York's Hispanics and African-Americans. It is the grimmest of inner-city areas, with large numbers of crack cocaine users and teenage prostitutes and with unimaginably high crime rates. Murder is common, including random murders, murders during simple robbery, murders that include decapitation and mutilation, and murders of children. Lots of children! Nearly 4,000 heroin injectors live in the area, many of whom are HIV infected, leading to the horrible statistic that one-fourth of all the Mott Haven women tested in obstetric wards in the region are positive for HIV. Thus, pediatric rates of HIV are very high. Death and despair are no strangers to the residents here:

> Depression is common among children in Mott Haven. Many cry a great deal but cannot explain exactly why.

Fear and anxiety are common. Many cannot sleep.

Asthma is the most common illness among children here. Many have to struggle to take in a good deep breath. Some mothers keep oxygen tanks, which children describe as "breathing machines," next to their children's beds.

The houses in which these children live, two thirds of which are owned by the City of New York, are often as squalid as the houses of the poorest children I have visited in rural Mississippi, but there is none of the greenness and the healing sweetness of the Mississippi countryside outside their windows, which are often barred and bolted as protection against thieves.

Some of these houses are freezing in the winter. In dangerously cold weather, the city sometimes distributes electric blankets and space heaters to its tenants. In emergency conditions, if space heaters can't be used, because substandard wiring is overloaded, the city's practice is to pass out sleeping bags.

"You just cover up . . . and hope you wake up the next morning," says a father of four children, one of them an infant one month old, as they prepare to climb into their sleeping bags in hats and coats on a December night.

In humid summer weather, roaches crawl on virtually every surface of the houses in which many of the children live. Rats emerge from holes in bedroom walls, terrorizing infants in their cribs. In the streets outside, the restlessness and anger that are present in all seasons frequently intensify under the stress of the heat. . . .

What is it like for children to grow up here? What do they think the world has done to them? Do they believe that they are being shunned or hidden by society? If so, do they think that they deserve this? What is it that enables some of them to pray? When they pray, what do they say to God? (pp. 4–5)

While Kozol raises moral issues that every society must address, some educational questions are also appropriate to ask. For example:

How well can we teach such children in our public schools? (Not well, I think.)

Would we have a better chance to teach these children all that we would like to teach them if the quality of their lives were enhanced? (Yes, I think we would.)

Then shouldn't teacher education programs produce teachers as adept at changing social conditions as they are at teaching social studies? (Yes, I think they should.)

Thus, it is my belief that the moral dimension of our profession now needs more emphasis in our teacher education programs. We cannot have as many successful students and schools as we want and need unless teachers can be enlisted in changing the social conditions that are negatively affecting too many of our youth. In teacher education we need to develop what my colleagues and I call *strong professionals* (Barone, Berliner, Blanchard, Casanova, & McGowan, 1996). Strong professionals are concerned about social justice for children and their families. Strong professionals are not silent on issues of social justice when so many children and families are being hurt so badly in a country with riches unimagined by any previous civilization on earth.

Characteristics of a Strong Professional

Every teacher preparation program struggles with some of the same issues. We all try to teach novices subject-specific teaching methods, organizational and management systems, ways of working effectively in a multicultural setting, something about the foundational fields needed for a career in education, and so forth. But when all is said and done, when our programs are specified and approved by whatever oversight authorities we have, we should ask whether *one* overarching disposition has been learned. We should ask if our novice teachers have developed an ideology for interpreting education, and if we accomplish that, we must then ensure that our novice teachers have the propensity to act on their ideology.

As Thomas Barone (Barone et al., 1996) eloquently argues, besides the knowledge and skills we ordinarily teach, *we owe our students an ideology*. Not our personal ideology, necessarily, but *an* ideology, one that is compatible with the best thinking we have about children, teaching, learning, and schooling. When a teacher we have trained has that kind of ideology, we hold that we have developed a strong professional educator. The moral as well as the technical aspects of that person's craft will be visible. Strong professional educators are recognized by their abilities in three dimensions: the *articulative,* the *operational,* and the *political.*

The Articulative Dimension of Strong Professionalism

The first dimension of strong professionalism is the articulative. Professionals are said to be strong when they are free and able to articulate—that is, to profess—what they hold to be beneficial and effective within their particular fields of endeavor. Schoolteachers who are strong professionals engage in the kind of critical reflection that enables them to make and express informed judgments about a variety of curricular and educational phenomena. Silence by teachers in these times is not good for our nation.

The educational ideas and practices about which strong education professionals make judgments are partially theoretical. That is, strong professionals have formulated sensible positions with regard to such enduring, classic philosophical questions as, What should I teach, to whom, and why? They have some kind of answer to the question, What knowledge is of most worth? (Or, as recently amended, *Whose* knowledge is of most worth—a teacher's, a student's, a test publisher's, business persons', Christian fundamentalists'? Whose knowledge will be accorded respect and given status?) But a professional teacher's beliefs about what constitutes good education are not just decontextualized, abstract, and theoretical. Strong professional educators are also able to articulate positions concerning the wisdom of particular local practices. For example, they may ask:

- Is it *sensible* for us to have this school open so few hours when so many children are in need of a safe place to work and be cared for?

- Is it *wise* for us at this school to use curricular and instructional tracking for our students?

- Is it *appropriate* for us to aid and abet the school nurse in dispensing Ritalin to some of these children, as their parents wish?

- Should I continue to teach in a school where the paddling of students occurs frequently?

- Why should I label all these children "at risk" when I truly believe they are all "at promise"?

- Should the content I use in teaching my second-grade Hispanic students to read arise from their own experiences and culture?

Each informed judgment about local practice implies a value position. Each requires that the teacher have an idea of what is good, of what ought to be. Strong professionals have acquired a more or less coherent system of beliefs about what constitutes educational virtue. This system of beliefs constitutes an educational ideology; it determines who one is as an educator. It is this ideology that compels teachers to ask, and formulate answers to, value-laden questions about their jobs. And if that is what we want our teachers to do, then teacher education programs must legitimate asking and exploring answers to such questions during training. But questions about the moral aspects of teaching, rather than the technical aspects of teaching, do not constitute a major part of any of the teacher education programs I know about.

Teachers have usually *not* been encouraged to articulate for themselves a personal stance on curricular and educational matters. While teachers play a prominent role in implementing the curriculum, others have assumed greater responsibility for creating curriculum content and setting educational priorities. It is not the professional judgment of teachers that informs decisions about what and how children should be taught. Federal and state politicians, organized groups of parents, university professors, test developers and publishers, the business community, and the courts all seem to have greater authority. A short while ago, in my state, the new chief state school officer, by fiat, threw out five years of intensive effort by teachers to develop new assessment instruments, and went back to standardized, multiple-choice, paper-and-pencil, norm-referenced achievement tests, in opposition to virtually all the new testing standards that our professional groups have struggled to develop.

This complete takeover of educational decision making by political and business leaders; test developers and publishers; narrow, special-interest parent groups; and others is a consequence of the inability of teachers to articulate a curriculum platform. Teachers have been encouraged to view themselves as servants of various political forces rather than as curriculum leaders. They have been told, in the language of business, that they must serve their "clients," that they are molders of "raw materials," that "customer satisfaction" must be maintained, and that "efficiency" and "effectiveness" and "total quality management" are important criteria in judging their merit. In this cultural milieu, too many teachers have lost their voices; too many forget to say that they are educators of human beings, not manufacturers of widgets. Their personal visions of educational virtue have come to be regarded as annoying distractions rather than as sources of professional wisdom. How much longer should this be allowed to continue unresisted?

The Operational Dimension of Strong Professionalism

Influence over the curriculum by agents outside the classroom has always been present to some degree, but it has become stronger and more pervasive since the 1970s. Since that time, teachers have increasingly been imagined as conduits of mandated curriculum content rather than as creative practitioners who are capable of developing original material and activities. Too many teachers now have a diminished sense of ownership of their craft. Too many teachers are now prevented from realizing their pedagogical preferences, for the states and the districts have imposed ever more regulations about what should be taught and tested. In too many districts now, the teacher is a semiprofessional functionary locked into a "top-down" bureaucratic organizational arrangement. Each teacher remains in a separate classroom, isolated from other professionals by packed teaching schedules. In this system, each teacher is expected to behave in accordance with predetermined administrative policy designed to heighten efficiency, that is, to maximize output at minimum cost. Such procedures weaken the ability of teachers to realize a professional ideology. And this weakens the teachers' chances of practicing their profession in a manner consistent with their ideology. It is the issue of practice that is of concern here. What we seek is a teacher that can both *articulate* an educational vision and carry that vision out in his or her classroom. The carrying out of one's ideology is the operational dimension needed by a strong professional.

The Political Dimension of Strong Professionalism

Teachers must always be mindful that they live and work within a democratic culture, a culture in which power must be shared rather than hoarded and lorded over others. Teachers must *never* assume that professional autonomy means a cavalier disregard for the judgments of members of other educational constituencies. Thus, teachers must engage in politics.

Recall that a strong professional teacher will have acquired, first, an ability to *articulate* a personal perspective on educational matters and, second, the talents to put that perspective into *operation* in a classroom. But what about teachers who experience an incongruity between their own perspectives on what is educationally proper, good, and virtuous and the hostile educational environment in which they find themselves? What are they to do? As strong professionals, they must struggle to alter those surroundings. That is the third element of strong professionalism: the political efforts of teachers. Teachers must negotiate ways to implement their ethically based curriculum platforms.

The sources of constraint on the implementation of one's educational platform are as numerous as the educational constituencies that exist in a democratic society. These constituencies include those already mentioned (state legislators, textbook and test publishers) and others, such as external and on-site administrators, parents, fellow teachers, students, and even maintenance personnel who refuse to rearrange furniture for alternative teaching modes. Teachers who are forced to assume subordinate positions within a "top-down" organizational arrangement are in special need of an arsenal of strategies for resisting the constraints on their professional prerogatives.

Our vision of strong professionals is about teachers who possess such strategies and are adept at using them. The political dimension of teaching has long been ignored by teacher education programs. In our vision it is not ignored; we think it deserves a much bigger role in the teacher education programs of our times. Teachers in my state are virtually silent as, one after another, state officials attempt to decertify teachers, cut public school budgets, develop private-school voucher plans, and in other ways impose their antiprofessional and antidemocratic visions on the educational system of the state. The silence of the teaching community is the clearest indicator I have that our schools of education have failed to develop the political dimension of a strong professional in the teachers they graduate.

In sum, beginning teachers are strong professionals if, after carefully examining the nature of what is educationally good and virtuous, they have acquired the ability to discuss an educational platform, have developed competence in putting that platform into practice, and are able to persuade others to respect their ethically grounded sets of beliefs and practices. But the articulative, operational, and political components of strong professionalism are not built merely out of self-reflection and deep philosophical discussions at school and at the local pub. An educational ideology also requires professional knowledge, and that knowledge, like an ideology, is also acquired in our programs of teacher education.

A Knowledge Base for Teacher Education

Of course, what constitutes the appropriate knowledge base for a teacher education program cannot be decided without controversy. For me, one of the many legitimate sources of knowledge about teaching and learning derives from traditional scientific methods, now in some need of defense in the postmodern world, an era marked by much antiscientific rhetoric in education. I believe that the scientific knowledge generated in sociology, educational psychology, anthropology, economics, and research on teaching, to name a few areas of the social sciences, provides a rich, legitimate, and potentially useful source of knowledge for prospective teachers to use in developing their visions of what is good and virtuous in education. A good deal of scientific knowledge is not neutral, but laden with implications for deciding what is proper to do for or with children. It is this value-laden part of the knowledge base that we need to promote much more, for it will help teachers to develop and then articulate their preferences for what is good and virtuous.

Scientific knowledge must be taught in a way that allows prospective teachers to examine it, question it, and reflect on it, rather than simply as authoritative findings to be implemented. A strong professional cannot emerge unless *all* knowledge is seen as open to question. Strong professionals emerge when they have license to use their own personal experience and professional ideology as filters for the evaluation of new knowledge.

But there is research that is reasonable to accept as trustworthy, and promoting that research in our colleges of education will help give teachers a stronger professional voice in contemporary educational debates. We live in an age that respects evidence, that expects professionals to have such evidence for their actions. I believe that teachers who can articulate and put into action research findings that contribute to social justice—to the betterment of the lives of children and families—are more likely to see an increase in their personal sense of efficacy and the respect in which the profession of teaching is held. These are significant secondary consequences of speaking out and doing something for children and families. But the primary reason for educating teachers to speak out is that research suggests that some contemporary educational practices are harmful to children and their families.

Let me suggest a few good fights in which teachers, armed with social science knowledge, can find their professional moral voice and enter the public debate that now is so harmful for children and destructive of their families.

Knowledge About the Effects of Punishment

We might start, for illustrative purposes, with the issue of punishment. Adults get frustrated with young people and want to punish them—for graffiti, disrespect, poor grades, to say nothing of more serious actions. People want to punish children even though all of behavioral psychology agrees that the use of positive reinforcement of alternative behaviors results in greater and longer-lasting behavioral change than the use of punishment. Although we can persuasively argue this point and can muster much evidence to support it, most Americans believe there are times when it is right and proper to punish youthful offenders. It is the nature of that punishment I want to comment on, because some of the recommendations for punishment include physical punishment. A contemporary example is the recent wave of parents and legislators pushing for the paddling of youthful offenders. This is morally and scientifically wrong. It is harmful. It is dangerous in its long-term effects.

In 1995 in California, a bill to "paddle" children (AB 7) was defeated (California AB 7, 1995). It was introduced and supported by 15 members of the state assembly and cosponsored by 5 state senators. So we are not talking about a single crank in the legislature. Assembly Bill 7 would have mandated paddling, the use of physical punishment, the systematic beating of children and youth. The 1995 legislation, sounding more like the legislation of the year 1695, specified that "The paddle shall be made of hardwood that is one-half inch thick. The handle of the paddle shall be six inches long and one and one-half inches wide. The paddle area shall be 18 inches long and six inches wide."

The legislation went on to state that parents must administer this punishment but if they refused, a bailiff would. The state would pay up to $1,000,000 to reimburse local governments for implementing these procedures.

Recently in my state, Arizona, the newspapers reported on a local Christian school where the principal had been whipping children, with the full and willing support of the parents and the local education authorities—at least until the story make the press (Sowers, 1995). Then this particular principal's violent and perverse sexual needs apparently went even beyond the authority he was ordinarily granted. A 15-year-old girl got the police to arrest him and then went on TV to show her scarred buttocks. She charged that the principal had stripped her and then beaten her in front of her mother as they all prayed together. The mother confirmed the story. The principal was then found to have a police record of child abuse of this kind in one other state and in one other country. Such behavior is not called abuse by some of my fellow Arizonans, but was, instead, called "discipline" by the parents of that particular Christian school.

Shouldn't there be some mechanism for teachers and teacher educators to bring in the name of Albert Bandura and the theory of social learning that convinces almost all of our profession that violence begets violence? The research literature is remarkably clear on this issue: The vast majority of those that physically abuse their spouses and their children were themselves physically punished *often* and *strongly* (Bandura, 1977). A few individuals will speak up about this issue, and they will be labeled bleeding-heart liberals by the community of parents that support this kind of school, parents who are committed to the belief that if you spare the rod you will spoil the child. This enduring biblical injunction is simply wrong in light of what we know about the roots of violence and the ways to bring up mentally healthy children (Berliner, 1997).

Shouldn't the massive body of literature we have on the origins of violence among young people be used to challenge state policies that permit such violence? Surely we have something to say about this as an organized group of scholars and practitioners. Silence is complicity. We should be speaking authoritatively and with consensus, though probably not with unanimity. We should also ask ourselves why we can't graduate from our schools of education an extremely high percentage of novice teachers who can articulate this overwhelmingly persuasive body of research, and who can, through political means, change schools and states that allow physical violence against children.

Knowledge About Retaining Children in Grade

Let us move to another issue where the research is compelling and the practice is in opposition to that research. I believe that there are very few more coherent bodies of knowledge in our field than the one relating to retention in grade, an action that year after year *fails* to accomplish its purpose for most of the students who are left back. Furthermore, retention in grade is enormously costly. Each year, it is estimated that more than 1 million students are left back. Providing an extra year of schooling for each of them costs a minimum of $5 billion a year! But, of course, that is only if those students stay in school long enough to graduate high school. Being overage for grade is usually the strongest predictor of dropping out of school; thus, the costs estimated for educating these students may actually be a bit lower, since many of them do not stay in school. On the other hand, the costs to society in general will be markedly greater, since individuals without high school diplomas cost more to support throughout their adult lives.

Where will professional educators learn about this coherent body of knowledge if not in their programs of teacher education? Why can't we develop an education community that can articulate and carry out policies in accordance with the research and the moral issues involved? And there are moral issues involved, for to leave a child back is to stigmatize that child and diminish that child in the eyes of his or her parents and friends. The vast majority of the children that are retained in grade will be hurt, not helped, by that decision (Smith, 1983). In addition, such children are much more likely to be from the powerless families, not the "school-smart" families (Smith, 1983). Surely we have something to say about this as an organized group of scholars and practitioners speaking authoritatively and with consensus, though again probably not with unanimity. What have schools of education done to teach novice teachers to be politically active and argue with citizens in thousands of local school districts that the practice of retention in grade is almost always wrongheaded—educationally, socially, and fiscally? There are always individuals arguing this case at the local level, but where is the advocacy by the organized professional community of teachers?

Knowledge About Bilingual Education

Another, more controversial example comes to mind. We have a reasonably coherent body of research on the lasting benefits of early-entry, late-exit bilingual education for children, as well as a remarkably coherent body of knowledge attesting to the cognitive, social, and economic benefits for those with balanced bilingual abilities (Hakuta & McLaughlin, 1996). Where will teachers learn about the scientifically compelling data that support these beliefs? Where will teachers learn to reflect on the meaning of these social-scientific truths in light of their own, perhaps strongly held, beliefs to the contrary? Either they will learn about these issues in their teacher education programs, or they will probably not learn them at all. If we strive to create strong professionals, and they learn the facts in this matter, then there will be outrage in the professional community when we continue to deny bilingual education to hundreds of thousands of eligible students, in violation of laws passed more than 20 years ago. But without strong professionals to argue for the rights of politically weak constituencies, legally required programs are denied.

The lack of strong professionals may explain why, for example, the education community let English-only advocates get newspaper space reporting things that are both racist and *not* true. In a magazine ad in March 1995, the headline screamed, "Millions of children abused in school!" The text of the ad referred to the fact that millions of children were enrolled in bilingual education programs. Where are the strong professionals to take these educational issues on and articulate what is good for immigrant children and their families? And if these families are important, then bilingual education is useful in another way. It demonstrates the schools' respect for immigrants' native culture and language, as the immigrants make the difficult transition to life in the United States. Are these issues without moral aspects? Are these issues to be decided strictly by fiscal exigency, or by what is educationally best for the children?

The question is why the educational community is not organized politically to argue with citizens in thousands of local school districts that denial of high-quality bilingual educational programs is wrongheaded—legally, educationally, socially, and fiscally. I don't think we should leave this issue just to the Hispanics, the Vietnamese, and the bilingual teachers. I am concerned about the response of the professional community of teachers and teacher educators when that community has coherent and persuasive bodies of knowledge that could lead to sensible and humane recommendations in areas of heated public debate. Our professional community of teachers and teacher educators is not visible enough in the public arena, because our teachers and teacher educators are not developing strong ideological platforms. Of course, there will always be teachers who are against bilingual education. But if the whole complement of sociolinguistic research and theory were presented in an environment that fostered reflection, it would be very hard for many teachers to hold such negative opinions. More teacher education programs need to be concerned with the creation of environments for understanding the charged nature of this research and its inexorable links to ideology.

Knowledge About Tracking

Another example of research with ideological implications is the research on tracking. Individual members of our community have been fighting this practice for some time. The preponderance of evidence, as I read it, is that placing young children on a low track affects them negatively for their entire lives (Oakes, 1985). And who are the low-track young children? Too often they are the poorest children of our communities. If we believe that socioeconomic classes are organized on Darwinian principles, then early placement in the lowest track reflects students' biology and, thus, their destinies. With that kind of thinking, there is no dilemma. But if we see people of low socioeconomic class as possessing malleable abilities, if we believe that their poverty is due more to outside forces than to genetically determined abilities, then the practice of early segregation into tracks is immoral.

How visible are the protestations of the teaching and teacher education communities against the practice of tracking, a practice that more often than not adds to the social handicaps of the already poor and powerless in our society? Where will teachers learn to think about these issues and recognize that the data are not as clear as those that make policy believe they are? Where will teachers learn that tracking is only one of a number of ways to accommodate the large spread of individual differences among students?

Shouldn't it be the teachers that inform school boards about the many alternatives to tracking, alternatives that do not penalize the faster or more motivated children? Teacher educators need not fear that such issues will be ignored if they concentrate on developing strong professionals. Strong professionals will find ways to monitor programs that segregate children—programs that track the gifted as well as the less able—to ensure that they do not accomplish more harm than good. Strong professionals do not just profess moral concern about programs designed to segregate children in a democracy; they also institute political action if those programs are likely to do harm.

Other Knowledge with Moral Implications

There are many other areas in which strong professionals can be armed with social science knowledge that supports moral stands. Many, if not most, members of the teacher education community would agree with the following statements:

● Strong professionals might want to comment on the testing of the "readiness" of kindergartners with instruments so flawed that they would be laughable if it were not for the awful consequences of their results. Some school districts in Arizona test children in the spring of the year before they are to enter school. So now young people are being identified as "slow" even before they arrive at school! Can any sane professional defend these practices? Why do we bother to teach education students the concept of test validity if we never teach them how to apply that knowledge in a way that will protect children and their families?

● Strong professionals might want to comment on the fiscal and social benefits to society of high-quality preschool programs for children who are poor. The research on the long-term benefits of such programs is quite remarkable, showing a reduction of costs to society in the long run (Berliner & Biddle, 1995). For example, poor children who have attended high-quality preschools show lower rates of assignment to special education. They show higher levels of school achievement, higher rates of school graduation, greater employment stability, and greater income earned, thereby increasing the taxes they pay and their consumption of goods, while decreasing their need for unemployment insurance and welfare payments. But society is not investing in such programs for the young.

● Strong professionals might want to comment about the importance of the after-school social groups (Girl Scouts, boys' clubs, church groups, etc.) that serve as physical and psychological "urban sanctuaries" for children in poor neighborhoods (McLaughlin, Irby, & Langman, 1994). These groups foster prosocial behavior and help students bond with school life (McLaughlin et al., 1994). They appear to promote the values we cherish in our schools and nation. Educators already know that families are stressed. Many children are being raised by single parents or in two-parent families in which both parents are working for a living. That means too many of our youth have too much unsupervised time. We end up blaming families for not doing the job we want them to do, though they are struggling to survive economically and the communities are doing nothing to help. If educators don't help support and organize the kinds of "gangs" we want our youth to be in, young people will find other kinds of gangs that meet their basic needs for survival in mean environments. And they will endanger us all.

● Strong professionals might want to comment on the inappropriate form staff development efforts take in most districts. Dissemination of ideas and practices in education too often wastes district money and staff time. The accumulated knowledge in this area suggests that other and better mechanisms for disseminating information are available (Fenstermacher & Berliner, 1985). In addition, the professional education community needs to speak out when charlatans among the professional-development and in-service education providers (for example, the split-brain people and the aura color readers) do workshops for teachers and administrators, wasting public money and professional time.

- Strong professionals might want to comment on the efforts of some citizens and local politicians to intensify the curriculum and increase the work of teachers and students, when research suggests that most of this zeal is misplaced (Berliner & Biddle, 1995). I know of no one who studies the lives of teachers and the ways of classrooms who believes that mandates for intensification have a chance of working.

- Strong professionals might want to point out the remarkably consistent findings of positive effects of peer and cross-age tutoring (Gage & Berliner, 1998) and to question the apparent inability of schools to organize themselves to try or sustain such programs.

- Strong professionals might want to make a commentary about the problems associated with competitive grading (Gage & Berliner, 1998). Contemporary American classrooms are designed to allow a few winners and make losers of the rest of the students, though alternatives exist.

- Strong professionals might want to comment on the use of homework. The evidence is that it is not as simple a solution to the problems of achievement as parents and school board members believe. Apparently, homework does not always have positive effects (Cooper, 1994).

What I hope we can develop is a teaching and teacher education community that engages in advocacy concerning issues on which it has a reasonable consensus. Or, in lieu of that, I seek from the organized educational-research community a reasoned explanation of the complexity of the issues that many of the 15,700 local boards and the 50 state boards of education confront. In particular, I would use research findings, where it is fair to do so, to promote social justice, for it is clear to me that teachers and teacher educators are remaining silent while our society, which includes our schools, is becoming a harsher one for our children.

Our nation, currently the richest nation that ever existed, has found new ways to keep wealth from the many and concentrate it in the hands of the few. At this point, about 1 percent of our nation's individuals own 40 percent of the nation's wealth (Berliner & Biddle, 1995). It is a worldwide phenomenon, in part a product of the globalization of trade and the ascent of market-driven economies. In fact, one recent U.N. estimate is that the 400 richest people in the world have accumulated personal wealth equivalent to that of the bottom 40 percent of the entire world's population (Berliner & Biddle, 1995)!

But not every nation competing in the global marketplace is suffering such appalling changes as ours. Other nations run better systems. I have lived in two other nations and have visited a number of others at length. Though they are vastly different and none are without problems, each of those other nations seems to believe more than we do in equity and communitarian values and has proved that social welfare and capitalism are not mutually exclusive philosophies. In any of those countries (e.g., Finland, Australia, Canada), for persons with only modest incomes, *and for their children*, things are currently working better than in our own country. If we use the usual indicators of the standard of living—rates of homicide, infant mortality, low-birth-weight children, teen pregnancy, AIDS, children in poverty, children who are economically active, single-woman heads of households in poverty, and so forth—our nation is not doing as well as some others.

The questions are these: Who will be the ones to articulate a better vision of what could be? Who will put into operation programs that help change our direction? Who will form the political alliances needed to change the trends that are now so destructive of children and their families? Strong professional teachers, as the citizens with the greatest concerns about these subjects, should be the citizens who most frequently organize to respond to these concerns, and that means that teacher education institutions must have a greater impact on their novice teachers as they socialize, train, and educate those who will educate the next generation.

Conclusion

Horace Mann, the most vigorous promoter of public education in the United States during the 19th century, recognized clearly that teachers are the nation's leaders in the fight for social justice. And he reasoned, with logic as true today as it was 150 years ago, that teacher educators have an enormously important role to play in developing teachers' motivation to fight for a just society. Horace Mann spoke at the opening of one of the earliest normal schools, in Bridgewater, Massachusetts, in 1846 (M. Mann, 1891). Schools for the education of teachers were then a new American invention, enthusiastically endorsed by Mann:

> I believe that, without them, free schools themselves would be shorn of their strength and their healing power, and would at length become mere charity schools, and thus die out in fact and in form. Neither the art of printing, nor the trial by jury, nor a free press, nor free suffrage, can long exist, to any beneficial and salutary purpose, without schools for the training of teachers; for if the character and qualifications of teachers be allowed to degenerate, the free schools will become pauper schools, and the pauper schools will produce pauper souls, and the free press will become a false and licentious press, and ignorant voters will become venal voters, and through the medium and guise of republican forms, an oligarchy of profligate and flagitious men will govern the land. (p. 219)

Horace Mann has given teachers and teacher educators no less a charge than to stop the development of pauper schools and pauper souls, to lift up the quality of our press, to remind our voters of their social obligations, and to prevent the development of a self-interested oligarchy whose greed will ruin our land. Horace Mann could clearly envision both Mott Haven and strong professional educators. He understood that the only counter to the one is the other.

References

Bandura, A. (1977). *Social learning theory.* Upper Saddle River, NJ: Prentice Hall.

Barone, T., Berliner, D. C., Blanchard, J., Casanova, U., & McGowan, T. (1996). A future for teacher education: Developing a strong sense of professionalism. In J. Sikula, T. J. Buttery, & E. Guyton (Eds.), *Handbook of research on teacher education* (2nd ed., pp. 1108–1149). New York: Macmillan.

Berliner, D. C. (1997, Spring). Educational psychology meets the Christian Right: Differing views of children, schooling, teaching, and learning. *Teachers College Record, 98,* 381–416.

Berliner, D. C., & Biddle, B. J. (1995). *The manufactured crisis.* Reading, MA: Addison-Wesley.

Berliner, D. C., & Rosenshine, B. (Eds.). (1987). *Talks to teachers.* New York: Random House.

Berliner, D. C., & Rosenshine, B. (1977). The acquisition of knowledge in the classroom. In R. C. Anderson, R. J. Spiro, & W. E. Montegue (Eds.), *Schooling and the acquisition of knowledge.* Hillsdale, NJ: Erlbaum Associates.

California AB 7. (1995). Juveniles: paddling.

Cooper, H. M. (1994). *The battle over homework.* Thousand Oaks, CA: Corwin Press.

Fenstermacher, G. D., & Berliner, D. C. (1985). A conceptual framework for evaluating staff development. *Elementary School Journal, 85,* 281–314.

Gage, N. L., & Berliner, D. C. (1998). *Educational Psychology,* 6th ed. Boston: Houghton Mifflin.

Hakuta, K., & McLaughlin, B. (1996). Bilingualism and second language learning: Seven tensions that define the research. In D. C. Berliner & R. C. Calfee (Eds.), *Handbook of educational psychology* (pp. 603–621). New York: Macmillan.

Kozol, J. (1995). *Amazing grace: The lives of children and the conscience of a nation.* New York: Crown.

Mann, M. (Ed.). (1891). *Life and works of Horace Mann* (Vol. 5). Boston: Lee & Shepard.

McLaughlin, M. W., Irby, M. A., & Langman, J. (1994). *Urban sanctuaries.* San Francisco: Jossey-Bass.

Oakes, J. (1985). *Keeping track: How schools structure inequality.* New Haven, CT: Yale University Press.

Rainwater, L., & Smeedling, T. M. (1995). *Doing poorly: The real income of American children in a comparative perspective* (Luxembourg Income Study Working Paper No. 127). Syracuse, NY: Syracuse University, Maxwell School of Citizenship and Public Affairs.

Smith, M. L. (1983). *How educators decide who is learning disabled.* Springfield, IL: Charles C. Thomas Publishing.

Sowers, C. (1995, March 25). Headmaster faced other abuse charges. *Arizona Republic,* p. A1.

4

Theory, Norms, and Intentionality in Process-Product Research on Teaching

N. L. Gage
Stanford University

Barak Rosenshine was an early contributor to the best aspects of process-product research on teaching (PPRT). In PPRT, investigators seek correlational and causal relationships between classroom processes and student achievement of instructional objectives. Rosenshine's doctoral dissertation, *Behavioral Predictors of Effectiveness in Explaining Social Studies Material* (1968; see also Rosenshine, 1971a) set a new standard for the ingenious and detailed analysis of videotaped recordings of teacher discourse. His *Teaching Behaviours and Student Achievement* (1971b) set a new standard for the detailed review of PPRT methods and findings. Since then, he has contributed a steady flow of scholarship in research on teaching. So it seems fitting that the following examination of the most recent critiques of PPRT should appear in this volume.

Process-Product Research on Teaching

Classroom processes consist of teacher actions, student actions, and teacher-student interactions. The ancient idea that process (what teachers and students do in

---

I am greatly indebted to Ray L. Debus for valuable criticisms and suggestions.

the classroom) should be related to product (what students learn) has had an enduring appeal to researchers on teaching. Research on that relationship was pioneered by Rice (1896, cited in Rice, 1913), who discovered that "the spelling grind," or teachers' spending a lot of time drilling pupils in spelling, did *not* improve achievement in spelling.

During subsequent decades, such correlational research had considerable success in finding teaching process related to student outcomes. Experiments applying the findings of such research yielded substantial improvements in student achievement. In such experiments, researchers took the findings of correlational studies as hypotheses. For example, they might decide to test a finding that teachers who used ways to reduce off-task time had classes that learned more. Then the researchers would train experimental-group teachers to use practices that reduced wasted (off-task) time. They temporarily withheld such training from the control-group teachers. Then they observed both groups of teachers to see whether the training had been effective. Finally, they measured the achievement of the students of both groups of teachers. Typically, researchers found that the training *was* effective and that the superiority in achievement of the experimental-group classes was substantial (see the reviews by Gage & Needels, 1989; Needels & Gage, 1991; Walberg, 1986, 1991; Waxman & Walberg, 1982).

Findings of PPRT were enthusiastically received by many teachers. Thus, in the early 1980s, on its own initiative, the American Federation of Teachers developed for its members a nationwide teacher-education program (Biles, Billups, & Veitch, 1982) based in large part on process-product research findings. That program was still operating in 1998.

Nonetheless, because such research required relatively large amounts of money and much technical expertise, it became less feasible when funds for educational research became harder to obtain in the United States and elsewhere in the 1980s and 1990s. Also, other research interests became popular. The result was less PPRT.

Criticisms of PPRT

Meanwhile, a variety of criticisms of PPRT were made. Those criticisms were summarized and rebutted by Gage and Needels (1989) and Needels and Gage (1991). Recently, the debate was reopened by the two most frequent critics of PPRT: Garrison and Macmillan (1994). The present essay examines their recent arguments in the context of related writings by them and others. Such an examination is important to the degree that PPRT is important. And even Garrison and Macmillan (1994, p. 397) recognized that importance.

Garrison and Macmillan have exhibited an interesting progression from condemnation to approval of PPRT. In their first critique, they wrote, "We do believe . . . that a combination of reasons weighs heavily in favor of searching for new approaches" (p. 256), and they called for "an adequate *replacement* [italics added] for the process-product tradition" (Garrison & Macmillan, 1984, p. 274; reprinted in Macmillan & Garrison, 1988, p. 78).

In their second critique (Macmillan & Garrison, 1984), they contradicted themselves:

> The rigor of the process-product approach, which we think is somewhat misguided at moments, is at the same time a model for anyone who would seriously investigate the nature of teaching. . . . It is *not to replace* [italics added] these strong aspects of the process-product tradition that we examine its foundations—it is rather to suggest ways for improving in just these areas. (p. 16)

Finally, they concluded their third critique (Garrison & Macmillan, 1994) by asserting, "Gage and Needels [1989, p. 295] conclude their paper as follows: 'In the long run, educators should insist on process-product research. They need knowledge of the connections between what teachers do [process] and what students learn [product].' *We certainly agree* [italics added]" (p. 397).

Their three-word final sentence amounts to a reconsideration of their position on the main issue, which is whether PPRT is desirable and important. The essence of PPRT is the search for relationships between classroom processes and student achievement. Beyond that essence, the rest is a matter of incidental, though sometimes important, features of conceptualization, method, interpretation, and application. Such features are incidental in the sense that they can be altered and improved without changing the essential nature of the PPRT enterprise.

Despite their final acceptance of PPRT, Garrison and Macmillan (1994) have again criticized PPRT—this time on four grounds: (a) that its posture is atheoretical, (b) that it neglects "normative issues," (c) that its results are not significant, and (d) that it is unable to deal with intentionality. The following discussion takes up each of these criticisms in turn.

The Criticism of Atheoretical Posture

Garrison and Macmillan's (1994) criticism of atheoretical posture has been rebutted in two papers (Gage, 1994a, 1994b) that appeared in the same year as that of Garrison and Macmillan. So it is considered only briefly here.

First, these critics ignore the implicit theories underlying PPRT, theories that are not distinctly expressed in any formal and rigorous way at first. To illustrate, one such implicit theory is that students achieve instructional objectives better if they are engaged longer in working toward those objectives at a nonconfusing level of difficulty (Carroll, 1963; Berliner, 1990). Another implicit theory is that students understand generalizations better if given examples.

Second, the critics ignore the agreement among philosophers of science on the impossibility of any rigid definition of scientific method, including any stipulating that scientific research must always be theory-driven. The history of science is full of examples of great discoveries made with no prior theory—discoveries such as continental drift, X-rays, penicillin, radar, and the positive correlation between the distance and velocity of galaxies. The role of serendipity in the history of scientific discovery is well recognized (see, e.g., Kanterovich & Ne'eman, 1989). Similarly, in research on teaching, there has been the serendipitous (and counterintuitive) discovery that a teacher's asking questions during a discussion session tends to stifle, not stimulate, student discussion (Dillon, 1985).

The Criticism on "Normative" Grounds

The Garrison-Macmillan (1994) criticism concerning normative issues amounts to a guess about something that might happen, not an observation of something that has happened:

> The theories of the researchers on teaching *may be* [italics added] largely incommensurable with the subjectively reasonable theories of the teacher practitioners. Simply turning research facts over to practitioners *is likely to* [italics added] lead to objective facts being subjectively interpreted and applied in idiosyncratic and inconsistent ways. (p. 395)

Here these critics (see also Fenstermacher, 1979) refer to *logical* possibilities for which they offer no *empirical* evidence. But abundant empirical evidence does indicate that the dire possibilities to which they refer have not come about. The evidence comes from *experiments* in which PPRT findings have been, in Garrison and Macmillan's words, "turned over" to teachers (Gage & Needels, 1989, pp. 268–286; Needels & Gage, 1991, pp. 11–18).

Before turning to those experiments, I will first explain the very important difference between experiments and correlational studies. Macmillan and Garrison (1984) do not explicitly recognize this difference. Thus they write, "Within the process-product tradition, teaching is viewed as the causation of student achievement by teacher behavior; the causes are discovered by statistical *correlations* [italics added] of measures of teacher behavior and measures of student outcomes" (p. 17). But the causes are not discovered through correlations. Rather, they are demonstrated through experiments. An experiment requires a deliberate manipulation of an independent variable. In PPRT, the manipulation of classroom processes is done through teacher education. Experiments can yield much more than correlations. They can yield differences in outcomes between experimental and control groups of teachers—*differences that can justifiably be causally attributed to differences in classroom processes.* The causal attribution is justified because other possible sources of the difference in outcomes can be ruled out by virtue of (a) random assignment of teachers to experimental and control groups (e.g., by tossing a coin) and (b) other features of the experiment's design.

At least 17 such randomized experiments have been conducted with regular teachers engaged in teaching the regular curriculum in regular classrooms over periods ranging from a school term to a school year (see summaries by Gage & Needels, 1989, pp. 268–286; Needels & Gage, 1991, pp. 11–18). Those experiments showed that experimental-group teachers who were taught to use practices derived from correlational findings did use them to a substantially greater degree than the control-group teachers. Further, and of even greater importance, the experimental-group teachers produced substantially higher *achievement* than the control-group teachers (who were not given such knowledge and understanding). (Technically, the median effect size was 0.60, which statisticians regard as substantial.) Some of the experiments studied, and found desirable effects on, student attitude and conduct.

These results indicate that the research findings "turned over" to the teachers were not interpreted in "idiosyncratic and inconsistent ways" and that the findings fitted readily into teachers' "subjectively reasonable theories." The "turning over" to the teachers usually took the form of substantial and intensive in-service teacher education sessions and supporting services. These sessions included emphasis on the rationale of the recommended teaching practices.

The Criticism of Significance of Results

Macmillan and Garrison have invested much in their frequently repeated claim that "A healthy, progressive research tradition should have come up with more significant results than this one has" (1984, p. 18). But in Garrison and Macmillan's 1994 criticism, they ignored the 17 experimental successes of PPRT, even though they wrote it several years after the reviews of those studies were published.

Critics owe it to the field of education to look at those experiments rather than, as these critics do, to continue to quote obsolete characterizations of the field of *presage*-product research (not process-product research) as it stood *in 1963*. (In presage-product research, investigators studied presage variables—dimensions of teacher personality, such as teacher intelligence, as rated, tested, and inventoried.) Garrison and Macmillan (1994) should follow their own advice to other philosophers: "Arguments among philosophical commentators on educational research often seem to be above the fray; much is said about how teaching or learning ought to be studied, for example, but *little by way of examination of actual research in those areas is found* [italics added]" (Macmillan & Garrison, 1984, p. 15).

Garrison and Macmillan also fail to compare PPRT achievements with those of other kinds of research. In 1984 they realized that "one does not evaluate a theory or research tradition *in vacuo*, but always against the example of others" (p. 272). Accordingly, when they wrote in 1994, a decade after their first critique, these critics should have pointed to other programs, approaches, or paradigms that have yielded, or promise to yield, results more "progressive" for the understanding of teaching and for the improvement of student outcomes. They have failed to do so.

Their own apparent candidate is an "erotetic theory," which conceives of teaching as a reply to students' actual or implied questions (Macmillan & Garrison, 1983). But "erotetic theory" is not a theory in the sense of characterizing or predicting relationships between variables. Rather, it is a *conception* of teaching that *may* have heuristic value. Thus far, in the 15 years since its publication, it has not led to empirical research that supports any claim of improvement in student outcomes.

The Criticism of Disregard of Intentionality

Intentionality includes the having of intentions but also much more—the having of beliefs, desires, ideas, feelings, and moods, for example. As philosophers use the term, it means that mental content is always *about something.*

The criticism that PPRT is unable to deal with intentionality dates at least from Phillips (1981):

> In the writings of Descartes, animals were treated as "conscious automata"—they had awareness, but nevertheless they were machines. Their awareness, in other words, was not causally efficacious. Cartesianism did not die out; it persisted over the centuries, and at present it is alive and well and flourishing in the field of educational research.
>
> Consider one of the main traditions in research on teacher effectiveness in which the process-product mode has been adopted. Aspects of the teacher's behavior are observed, and then the attempt is made to find correlations with pupil outcomes. The procedure is as much at home in the elementary or high-school classroom as it would be in the primate enclosure at the municipal zoo—at best, the subjects of the researcher's attention are treated as conscious automata. (p. 99)

Noel (1993) elaborated the criticism as follows:

> The research program commonly known today as "process-product" has contributed a large body of research which exemplifies both a conceptual and methodological lack of consideration of the intentionality of teachers. Simply stated, this is the result of the basic tenets of this research program: the examination only of teacher behaviors (processes) and their effects on student achievement (products). . . . The development of research . . . culminated in a focus on finding lawlike generalizations . . . and *a lack of consideration of the teacher's beliefs, desires, emotions, and intentions* [italics added]. (p. 129)

Garrison and Macmillan (1984, 1994; see also Macmillan & Garrison, 1984, 1988) have made the same allegation repeatedly. They state:

> The process-product tradition explicitly ignores the intentions of teachers and learners in its investigations. In part this is for reasons having to do with basic methodological assumptions. Intentions cannot be investigated by the usual low-inference methods embraced by this tradition. But teaching is a human activity, and like all human activities it is intentional, a matter of moods and tenses. (Macmillan & Garrison, 1984, p. 18)

My consideration of this criticism addresses five questions: (a) What does intentionality mean in this context? (b) Is there abundant evidence that intentionality *has* been dealt with in PPRT? (c) What causes the critics' erroneous view that PPRT neglects intentionality? (d) What are some problems in dealing with intentionality? (e) What are the intentions of *researchers,* or where has intentionality fitted into the framework of research on teaching until now, and what is its potential place in such research?

The meaning of intentionality. The term *intentionality,* in everyday parlance, refers to intention or purpose. But, as used in philosophy, it can refer to the quality, in states of mind, of being "about," or directed toward, something. We cannot believe, wish, hope, or desire without believing, wishing, hoping, or desiring *something,* which may or may not exist. Thus, intentionality is not necessarily, in this philosophical usage, the same as intention or purpose. "Intentionality is directedness; intending to do something is just one kind of Intentionality [capitalization in original] among others" (Searle, 1983, p. 3). Broadly speaking, this meaning of intentionality seems similar to the meaning of "being mental."

The large philosophical literature on intentionality (see, e.g., Dennett, 1987; Lyons, 1995; Searle, 1983) varies widely in its concerns. Lyons (1995) described, categorized, and analyzed several major philosophical conceptions of intentionality. But the critics discussed here have never stated explicitly which of these they have in mind. So the present discussion must be restricted to inferences of their definitions of intentionality from their writings as philosophers of education who have brought the concept to bear on PPRT.

Phillips (1981) implied his definition by referring to "factors internal to their [neobehaviorists'] experimental subjects. . . . (Why they [neobehaviorists] persist in maintaining an outmoded and misleading name for their position is a mystery. . . .)" (p. 99). He quotes developmental psychologists who had done better research by "attending to the 'meaning of the behavior'" (p. 100).

Thus, what Phillips means by "intentionality" is the internal factors that give meaning to human behavior. These factors would presumably include the beliefs, attitudes, values, and intentions of the person—all of which enable us to understand what the person does.

Noel (1993) set forth her conception as follows:

> Research on teaching throughout the twentieth century has focused on teacher effectiveness, often in terms of the effects of teachers' specific behaviors on student achievement. This research has been conspicuously lacking in consideration of the intentional nature of teaching and the intentionality of teachers. . . . As a result of shifts in conceptions of social science research, researchers have begun to recognize that teachers are intentional agents who have beliefs, desires, emotions, intentions, and goals that help make up their aims and actions in teaching. (p. 123)

Garrison and Macmillan (1984) considered concern with intentionality to be absent from PPRT because they attributed behaviorism to PPRT: "If one deals in one's scientific investigations solely with the directly observable 'behavior,' one need not solve the mysteries of the mind" (p. 262). (But Gage's definition of teaching, to which this sentence refers, did not include "directly observable.") In their most recent restatement (1994), we find the following:

> Teaching . . . is an intentional act. . . . Now, think about what it will take to understand the vicissitudes of human intentions. Finally, think about the essence of process-

product research. If intentionality is the essence of teaching . . . theories of teaching and research on teaching must display that essence at the very core of their methodology and logic. . . . While the process-product research program can stretch to accommodate intentionality "incidentally," it would be better to make it central in all consideration of teaching. (pp. 386–387)

Evidence of PPRT's regard for intentionality.   Has intentionality indeed been disregarded in the kinds of classroom-process observation used in PPRT? The best answer can be found in a source ignored by the critics. This source consists of the statements of researchers concerning what they have observed and how they have observed it in describing classroom processes. No such statement has been mentioned or quoted by these critics. If they had taken those statements into account, they would not have regarded PPRT as engaged in a "stretch to accommodate intentionality 'incidentally'" (Garrison & Macmillan, 1994, p. 387).

The researchers' statements manifestly appeal to any ordinary, commonsense comprehension as saturated with references to, and calls for assessments of, teachers' and students' intentions, feelings, hopes, desires, and so on. The reader should judge whether the following examples "avoid intentionality" and create the problem of "translating the findings from the nonintentional language into the language that dominates the practical settings of the classroom" (Garrison & Macmillan, 1984, p. 273). These examples come from research published in years ranging from the 1930s to the 1980s.

First, consider items about what teachers do in the observation system used relatively long ago by Wrightstone (as quoted in Medley & Mitzel, 1963), who supplemented each of these items with a paragraph of instructions:

- "Allows pupil to make a voluntary contribution" (p. 255)
- "Encourages pupil to make a contribution"
- "Proposes a question or thesis for pupil or class"
- "Refers pupil or pupils to sources of data or information"

Second, consider typical categories of teaching practice in an observation system (Flanders, 1965) widely used in the 1960s:

1. *Accepts feeling:* accepts and clarifies the feeling tone of the students in an unthreatening manner. Feelings may be positive or negative. Predicting or recalling feelings are included.

2. *Praises or Encourages:* praises or encourages student action or behavior. Jokes that release tension, but not at the expense of another individual, nodding head or saying, "um hm?" or "go on" are included. (p. 20)

Third, consider the following representative sets of directions to observers of teaching, drawn from two later research projects:

Confusion between academic questions and self-reference questions must be resolved by *determining the teacher's intent* [italics added]. Often the question as asked will be ambiguous ("What do you think would happen if . . . "), and the coder will have to await the teacher's feedback to the child's response in order to determine how he is going to treat the question. (Brophy & Good, 1969, p. 18)

Code 2 questions are those that *allow a free expression of ideas or feelings and invite opinions* [italics added]. Code 2 questions encourage responses that require: interpreting ideas, cause-and-effect establishing relationships, making comparisons, reasoning, . . . and describing a process." (Stallings, 1977, p. 269)

Fourth, consider the processes observed in the process-product study conducted in the 1980s in ten countries by the International Association for the Evaluation of Student Achievement (Anderson, Ryan, & Shapiro, 1989). Among the instructional practices observed were

(1) provision of cues to structure students' learning, (2) provision of directions (e.g., Here's how to work the problems on your worksheets) and directives (e.g., Take out your homework papers from yesterday), (3) explanation of content and subject matter, (4) use of instructional materials in support of their explanations, (5) demonstrations of some procedure or skill, and (6) use of examples to illustrate major points made during the explanations. (p. 106)

Furthermore, "data on student perceptions of the task-orientation of the classroom, their teacher's classroom management, and the nature of the instruction they were provided during the study were collected" (p. 116).

Observers could not classify what teachers do into these kinds of categories without making judgments as to teachers' intentions, hopes, concerns, desires, and feelings. The observers base their judgments not only on what the teacher does, but also on the total classroom situation—in all its complexity—in which the teacher does it.

These examples of ways in which process-product researchers describe classroom processes indicate that the process-product tradition does not ignore intentionality in describing what teachers and learners do. Yet, even after the publication by Gage and Needels (1989, p. 257) of the Brophy and Good (1969) and Stallings (1977) examples quoted here, Garrison and Macmillan (1994) were unable to see the concern with intentionality that saturates the kinds of observations done by process-product researchers. After noting that they had previously written, concerning process-product research, "The failure to come to grips with the essential intentionality of teaching is its greatest conceptual shortcoming" (Garrison & Macmillan, 1984, p. 18), they wrote, "We would like to reaffirm this claim" (Garrison & Macmillan, 1994, p. 388).

These writers do not suggest any method by which "coming to grips with intentionality" might be improved. Thus, they make no reference to literature, either early (e.g., Gage & Cronbach, 1955) or recent (e.g., Kenny, 1994), on interpersonal perception, or persons' (e.g., researchers') perceptions of other persons' intentions, motives, and actions. Which of Lyons's (1995) alternative conceptions of intentionality the critics have in mind is not made explicit. They call to mind what Dennett (1987) meant when he stated that there are "few scolds more tiresome than the philosopher trying to reform the linguistic habits of others" (p. 271).

Possible sources of the critics' erroneous assumption.   Where does this erroneous assumption of these critics—that PPRT does not regard the intentions of teachers as central—come from? What leads them to make that assumption? I offer three surmises.

A first surmise is that they *misinterpret the term "behavior."* What may mislead them is that the researchers (who are often psychologists) use the term *behavior,* rather than the philosophers' term *action,* for "intended behavior." Perhaps the critics conclude from that usage that the researchers are radical behaviorists (like, e.g., B. F. Skinner) who strip "behavior" of any reference to ideas, emotions, or inner mental experience and activity and that they attend to no phenomena other than those that are directly observable, such as the uninterpreted movements or words of teachers.

This explanation of the critics' inference of neglect of intentionality gains plausibility from the statement by Phillips (1981), quoted earlier, concerning neobehaviorism. Similarly, Macmillan and Garrison (1984) regard process-product research as "continuous with the (largely behavioristic) tradition that goes back to and through Thorndike" (p. 17). But Thorndike was not "largely behavioristic." He was a functionalist. His *Psychology of Wants, Interests, and Attitudes,* for example, was anathema to radical behaviorists (see Hilgard, 1987, p. 85). The classic behaviorists John B. Watson and B. F. Skinner would not have regarded process-product research as behavioristic. If PPRT has roots in a school or system of psychology, they reside in functionalism (see Berliner, 1989), not behaviorism.

Thus it seems that, to these critics, the term *behavior* has the connotation of disregard of inner, or mental, life. But that connotation has long been erroneous. No dictionary of psychology adheres to such a connotation. One classic dictionary (English and English, 1958) considers behavior to include "thinking" and "perceiving" (p. 61). A second dictionary (Heidenreich, 1970) states that behavior "is characterized by [among other things] goal-directed patterns of reaction" (p. 18), and, of course, goal-directedness is not directly observable in the Watsonian-Skinnerian sense. A third dictionary (Wolman, 1989) states, "Activities that qualify as behavior include ideas, thoughts, dreams, images" (p. 41). The *Encyclopaedia Britannica* ("Human Behaviour," 1995) defines human behavior as "the expressed and potential capacity for activity in the physical, *mental* [italics added], and social spheres of human life" (p. 133).

Nonetheless, the critics persist in imputing to PPRT a disregard of intentionality. They do so, perhaps, because PPRT (and much other social science) uses the term *behavior* in referring to what people, including teachers, do. We should discard this too-well-gnawed bone of contention. Then philosophers could correct their misinterpretation of the term *behavior.* Whatever the philosophers' misunderstandings of terminology may be, PPRT surely denies, indeed would regard as ridiculous, the charge that it neglects teachers' intentionality, that it focuses merely on teachers' uninterpreted words or movements, that it disregards the meaning and purpose of classroom behaviors.

The critics hold that "the interpretation of *meaning* is generally taken to involve interpretation of observations or perceptions, but the 'essence' of process-product research provides no such guidance for interpretation" (Garrison & Macmillan, 1994, p. 368). On the contrary, PPRT does provide its observers with guidance for interpretation of the actions of teachers and students. As was noted five years earlier (Gage & Needels, 1989, p. 257), it is easy to find references to teachers' intentions in PPRT's definitions of the classroom processes observed and in the instructions and training given to process observers. Recall the instruction, quoted earlier, that "confusion between academic questions and self-reference questions must be resolved by *determining the teacher's intent* [italics added]. . . . and the coder will have to await the teacher's feedback to the child's response in order to determine how he is going to treat the question" (Brophy & Good, 1969, p. 18). Recall also Stallings's (1977) instruction that "Code 2 questions are those that allow a free expression of ideas or feelings and invite opinions" (p. 269). Clearly, the observers are being instructed to take into account the intentions underlying the teaching activity they are recording.

Critics who allege that intentionality is disregarded in PPRT should find directions for classroom-process observation that support their allegations. Phillips (1981) used a merely hypothetical example of an intentionality—disregarding teacher behavior ("The teacher's arm goes up" [p. 101]) that he implied might be used in process-product research. The critics have given no *actual* examples of PPRT observation that disregards intentionality. They have neglected the details of what PPRT has actually done in describing and measuring classroom processes. The critics' writings suggest a serious shortcoming: they have not read the reports of the process-product research they criticize.

A second surmise is that the critics *misunderstand low-inference observation.* Low-inference observations require the observer, in describing teaching practices, to use *relatively* less inference, extrapolation, judgment, or deduction from what is directly observed. Thus, Macmillan and Garrison (1984) charge that "Intentions cannot be investigated by the usual low-inference methods embraced by this tradition" (p. 18).

One reason for studying low-inference behaviors is largely pragmatic: low-inference actions are assumed to be easier to communicate helpfully to the teachers addressed in teacher education programs. Low-inference actions are more readily understood and duplicated. For example, it is assumed that it is less helpful to teachers to tell them to "be clear" (a high-inference action) than to tell them the *relatively* low-inference actions (e.g., "use well-understood terms" and "give examples") they should take if they intend to be clear. But these low-inference actions are obviously intentionality-laden, as are the typical low-inference concerns of observers of teaching in PPRT.

A second reason for using low-inference behaviors is that they facilitate communication between researchers. One understands better what a fellow researcher has done when the classroom processes observed are couched in low-inference terms.

In any case, the use of low-inference actions does not signify, and does not result in, a disregard of teachers' intentionality. Hiller, Fisher, and Kaess (1969) defined the low-inference variable *vagueness* as a "psychological construct which refers to *the state of mind of a performer* [italics added] who does not sufficiently command the facts or understanding required for maximally effective communication" (p. 670). Similarly, Rosenshine (1968) defined the low-inference variable *familiarization procedures* as those that "give the subject specific cues [e.g., definitions of key terms] before the main material" (pp. 113, 116). Low-inference behaviors, such as the examples just given, are typically rich in meaning and content concerning the teachers' intentions; they are not mere uninterpreted words and movements. The critics have an obligation to quote instances of intention-disregarding low-inference variables actually used in PPRT.

A *third surmise* as to the source of confusion is the Garrison-Macmillan assumption that process-product researchers use low-inference variables *exclusively* in describing teachers' actions and thus fail to use high-inference observations. Thus they write, "One would expect an appeal to ethnographic research methods at this point, since intentions are central to that methodology, *but that would expand the research program beyond its stated essence* [italics added]" (Garrison & Macmillan, 1994, p. 389). In referring to ethnographic methods, they fail to recognize the problems with such methods, cogently identified by Phillips (1987).

In any case, the essence of PPRT—the search for relations between process and product variables (Gage & Needels, 1989, p. 291; Needels & Gage, 1991)—has never excluded *any* valid method of describing process or product. Garrison and Macmillan are mistaken in implying that PPRT is linked to the exclusive or even primary use of low-inference variables. Published reports show that PPRT has often described process by means other than low-inference observations. Even a cursory examination of representative research (see Gage & Needels, 1989, pp. 292–293, for illustrative citations) would reveal that low-inference variables are often absent from process-product studies. And when low-inference variables are used, they are often accompanied by (a) high-inference observations, (b) high-inference questionnaires and interviews with teachers and students, (c) high-inference *noninteractive,* or unobtrusive, methods of describing the complexities of classroom life (Webb, 1981), such as noting the placement of seats and tables, the frequency and length of homework assignments, and the amount of absenteeism, and (d) summary judgments (ratings) of photographs and videotapes as to high-inference variables, such as the teacher's warmth, clarity, task orientation, student-centeredness, and the students' time on task. Such variables have often been observed and rated in PPRT. Researchers have used well-defined schemes that call upon an observer to make and record complex judgments of the intentionality underlying teachers' actions. These judgments have often taken the form of ratings—that is, summaries of multifaceted impressions over long periods of time—of teachers' intentionality-permeated acts.

Also, some PPRT directly contradicts the Garrison-Macmillan misconception that ethnographic PPRT has not been done, that it "would expand the [process-product] research program beyond its stated essence" (Garrison & Macmillan, 1994, p. 389). Studies by Au and Jordan (1980), Barnhardt (1982), and Edelsky, Draper, and Smith (1984) used ethnographic descriptions of classroom processes. Although these researchers might not characterize themselves as process-product researchers, their research not only described classroom processes ethnographically, but also examined the relationships of those processes to student achievement. This research is PPRT because it was aimed at revealing a relationship between a process variable (cultural appropriateness) and a product variable (student achievement). As Erickson (1986) put it, in describing the first-mentioned two studies,

In both cases, as teachers have interacted with students in the classroom in ways that resemble those that are culturally appropriate in the home and community [a process variable], student achievement on standardized tests [a product variable] increases dramatically [a process-product relationship]. (p. 135)

Ethnographic methods of describing classroom processes may turn out to yield higher correlations with student achievement than the more highly structured and quantifiable methods used most often in PPRT. If so, those methods should be used more often in PPRT aimed at enhancing the explanation, prediction, and improvement of student achievement. But that is an empirical, not a "philosophical," issue—one on which sufficient knowledge is unavailable. In any case, ethnographic methods are not at all barred from PPRT.

Thus, the criticism of PPRT on the grounds that it neglects the intentionality of teaching seems to be based on a misunderstanding of terminology rather than a close examination and analysis of the details of the researchers' conceptualizations, methods, and interpretations of results, as described in their research reports. Nothing in the PPRT program, as it has been carried out, has excluded or worked against full attention to teachers' intentionality.

Problems in dealing with intentionality. All this is not to say that there are no problems in dealing with intentionality. It is not always easy to get at intentionality in seeking to understand the meanings of teachers' actions. Phillips (1981) appropriately pointed to possible difficulties in the direct approach of asking teachers to tell their intentions: (a) the teachers may be unaware of their own intentions, (b) the teachers may be unwilling to admit to socially undesirable intentions, and (c) teachers' actions may have unintended effects and side effects.

An example of these difficulties can be seen in examining the conscious or unconscious intentions that might underlie a teacher's comment, at the beginning of a lecture, that a researcher with whom she strongly disagrees has nonetheless done the most important work in the area of the lecture. What is the teacher's intention? Several alternatives can be imagined:

Stage-setting: to introduce immediately the subject of her lecture

Generosity: to offer disinterested, generous praise of the researcher

Kindness: to soften the blow of her subsequent criticism of the researcher

Self-aggrandizement: to appoint herself as an expert who knows enough about the subject to judge who its most important researcher is

Disingenuousness: to appear evenhanded and thus strengthen the force of her criticism of the researcher

Defensiveness: to defend herself, by inflating the importance of her target, against potential criticism for failure to pay attention to the work of other important researchers.

Other plausible interpretations of the intentions underlying this single statement are possible. Perhaps the correct interpretation is "all of the above." An interpretation of such a remark should, of course, be based on its immediate context, on the rest of the teacher's lecture, and on her prior statements on the same subject. Similarly varied interpretations can be formed for many of the intentions, feelings, desires, and hopes underlying all the actions of teachers, writers, and persons in general.

Just how Garrison and Macmillan would confront the difficulties of perceiving intentions in a valid way is unclear from what they have written about intentionality in the erotetic theory. In their 1994 work, they consider the intention of all teaching to be erotetic. That is, they believe "*it is the intention of teaching acts to answer the questions that the auditor (student) epistemologically ought to ask, given his or her intellectual predicaments with regard to the subject matter* [italics in original]" (p. 387). They regard this definition as indicating "that intentionality is part of the 'essence' of teaching" (p. 387).

Another example of how Macmillan and Garrison (1988) seek to take account of intentionality is their analysis of transcripts of classroom discourse as a way of illustrating their erotetic theory of teaching. In analyzing one bit of classroom discourse, they discover that

> when a teacher asks a question—even a relatively simple one like "who lives in that house?"—it might be for one of three different purposes: (1) as a diagnosis of the students' state of knowledge or intellectual predicament, (2) as a test of the students' knowledge or attentiveness to the ongoing lesson or of their learning, or (3) as a way of carrying on the lesson. . . . *The uses may overlap in practice* [italics added]. (p. 166)

Although these authors appropriately identify the problem of valid interpretation of the purpose of teachers' questions, they offer no help in solving it—no help of the kind developed by PPRT through methods of analyzing discourse (see, e.g., the quotations given earlier from Brophy & Good [1969] and from Stallings [1977]). Nor do they mention the quest for prediction and control (i.e., improvement) of achievement—two of the major purposes of PPRT—as bases for resolving issues and appraising the validity of perceptions of intentions.

Noel's (1993) approach also treats the problem of determining the intentions, beliefs, desires, and attitudes of teachers. She approvingly cites several studies (pp. 140–142). In one of these, transcripts of interviews of teachers were analyzed and computer-searched to find specific terms. These terms were then used as a basis for perceiving the teacher's metaphorical construction of the lesson as a "moving object" because of the teacher's use of such phrases as "ahead of time," "get through," "move on," and "got started." In a second study, transcripts of interviews of teachers by researchers were analyzed in a similar way to examine a teacher's personal, practical knowledge, with the finding that the teacher regarded her teaching as something like "running a house." A third example refers to the "reflective-teaching" research program, in which the intentional components are considered central, in that the teacher's beliefs, desires, intentions, and emotions are addressed. But in reflective-teaching research, the actual reasoning of the teacher is not laid out, says Noel, and the teacher is left merely thinking, without knowing how to incorporate the beliefs and so on into the next teaching act. Moreover, reflective-teaching research regards the teacher's intentionality as inaccessible because the teacher's tacit knowledge is considered indescribable, incommunicable, and unknowable. The result is that researchers must make their own interpretations of teachers' language and devise metaphors to portray teachers' thoughts and actions.

Noel's own "more complete conception of intentionality" (p. 142) has two components: the ideas that (a) "teachers have content-ful states, such as beliefs and desires" (p. 142) and (b) "practical reasoning is the process that turns these intentional components into active decision making" (p. 142). Such a conception, she writes, calls for studying a teacher through interviews, journals, and narratives to understand why the teacher feels that a certain approach is best for teaching a certain subject. A given image of teaching may help understand the teacher's overall approach.

"But it will not tell us why the teacher makes a particular decision in a specific teaching situation [italics in original]" (Noel, 1993, p. 144). Noel's insight here points to the inadequacy of any "intentionality" of the kind formulated by Garrison and Macmillan, with their conception that all teaching acts are intended to answer questions that students ask or should ask. That conception would not cope with the question of why, for example, a given teacher answered one question and ignored another. Here we need the psychologist's distinction between traits (long-lasting dispositions) and states (temporary dispositions). Traits have some cross-situational stability, whereas states are determined more by the immediate situation.

In any case, the methods Noel advocates for studying intentionality—examining journals, narratives, and transcripts of classroom discourse and interviews with teachers—have been used in many process-product studies (see, e.g., Rosenshine, 1971b). In those studies researchers also examined videotape records of what the teachers did, transcribed the verbal part of them, and counted various kinds of words, expressions, phrases, and movements. There is no fundamental difference between Noel's approach to learning about teachers' meanings, intentions, and actions and the approaches of the PPRT investigators whom Noel regards as inadequate students of intentionality. Both process-product researchers and intentionality-oriented researchers have paid close attention to the form, content, and context of what teachers said. But there *is* an important difference in focus between PPRT and the intentionality research described by Noel—a difference demonstrated and emphasized in the following section.

Despite all the problems in dealing with intentionality, most judgments of intentions in everyday life are correct. If they were not, human society—family life, school life, and work with others on the job and in the community—would be impossible. When a supermarket checkout clerk says, "That'll be twenty seventy-eight," no English-speaking adult in the United States misinterprets the clerk's intentions, expectations, beliefs, and desires.

Students usually interpret teachers' intentions correctly and easily. Perhaps they misinterpret teachers' intentions when new teaching methods are introduced or when teachers and students come from different cultural backgrounds (G. Morine-Dershimer, personal communication, September, 1996). But ordinarily, correct understanding of intentionality occurs easily every day in billions of human interactions around the world, including the interpretations made by PPRT observers using the observation schemes described earlier in this chapter. In short, it is easy to magnify beyond realistic limits the difficulties of making valid judgments of teachers' and students' intentionality for the purposes of PPRT. If the judgment of intentionality were as difficult in PPRT as critics contend, the research would not have obtained such meaningful results.

The Intentionality of Researchers on Teaching

Philosophical analysts of research on teaching should pay attention to the intentions—the purposes, goals, objectives, and interests—of researchers on teaching. For example, there has been a major difference in the intentions of two kinds of researchers: describers and improvers (Gage & Unruh, 1968). Describers, such as Noel's intentionality researcher, seek to portray, analyze, and interpret teaching, primarily to improve understanding of it. Improvers seek to discover process-product relationships for the purpose of improving teacher education and thus teacher effectiveness. The goals of process-product research go beyond those of the intentionality research described by Noel. Using Noel's data, PPRT would seek to identify which kinds of teacher intentionality occur more (or less) often in classes that learned more than in classes that learned less.

The Variety of Intentions in Research on Teaching

Those different kinds of research intentions can be seen in Figure 4–1, which displays (a) 6 categories (labeled A–F) of concepts, or variables, in research on teaching and (b) the 15 relationships (labeled 1–15), or connections, between pairs of categories. The model illustrated by this diagram has a considerable ancestry, traced with assistance from Burns (1994) and M. J. Dunkin (personal communication, October, 1996). That ancestry begins with Rice (1896, cited in Rice, 1913), who studied, as a process variable, the amount of time teachers devoted to spelling instruction and, as a product variable, student achievement in spelling. During the 1930s and 1940s, much research was conducted by the students of Barr (1948), but it was *presage*-product research, in that they studied presage variables—dimensions of teacher personality, such as teacher intelligence as rated, tested, and inventoried.

Then Mitzel (1957, cited in Gage, 1963, p. 121; see also Mitzel, 1960) identified and distinguished between four categories of variables: (a) *presage* variables, or possible predictors in teacher personality and training, (b) *context* variables, or contingency factors, in the form of school, classroom, and pupil characteristics, (c) *process* variables, namely, classroom actions of teachers and students, and (d) *product* variables, such as pupil achievement, attitudes, and classroom behavior.

This four-category scheme was used by Biddle (1964), who called the categories (a) teachers' "properties" and "formative experiences," (b) "school and community contexts" and "classroom situations," (c) "teacher behaviors" and "immediate effects

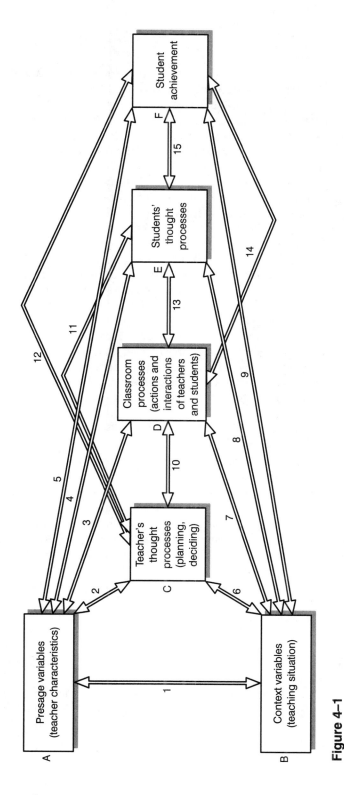

Figure 4–1

Six major categories of variables and the 15 possible two-category relationships in research on teaching.

on pupil responses," and (d) "long-term consequences," including pupil achievement and adjustment. The same scheme was also used by Dunkin and Biddle (1974) in their comprehensive and searching review of research on teaching.

Then Smith (1961) called attention in his "pedagogical model" to what he called the teacher's "intervening variables" (p. 92), namely, the teacher's thought processes. Shulman (1975) brought these to the fore, with the eventual result that Clark and Peterson (1986) were able to review a considerable body of research literature on that component of teaching activity. Smith also included in his model the students' thoughts—"memories, beliefs, needs, inferences, and associative mechanisms" (p. 91). Subsequently, Winne (1987) and Wittrock (1986) reviewed the pertinent research and developed in detail the theoretical rationale for a concern with such thought processes of students.

The arrows in Figure 4–1 denote relationships of the kind that can be revealed by case studies, correlational studies, or experiments. Of course, randomized experiments are what often produce the most persuasive knowledge of whether a relationship is causal, in the sense that deliberate change in the value of one variable—say, a teacher's belief or instructional practice—can cause improvement in the level of another variable, such as student achievement.

The six categories are arranged in Figure 4–1, from left to right, in a quasi-logical-psychological-chronological sequence. The sequence begins with *presage variables* and *context variables*. These factors are followed by the *teacher's thought processes* considered as states (not traits). These affect the teacher's and students' *classroom actions and interactions*. In turn, these occasion *students' thought processes*, which eventuate in, among other things, *student achievement* of the cognitive and other objectives of the teaching.

The two-way arrows indicate that the connections can go in both directions. For example, student achievement can affect subsequent student thought processes, and teachers' actions can influence their own subsequent intentions.

In greater detail, *presage variables* consist of such characteristics of the teacher as gender, age, years of experience, intelligence, knowledge of the subject matter being taught, knowledge about ways of teaching—both in general and in the specific subject matter (pedagogical content knowledge), and intentionality (somewhat stable intentions, beliefs, attitudes, values, appreciations, and the like) as a trait that the teacher has acquired from experience, including experience in teacher education programs.

Context variables refer to the setting in which teaching occurs. They include the community, the school, the grade level, the class size, and the subject matter. They also include the motivations, the values, and the economic, ethnic, ability, and background-knowledge characteristics of the students, as well as the homogeneity of the class in these respects.

The *teacher's thought processes* include intentionality as a relatively momentary state, in a particular situation, and thus the teacher's momentary beliefs and desires about selecting content, adapting text materials, making plans for teaching, and choosing methods of teaching, and the teacher's thoughts and decisions while interacting with students.

Classroom processes consist of the actions and interactions of teachers and students in the classroom. The actions and interactions can be verbal or nonverbal, be cognitive or social-emotional, and involve the whole class, subgroups of the class, or individual students. Verbal behavior takes such forms—identified by Bellack, Kliebard, Hyman, and Smith (1966)—as structuring (setting forth and organizing the subject matter), soliciting (asking questions) of various kinds, responding (typically by a student to a question), and reacting (typically by a teacher to a student's response).

Macmillan and Garrison (1984) erroneously claim that "process-product research cannot be content-specific because of the methodological constraints of correlational statistics" (p. 17). But whenever the product variable is student achievement, the research can be content-specific, to permit the measures of student achievement to be compared across teachers. Process variables can be as content-specific as the researcher's purposes require. Examples of possible content-specific process variables are the processes used in teaching paragraph analysis in reading, teaching the use of the semicolon in writing, teaching the addition of mixed numbers in arithmetic, teaching the gas laws in science, or teaching metaphors in Shakespeare. Product can take the form of student understanding of this specific content. The process-product relationships are then similarly content-specific. The various handbooks of research on teaching (e.g., Richardson, in press) review much content-specific PPRT.

Students' thought processes include students' perceptions, expectations, attendings, motivations, attributions, memories, learning strategies, and metacognitive (monitoring-their-own-thoughts) processes (all considered as states, not traits) in and out of the classroom.

Student achievement of educational objectives can be categorized by type of objective: intellectual, social-emotional, or motor-skill. Within each of these there are many subcategories. Thus, within the intellectual category, the distinction is often made between knowledge, or the ability to recall or recognize subject matter, and "higher-order" abilities, such as comprehension, analysis, synthesis, and evaluation capabilities within the subject matter. The term *higher-order* is sometimes misconstrued as implying that knowledge is "lower-order." But, of course, knowledge of subject matter is essential to any subsequent processing (application, analysis, etc.) of that subject matter.

Research Programs

We can distinguish three kinds of research programs that use these categories of variables. *Single-category* research programs work within one of these six categories of variables. Thus, studies are performed to describe and understand, say, teachers' intentionalities. The research summarized by Noel (1993), as mentioned above, seems to be of this kind, in that it makes no effort to relate intentionalities to other kinds of variables.

Two-category research programs focus on relationships between variables in two of the categories. Process-product research is one of the 15 possible programs of this kind. It is easy to formulate scientifically and socially important questions belonging to each of the 15 numbered lines shown in Figure 4–1. Thus, a Type 1 relationship might indicate whether teachers with certain levels of academic achievement (a presage variable) are found more often in school districts of greater or less wealth (a context variable). A Type 2 relationship might tell whether that presage variable is correlated with teachers' decisions about whether to give homework.

Three-or-more-category research examines the relationships between variables from more than two of these categories. Studies using such statistical methods as aptitude-treatment-interaction analysis, path analysis, and structural equations can answer such questions as, Does teacher clarity make more of a difference in achievement for low-ability students than high-ability students? and, Does student intelligence determine teacher thought processes that in turn determine classroom processes?

Adjacency of categories is likely to affect research results. The various correlations, or connections, will always be less than perfect. That is, some looseness, or slippage, is bound to occur in the relationships between variables within a category or between those in one category and those in another. Still, the connection between variables in adjacent categories is likely to be tighter (that is, the correlation or the experimental effect is likely to be greater) than that between variables in nonadjacent categories. So the Type 10 correlation, between teachers' intentions (Category C) and their actions (Category D), is likely to be higher than the Type 11 correlation, between teachers' intentions and students' thought processes (Category E), or the Type 12 correlation, between teachers' intentions and student achievement (Category F).

Most important for the present discussion, this scheme throws light on the differences between those who, according to Noel (1993), have emphasized intentionality in its own right and those who focus on PPRT. Noel's examples of studies of teachers' intentions, in all their variety and complexity, throw light on *why teachers teach as they do*. Thus, they are located in Category C of Figure 4–1 and are sometimes aimed at explaining the teacher actions located in Category D, or a relationship of Type 10. Research on intentionality—on the nature, determiners, and effects of teachers' beliefs, desires, values, and goals—can yield knowledge of great value, especially in teacher education.

But research on teacher intentionality has not been discussed by the critics in relation to the other categories of variables shown in Figure 4–1. In particular, discussions of teacher intentionality have not been concerned, at least not directly, with the relationships between teacher intentions and student thought processes or student achievement. In short, none of the critics who have urged consideration of teachers' intentionality has mentioned, much less elaborated on or emphasized, effects on students' thought processes or achievement.

Clearly, without knowledge of how the teaching resulting from teachers' intentions affects students, knowledge about teaching would be barren of what makes teaching important to education and society. Yet, intentionality-focused philosophers of education have seemed willing to leave research-based knowledge at the point where we gain understanding of teachers and why they teach as they do. They have not seemed interested in going beyond such knowledge to the relationships between what teachers do and what students think and achieve. They have seemed willing to leave the story at just the point where it begins to focus on the raison d'être of teaching: beneficial effects on students.

On the other hand, PPRT focuses on *how teaching relates to student outcomes*—on the Type 14 relationships between variables in Category D and those in Category F of Figure 4–1. And thus far PPRT has yielded the useful knowledge mentioned earlier. But there is, as always, much room for improvement. Winne (1987), in particular, has made a strong case for the value of incorporating data on students' thought processes (Category E) in a search for Type 13 and Type 15 relationships that will strengthen explanations of process-product relationships (Type 14). And Berliner (1989) has argued for the incorporation of contrasting groups of teachers into research on teacher thinking—groups selected for their differing degrees of effectiveness in producing beneficial effects on students. Such research could yield knowledge of Type 12 relationships, relationships between teachers' intentionality and student achievement. In the process, the research could also throw light on relationships of Type 10 (between teachers' thought processes and classroom actions) and Type 11 (between teachers' thought processes and students' thought processes).

Whether improved ways of addressing intentionality in research on teaching will improve our ability to explain, predict, and improve student achievement is an empirical question that awaits improved approaches to intentionality. By engaging in research on that question, the philosopher-critics of PPRT could clarify their ideas about such approaches.

References

Anderson, L. W., Ryan, D., & Shapiro, B. J. (Eds.). (1989). *The IEA classroom environment study.* Oxford: Pergamon.

Au, K. H., & Jordan, C. (1980). Teaching reading to Hawaiian children: Finding a culturally appropriate solution. In H. T. Trueba, G. P. Guthrie, & K. H. Au (Eds.), *Culture and the bilingual classroom* (pp. 139–152). Rowley, MA: Newbury House.

Barnhardt, C. (1982). "Tuning in": Athabaskan teachers and Athabaskan students. In R. Barnhardt (Ed.), *Cross-cultural issues in Athabaskan education* (Vol. 2, pp. 144–166). Fairbanks: University of Alaska, Center for Cross-cultural Studies.

Barr, A. S. (1948). The measurement and prediction of teaching efficiency: A summary of investigations. *Journal of Experimental Education, 16,* 203–283.

Bellack, A. A., Kliebard, H. M., Hyman, R. T., & Smith, F. L. (1966). *The language of the classroom.* New York: Teachers College Press.

Berliner, D. C. (1989). The place of process-product research in developing the agenda for research on teacher thinking. *Educational Psychologist, 24,* 324–344.

Berliner, D. C. (1990). What's all the fuss about instructional time? In M. Ben-Peretz & R. Bromme (Eds.), *The nature of time in schools* (pp. 3–35). New York: Teachers College Press.

Biddle, B. J. (1964). The integration of teacher effectiveness research. In B. J. Biddle & W. J. Ellena (Eds.), *Contemporary research on teacher effectiveness* (pp. 1–40). New York: Holt, Rinehart & Winston.

Biles, B. L., Billups, L. H., & Veitch, S. C. (1982). *Educational research and dissemination program: Training and resource manual.* Washington, DC: American Federation of Teachers. (ERIC Document Reproduction Service No. ED 236 125)

Brophy, J. E., & Good, T. L. (1969). *Teacher-child dyadic interaction: A manual for coding classroom behavior.* Austin: University of Texas, Research and Development Center for Teacher Education.

Burns, R. B. (1994). Teaching, paradigms for research on. In T. Husén & T. N. Postlethwaite (Eds.), *The international encyclopedia of education* (2nd ed., Vol. 10, pp. 6202–6208). Oxford: Pergamon.

Carroll, J. B. (1963). A model of school learning. *Teachers College Record, 64,* 723–733.

Clark, C. M., & Peterson, P. L. (1986). Teachers' thought processes. In M. C. Wittrock (Ed.), *Handbook of research on teaching* (3rd ed., pp. 255–296). New York: Macmillan.

Dennett, D. C. (1987). *The intentional stance.* Cambridge, MA: MIT Press.

Dillon, J. T. (1985). Using questions to foil discussion. *Teaching and Teacher Education, 1,* 109–121.

Dunkin, M. J., & Biddle, B. J. (1974). *The study of teaching.* New York: Holt, Rinehart & Winston.

Edelsky, C., Draper, K., & Smith, K. (1984). Hookin' 'em at the start of school in a "whole language" classroom. *Anthropology and Education Quarterly, 14,* 256–281.

English, H. B., & English, A. C. (1958). *A comprehensive dictionary of psychological and psychoanalytical terms: A guide to usage.* New York: David McKay.

Erickson, F. (1986). Qualitative methods in research on teaching. In M. C. Wittrock (Ed.), *Handbook of research on teaching* (3rd ed., pp. 119–161). New York: Macmillan.

Fenstermacher, G. D. (1979). A philosophical consideration of recent research on teacher effectiveness. *Review of Research on Education, 6,* 157–185.

Flanders, N. A. (1960). *Teacher influence, pupil attitudes, and achievement* (U.S. Office of Education Cooperative Research Project No. 397). Minneapolis: University of Minnesota.

Gage, N. L. (1963). Paradigms for research on teaching. In N. L. Gage (Ed.), *Handbook of research on teaching* (pp. 94–141). Chicago: Rand McNally.

Gage, N. L. (1994a). The scientific status of research on teaching. *Educational Theory, 44,* 371–383.

Gage, N. L. (1994b). The scientific status of the behavioral sciences: The case of research on teaching. *Teaching and Teacher Education, 10,* 565–577.

Gage, N. L., & Cronbach, L. J. (1955). Conceptual and methodological problems in interpersonal perception. *Psychological Review, 52,* 411–422.

Gage, N. L., & Needels, M. C. (1989). Process-product research on teaching: A review of criticisms. *Elementary School Journal, 89,* 253–300.

Gage, N. L., & Unruh, W. (1967). Theoretical formulations for research on teaching. *Review of Educational Research, 37,* 358–370.

Garrison, J. W., & Macmillan, C. J. B. (1984). A philosophical critique of process-product research on teaching. *Educational Theory, 34,* 255–274.

Garrison, J. W., & Macmillan, C. J. B. (1994). Process-product research on teaching: Ten years later. *Educational Theory, 44,* 385–397.

Heidenreich, C. A. (1970). *A dictionary of general psychology: Basic terminology and key concepts.* Dubuque, IA: Kendall/Hunt.

Hilgard, E. R. (1987). *Psychology in America: A historical survey.* New York: Harcourt Brace Jovanovich.

Hiller, J., Fisher, G. A., & Kaess, W. (1969). A computer investigation of verbal characteristics of effective classroom teaching. *American Educational Research Journal, 6,* 661–675.

Human behaviour. (1995). In *The new encyclopaedia Britannica* (Micropedia, Vol. 6, p. 113). Chicago: Encyclopaedia Britannica.

Kanterovich, A., & Ne'eman, Y. (1989). Serendipity as a source of evolutionary progress in science. *Studies of History and Philosophy of Science, 20,* 505–529.

Kenny, D. A. (1994). *Interpersonal perception.* New York: Guilford Press.

Lyons, W. (1995). *Approaches to intentionality.* Oxford: Oxford University Press.

Macmillan, C. J. B., & Garrison, J. W. (1983). An erotetic conception of teaching. *Educational Theory, 33,* 157–166.

Macmillan, C. J. B., & Garrison, J. W. (1984). Using the "new philosophy of science" in criticizing current research traditions on education. *Educational Researcher, 13*(10), 15–21.

Macmillan, C. J. B., & Garrison, J. W. (1988). *A logical theory of teaching: Erotetics and intentionality.* Boston: Kluwer.

Medley, D. M., & Mitzel, H. E. (1963). Measuring classroom behavior by systematic observation. In N. L. Gage (Ed.), *Handbook of research on teaching* (pp. 247–328). Chicago: Rand McNally.

Mitzel, H. E. (1957). *A behavioral approach to the assessment of teacher effectiveness* (mimeographed). New York: College of the City of New York, Division of Teacher Education.

Mitzel, H. E. (1960). Teacher effectiveness. In C. W. Harris (Ed.), *Encyclopedia of educational research* (3rd ed., pp. 1481–1486). New York: Macmillan.

Mitzel, H. E., & Gross, C. F. (1958). The development of pupil-growth criteria in studies of teacher effectiveness. *Educational Research Bulletin, 37,* 178–187, 205–275.

Needels, M. C., & Gage, N. L. (1991). Essence and accident in process-product research on teaching. In H. C. Waxman & H. J. Walberg (Eds.), *Effective teaching: Current research* (pp. 3–31). Berkeley, CA: McCutchan.

Noel, J. R. (1993). Intentionality in research on teaching. *Educational Theory, 43,* 123–145.

Phillips, D. C. (1981). Perspectives on teaching as intentional act. *The Australian Journal of Education, 25*(2), 99–105.

Phillips, D. C. (1987). Validity in qualitative research: Why the worry about warrant will not wane. *Education and Urban Society, 20,* 9–24.

Rice, J. M. (1913). *Scientific management in education.* New York: Hinds, Noble & Eldredge.

Richardson, V. (Ed.). (in press). *Handbook of research on teaching* (4th ed.). New York: Macmillan.

Rosenshine, B. (1968). *Behavioral predictors of effectiveness in explaining social studies material.* Unpublished doctoral dissertation, Stanford University, Stanford, CA.

Rosenshine, B. (1971a). Explorations of the teacher's effectiveness in lecturing: Study III. Objectively measured behavioral predictors of effectiveness in explaining. In I. Westbury & A. A. Bellack (Eds.), *Research into classroom processes* (pp. 201–209). New York: Teachers College Press.

Rosenshine, B. (1971b). *Teaching behaviours and student achievement.* Slough, UK: National Foundation for Educational Research in England and Wales.

Searle, J. R. (1983). *Intentionality: An essay in the philosophy of mind.* New York: Cambridge University Press.

Shulman, L. S. (Chair). (1975). *Teaching as clinical information processing* (Report of Panel 6, National Conference on Studies in Teaching, National Institute of Education). Washington, DC: U.S. Department of Health, Education and Welfare.

Smith, B. O. (1961). A concept of teaching. In B. O. Smith & R. Ennis (Eds.), *Language and concepts in education* (pp. 86–101). Chicago: Rand McNally.

Stallings, J. (1977). *Learning to look: A handbook on classroom observation and teaching models.* Belmont, CA: Wadsworth.

Walberg, H. (1986). Synthesis of research on teaching. In M. C. Wittrock (Ed.), *Handbook of Research on teaching* (3rd ed.). New York: Macmillan.

Walberg, H. (1991). Productive teaching and instruction: Assessing the knowledge base. In H. Waxman & H. Walberg (Eds.), *Effective teaching: Current research* (pp. 33–62). Berkeley, CA: McCutchan.

Waxman, H. C. & Walberg, H. (1982). The relation of teaching and learning: A review of reviews of process-product research. *Contemporary Education Review, 1*(2), 103–120.

Webb, E. J. (1981) *Noninteractive measures in the social sciences.* Boston: Houghton Mifflin.

Winne, P. H. (1987). Why process-product research cannot explain process-product findings and a proposed remedy: The cognitive-mediational paradigm. *Teaching and Teacher Education, 3,* 333–356.

Wittrock, M. C. (1986). Students' thought processes. In M. C. Wittrock (Ed.), *Handbook of research on teaching* (3rd ed., pp. 297–314). New York: Macmillan.

Wolman, B. (Ed.). (1989). *Dictionary of behavioral science* (2nd ed.). San Diego, CA: Academic Press.

Wrightstone, J. W. (1934). Measuring teacher conduct of classroom discussion. *Elementary School Journal, 34,* 454–460.

Direct Instruction and Diversity

Russell Gersten
Eugene Research Institute/University of Oregon

Robert Taylor
Memphis City Schools

Anne Graves
San Diego State University

T he direct-instruction movement began with the pioneering research of Bereiter and Engelmann (1966) with African-American preschool children. The structured approach to teaching—with a heavy emphasis on developing knowledge and skills related to academic success (such as phonemic awareness, conventions of print, abstract concepts, and basic mathematical concepts and relationships), with high expectations and standards, and with a minimal emphasis on "hands-on," inductive, experiential learning—was extremely controversial at the time. It remains controversial to this day (Cazden, 1983; Heshusius, 1991; Schweinhart & Weikart, 1986), although the crucial need for direct instruction for culturally and linguistically diverse

This research was supported in part by grants HO0023HO0014Q and HO0023C20111 from the Research-to-Practice Division, Office of Special Education Programs, of the United States Department of Education. The authors wish to thank Dorothy Dilliplane, Susan Brengelman, Scott Baker, Joseph Dimino, and Damion Jurrens for their considerable assistance in the preparation of this manuscript.

students has become an increasing refrain from minority educators such as Delpit (1988), Reyes (1992), and McElroy-Johnson (1993).

One of the most lucid definitions of direct instruction comes from a researcher and thinker who, until recently, was one of direct instruction's staunchest critics, Courtney Cazden. Cazden (1992) notes that the key feature of direct instruction is "explicitness. . . . Direct instruction means being explicit about what needs to be done, or said, or written—rather than leaving it to learners to make inferences from experience that are unmediated by such help" (p. 111).

For three decades, research has consistently supported the assertion made by Bereiter and Engelmann in 1966 that many low-income learners, from diverse cultures, enter school with backgrounds highly dissimilar to those of their middle-class peers and need explicit instruction to meet the demands of school. In particular, many lack familiarity with print conventions (Teale & Sulzby, 1986) or the formal language used in schools, or both. Students also may not have sufficient background knowledge and may have difficulty drawing inferences and extrapolating information on their own. Unless instruction is adapted to meet the specific needs of these students (Heath, 1983), many will flounder in classrooms.

In reviewing two decades of research on effective teaching of learners from a variety of cultural backgrounds, Stein, Leinhardt, and Bickel (1989) noted that real learning does "not materialize from brief encounters" (p. 164) with new material, but rather develops with the type of systematic guidance and structure provided by a system such as direct instruction. Direct instruction strives to provide a structure or framework so that students can make sense of new concepts, relationships, and learning experiences. With this approach, students are provided with models of reasonable ways to solve problems or follow procedures, are supported amply during the stages of the learning process, and then are provided with adequate practice.

The purpose of this essay is to enhance understanding of the virtually three decades of research in the direct-instruction tradition. In particular, we wish to focus on ways direct instruction can be used to improve the learning performance of culturally and linguistically diverse students with and without disabilities. In so doing, we will discuss the evolution of direct instruction. We will also explore its application to new approaches, such as sheltered English.

What Is Direct Instruction?

The great physicist Helmholtz (cited in Cline, 1987) once remarked, "The originator of a new concept . . . finds, as a rule, that it is much more difficult to find out why other people do not understand him than it was to discover the new truths" (p. 31).

Those involved with direct instruction know well what Helmholtz meant. Direct instruction has often been attacked for stifling students' independence and ability to think independently, forcing values of mainstream culture onto minority students, and decreasing students' motivation (Cazden, 1983; Heshusius, 1991; Katz, 1988; Palincsar, David, Winn, & Stevens, 1991). Yet, the true picture is much more complex, as research by educators working with minority students has begun to help us all understand.

Core Components of Direct Instruction

Longitudinal research by McKinney, Osborne, and Schulte (1993) has highlighted a major problem experienced by many students with learning disabilities: the lack of task persistence and a pervasive lack of motivation. In a sense, many of these students simply give up before even trying to grapple with an instructional activity. Similar problems were noted in observational research of language-minority students (Gersten & Woodward, 1994; Moll, 1988) and African-American students (Gay, 1988).

The overarching principle in direct instruction is deceptively simple: to ensure that *all* students learn (including those from other cultures and those entering school with limited exposure to print), both the curriculum and the presentation of the curriculum must be clear and unambiguous. Once, the senior author of this chapter described this principle as "the pursuit of clarity" (Gersten, Carnine, & White, 1984, p. 38). This pursuit of clarity entails probing as to what are the crucial, essential concepts in a given body of knowledge (be it chemistry or primary-grade mathematics) and sensitivity to possible differences in relevant background knowledge between the student and the teacher (or the middle-class "target audience" of most textbook publishers). A central aim of direct instruction is to ensure high levels of student success, in large part to increase students' self-confidence and their willingness to take risks and grapple with conceptual thinking. Gersten and Dimino (1993) noted that, ideally, direct instruction promises students a virtually constant series of successful experiences—regardless of a student's competence with the English language, home background, or familiarity with conventions of print and abstract use of languages.

Figure 5–1 depicts the five essential components of contemporary conceptions of direct instruction. Each will be introduced in the remainder of this section.

Providing Explicit Strategies or Frameworks

Analysis reveals that textbooks are rarely organized around big ideas (Beck, McKeown, & Gromoll, 1989; Tyson & Woodward, 1989), that is, the knowledge structures and causal relationships that are essential for understanding a subject area. Even when textbooks are organized in such a way, they rarely make these big ideas explicit (see also Brophy & Alleman, in this volume). Observational research indicates that only a small percentage of teachers are able to make big ideas explicit without any assistance from textbooks or teachers' guides (Ball, 1990; Barksdale-Ladd & Thomas, 1993; Gersten, 1996b). The need to reform curricula so that these underlying concepts and ways of thinking are made explicit and clear to students is an academic life-and-death issue for many learners (Carnine, Crawford, Harniss, Hollenbeck, & Miller, 1998).

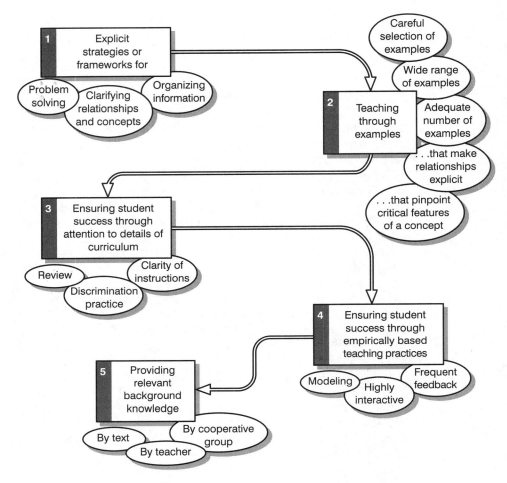

Figure 5–1
Critical components of direct instruction.

As Cazden (1992) noted, the use of explicit strategies and frameworks is a key component of direct instruction. An example of an explicit strategy or framework is the story grammar strategy used by Dimino, Gersten, Carnine, and Blake (1990) to teach students to better comprehend narrative passages. Students were taught to note story grammar elements as they read a passage and to revise their findings as they read further. The story grammar elements include (a) the main character, (b) a problem the main character encounters, (c) characteristics of the main character pertaining to the solution of the problem, (d) attempts by the main character to solve the problem, (e) resolution of the problem, (f) any unexpected twists the story may take, and (g) the theme of the story. After identifying the elements in a particular passage, students use them to summarize the story without becoming bogged down in less important details. Initially, teachers can support the students in applying this framework to a passage, by sharing their understanding of these elements. The strategy was more effective than more traditional comprehension questions with high school students with comprehension difficulties. Clearly, the strategy works better with some narrative passages (i.e., those that follow traditional story grammar structure) than with others. Yet, even for stories that use a less traditional structure, a strategy for identifying story grammar elements still provides students, especially those with comprehension difficulties, with an explicit procedure for understanding a passage.

To teach this framework, the teacher begins by explaining the story grammar elements. Then the teacher provides a model for the process of finding and refining the elements in a passage and writing them on a note sheet. For example, for de Maupassant's "The Necklace," after having students read to the appropriate point, the teacher would say, "That sounds like a problem—the borrowed necklace is lost. I'll write that down here, next to *Problem*. Let's read on and see what other elements we can find." In later passages, teachers remove more and more of the support they provide, with the students doing progressively more of the work. Some of the elements are more difficult than others and need more instruction. Likewise, some examples or passages are more difficult and require more teacher direction. Eventually, students gather the information independently and practice retelling the story with their note sheets. The instructional process takes several weeks.

There are also text structures for expository passages. Researchers have used them to explicitly teach comprehension (Armbruster, Anderson, & Ostertag, 1987) and study skills (Scanlon, Duran, Reyes, & Gallego, 1992), which serve as a basis for writing processes (Englert, 1991), and they have used them as a basis for development of textbooks (Carnine et al., 1995). At best, explicit strategies can "create a shared language between teachers and students" (Gersten & Carnine, 1986, p. 77), which teachers can use to guide students to formulate their own thoughts, to pursue a theme or an idea, or to provide evidence to support an assertion.

Teaching Through Examples

Achieving clarity of instruction requires great care in the generation and selection of examples. Additionally, practice using a wide range of examples is a critical aspect of direct instruction, and of learning in general. In a synthesis of reading research and an analysis of why so many students experience difficulty in the intermediate grades and middle school, Idol (1988) concluded that when "concepts are presented briefly and are not followed by sufficient practice opportunity, the poor reader is likely to flounder" (p. 10). *Becoming a Nation of Readers* (Anderson, Hiebert, Scott, & Wilkinson, 1984) noted that this lack of opportunity to apply new principles or concepts is a major flaw in commonly used reading series. Mathematics educators (Silbert, Carnine, & Stein, 1989) have found analogous problems in mathematics textbooks. A range of culturally relevant examples is critical for students to generalize the use of the concept or strategy (Gay, 1988; Gilbert & Gay, 1985).

Ensuring Student Success Through Attention to Details of Curriculum

Gersten and Carnine (1986) noted that direct instruction often "focused on what many would consider mundane decisions: the best wording for teachers to use in demonstrating a comprehension (strategy) . . . the most effective way to deal with student misconceptions . . . the number and range of examples necessary to ensure mastery of a new concept" (p. 70). This concern with the *details* of curriculum design is most assuredly a distinguishing feature of direct instruction.

Many experimental studies have demonstrated how these details of curriculum design can significantly reduce students' misconceptions. For example, when teaching fractions, traditional curriculum series provide exercises in which students need to discriminate between addition problems and subtraction problems and between division problems and multiplication problems, *but never between addition problems and multiplication problems.* Experimental research by Kelly, Gersten, and Carnine (1990) examined how a conventional sequence for teaching fractions, taken from a major basal series, and a sequence in which students were taught early on to distinguish simple multiplication problems from addition problems affected the learning performance of students with learning disabilities and of remedial high school students. Results indicated that students taught with the conventional sequence *made four times as many errors* as those taught with the more carefully designed sequence. Most of the misconceptions could be linked to flaws in the curriculum. For example, students explicitly taught to distinguish multiplication problems from addition problems rarely confused them, whereas students never provided with such practice often did. (See Woodward, 1991, for further examples.)

Curricula for diverse learners must focus on key concepts, relationships, and operations, must accommodate the range of background knowledge that these students bring to the learning tasks, and must attend to the important details of instructional design. Yet, direct instruction (Engelmann and Carnine, 1982) recognizes that educators working with diverse student populations face two sets of challenges. Not only must they utilize (or modify) effective, relevant curricula for teaching academic content and learning strategies, but they must also utilize a set of effective instructional approaches. Gersten and Carnine (1986) noted that "whereas researchers often treat these topics as separate strands, practitioners play them in concert" (p. 70).

Ensuring Student Success Through Empirically Based Teaching Practices

A critical component of direct instruction is the inclusion of a range of empirically based teaching practices, such as the use of modeling, the promotion of high rates of student interactions, and the provision of frequent feedback. These teaching practices are incorporated as a means of ensuring student success in learning.

A naturalistic observational study conducted by Gersten, Carnine, and Williams (1982) clearly indicates the critical importance of these empirically based teaching practices on how reading is taught. Ten teachers were all using the same reading curriculum for the academic year. They were teaching similar students, low socioeconomic-status African-American and Hispanic first graders. This was the students' first year of formal reading instruction. The amount of time allocated to instruction in reading and language arts each day was virtually identical in every classroom.

Yet, at the end of the year, the average reading score (as measured by the Comprehensive Test of Basic Skills [CTBS]) was at grade level for some classes and was at the 22nd percentile for others. Using a contrasted-groups design, the researchers observed instructional interactions of the two teachers whose students made the most growth (having mean scores at the 52nd and 57th percentiles) and two teachers whose students made minimal growth (having mean scores at the 2nd and 22nd percentiles).

The teachers whose students were reading at grade level by the end of the year tended to (a) respond to student errors and problems immediately and (b) maintain an oral-reading success rate of at least 85 percent during the lesson with all students (even those placed in the lowest reading group). For teachers whose students made virtually no growth in reading during the entire year, student success ranged from 50 to 65 percent. The students of those teachers were rarely provided with feedback when they encountered difficulties. These findings were replicated (Gersten, Carnine, Zoref, & Cronin, 1986) with a larger sample of teachers the following year. Stallings (1980), Leinhardt, Zigmond, and Cooley (1981), and Brophy and Good (1986) have documented the importance of these two instructional variables—feedback and student success.

Because of the explicit approach commonly used in direct instruction, and the abundant active responding of students, the teacher is in an excellent position to diagnose any problems a student may be having, for example, when learning a concept or beginning to understand a mathematical relationship. If a student experiences difficulty, or fails to respond at all, the teacher can immediately intervene with a model of how to answer correctly or can provide an instructional prompt based on previous instruction. Once students are again secure in their knowledge of the steps in the problem-solving strategy, the additional teacher questions and instructions can be gradually dropped from the instructional presentation.

Providing Relevant Background Knowledge

To ensure clarity and comprehension by all students, direct instruction assumes very little about the students' prior knowledge. For example, when teaching reading, there must be provision for systematic teaching of necessary vocabulary. This is truly essential when teaching students from other cultures, for whom massive comprehension problems arise from the assumptions conventional textbooks make about students' understanding of American culture (Gersten & Jiménez, 1994; Yates & Ortiz, 1991). More broadly, research has consistently shown that adequate coverage of requisite background knowledge and related skills (e.g., left-right orientation for kindergartners) is critical in teaching diverse learners (Delpit, 1988; Durkin, 1984; Greene, 1993). Often, subsequent learning problems can be traced to assumptions middle-class teachers or middle-class textbooks have made about the knowledge students possess.

Examples of Problems With Conventional Curricula

Here we present an example from a conventional basal program, for several reasons. The first is that it serves as a point of departure for understanding direct instruction. The second is that the senior author observed this lesson actually being used with a culturally and linguistically diverse group of learners and saw a low level of student cognitive engagement and a high level of confusion; the result was that students did not possess adequate knowledge to engage in an instructional conversation. The third is that subsequent research conducted with students with learning disabilities demonstrated significantly higher performance when students were taught with a direct-instruction approach than when they were taught with an approach similar to the conventional one described here. This example, from the teacher's guide of a commonly used series (Durr, LePere, Bean, Glaser, & Evanhardt, 1983), leads up to a passage on oceanography:

> Write *oceanographer* on the chalkboard, and explain that oceanographers are scientists who study the ocean. Encourage students to speculate about the specific subjects that these scientists explore. Mention any of the following that students don't name: waves, currents, and tides; the chemicals in the sea water; marine plants and animals; the structure of the ocean bottom and shores. (p. 47)

Although these directions attempt to facilitate student interest and motivation, they fail to convey any systematic information about instruction. Different teachers will interpret these directions in different ways. Soliciting student-generated definitions leaves open exactly how concepts and relationships will be explained. The discussion may meander at times, resulting in confusion for low-performing students as to what is salient. Whereas highly skilled teachers will tend to redirect students to the most salient content and to provide relevant examples as a basis for discussion and clarification, many teachers will not (Gersten, 1992; Leinhardt & Greeno, 1986).

Further, if and how these definitions, concepts, and relationships will be reviewed is not at all clear. It becomes apparent that teacher instructions—as well as the curriculum—must be much more focused and precisely crafted for instructional sequences to be effective with all students. Many teachers need help knowing how, in Cazden's (1992) phrase, to make the core concepts "explicit" (p. 111) to all.

Summary

In attempting to describe direct instruction, we have focused on components that distinguish it from other approaches and are relevant to students from a variety of cultural backgrounds. Explicit frameworks and problem-solving strategies enable students to solve many problems they have never seen and allow teacher and student to develop a shared language that facilitates all aspects of learning. The careful selection of examples makes critical distinctions explicit to learners. Attention to detail—e.g., in the selection of discrimination practice exercises and review exercises—helps give students the greatest chance of success, which is essential for learners who are culturally and linguistically diverse. The use of effective teaching practices—such as monitoring instruction, providing frequent and specific feedback, modifying instruction as student problems are observed, and providing adequate practice—is essential to improving communication between teachers and students. Finally, the concern for relevant background knowledge is important whether the material being taught is the initial conceptual introduction to addition or a working understanding of the concept of specific gravity. These five components—explicit frameworks and problem-solving strategies, teaching through examples, attention to relevant curriculum details, effective teaching practices, and the provision of relevant background knowledge—have been the foundation of direct instruction since the 1960s.

Major Implementation Research

Bereiter and Engelmann (1966) realized that many students entering school from low-socioeconomic-status family backgrounds had not had the same experiences with print materials as their middle-class peers had. Bereiter and Engelmann reasoned that it was the responsibility of schools to explicitly teach these early literacy strategies, skills, and conventions. Another central tenet of their philosophy was that students should be explicitly taught the more formal, academic language used in the school, as well as conventions of mathematics and basic arithmetic relationships.

Early evaluations of the Bereiter-Engelmann preschool program showed significant cognitive growth for students in vocabulary, reasoning, and math concepts; however, the effects were not maintained once students entered mainstream primary-grade classrooms (Lazar, Darlington, Murray, Royce, & Snipper, 1982). Although every effort was made to make these learning activities fun and to ensure that students felt successful much of the time, the major goal was academic and cognitive growth. The traditional concerns of early childhood educators—including the creation of personally meaningful learning environments, encouragement of hands-on learning, and the development of a sense of inquiry—were secondary. (For further discussion, see Gersten, 1992; Gersten, Darch, & Gleason, 1988.) The program's concern with the precise details of teaching each concept was particularly alien to the educational thinking of the 1960s.

The seeming success of the preschool intervention—even if it was short-lived—led to the development of a comprehensive primary-grade (K–3) educational model. This instructional model was rigorously field-tested in Project Follow Through, which was supported by the U.S. Department of Education. From the late 1960s to the 1980s, the direct-instruction model was implemented with African-American, Latino, and Native American children in both urban and rural areas. The 20 communities involved in the program were among the poorest communities in the United States. Many students entered the program with little exposure to conventional, mainstream literacy and language concepts that most middle-class school personnel assumed students understood.

On average, the students who participated in the four years of the program completed third grade with reading, math, and language achievement scores at or near grade level—often significantly higher than those of their peers who had been taught with more conventional methods. The sample was approximately 70 percent African-American, 15 percent Latino, 10 percent Native American, and 5 percent white. (See Engelmann, Becker, Carnine, & Gersten, 1988, for details of analysis.) The mean performance of these students at the end of the third grade on all subtests of the Metropolitan Achievement Test was at, near, or above the national median in math, language, and spelling (53rd, 51st, and 49th percentiles, respectively). In reading, performance corresponded to the 40th percentile, within 10 percentile points of the national norm. Thus, in math, language, and spelling, the model succeeded in bridging the gap in skills between low-socioeconomic-status students and their middle-socioeconomic-status peers. In reading, the program came very close to reaching this goal. In contrast, typical performance for comparable students was at the 25th to 30th percentile.

In some communities, dropout rates and grade-level retention rates were significantly reduced (Gersten, Keating, & Becker, 1988). Unlike the earlier finding of "fadeout," or no generalization, from the Bereiter-Engelmann preschool to second or third grade, in Follow Through there was evidence that effects on reading achievement lasted through high school.

Mean scores can be deceptive, however. They do not really explain how the very-low-performing students did, since the mean can be heavily influenced by extremely high scores. Gersten, Becker, Heiry, and White (1984) performed secondary analyses on the achievement data from the Follow Through study to see whether the academic growth of minority students at risk of special-education placement was different from the growth of their peers.

The hypothesis tested was that yearly academic growth rates would be no different for the at-risk group (i.e., those entering kindergarten with low scores on the Slosson Intelligence Test) than for the other students. Though the at-risk students enter kindergarten at lower academic levels than their peers and would tend to exit third grade at a lower level, we believed that their yearly growth—that is, their ability to profit from schooling—would be roughly the same as their peers'.

The analyses found no significant interactions between entry IQ level and growth in reading performance on the Wide Range Achievement Test (WRAT), a measure of word identification, or growth in Total Math on the Metropolitan Achievement Test (MAT), a measure of math problem solving, concepts, and computation. On WRAT reading, the students with IQ scores below 70 who began at the 5th percentile were at normal levels (the 47th percentile) by the end of kindergarten and continued to make slow but steady growth. By the end of third grade, performance corresponded to the 70th percentile, or a 4.3 grade level. A similar pattern was found for the group with IQ scores from 71 to 90.

For MAT math, the growth rates for both the below-70 group and the 71-to-90 group corresponded to 1.0 grade equivalent unit for each year in school. These at-risk students (with low entry IQs on the Slosson) demonstrated one year's growth in mathematics for each year in school.

The picture was less promising in the area of reading comprehension and vocabulary. In this domain, although second-grade growth was comparable for all groups, third-grade gains by the students deemed "at risk" at entry were significantly smaller than gains by their peers. Although the low-ability students seemed to adequately learn the decoding skills and literal comprehension, these children *needed more intensive instruction* in vocabulary concepts and comprehension strategy as they progressed through school.

It is important to remember that all instruction took place in general-education classrooms with general-education teachers in some of the poorest districts in the country. Under current conditions, many of the "at-risk" children would qualify for special-education services, but this study was conducted prior to the Education of the Handicapped Act. Thus, the children were "mainstreamed" in a de facto fashion. Teachers were responsible for the success of *all* students in their classrooms and received extensive in-class coaching and consultation on working with students experiencing difficulty.

Future Research: Contemporary Trends

As direct-instruction research enters its third decade, there have been several subtle shifts in emphasis. Perhaps the primary one is that the concept of explicitness is defined more broadly than in the 1960s, when step-by-step breakdowns of all learning activities and every strategy were deemed essential. Direct-instruction research is focusing more on strategies, relationships, and concepts; more on such topics as understanding of literary classics (Dimino et al., 1990), history (Carnine et al., 1998), and chemistry (Woodward & Noell, 1991); and less on rudimentary academic skills. However, there remains an emphasis on students' development of phonological awareness, automatic knowledge of key number facts, and knowledge of relevant facts essential for solving problems or understanding stories.

There is a growing understanding that often when students are presented with an explicit strategy, they will adapt and personalize it. At times, their adapted version may be more effective than the teacher's. This was first brought to light in research that Adams, Carnine, & Gersten (1982) conducted on study skills.

This brings us directly to a current question in instruction for students with learning disabilities and for students from a variety of linguistic backgrounds: Can principles of direct instruction be merged with more constructivist or open-ended approaches in the areas of language arts, language development, expressive writing, and the teaching of problem solving to culturally and linguistically diverse students?

Traditional direct instruction, as developed to teach basic academic skills to young children, does not make sense for topics and content areas in which the knowledge base is not well defined or well articulated. For example, if the instructional goal is to teach students how to generate questions when they read, then a teacher cannot provide a clear, explicit model. Rather, the teacher can provide and generate a range of models of questions, can encourage students to share the questions they've generated, and can—in an informal but conspicuous fashion—provide students with feedback on the conciseness, relevance, and clarity of the questions they generate. Such an approach has been found to be successful in building reading comprehension and expressive writing abilities (Palincsar & Brown, 1984; Palincsar et al., 1991).

Traditional direct instruction was conceived for small-group instruction. For the increasingly heterogeneous groups found in contemporary classrooms, some adaptations and modifications need to be made. For example, Schumm, Vaughn, and Leavell (1994) provide a framework for assisting teachers who work with heterogeneous groups of students in their classes to specify the "concepts/principles/facts" that *all students need to know*. Schumm, Vaughn, and Leavell emphasize that core concepts are not necessarily lower-order, factual, or "basic" concepts. Often they include abstract, but crucial, concepts like equilibrium and compromise. Yet, in some cases, such as elementary school mathematics, this critical material includes automaticity of basic skills (e.g., number facts). In either case, the goal is to identify what is crucial for students to know. Then instruction focused on that crucial knowledge is provided, and students receive feedback on their emerging sense of critical concepts and their emerging proficiencies. In many cases, alternative instructional procedures, such as cooperative learning, can be used to ensure that all students have mastered the material.

Relationship Between Direct Instruction and Authentic Problem Solving

A small but growing number of studies are demonstrating that students with learning disabilities seem to benefit from simulations and authentic problem-solving activities only when they are first directly taught the salient facts and concepts that underlie the activities and then are provided with a structure to help them understand how to apply the facts and concepts to authentic problem solving (Bottge & Hasselbring, 1993; Kinder & Bursick, 1993; Woodward, Carnine, & Gersten, 1988).

Two studies, by Hollingsworth and Woodward (1993) and Woodward et al. (1988), attempted to apply many of the principles of direct instruction to helping students with learning disabilities develop a complex, higher-order problem-solving ability: the ability to set priorities and to rank items by importance. The topic was understanding the relationship of diet, exercise, and health. Students who were given an explicit framework for making decisions tended to benefit significantly more from the series of simulation exercises than those who merely received feedback and support (Hollingsworth & Woodward, 1993). It is important to note that students' knowledge of basic facts related to health did not differ significantly between the two groups before or after the intervention, *but their ability to apply this knowledge* was significantly aided by their use of an explicit strategy in the computer simulations.

Relationship of Direct Instruction to Culturally Relevant Instruction

A series of observational research studies of minority students conducted over a seven-year period (Delpit, 1988; Gersten & Jiménez, 1994; Goldenberg & Gallimore, 1991; Goldenberg & Sullivan, 1995; Reyes, 1992) support the need for some type of explicit *culturally relevant* (Ladson-Billings, 1995) instruction. Although the researchers utilized different methodologies and approached the subject from different orientations, certain commonalities emerged.

Students seemed to crave some type of explicit instruction and clear feedback on the quality of their work at some time during the day (Reyes, 1992). In research with intermediate-grade language-minority students taught with a process approach, Reyes noted that some students felt betrayed when teachers pointed out grammatical and spelling errors in their final written work in English. The students had assumed that because the teacher had not commented on their spelling or grammar in earlier drafts, their work was acceptable. Delpit (1988) has also talked about the need for explicit instruction in core academic areas as a prerequisite of minority students' access to subsequent high-quality educational opportunities.

Similarly, in Goldenberg and Gallimore's (1991) action research, spending some time each day explicitly teaching comprehension significantly improved the reading performance of kindergartners and first graders. Goldenberg and Gallimore felt that the traditional Spanish-language reading series did not explicitly teach comprehension and that explicit instruction in this area was essential. The explicit comprehension instruction was augmented by much more loosely structured "instructional conversations," which allowed students to practice expressing thoughts linking what they read or learned to their home lives, and to practice using and internalizing the more abstract language of academic contexts.

One could argue that the students in the Goldenberg and Gallimore project, the Bottge & Hasselbring (1993) authentic-learning-in-mathematics project, the Woodward et al. (1988) simulation study, and the Dimino et al. (1990) literature study received the best of both worlds. They received clear instruction in relevant facts and were provided with a framework for using this knowledge as they engaged in more loosely structured authentic-learning tasks. The teachers had a structure to help them mediate any difficulty students experienced. Observational research of teachers of language-minority students has revealed numerous instances of teachers who provide explicit support structures while using a constructivist orientation toward the teaching of reading (Gersten & Jiménez, 1994; Gersten, 1996a). In each case, explicit support structures were provided to students.

Content-Area ESOL Instruction

As an alternative or a supplement to native-language instruction, content-area ESOL instruction (also known as *sheltered English instruction*) is often recommended for linguistically diverse learners (Baca & Cervantes, 1989; Saville-Troike, 1984). Learners who have developed a sufficient academic foundation in their native language and who have strong receptive and basic conversational language skills in English generally benefit most from content-area ESOL instruction. It is typically used in content areas such as social studies and science (Chamot & O'Malley, 1989).

Content-area ESOL instruction is designed to provide comprehensible, clear, and meaningful instruction to students who have good receptive language skills in English. The emphasis is on simultaneously providing content-area instruction in

English while developing English language competence (Saville-Troike, 1984; Krashen, 1985). Inspired by the work of Krashen (1985) and Cummins (1981, 1984), both second-language acquisition researchers and pedagogical researchers have concluded that a second language is acquired by

- using language in meaningful contexts,
- receiving *comprehensible input* when academic subjects are taught, and
- focusing on *clear, concise, consistent* language and controlled vocabulary (Baca & Cervantes, 1989; Echevarria-Ratleff, 1988).

Typically, recommendations for the design and delivery of content-area ESOL lessons are congruent with many of the essential elements of direct instruction (Acosta, 1985; Baca & Cervantes, 1989; Echevarria, 1998):

1. careful selection of key concepts, vocabulary, and topics (Chamot & O'Malley, 1989);
2. activation of existing relevant background knowledge (Gay, 1988; Krashen, 1985);
3. opportunities for students to explicitly learn necessary skills in prereading and prewriting activities (Baca & Cervantes, 1989; Gay, 1988; Reyes, 1992);
4. use of demonstrations and modeling across a range of modalities to make instruction highly explicit (Cummins, 1984; Gilbert & Gay, 1985);
5. use of repetitions and, at times, verbal saturation to improve accuracy and fluency (Krashen & Terrell, 1983);
6. emphasis on active involvement (Baca & Cervantes, 1989); and
7. provision of extensive practice by asking many questions in a variety of applications (Cummins, 1984; Krashen, 1985).

We envision an emerging body of research on understanding the principles of content-area ESOL instruction that enhances student learning. To date, research has been primarily qualitative (Gersten, 1996a).

In summary, both direct instruction and content-area ESOL instruction are essentially explicit instructional approaches that maximize precision in teaching and active learning. Both direct instruction and content-area ESOL instruction urge teachers to speak clearly and precisely. References to reading materials and cultural information unknown to students are also discouraged—unless time is taken to explain the material and help make the prerequisite connections. In both approaches, it is recommended that teachers initially write out the exact wording they will use to model or demonstrate, to avoid confusion or inconsistent language use (see Figure 5–2).

In both content-area ESOL and direct instruction, explicit instruction is utilized to ensure that students learn essential concepts, vocabulary, rules, and strategies. In content-area ESOL instruction, content-related skills are taught explicitly, and in an

Objective: Students will be able to state the meaning of *migration* and will be able to give examples of animals that migrate.

Review: The teacher will have students brainstorm about animals they know of that live in groups in the wild. Pictures of some of these animal groups will be conveniently posted during this time (to activate relevant background knowledge). The teacher then might show a short video about gray whales traveling from Alaska to the Baja, California, and back to Alaska (whales are chosen in a coastal city in Southern California because students have been on whale-watching field trips in school). After the video, the teacher asks how many have seen whales. Then the teacher asks students to brainstorm again about characteristics of whales. The final point that the teacher will make is that whales move from place to place to find food and to have babies. (If the teacher deems it appropriate for the experience and language level of learners, the teacher might allude to migration of people from Cuba, Cambodia, Mexico, etc.)

Goal: The teacher will state that today students will learn that many animals *move from place to place, or migrate* (write italicized portion on the board).

Modeling, Examples and Nonexamples, and Verbal Saturation: (**This portion is scripted so that teachers can use the same careful wording over and over to ensure clear, precise understanding of the concept.**)

Some groups of animals move from place to place. When animals move from place to place, we say they migrate. Everyone say "migrate." So, when groups of animals move from place to place, they (migrate) which means (move from place to place). Look at these gray whales (show a clip from the video once again). They are moving from Alaska to Mexico (show movement on a map) to find food and to have babies. So, the whales migrate, because they move from place to place. What do these whales do? Yes, they move from place to place. Say it another way. Yes, they migrate.

Every year birds called swallows fly from north to south and land in San Juan Capistrano (point to this place on the map and show pictures of birds landing) to find food and to stay warm. So swallows move from place to place. Everyone get ready to tell me another way of saying that swallows migrate. Swallows move from _____ to _____. Yes, swallows move from place to place, or they _____. Yes, swallows migrate.

In Africa, elephants (show pictures of elephants in a herd and at watering holes) move from north to south each year to find food and water. So, in Africa, elephants move from _____ to _____, or _____. Yes, elephants move from place to place, or migrate.

In Oregon, salmon (show pictures of salmon swimming in a river) swim upstream to have babies each year. So, we can say that salmon what? Yes, they migrate.

Closing Activity: The teacher will assign one migrating animal group to each table (giving a large picture of animal group to students at that table). The teacher will ask each student to draw a picture of the animal assigned to the table and to write about the animal, including a statement about whether the animal migrates.

Figure 5–2
Example of a content-area ESOL lesson on migration.

attempt to build intrinsic motivation for learning, there is greater focus on spontaneous language production than was typical of earlier models of direct instruction. Both approaches are most concerned with maximizing learning and providing successful school experiences for students by explicitly teaching them essential information, stressing high rates of interaction, and attempting to be as clear as possible.

Summary

This chapter has presented a historical overview of some of the shifts in the evolution of direct instruction as a means of enhancing the achievement of students from a variety of cultural and linguistic backgrounds. Figure 5–3 presents an overview of this evolution, including a delineation of the major influences on the evolution of the model.

Note, for example, that small, homogeneous groups based on students' current ability or skill levels were the sine qua non of direct instruction in the 1960s and 1970s, whereas the research and development work in the late 1980s and 1990s often incorporated more heterogeneous groups (often involving cooperative learning). Increasingly, we have realized that students can learn a good deal from one another. Note, too, that early efforts involved core academic skills—such as the development of phonemic awareness, beginning reading, and understanding of basic arithmetic concepts and operations—whereas in the 1980s and 1990s, research moved into more advanced topics, such as chemistry, algebraic word problems, and American history. Recent efforts have more directly addressed the needs of language-minority students.

During the 1980s, innovations from cognitive psychology played a large role in shaping the conceptualization of curriculum design and research interventions. Some of the innovations of the 1980s involved the use of technology. Several researchers began to conceptualize learning much more holistically than was common in earlier research. Despite the diversity of curriculum topics, the key underlying principles presented in Figure 5–1 continued, and still continue, to be central to direct instruction.

Most important, the concerns with explicitness and with exactly how concepts are taught, exactly which words are used, and how words are used (as in some of the content-area ESOL research) remain critical, as does the concern for clarity and precision that Gersten, Carnine, and White (1984) highlighted in a review over a decade ago.

In 1970 the Swedish filmmaker Ingmar Bergman received an honorary Academy Award for distinguished lifetime achievement. He seemed out of place amid such glitzy stars such as Diana Ross, Goldie Hawn, and Warren Beatty. His speech was as stark and unsentimental as his films. He merely said that the one thing he had tried to accomplish in his films was to attend correctly to all the details—lighting, camera angle, setting, and costumes—as well as the big picture. He felt that if he succeeded in doing that, his films would be remembered.

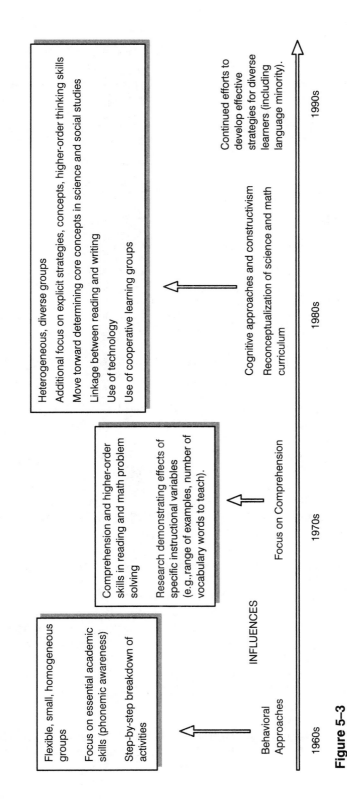

Figure 5-3
Evolution of direct-instruction research and development.

97

The legacy of direct instruction is a continual examination and understanding of the crucial aspects necessary for instruction to be effective for all students. There continues to be a strong indication that the five components outlined in this chapter—providing explicit frameworks and problem-solving strategies, teaching through examples, giving attention to curriculum details, using effective teaching practices, and providing relevant background knowledge—remain critical for student academic success.

References

Acosta, C. (1985). *Sheltered English: Content area instruction for limited English proficient students.* Los Angeles: Los Angeles Board of Education, Division of Curriculum and Instructional Programs.

Adams, A., Carnine, D., & Gersten, R. (1982). Instructional strategies for studying content area texts in the intermediate grades. *Reading Research Quarterly, 18,* 27–55.

Anderson, R. C., Hiebert, E. H., Scott, J. A., & Wilkinson, I. A. G. (1984). *Becoming a nation of readers: The report of the commission on reading.* Washington, DC: National Institute of Education.

Armbruster, B. B., Anderson, T. H., & Ostertag, J. (1987). Does text structure/summarization instruction facilitate learning from expository text? *Reading Research Quarterly, 22*(3), 331–346.

Baca, L. M., & Cervantes, H. T. (1989). *The bilingual special education interface* (2nd ed.). Upper Saddle River, NJ: Merrill/Prentice Hall.

Ball, D. L. (1990). Reflections and deflections of policy: The case of Carol Turner. *Educational Evaluation and Policy, 12,* 247–249.

Barksdale-Ladd, M. A., & Thomas, K. F. (1993). Eight teachers' reported pedagogical dependency on basal readers. *The Elementary School Journal, 94*(1), 49–72.

Beck, I. L, McKeown, M. G., & Gromoll, E. W. (1989). Learning from social studies texts. *Interchange, 17*(2), 10–19.

Bereiter, C., & Engelmann, S. (1966). *Teaching disadvantaged children in the preschool.* Upper Saddle River, NJ: Prentice Hall.

Bottge, B., & Hasselbring, T. (1993). A comparison of two approaches for teaching complex, authentic mathematics problems to adolescents in remedial math classes. *Exceptional Children, 59*(6), 556–566.

Brophy, J., & Good, T. L. (1986). Teacher behavior and student achievement. In M. Wittrock (Ed.), *The third handbook of research on teaching* (pp. 328–375.). New York: Macmillan.

Brophy & Alleman, in this volume.

Carnine, D., Crawford, D., Harniss, M., & Hollenbeck, K. (1995). *Understanding U.S. history: Vol. 1. Through the Civil War.* Eugene, OR: Considerate Publishing.

Carnine, D., Crawford, D., Harniss, M., Hollenbeck, K., & Miller, S. (1998). Effective strategies for teaching social studies. In E. Kaméenui & D. Carnine (Eds.), *Strategies for teaching students with diverse learning needs* (139–160). Upper Saddle River, NJ: Merrill/Prentice Hall.

Cazden, C. B. (1983). Can ethnographic research go beyond the status quo? *Anthropology and Education Quarterly, 14,* 33–41.

Cazden, C. B. (1992). *Whole language plus: Essays on literacy in the United States & New Zealand.* New York: Teachers College Press.

Chamot, A. U., & O'Malley, J. M. (1989). The cognitive academic language learning approach. In P. Rigg & V. Allen (Eds.), *When they don't all speak English* (pp. 108–125). Urbana, IL: National Council of Teachers of English.

Cline, B. L. (1987). *Men who make a new physics.* Chicago: University of Chicago Press.

Cummins, J. (1984). *Bilingualism and special education: Issues in assessment and pedagogy.* San Diego, CA: College-Hill Press.

Delpit, L. D. (1988). The silenced dialogue: Power and pedagogy in educating other people's children. *Harvard Educational Review, 58*(3), 280–298.

Dimino, J., Gersten, R., Carnine, D., & Blake, G. (1990). Story grammar: An approach for promoting at-risk secondary students' comprehension of literature. *The Elementary School Journal, 91*(1), 19–32.

Durkin, D. (1984). Do basal manuals teach reading comprehension? In R. C. Anderson, J. Osborn, & R. J. Tierney (Eds.), *Learning to read in American schools: Basal readers and content texts* (pp. 29–38). Hillsdale, NJ: Erlbaum.

Durr, W. K., LePere, J. M., Bean, R. M., Glaser, N. A., & Evanhardt, K. S. (1983). *Beacon teacher's guide.* Boston: Houghton-Mifflin.

Echevarria, J. (1998). Preparing text and classroom materials for English language learners: Curriculum adaptations in secondary school settings. In R. G. R. Jiménez (Ed.), *Promoting learning for culturally and linguistically diverse students: Classroom applications from contemporary research* (pp. 210–229). Pacific Grove, CA: Brooks/Cole.

Echevarria-Ratleff, J. (1988). *Instructional strategies for crosscultural students with special education needs.* Sacramento, CA: Resources in Special Education.

Engelmann, S., & Carnine, D. (1982). *Theory of instruction.* New York: Irvington.

Engelmann, S., Becker, W. C., Carnine, D., & Gersten, R. (1988). The direct instruction Follow Through model: Design and outcomes. *Education and Treatment of Children, 11*(4), 303–317.

Englert, C. S. (1991). Unraveling the mysteries of writing through strategy instruction. In T. Scruggs & B. Wong (Eds.), *Intervention research in learning disabilities* (pp. 186–223). New York: Springer-Verlag.

Gay, G. (1988). Designing relevant curricula for diverse learners. *Education and Urban Society, 20,* 327–340.

Gersten, R. (1992). Passion and precision: Reflections on "Curriculum-based assessment and direct instruction: Critical reflections on fundamental assumptions." *Exceptional Children, 58*(5), 464–467.

Gersten, R. (1995). Lost opportunities: Observations of the education of language minority students. Manuscript submitted for publication.

Gersten, R. (1996a, February). The double demands of teaching English language learners. *Educational Leadership,* pp. 18–22.

Gersten, R. (1996b). Literacy instruction for language-minority students: The transition years. *Elementary School Journal, 96*(3), 227–244.

Gersten, R., Becker, W. C., Heiry, T. J., & White, W. A. T. (1984). Entry IQ and yearly academic growth of children in Direct Instruction programs: A longitudinal study of low SES children. *Educational Evaluation and Policy Analysis, 6*(2), 109–121.

Gersten, R., & Carnine, D. (1986). Direct instruction in reading comprehension. *Educational Leadership, 43*(7), 70–78.

Gersten, R., Carnine, D. W., & White, W. A. (1984). The pursuit of clarity: Direct Instruction and applied behavior analysis. In W. Heward, T. E. Heron, D. S. Hill, & J. Trap-Porter (Eds.), *Focus on behavior analysis in education* (pp. 38–57). Upper Saddle River, NJ: Merrill/Prentice Hall.

Gersten, R., Carnine, D., & Williams, P. (1982). Measuring implementation of a structured educational model in an urban setting: An observational approach. *Educational Evaluation and Policy Analysis, 4,* 67–79.

Gersten, R., Carnine, D., Zoref, L., & Cronin, D. (1986). A multifaceted study of change in seven inner city schools. *Elementary School Journal, 86*(3), 257–276.

Gersten, R., Darch, C., & Gleason, M. (1988). Effectiveness of a direct-instruction academic kindergarten for low income students. *Elementary School Journal, 89*(2), 227–240.

Gersten, R., & Dimino, J. (1993). Visions and revisions: A perspective on the whole language controversy. *Remedial and Special Education, 14*(4), 5–13.

Gersten, R., & Jiménez, R. (1994). A delicate balance: Enhancing literacy instruction for students of English as a second language. *The Reading Teacher, 47*(6), 438–449.

Gersten, R., Keating, T., & Becker, W. C. (1988). The continued impact of the direct instruction model: Longitudinal studies of Follow Through students. *Education and Treatment of Children, 11*(4), 318–327.

Gersten, R., & Woodward, J. (1994). The language minority student and special education: Issues, themes, and paradoxes. *Exceptional Children, 60*(4), 310–322.

Gilbert, S., & Gay, G. (1985). Improving the success in school of poor black children. *Phi Delta Kappan, 66,* 133–137.

Goldenberg, C., & Gallimore, R. (1991). Local knowledge, research knowledge, and educational change: A case study of early Spanish reading improvement. *Educational Researcher, 20*(8), 2–14.

Goldenberg, C., & Sullivan, J. (1995, April). The role of leadership in promoting coherence and change. Paper presented at the annual meeting of the American Educational Research Association, San Francisco.

Greene, M. (1993). The passions of pluralism: Multiculturalism and the expanding community. *Educational Researcher, 22*(1), 13–18.

Heath, S. B. (1983). *Ways with words.* New York: Cambridge University Press.

Heshusius, L. (1991). Curriculum-based assessment and direct instruction: Critical reflections on fundamental assumptions. *Exceptional Children, 57*(4), 315–328.

Hollingsworth, M., & Woodward, J. (1993). Integrated learning: Explicit strategies and their role in problem-solving instruction for students with learning disabilities. *Exceptional Children, 59*(5), 444–455.

Idol, L. (1988). Johnny can't read: Does the fault lie with the book, the teacher, or Johnny? *Remedial and Special Education, 9*(1), 8–25.

Katz, L. G. (1988). Engaging children's minds: The implications of research for early childhood education. In C. Warger (Ed.), *A resource guide to public school early childhood programs* (pp. 32–52). Alexandria, VA: ASCD.

Kelly, B., Gersten, R., & Carnine, D. (1990). Student error patterns as a function of curriculum design. *Journal of Learning Disabilities, 23*(1), 23–32.

Kinder, D., & Bursick, W. (1993). History strategy instruction: Problem-solution-effect analysis, timeline, and vocabulary instruction. *Exceptional Children, 59*(4), 324–335.

Krashen, S. D. (1985). *The input hypothesis: Issues and implications.* New York: Longman.

Krashen, S. D., & Terrell, T. D. (1983). *The natural approach.* Oxford, England: Pergamon Press.

Ladson-Billings, G. (1995). Toward a theory of culturally relevant pedagogy. *American Educational Research Journal, 32*(3), 465–491.

Lazar, I., Darlington, R., Murray, H., Royce, J., & Snipper, A. (1982). Lasting effects of early education. *Monographs of the Society for Research in Child Development, 47*(Serial No. 194), 1–2.

Leinhardt, G., & Greeno, J. G. (1986). The cognitive skill of teaching. *Journal of Educational Psychology, 78*, 75–95.

Leinhardt, G., Zigmond, N., & Cooley, W. (1981). Reading instruction and its effects. *American Educational Research Journal, 18*, 343–361.

McElroy-Johnson, B. (1993). Giving voice to the voiceless. *Harvard Educational Review, 63*(1), 85–104.

McKinney, J. D., Osborne, S. S., & Schulte, A. C. (1993). Academic consequences of learning disability: Longitudinal prediction of outcomes at 11 years of age. *Learning Disabilities Research and Practice, 8*(1), 19–27.

Moll, L. C. (1988). *Social and instructional issues in educating "disadvantaged" students.* Commissioned paper prepared for SRI's Committee on Curriculum and Instruction of the Study of Academic Instruction for Disadvantaged Students, Washington, DC.

Palincsar, A. S., & Brown, A. L. (1984). Reciprocal teaching of comprehension-fostering and comprehension-monitoring activities. *Cognition and Instruction, 1*(2), 117–175.

Palincsar, A. S., David, Y. M., Winn, J. A., & Stevens, D. D. (1991). Examining the context of strategy instruction. *Remedial and Special Education, 12*(3), 43–53.

Reyes, M. de la luz. (1992). Challenging verable assumptions: Literacy instruction for linguistically different students. *Harvard Educational Review, 62*(4), 427–446.

Saville-Troike, M. (1984). What really matters in second language learning for academic achievement. *TESOL Quarterly, 18*(2), 199–219.

Scanlon, D. J., Duran, G. Z., Reyes, E. I., & Gallego, M. A. (1992). Interactive semantic mapping: An interactive approach to enhancing LD students' content area comprehension. *Learning Disabilities Research and Practice, 7*(3), 142–146.

Schumm, J. S., Vaughn, S., & Leavell, A. G. (1994). Planning pyramid: A framework for planning for diverse student needs during content area instruction. *The Reading Teacher, 47*(8), 608–615.

Schweinhart, L., & Weikart, D. (1986). Early childhood development programs: A public investment opportunity. *Educational Leadership, 44*(3), 4–13.

Silbert, J., Carnine, D., & Stein, M. (1989). *Direct instruction mathematics* (2nd ed.). Upper Saddle River, NJ: Merrill/Prentice Hall.

Stallings, J. (1980). Allocated academic learning time revisited, or beyond time on task. *Educational Researcher, 9*(11), 11–16.

Stein, M. K., Leinhardt, G., & Bickel, W. (1989). Instructional issues for teaching students at risk. In R. E. Slavin, N. L. Karweit, & N. A. Madden (Eds.), *Effective Programs for Students at Risk* (pp. 145–194). Boston: Allyn & Bacon.

Teale, W. H., & Sulzby, E. (Eds.). (1986). *Emergent literacy: Writing and reading.* Norwood, NJ: Ablex.

Tyson, H., & Woodward, A. (1989). Why students aren't learning very much from textbooks. *Educational Leadership, 47*(3), 14–17.

Woodward, J. (1991). Procedural knowledge in mathematics: The role of the curriculum. *Journal of Learning Disabilities, 24*, 242–251.

Woodward, J., Carnine, D., & Gersten, R. (1988). Teaching problem solving through computer simulations. *American Educational Research Journal, 25*(1), 7–28.

Woodward, J., & Noell, J. (1991). Science instruction at the secondary level: Implications for students with learning disabilities. *Journal of Learning Disabilities, 24*(5), 277–284.

Yates, J. R., & Ortiz, A. A. (1991). Professional development needs of teachers who serve exceptional language minorities in today's schools. *Teacher Education and Special Education, 14*(1), 11–18.

Educating Young Students at Risk of School Failure: Research, Practice, and Policy

Robert E. Slavin
Center for Research on the Education of Students Placed at Risk

T his is a remarkable period in the history of American education. For more than a decade, a clamor for fundamental change in schooling has been heard among policy makers, educators, and the general public. Recent policy changes have made classroom reforms both more imperative and more possible. For example, new assessments being adopted in many states are raising standards and greatly broadening definitions of normative performance, shifting from narrow multiple-choice assessments of reading and mathematics to performance measures in all major subjects. Changes in regulations are focusing Title I, a key resource in high-poverty schools, on professional development, prevention, and early intervention, rather than remediation. Similar changes are contemplated for special-education regulations. These and other trends create both the motive and the opportu-

This chapter was written under a grant from the Office of Educational Research and Improvement of the U.S. Department of Education (No. OERI-R-117-D40002). However, any opinions expressed are my own and do not necessarily represent OERI positions or policies. Portions of this chapter are adapted from Slavin, Karweit, and Wasik (1994).

nity for serious, lasting change. Even in a time of funding cutbacks for Title I and other educational programs, the potential for change is great.

One area in which change is particularly possible is the education of children in preschools and elementary schools who are at risk for school failure. These students have long received the bulk of Title I and Chapter 1 funding, and they are most affected by the trend toward prevention and early intervention. Further, research on effective programs for this age group has made enormous strides over the past 20 years, providing a strong basis for reform. Process-product studies in the 1970s and 1980s (Rosenshine & Stevens, 1986), done mostly in elementary schools, identified "master teacher" behaviors associated with achievement gains above expectations. Development and evaluation of many replicable "master developer" programs (Rosenshine, 1983), also primarily in elementary schools, have increased confidence that schools can reliably make significant differences in student achievement.

Yet despite growing knowledge of how preschools and elementary schools could ensure the success of many more children, the application of this knowledge is still far from routine. Public policies are becoming more permissive of research-based reform, but are still far from actively promoting such change.

The purpose of this chapter is twofold. First, it is to briefly review research on effective prevention and early-intervention programs and practices for children in preschool and elementary school. Second, it is to describe policy objectives designed to support the widespread, intelligent use of research-based instructional strategies with young children, and to lay out the "critical path" of research and policy changes needed to bring about these objectives.

Prevention and Early Intervention

Despite some improvements and a growing acceptance of the idea that prevention and early intervention are preferable to remediation, the overwhelming emphasis of programs (and funding) for at-risk students remains on remediation. The unspoken assumption behind policies favoring remediation and retention over prevention and early intervention is that there are substantial numbers of students who, because of low IQs, impoverished family backgrounds, or other factors, are unlikely to be able to keep up with their classmates and will therefore need long-term supportive services to keep them from falling further behind. However, there is a growing body of evidence that refutes the proposition that school failure is inevitable for those children, except for the most developmentally delayed. Further, the programs and practices that, either alone or in combination, have the strongest evidence of effectiveness in preventing school failure for virtually all students are currently available and broadly replicable.

Failure in any school subject is a serious matter, but the consequences of failing to learn to read in the early grades are particularly severe. Longitudinal studies find that disadvantaged third graders who have failed one or more grades and are reading below grade level are extremely unlikely to complete high school (Lloyd, 1978; Kelly, Veldman, & McGuire, 1964). As early as the end of first grade, however, it is possible to identify children who will be poor readers throughout elementary school (Juel, 1988). Remedial programs, such as most Title I programs, have few if any effects on students above the third-grade level (see Puma, Jones, Rock & Fernandez, 1993; Kennedy, Birman, & Demaline, 1986). Many students are referred to special-education programs largely on the basis of reading failure, and then remain in special education for many years, often for their entire school careers.

Almost all children, regardless of social class or other factors, enter first grade full of enthusiasm, motivation, and self-confidence, fully expecting to succeed in school. By the end of first grade, many of these students have already discovered that their initial high expectations are not coming true, and have begun to see school as punishing and demeaning. Trying to remediate reading failure later on is very difficult, because by then students who have failed are likely to be unmotivated, to have poor self-concepts as learners, and to be anxious about reading. Reform is needed at all levels of education, but no goal of reform is as important as seeing that all children start off their school careers with success, confidence, and a firm foundation in reading. Success in the early grades does not guarantee success in later schooling, but failure in the early grades virtually ensures failure in later schooling. This is one problem that must be solved.

If there is a chance to prevent the negative spiral that begins with early reading failure, then it seems necessary to take that chance. Even very expensive early interventions can be justified by cost-effectiveness alone if they reduce the later need for continuing remedial and special-education services, retentions, and other costs (Barnett & Escobar, 1977). Although the cost-effectiveness estimates associated with the High/Scope (Perry Preschool) Model (Berrueta-Clement, Schweinhart, Barnette, Epstein, & Weikart, 1984) have been criticized as unrealistic by many researchers (see Holden, 1990), they have contributed to a widespread acceptance of the idea that early intervention, even if expensive, ultimately pays back its costs. Given, then, that there is growing agreement on the proposition that investments in early intervention are worthwhile, the next question should be, which forms of early intervention are likely to have the greatest impact?

This chapter, a review of research on the effects of programs intended to prevent early school failure (see Slavin, Karweit, & Wasik, 1994), focuses on a variety of indicators of success and failure. Most early-intervention programs involving students from birth to age four have measured their results by assessing IQ, language proficiency, and other indicators that predict school success. I report those outcomes but place greater emphasis on measures of actual school success or failure: reading performance, retention, and placement in special education. Whenever possible I emphasize long-term effects of early interventions.

This review covers several types of early-schooling programs. One important feature most of these programs have in common is that they are expensive, and most have costs of a similar magnitude. For example, reducing class size by half (e.g., from 30 to 15) involves hiring an additional certified teacher for each class. Other ways an additional teacher could be used are to teach a preschool class, to increase the kindergarten staff to enable a school to move from half-day to full-day kindergarten, or to tutor about 15 low-achieving first graders 20 minutes each per day. Retention or provision of extra-year programs for kindergartners or first graders adds one year's per-pupil cost per child—about $6,000 in round numbers. Writing to Read and other integrated computer-assisted instruction programs require at least one additional aide per school, plus initial and continuing costs, for a total roughly comparable to the cost of an additional certified teacher. The popularity of all these programs indicates that we are willing to spend money to prevent early school failure, but which of these investments are most likely to succeed?

Interventions From Birth to Age Three

Both child-centered and family-centered interventions with at-risk children from birth to age three can make a substantial and, in many cases, lasting difference in the children's IQ scores (Wasik & Karweit, 1994). The child-based interventions are ones in which infants and toddlers are placed in stimulating, developmentally appropriate settings for some portion of the day. Family-centered interventions provide parents with training and materials to help them stimulate their children's cognitive development, to help them with discipline and health problems, and to help them with their own vocational and home management skills.

The IQ effects of the birth-to-three programs have mostly been seen immediately after the interventions were implemented, but in a few cases longer-lasting effects have been found. The extremely intensive Milwaukee Project (Garber, 1988), which provided 35 hours of infant stimulation per week, including one-to-one interaction with trained caregivers, followed by high-quality preschool, parent training, and vocational skills training, found particularly large, lasting effects. At age ten, the children (whose mothers were mildly retarded) had IQs comparable to those of low-risk children and substantially higher than those of a randomly selected control group of at-risk children. As the project children reached the fourth grade, they were reading a half year ahead of the control group. Special-education referrals were also reduced.

The Gordon Parent Education Program (Jester & Guinagh, 1983) provided impoverished parents with intensive training in child stimulation. A study of this program found that at age ten, children who had been in the program at least two years still had higher IQs than children in a randomly selected control group, and had less than half the rate of special-education placements (23 percent vs. 53 percent).

The Carolina Abecedarian Project provided at-risk children with intensive infant stimulation and preschool programs seven hours a day for at least five years, along with services to families. A longitudinal study (Ramey & Campbell, 1984; Campbell & Ramey, 1994) found that in kindergarten, first grade, and second grade, children in the program had higher IQs and fewer retentions than similar control students.

The studies of birth-to-three interventions have demonstrated that IQ is not a fixed attribute of children but can be modified by changing the child's environment at home or in special center-based programs. They also show that special-education referrals and retention can be significantly affected. It apparently takes intensive intervention over a period of several years (continuing into the early elementary years) to produce *lasting* effects on measures of cognitive functioning, but even the least intensive models, which often produced strong immediate effects, may be valuable starting points for an integrated combination of age-appropriate preventive approaches over the child's early years.

Preschool Interventions

In comparison with similar children who do not attend preschool, those who do have been found to have higher IQ and language proficiency scores immediately after the preschool experience, although follow-up assessments typically find that these gains do not last beyond the early elementary years (see Karweit, 1994a; McKey et al., 1985). In addition, there is little evidence to indicate that preschool experience has any effect on elementary reading performance. The most important lasting benefits of preschool are on other outcomes. Several studies have found that preschool experience has lasting effects on retention and on placement in special education. Very long-term impacts of preschool on dropout rate, delinquency, and other behaviors have also been found (Berrueta-Clement et al., 1984; Schweinhart, Barnes, & Weikart, 1993). It may be that the effects of preschool on outcomes for teenagers are due to the relatively shorter-term effects on retention and special-education placement in the elementary grades. Retention and special-education placement in elementary school have been found to be strongly related to dropping out in high school (Lloyd, 1978).

Attending a high-quality preschool program apparently has long-term benefits for children, but it is clear that preschool experience in itself is not enough to prevent early school failure, particularly because preschool effects on student reading performance have not been seen. Preschool experiences for four-year-olds should be part of a comprehensive approach to prevention and early intervention, but a one-year program, whatever its quality, cannot be expected to solve all the problems of at-risk children.

Kindergarten Interventions

Since the great majority of children now attend kindergarten or other structured programs for five-year-olds, the main questions about kindergarten in recent years have concerned the relative benefits of full-day and half-day programs and the effects of particular instructional models for kindergarten. Research comparing full- and half-day programs generally finds positive effects for full-day programs on end-of-year measures of reading readiness, language, and other objectives. However, the few studies that have examined long-term effects of full-day kindergarten have failed to find evidence that these effects last, even to the end of first grade (see Karweit, 1994b).

Several specific kindergarten models have been found to be effective in end-of-kindergarten assessments. Among these were Alphaphonics, Early Prevention of School Failure, and TALK. These are all structured, sequenced approaches to building prereading and language skills felt to be important predictors of success in first grade. However, of these, only Alphaphonics presented evidence of long-term effects on student reading performance (Karweit, 1994b). The Writing to Read computer program from IBM has had small positive effects on end-of-kindergarten measures, but longitudinal studies have failed to show any carryover to first- or second-grade reading (Freyd & Lytle, 1990; Slavin, 1991).

Retention, Developmental Kindergarten, and Transitional First Grades

Many schools attempt in one way or another to identify young children who are at risk for school failure and to give them an additional year before second grade to catch up with grade-level expectations. Students who perform poorly in kindergarten or first grade may simply be retained and recycled through the same grade. Alternatively, students who appear developmentally immature may be assigned to a two-year "developmental kindergarten" or "junior kindergarten" sequence before entering first grade. Many schools have a "transitional first grade" or "pre-first" program designed to provide a year between kindergarten and first grade for children who appear to be at risk.

Interpreting studies of retention and early extra-year programs is difficult. Among other problems, it is unclear whether the appropriate comparison group should be similar children of the *same age* who were promoted or similar children in the *same grade* as the students who were retained. That is, should a student who attended first grade twice be compared with second graders (his original classmates) or first graders (his new classmates)?

Studies that have compared students who experienced an extra year before second grade have generally found that these students appear to gain on achievement tests in comparison with their same-grade classmates, but not in comparison with their age-mates. Further, any positive effects extra-year programs have in the year following the retention or program participation consistently wash out in later years (Karweit & Wasik, 1994; Shepard & Smith, 1989). Clearly, the experience of spending another year in school before second grade has no long-term benefits. In contrast, studies of students who have been retained before third grade find that, when achievement is controlled for, such students are far more likely than similar nonretained students to drop out of school (Lloyd, 1978).

Class Size and Instructional Aides

A popular policy in recent years has been to reduce class size markedly in the early elementary grades. Because it is so popular politically and so straightforward (albeit expensive) to implement, class size reduction should in a sense be the standard against which all similarly expensive innovations are judged.

Decades of research on class size have established that small reductions in class size (e.g., from 25 to 20) have few if any effects on student achievement. However, research has held out the possibility that larger reductions (e.g., from 25 to 15) may have educationally meaningful impacts (see Slavin, 1994).

The largest and best-controlled study ever done on this question was a recent statewide evaluation in Tennessee (Word et al., 1990) in which kindergarten students were randomly assigned to classes of 15, 25 with an aide, or 25 with no aide and were then kept in the same class configurations through third grade. This study found moderate effects in favor of the small classes at the end of third grade. A year after the study, when the children were in fourth grade, the difference was still positive but very small (Nye, Zaharias, Fulton, Achilles, & Hooper, 1991). Other statewide studies of class size reduction in the first grade, in South Carolina (Johnson, Mandeville, & Quinn, 1977) and Indiana (Farr, Quilling, Bessel, & Johnson, 1987), found even smaller effects for substantial reductions in class size.

The Tennessee class size study also evaluated the effects of providing instructional aides to classes of 25 in grades K–3. The effects of the aides were near zero in all years (Folger & Breda, 1990). This result is consistent with the conclusions of an earlier review by Schuetz (1980) and of other studies (Slavin, 1994). However, there is evidence, cited in a later section of this chapter, that aides can be effective in providing one-to-one tutoring to at-risk first graders.

Reducing class size may be a part of an overall strategy for getting students off to a good start in school, but it is clearly not an adequate intervention in itself.

Nongraded Primary Programs

The nongraded primary program is a form of school organization in which students are flexibly regrouped according to skill levels, across grade lines, and proceed through a hierarchy of skill at their own pace (Goodlad & Anderson, 1963). This was an innovation of the 1950s and 1960s that has made a comeback in the 1990s.

Research from the first wave of implementation of the nongraded primary approach supports the use of simple forms of this strategy but not complex ones (Gutiérrez & Slavin, 1992). Simple forms are ones in which students are regrouped across grade lines for instruction (especially in reading and mathematics) and are taught in whole-class groups. These simple nongraded programs allow teachers to accommodate instruction to individual needs without requiring students to do a great deal of seat work (as they must when teachers use traditional reading groups, for example). In contrast, complex forms of the nongraded primary approach, which make extensive use of individualized instruction, learning stations, and open space, have generally been ineffective in increasing student achievement (Gutiérrez & Slavin, 1992).

One-to-One Tutoring

Of all the strategies reviewed in this chapter, the most effective by far in preventing early reading failure are approaches incorporating one-to-one tutoring of at-risk first graders. Wasik & Slavin (1993) reviewed research on five specific tutoring models. One of those, the model used in Success for All, will be discussed in a separate section. Success for All, Reading Recovery (Pinnell, DeFord, & Lyons, 1988), and Prevention of Learning Disabilities (Silver & Hagin, 1990) are programs that use certified teachers as tutors; the Wallach tutoring program (Wallach & Wallach, 1976) and Programmed Tutorial Reading (Ellison, Harris, & Barber, 1968) use paraprofessionals, and are consequently much more prescribed and scripted. Some programs use volunteers as tutors (Wasik, 1997). The immediate reading outcomes for all forms of tutoring are very positive, but the largest and longest-lasting effects have been found for the three programs that use teachers rather than aides or volunteers as tutors.

Reading Recovery is a highly structured model requiring a year of training and feedback. It emphasizes direct teaching of metacognitive strategies, "learning to read by reading," teaching of phonics in the context of students' reading, and integration of reading and writing. Two follow-up studies of this program have found that the strong positive effects seen at the end of first grade do continue into second and third grade, but because of increasing standard deviations in each successive grade, effect sizes diminish. A reduction in the retention rate was found in second grade in one study, but the effect had mostly washed out by third grade.

Prevention of Learning Disabilities focuses on remediating specific perceptual deficits as well as improving reading skill, and it usually operates for two school years (Reading Recovery rarely goes beyond first grade). Two of three studies found substantial effects on children's reading performance at the end of the program, and in one follow-up study, the effects remained very large at the end of third grade (see Wasik & Slavin, 1993).

Improving Curriculum, Instruction, and Classroom Management

One strategy for enhancing early reading performance is, of course, to improve curriculum and instruction in the early grades. All of the tutoring programs cited in the preceding section used a particular curriculum and set of instructional methods, and it is therefore impossible to separate the unique effects of tutoring from those of the materials and procedures used. Further, any comprehensive approach to prevention and early intervention must include an effective approach to curriculum and instruction in beginning reading.

The definitive review of research on beginning reading was conducted by Marilyn Adams (1990). Her conclusion was as follows:

> In summary, deep and thorough knowledge of letters, spelling patterns, and words, and of the phonological translations of all three, are of inescapable importance to both skillful reading and its acquisition. By extension, instruction designed to develop children's sensitivity to spellings and their relations to pronunciations should be of paramount importance in the development of reading skills. This is, of course, precisely what is intended of good phonic instruction. (p. 416)

Adams goes on to define "good phonic instruction" as instruction that teaches word attack skills in the context of meaning, not in isolation from real reading.

There are several specific approaches to curriculum, instruction, and classroom management that have consistent evidence of effectiveness in the early grades. For example, dozens of studies have found that cooperative learning methods incorporating group goals and individual accountability increase student achievement (Slavin, 1995). Reciprocal teaching, a technique for teaching students to generate their own questions and take increasing control of their own metacognitive processes, also has a strong research base (Palincsar, Brown, & Martin, 1987; Rosenshine & Meister, 1994). Constructivist approaches to early mathematics instruction, such as cognitively guided instruction, have been found to increase performance on traditional, as well as innovative, measures of mathematics performance (Carpenter, Fennema, Peterson, Chiang, & Loef, 1989). School and classroom management programs developed and evaluated by Freiberg, Stein, and Huang (1995), by Evertson and Harris (1993), and by others have been found to have positive effects, not only on time on task and positive behavior, but also on achievement. Professional development in these and other proven instructional strategies should be a critical part of any comprehensive plan to ensure the success of young children at risk of school failure. High-quality professional development in research-based strategies, incorporating extensive follow-up and coaching, is almost certainly the most cost-effective of the strategies discussed in this chapter; even the most elaborate professional development programs are inexpensive compared with the costs of additional personnel.

Combining Multiple Strategies

Each of the strategies presented here has focused on one slice of the at-risk child's life: birth to age 3, age 4 (preschool), age 5 (kindergarten), and ages 6 to 11 (first to fifth grades). Although birth-to-age-3 and preschool programs have often integrated services to children with services to parents, the programs for older young-sters have tended to focus only on academics and, in most cases, only on one aspect of the academic program, such as class size, length of day, grouping, or tutoring in reading.

How much could school failure be reduced if at-risk children were provided with a coordinated set of interventions over the years, designed to prevent learning problems from developing in the first place and to intervene intensively and effectively when they do occur? This is the question posed in research on Success for All.

Success for All

The idea behind Success for All (Madden, Slavin, Karweit, Dolan, & Wasik, 1993; Slavin, Madden, Dolan, & Wasik, 1996; Slavin, Madden, et al., 1994; Slavin, Madden, Karweit, Dolan, & Wasik, 1992) is to provide children with whatever programs and resources they need to succeed throughout their elementary years. The emphasis is on prevention and early intervention. Prevention includes the provision of high-quality preschool or full-day kindergarten programs or both; research-based curriculum and instructional methods in all grades, preschool to fifth; reduced class size and non-graded organization in reading; the building of positive relationships and involvement with parents; and other elements. Early intervention includes one-to-one tutoring in reading, by certified teachers, for students who are beginning to fall behind in first grade, as well as family support programs to solve any problems of truancy, behavior, or emotional difficulties and any health or social service problems. In essence, Success for All combines the most effective interventions identified in this chapter and adds them to extensive staff development in curriculum and instruction and a school organizational plan that uses resources flexibly to provide whatever it takes to see that students read, stay out of special education, and are promoted each year.

Research on Success for All has found substantial positive effects on the reading performance of all students in grades 1–5 and substantial reductions in the rates of retention and special-education placement (Slavin et al., 1992, 1996). Differences between Success for All and control schools have averaged more than 50 percent of a standard deviation in grades 1–5 for students in general, and more than a full standard deviation for at-risk students, those in the lowest 25 percent of their grades. Outcomes have been particularly positive for a Spanish version of the program used in bilingual schools (Slavin et al., 1996). The lasting effects of Success for All into fifth grade are the largest of any of the strategies reviewed in this chapter, but those results cannot be interpreted as maintenance assessments, as the program continues through the elementary grades. However, with few exceptions, the program beyond the first grade consists of improved curriculum, instruction, and family support services, not continued tutoring. A follow-up study in middle grades, grades 6 and 7, did find lasting effects of Success for All, averaging 40 percent of a standard deviation at each grade level.

Implications for Practice

There is a consistent pattern seen across most of the programs and practices reviewed in this chapter. Whatever their nature, preventive programs tend to have their greatest impacts on outcomes closely aligned with the intervention and in the years immediately following the intervention period. The long-term research on effects of preschool on dropout rates and related variables is one exception to this, but on measures of IQ, reading, special-education placements, and retention, preschool effects were like those of other time-limited interventions. The positive effects seen on these variables were strongest immediately after the program and then faded over time.

Some might take the observation that effects of early interventions often fade in later years as an indication that early intervention is ultimately futile. Yet such a conclusion would be too broad. What research on early intervention suggests is that there is no magic bullet, no program that, administered for one or two years, will ensure the success of at-risk children throughout their school careers and beyond. However, it is equally clear that there are key developmental hurdles that children must successfully negotiate in their first decade of life, and that *we know how to ensure that virtually all of them do so.*

The first hurdle, for children from birth to age five, is development of the cognitive, linguistic, social, and psychological basis on which later success depends. Second, by the end of first grade, students should be well on the way to reading. Each year afterward, students need to make adequate progress in basic and advanced skills, at least enough to be promoted each year and to avoid any need for remedial or special education.

Research on birth-to-age-three programs, on preschool, and on kindergarten shows that we know how to ensure that children enter first grade with good language skills, cognitive skills, and self-concepts, no matter what their family backgrounds or personal characteristics may be. Research on tutoring and on instruction, curriculum, and organization of early-grade education shows that we know how to ensure that children are reading when they enter fourth grade, regardless of their family and personal backgrounds. This chapter focuses on early interventions, but it is important to note that there are many programs and practices with strong evidence of effectiveness for at-risk students throughout the grades (see Slavin, Karweit, & Madden, 1989). Rather than expecting short-term interventions to have long-term effects, we need to provide at-risk children with the services they need at each age or developmental stage.

Does this mean that we need to provide intensive (and therefore expensive) "preventive" services to at-risk students forever? For a very small proportion of students, a portion of those now served in special education, perhaps we do. But for the great majority of students, including nearly all of those currently served in compensatory education programs and most of those now called "learning disabled," only a brief period of *intensive* intervention may be needed, primarily one-to-one tutoring in first grade. After these students are well launched in reading, they still need high-quality instruction and other services in the later elementary grades to continue to build on their strong base. Improving instruction is relatively inexpensive.

The best support for this perspective comes from research on Success for All. This program usually begins with four-year-olds, giving them high-quality preschool and kindergarten experiences. These are enough for most children, but for those who have serious reading problems, the program provides one-to-one tutoring, primarily in first grade. After that, improvements in curriculum and instruction, plus long-term family support services, are used to maintain and build on the substantial gains students have made in tutoring. The program's findings have shown the effectiveness of this approach; not only do at-risk students perform far better than matched control students at the end of first grade, but their advantage continues to grow in second, third, fourth, and fifth grades, and is maintained at least through seventh grade. This is not to say that every element of Success for All has been proven to be optimal or essential. Other preschool or kindergarten models, reading models, or tutoring models could perhaps be more effective, and outcomes for the children most at risk could probably be enhanced by intervention before age four. Success for All is only one demonstration of the idea that linking prevention, early intervention, and continuing instructional improvement can prevent school failure for nearly all students.

How Many Students Can Succeed, at What Cost?

What the research summarized in this chapter shows is that virtually every child can succeed in the early grades, *in principle*. The number who will succeed in fact depends on the resources we are willing to devote to ensuring success for all and on our willingness to reconfigure the resources we already devote to remedial and special-education services.

We have evidence (particularly from the Success for All research) to suggest that we can ensure the school success of the majority of disadvantaged, at-risk students by using the local Title I funds already allocated to schools, but using them in different ways (primarily to improve curriculum, instruction, and classroom management in the regular classroom). However, ensuring the success of *all* at-risk students takes a greater investment. There is a large category of students who would fail to learn to read without intervention, but who succeed with good preschool and kindergarten experiences, improved reading curriculum and instruction, and perhaps brief tutoring at a critical juncture, plus family support, health services, eyeglasses, or other relatively inexpensive assistance. A much smaller group of students might require extended tutoring, more intensive family services, and so on. An even smaller group might need intensive intervention before preschool, as well as improved early childhood education, tutoring, and other services, to make it in school. One can imagine that any child who is not severely delayed could succeed in school if he or she had some combination of the intensive birth-to-age-three services used in the Abecedarian project, the high-quality preschool programs used in the High/Scope model, the tutoring provided by Reading Recovery or other models, and the improvements in curriculum, instruction, family support, and other services (along with tutoring) provided throughout the elementary grades by Success for All. The cost of ensuring the success of children who are extremely at risk would, of course, be substantial. Yet, a multiple-risk child (such as a child from an impoverished and disorganized home who has a low IQ and poor behavior) will, without effective intervention, cost schools and society an equally enormous amount. Even in the midterm, excess costs for special or remedial education during the elementary years are themselves staggering. This leaves aside the likely long-term costs of dropouts, delinquency, early pregnancy, and so on (see Barnett & Escobar, 1977). The key issue for at-risk students is not *whether* additional costs will be necessary, but *when* they should be provided. By every standard of evidence, logic, and compassion, dollars used preventively make more sense than the same dollars used remedially.

Future Research and Policy

The most important work yet to be done on effective practices for children at risk of school failure is additional development and evaluation of replicable programs capable of ensuring that students succeed at each of the critical stages of development. Not until educators have available a variety of well-designed, rigorously evaluated, replicable, and cost-effective programs capable of significantly accelerating the achievement of all children will we truly be able to ensure that all children achieve their full potential. In particular, there is a need for development and evaluation of preschool and kindergarten models, of first-grade reading and mathematics programs, of content reading programs for the upper grades, and of methods of ensuring a successful transition from elementary school to middle or high school.

One means of focusing research and development on these topics might be to have the federal government or private foundations sponsor a series of "design competitions." Groups of developers and educators would be funded to develop, implement, and formatively evaluate pilot programs capable of meeting well-specified criteria for student outcomes and for cost and replicability. For example, a number of design teams might be funded to create and evaluate alternative approaches to beginning reading or early mathematics. Promising programs might then receive third-party evaluations (see Slavin, 1990, 1996). In this way, the number of proven, replicable approaches to instruction would constantly be increasing, not only offering educators new solutions to longstanding problems, but also eliminating all excuses for the unnecessary school failure of so many children.

As we gain ever greater confidence in our ability to ensure the success of all children, other education policies must come to support adoption of effective practices. In particular, there is enough evidence now, of both the ineffectiveness of traditional uses of compensatory education funds (pullouts, aides) and the effectiveness of practical alternatives, to justify focusing Title I on proven practices, and as the number of high-quality or proven programs grows, the rationale for doing so becomes even stronger. The same reasoning applies to other programs that fund services to students placed at risk, professional development, adoption of instructional materials, and so on. Just as standards of medical practice are continually being raised in response to rigorous, widely respected third-party evaluations, so must educational standards begin to take into account evidence supporting effective practices.

Even though additional research and development are desperately needed, there is enough evidence today to indicate that school failure, especially in the early elementary grades, is fundamentally preventable for nearly all students. The implications of that conclusion should be revolutionary. What it means is that, as a policy, we can choose to eradicate school failure, or we can allow it to continue. What we cannot do is pretend we do not have a choice.

References

Adams, M. J. (1990). *Beginning to read: Thinking and learning about print.* Cambridge, MA: MIT Press.

Barnett, W. S., & Escobar, C. M. (1977). The economics of early educational intervention: A review. *Review of Educational Research, 57,* 387–414.

Berrueta-Clement, J. R., Schweinhart, L. J., Barnette, W. S., Epstein, A. S., & Weikart, D. P. (1984). *Changed lives.* Ypsilanti, MI: High/Scope.

Campbell, F. A., & Ramey, C. T. (1994). Effects of early intervention on intellectual and academic achievement: A follow-up study of children from low-income families. *Child Development, 65,* 684–698.

Carpenter, T. P., Fennema, E., Peterson, P. L. Chiang, C.-P., & Loef, M. (1989). Using knowledge of children's mathematics thinking in classroom teaching: An experimental study. *American Educational Research Journal, 26,* 499–531.

Ellison, D. G., Harris, P., & Barber, L. (1968). A field test of programmed and directed tutoring. *Reading Research Quarterly, 3,* 307–367.

Evertson, C. M., & Harris, A. H. (1993). What we know about managing classrooms. In K. M. Cauley, F. Linder, J. H. McMillan (Eds.), *Annual Editions: Educational Psychology 93/94* (pp. 211–220). Guilford, CT: Dushkin Publishing Group.

Farr, B., Quilling, M., Bessel, R., & Johnson, W. (1987). *Evaluation of PRIMETIME: 1986–87 final report.* Indianapolis, IN: Advanced Technology.

Folger, J., & Breda, C. (1990, April). *Do teacher-aides improve student performance? Lessons from Project STAR.* Paper presented at the annual convention of the American Educational Research Association, Boston.

Freiberg, H. J., Stein, T. A., & Huang, S. (1995). Effects of a classroom management intervention on student achievement in inner-city elementary schools. *Educational Research and Evaluation, 1*(1) 33–66.

Freyd, P., & Lytle, J. (1990). Corporate approach to the 2 R's: A critique of IBM's Writing to Read program. *Educational Leadership, 47*(6), 83–89.

Garber, H. L. (1988). *The Milwaukee Project: Preventing mental retardation in children at risk.* Washington, DC: American Association on Mental Retardation.

Goodlad, J. I., & Anderson, R. H. (1963). *The nongraded elementary school* (Rev. ed.). New York: Harcourt, Brace, & World.

Gutiérrez, R., & Slavin, R. E. (1992). Achievement effects of the nongraded elementary school: A best-evidence synthesis. *Review of Educational Research, 62,* 333–376.

Holden, C. (1990). Head Start enters adulthood. *Science, 247,* 1400–1402.

Jester, E. R., & Guinagh, B. J. (1983). The Gordon Parent Education Infant and Toddler Program. In Consortium for Longitudinal Studies (Ed.), *As the twig is bent . . . : Lasting effects of preschool programs* (pp. 103–132). Hillsdale, NJ: Erlbaum.

Johnson, L. M., Mandeville, G. K., & Quinn, J. L. (1977). *South Carolina first grade pilot project 1975–1976: The effects of class size on reading and mathematics achievement.* Columbia: South Carolina Department of Education.

Juel, C. (1988). Learning to read and write: A longitudinal study of 54 children from first through fourth grades. *Journal of Educational Psychology, 80,* 437–447.

Karweit, N. L. (1994a). Can preschool alone prevent early learning failure? In R. E. Slavin, N. L. Karweit, & B. A. Wasik (Eds.), *Preventing early school failure: Research on effective strategies* (pp. 58–77). Boston: Allyn & Bacon.

Karweit, N. L. (1994b). Issues in kindergarten organization and curriculum. In R. E. Slavin, N. L. Karweit, & B. A. Wasik (Eds.), *Preventing early school failure: Research on effective strategies* (pp. 78–101). Boston: Allyn & Bacon.

Karweit, N. L., & Wasik, B. A. (1994). Extra-year kindergarten programs and transitional first grades. In R. E. Slavin, N. L. Karweit, & B. A. Wasik (Eds.), *Preventing early school failure: Research on effective strategies* (pp. 102–121). Boston: Allyn & Bacon.

Kelly, F. J., Veldman, D. J., & McGuire, C. (1964). Multiple discriminant prediction of delinquency and school dropouts. *Educational and Psychological Measurement, 24,* 535–544.

Kennedy, M. M., Birman, B. F., & Demaline, R. E. (1986). *The effectiveness of Chapter 1 services.* Washington, DC: U.S. Department of Education, Office of Educational Research and Improvement.

Lloyd, D. N. (1978). Prediction of school failure from third-grade data. *Educational and Psychological Measurement, 38,* 1193–1200.

Madden, N. A., Slavin, R. E., Karweit, N. L., Dolan, L., & Wasik, B. A. (1993). Success for *All:* Longitudinal effects of a restructuring program for inner-city elementary schools. *American Educational Research Journal, 30,* 123–148.

McKey, R., Condelli, L., Ganson, H., Barrett, B., McConkey, C., & Plantz, M. (1985). *The impact of Head Start on children, families, and communities.* Washington, DC: CSR.

Nye, B. A., Zaharias, J. B., Fulton, B. D., Achilles, C. M., & Hooper, R. (1991). *The lasting benefits study: A continuing analysis of the effect of small class size in kindergarten through third grade on student achievement test scores in subsequent grade levels.* Nashville, TN: Tennessee State University.

Palincsar, A. S., Brown, A. L., & Martin, S. M. (1987). Peer interaction in reading comprehension instruction. *Educational Psychologist, 22,* 231–253.

Pinnell, G. S., DeFord, D. E., & Lyons, C. A. (1988). *Reading Recovery: Early intervention for at-risk first graders.* Arlington, VA: Educational Research Service.

Puma, M. J., Jones, C. C., Rock, D., & Fernandez, R. (1993). *Prospects: The congressionally mandated study of educational growth and opportunity* (Interim Report). Bethesda, MD: Abt Associates.

Ramey, C. T., & Campbell, F. A. (1984). Preventive education for high-risk children: Cognitive consequences of the Carolina Abecedarian Project. *American Journal of Mental Deficiency, 88,* 515–523.

Rosenshine, B. (1983). *The master teacher and the master developer.* Champaign: University of Illinois.

Rosenshine, B., & Meister, C. (1994). Reciprocal teaching: A review of the research. *Review of Educational Research, 64,* 479–530.

Rosenshine, B., & Stevens, R. J., (1986). Teaching functions. In M. C. Wittrock (Ed.), *Handbook of Research on Teaching* (3rd ed., pp. 376–391). New York: Macmillan.

Schuetz, P. (1980). *The instructional effectiveness of classroom aides.* Pittsburgh, PA: University of Pittsburgh, Learning Research and Development Center.

Schweinhart, L. J., Barnes, H. V., & Weikart, D. P. (1993). *Significant benefits: The High/Scope Perry Preschool Study through age 27.* Ypsilanti, MI: High/Scope.

Shepard, L. A., & Smith, M. L. (Eds.). (1989). *Flunking grades: Research and policies on retention.* New York: Falmer.

Silver, A. A., & Hagin, R. A. (1990). *Disorders of learning in childhood.* New York: Wiley.

Slavin, R. E. (1990). On making a difference. *Educational Researcher, 19*(3), 30–34.

Slavin, R. E. (1991). Reading effects of IBM's "Writing to Read" program: A review of evaluations. *Educational Evaluation and Policy Analysis, 13,* 1–12.

Slavin, R. E. (1994). School and classroom organization in beginning reading: Class size, aides, and instructional grouping. In R. E. Slavin, N. L. Karweit, & B. A. Wasik (Eds.), *Preventing early school failure: Research on effective strategies.* Boston: Allyn & Bacon.

Slavin, R. E. (1995). *Cooperative learning: Theory, research, and practice* (2nd ed.). Boston: Allyn & Bacon.

Slavin, R. E. (1996). *Education for All.* Lisse, Netherlands: Swets.

Slavin, R. E., Karweit, N. L., & Madden, N. A. (1989). (Eds.). *Effective programs for students at risk.* Boston: Allyn & Bacon.

Slavin, R. E, Karweit, N. L., & Wasik, B. A. (1994). *Preventing early school failure: Research on effective strategies.* Boston: Allyn & Bacon.

Slavin, R. E., Madden, N. A., Dolan, L. J., & Wasik, B. A. (1996). *Every child, every school: Success for All.* Newbury Park, CA: Corwin.

Slavin, R. E., Madden, N. A., Dolan, L. J., Wasik, B. A., Ross, S., & Smith, L. (1994). "Whenever and wherever we choose . . . ": The replication of Success for All. *Phi Delta Kappan, 75,* 639–647.

Slavin, R. E., Madden, N. A., Karweit, N. L., Dolan, L., & Wasik, B. A. (1992). *Success for All: A relentless approach to prevention and early intervention in elementary schools.* Arlington, VA: Educational Research Search.

Wallach, M. A., & Wallach, L. (1976). *Teaching all children to read.* Chicago: University of Chicago Press.

Wasik, B. A. (1997). Volunteer tutoring programs: Do we know what works? *Phi Delta Kappan, 79*(4), 282–287.

Wasik, B. A., & Karweit, N. L. (1994). Off to a good start: Effects of birth to three interventions on early school success. In R. E. Slavin, N. L. Karweit, & B. A. Wasik (Eds.), *Preventing early school failure: Research on effective strategies* (pp. 13–57). Boston: Allyn & Bacon.

Wasik, B. A., & Slavin, R. E. (1993). Preventing early reading failure with one-to-one tutoring: A best-evidence synthesis. *Reading Research Quarterly, 28,* 178–200.

Word, E., Johnston, J., Bain, H. P., Fulton, B. D., Zaharias, J. B., Lintz, M. N, Achilles, C. M., Folger, J., & Breda, C. (1990). *Student/Teacher Achievement Ratio (STaR): Tennessee's K–3 Class Size Study, Final Report.* Nashville: Tennessee Department of Education.

Teaching Effective Discourse Patterns for Small-Group Learning

Alison King

California State University, San Marcos

In recent years much emphasis has been placed on small-group learning in the classroom, and many schools have embraced the use of cooperative learning, peer tutoring, and other collaborative approaches to learning. A large body of research over the past two decades has documented the effectiveness of these approaches in producing achievement gains, promoting critical thinking and problem solving, and enhancing interpersonal skills (Allen, 1976; Johnson & Johnson, 1990; Sharan, 1980; Slavin, 1990). However, there is a great deal of variability in the findings of research on small-group learning, because learning outcomes vary with such factors as the nature of the task, the type of learning called for, the age of the participants, the group structure, and the resources used by the group. Because of this inconsistency in research results, there is still ambiguity about the specific mechanisms involved in successful group work and the ideal conditions under which collaboration can be an effective way to learn.

Both motivational and cognitive theoretical explanations have been advanced to help account for the effectiveness of collaborative learning. According to a motivational theoretical perspective, students' motivation increases as a function of working with each other in a group, particularly when group goals and group rewards are present, and their increased motivation in turn improves performance. Slavin (1992) contends that when individual rewards are contingent on the group's success, members will do whatever it takes to make the group succeed, including

121

helping each other and encouraging and praising each other's efforts. (See Slavin, 1992, for an extended discussion of motivational views of cooperative learning.)

In contrast to motivational theorists' focus on goals and rewards, cognitive theorists attribute the beneficial effects of small-group learning to the groups' interaction per se. From a cognitive perspective, learning is defined as cognitive change. During the process of interaction with others, individuals change their own knowledge structures, and that change is reflected in subsequent performance. According to this view, cognitive change occurs during interaction with others, through the process of cognitive mediation. In collaborative learning, interaction with others, either in pairs or in small groups, provides opportunities for individuals to discuss the material to be learned. In doing so, they elaborate on it, reformulate it, or in some other manner process the material more effectively than if they worked alone. Thus, through their interaction with each other, group members are said to *mediate* each other's learning. Modeling also plays a role in the mediation process because group learning contexts provide opportunities for students to model their thinking, reasoning, and problem-solving skills on those of their peers.

Interaction and Learning

Although cognitive theorists and researchers agree that interaction among members of a collaborating group is beneficial to learning, it appears that different types of interaction facilitate different kinds of learning. For example, learning factual material may simply require rehearsal and reproduction of that material by group members, and applying facts in a routine manner may call for group conversation that consists merely of requesting and providing information. In contrast to fact learning, which consists of *reproduction of information,* generative learning (e.g., Wittrock, 1974, 1990) involves *production of knowledge.* Generative learning includes analyzing and integrating ideas, constructing new knowledge, and solving ill-structured problems. For groups to be successful in such generative learning tasks, they must go beyond memorizing facts to actually thinking *with* those facts and thinking about *how* those facts relate to each other and to what the group members already know. To engage in such higher-level learning effectively as a group, the discourse within the group must be of a comparably high cognitive level. It is through such high-level discourse that cognitive change occurs (Noddings, 1989; Tudge, 1990; Vygotsky, 1978). In short, generative learning requires interaction among group members that includes mutual exchange of ideas, explanations, justifications, speculations, inferences, hypotheses, conclusions, and other high-level discourse.

This relationship between the level of discourse within a collaborating work group and the level of achievement or productivity of group members has been observed in classroom learning contexts by several researchers. In her studies of interaction in small-group learning, Webb (1989) consistently found that giving detailed, elaborate explanations to others in the group is a strong predictor of achievement; that is, the student who does the explaining is the one who achieves the most. Other researchers have found similar positive effects for explanation giving (Chi & VanLehn, 1991; King, 1990; Swing and Peterson, 1982). In my analysis of naturally occurring group interaction during problem solving (King, 1989b), I found a positive relationship between children's level of verbal interaction and their problem-solving success. I analyzed the interaction of groups of fourth graders as they attempted to solve the problem of replicating a given design by using a computer graphics program. I found that the groups that were successful in the task were the ones that asked more task-related questions of each other and reached higher levels of strategy elaboration than did unsuccessful groups. Subsequent studies (e.g., King, 1990, 1991, 1992, 1994b; King & Rosenshine, 1993) showed that when students are taught various strategies for asking such thought-provoking, task-related questions of others in the group, those questions elicit explanations, inferences, speculations, and other such elaborated responses, which in turn have a direct positive effect on individual achievement. Chan, Burtis, Scardamalia, and Bereiter (1992) also analyzed the constructive cognitive activity of children and assessed the contribution that activity made to learning. After giving the children instruction in "deep thinking" in response to text statements, the researchers read a series of text statements to each child individually and asked the child to respond. Deep thinking was defined as generating "thinking ideas" (describing a new realization, attempting to solve a problem, or trying to understand a difficult point), as opposed to "easy ideas." Chan et al. found clear evidence that the level of cognitive constructive activity a child engaged in, from simple retelling of details and knowledge from the text (low) to problem solving and extrapolation beyond the text (high), had a direct effect on the level of learning.

Why is this higher-level interaction so effective for analytical and generative learning, and what are the cognitive mechanisms involved? Interaction between the individuals in a group promotes learning through several processes. First of all, in a group learning context, members of a group must talk to each other about the task, presenting their ideas and perspectives, asking questions, providing information, suggesting plans of action, and so on. Externalizing their thinking by verbalizing it to the group is a meaning-making process in itself. Even without any responses from others, thinking aloud in this way can alter the individual's knowledge structures (at least to some extent) because it forces individual members to clarify their own ideas, elaborate on them, evaluate their existing knowledge for accuracy and gaps, integrate and reorganize knowledge, or in some manner reconceptualize the material (Bargh & Schul, 1980; Brown & Campione, 1986). This sort of cognitive change affects subsequent learning and performance.

Furthermore, making their thinking explicit and available to the group in this way also sets the stage for *group* evaluation and revision of ideas and plans, for dealing with conceptual discrepancies that emerge within the group, and for the *negotiation* of meanings in general. According to theories of the social construction of knowledge (e.g., Bearison, 1982; Damon, 1983; Mugny & Doise, 1978; Perret-Clermont, 1980; Vygotsky, 1978), when individuals interact in a cooperative discussion, they discover that their own perceptions, facts, assumptions, values, and general understandings of the material differ to some extent from those of others with whom they are interacting. When these conceptual discrepancies emerge, the individuals want to reconcile them. To do so, they must negotiate understanding and meaning with each other. This negotiation, this co-construction of meaning, occurs through individuals' explaining concepts to the group, defending their own views to each other, asking thought-provoking questions, hypothesizing, speculating about alternative interpretations, evaluating suggestions for feasibility, revising plans, and in general arriving at agreed-upon meanings and plans. As Cobb (1988) pointed out, individuals engaged with others in such negotiation of meaning are continually reorganizing and restructuring their own thinking. Working alone would not result in the same extent of cognitive change; therefore, cognitively speaking, it is said that through interaction that is characterized by such a high level of discourse, group members are *mediating* each other's learning.

Unfortunately, students do not often engage in this level of discourse spontaneously. A number of researchers (Britton, Van Dusen, Glynn, & Hemphill, 1990; Pressley, Symons, McDaniel, Snyder, & Turnure, 1988; Spires, Donley, & Penrose, 1990) have been disappointed to find that learners generally do not elaborate on material unless they are prompted to do so. Nor do they ask many thought-provoking questions during discussion without specific training in questioning skills (King, 1990, 1992, 1994b). In fact, without being prompted in some way, students often do not even spontaneously activate and use their relevant prior knowledge (Pressley, McDaniel, Turnure, Wood, & Ahmad, 1987). Some researchers have observed that students working in groups are more focused on finding the right answer than in mediating each other's problem solving (e.g., Vedder, 1985) and that problem-solving groups operate at a concrete, specific level in a step-by-step manner (rather than at an abstract, planful level) unless the teacher intercedes with explicit guidance in how to interact (e.g., Webb, Ender, & Lewis, 1986). In general, then, it appears that students will interact with each other at a very basic level unless they are taught specific skills of higher-level discourse.

Promoting Effective Discourse

Some attempts have been made to promote effective discourse within collaborating groups by structuring the interaction in some manner so that students are compelled to follow a particular pattern of talk. The resulting discourse patterns are intended to control student mediation of learning. For example, Dansereau's (1988) scripted cooperation procedure (in which the script specifies and directs the processing activities students engage in during learning) forces students into a specific sequence of discourse: summarizing, error feedback, and elaboration. However, the focus of the structure of scripted cooperation (and the resulting discourse) is on learning *factual* material, primarily through simple rehearsal; scripted cooperation was not designed for mediating generative learning and problem solving. Reciprocal teaching (Palincsar & Brown, 1984) also relies on structuring the interaction to induce specific types of discourse (in this case questioning, summarizing, clarifying, and predicting). Although reciprocal teaching can be effective for understanding and remembering prose and for simple skill acquisition, the interaction it induces, like that of scripted cooperation, is formulaic and too limited and constrained by the procedure's structure to be conducive to the higher-order thinking required for generative learning (Cohen, 1994; Rosenshine & Meister, 1994; Salomon & Globerson, 1989). In both of these procedures, group members mediate each other's learning. However, the kind of learning they facilitate is recall of factual material and application of it in a routine manner. Although the highly structured interaction dictated by these two procedures facilitates fact learning, that same structure thwarts the independent thinking necessary for analytical and generative learning and impedes the kind of free exploratory activity needed for solving ill-structured problems (see Salomon & Globerson, for a discussion of this point). Cohen also cautions about the danger of overstructuring group interaction. Clearly, if problem solving and generative learning are to take place through peer mediation in cooperative groups, peer interaction must be structured to promote high-level discourse; however, that structure must somehow be flexible enough to allow students freedom to adapt those discourse skills and patterns to task demands and group needs. Such freedom within structure is a delicate balance, but it holds promise for learning in group contexts.

Discourse Patterns for Mediating Generative Learning

I have developed procedures for structuring group discourse into patterns that are effective in promoting higher-level generative learning in small groups. In a comprehensive program of research, I have assessed and refined discourse patterns that support peer-mediated learning for the following three types of learning: problem solving (King, 1991), peer tutoring (King, 1994c, 1998), and construction of complex knowledge (King, 1989a, 1994b). My research has shown that these patterns of discourse can be readily taught to students, that students can easily adapt them for flexible use, that intentional use of these discourse patterns in groups guides and supports students' mediation of each other's learning; and that use of these particular discourse patterns promotes learning characterized by problem solving and extrapolation well beyond any facts or concepts provided to the students. In this chapter, I discuss only my discourse patterns for construction of complex knowledge.

Discourse Patterns for Mediating Knowledge Construction

I have developed (King, 1989a, 1992, 1994a) a guided questioning-responding procedure for small-group learning, in which students are taught how to ask and answer thought-provoking questions. The central component of this procedure is a set of open-ended, thought-provoking questions, such as, "Why is _____ important?" "How is _____ similar to _____?" "How does _____ relate to _____?" "What is an example of _____?" and "What does _____ remind you of? Why?" Students are trained to use these content-free questions to guide them in generating their own specific questions on the material being studied. They are also taught how to provide elaborated responses (such as explanations, speculations, and rationales) to questions they are asked (King, 1994b). In using this procedure, each student selects a few of the open-ended, content-free questions from a larger list and generates several content-specific questions by filling in the blanks. Then the students take turns posing their specific questions to the group to stimulate group discussion. After students have learned to generate the thought-provoking questions, they are taught to base their selection of generic questions on their own perceived learning needs and those of the group, as well as on their own curiosity.

In a series of studies (King, 1989a, 1990, 1992, 1994b; King & Rosenshine, 1993), I found that when students were taught to ask each other particular forms of these questions during learning, their questions elicited predictable kinds of responses. I found (King, 1994b; King & Rosenshine, 1993) that during peer interaction, clear patterns of discourse emerged that were dictated by the particular form of the original open-ended question. Results of both studies (King, 1994b; King & Rosenshine, 1993) showed that these discourse patterns mediated learning as measured by tests of inference and factual recall and by knowledge mapping.

Knowledge Construction Discourse

Most of the generic, open-ended questions were classified as integration questions, that is, ones that called for the responder to go beyond what was explicitly stated in the material presented in class, by connecting two or more ideas or by providing explanations, inferences, speculation, or justifications. The integration questions were of various forms: comparison-contrast, analysis-inference, cause-effect, evaluation-evidence, problem-solution, rule-example or principle-example, application to the real world, argument-support, case-metaphor or case-analogy, analysis-speculation, and analysis-hypothesis/prediction (King, 1991, 1992). Figure 7–1 contains examples of these question forms. Analysis of peer interaction in two studies (King, 1994b; King & Rosenshine, 1993) revealed that these integration questions elicited highly elaborated responses that corresponded to the form of question posed.

For example, when a content-free integration question of the comparison-contrast form, such as "Compare and contrast _____ with _____," was used by an upper-elementary-grade student to generate a content-specific integration question, such as "Compare and contrast tide pools with inland pools," and the student posed that specific question to a learning partner, the question elicited a highly elaborated comparison based on the material being studied. These discourse patterns were categorized as knowledge-construction discourse patterns because they showed evidence of new knowledge being constructed in the course of the partners' interaction.

Question Form	Examples
comparison–contrast	Compare and contrast _____ with _____.
	What is the difference between _____ and _____?
	How are _____ and _____ similar?
	Compare _____ and _____ with regard to_____.
analysis–inference	What are the implications of _____?
	What are the strengths and weaknesses of _____?
	Explain why _____. *or* Explain how _____.
	Why is _____ important?
	What is the significance of _____?
cause–effect	How does _____ affect _____?
	What do you think causes _____? Why?
	What could cause _____?
analysis–speculation	What do you think might happen if _____?
	How do you think _____ would see the issue of _____?
analysis–prediction/hypothesis	What do you predict would happen if _____?
argument–support	What are some reasons for _____?
	Explain why _____ and justify your answer.
	What is a counter-argument for _____?
evaluation–evidence	What is the best _____, and what are your reasons?
	Which is a better _____: _____ or _____? Why?
	Is it possible that _____? Why or why not?
	Do you agree or disagree with this statement: _____? What evidence is there to support your answer?
rule–example (or principle–example)	What is a new example of _____?
application to the real world	How could _____ be used to _____?
	How does _____ apply to everyday life?
problem–solution	What are some possible solutions to the problem of _____?
case–metaphor (or case-analogy)	What is _____ analogous to?
	What does _____ remind you of?

Figure 7–1
Forms of integration questions.

The following exchange is an example of such a knowledge-construction discourse pattern, taken from the transcript of a recording of the interaction of a pair of fifth graders discussing a lesson on zonation in tide pools (King & Rosenshine, 1993). These students had been trained to use the content-free integration and comprehension questions and were provided with prompt cards containing those questions to prompt and guide their discussion.

Janelle: What do you think would happen if there weren't certain zones for certain animals in the tide pools?

Katie: They would all be, like, mixed up—and all the predators would kill all the animals that shouldn't be there and then they just wouldn't survive. 'Cause the food chain wouldn't work—'cause the top of the chain would eat all the others and there would be no place for the bottom ones to hide and be protected. And nothing left for them to eat.

Janelle: OK. But what about the ones that had camouflage to hide them?

Although at first glance this knowledge-construction discourse pattern appears similar to the initiation-response-evaluation discourse pattern commonly seen in classroom discussion (Cazden, 1988; Mehan, 1979), there are important differences in both content and process. The typical initiation-response-evaluation discourse pattern is teacher-led. The teacher initiates by asking a question, the student responds by answering the question, the teacher evaluates that response, and the sequence is repeated (Cazden; Mehan). Those teacher questions are often low-level ones (Dillon, 1988; Graesser, 1992), and the responses generally consist of retelling (reproducing) information learned and such responses can be readily evaluated as right or wrong. In contrast, these knowledge-construction discourse patterns are initiated by *student*-generated questions that are high-level, integrative, thought-provoking ones. Further, those questions generally elicit thoughtful, elaborated student responses that are characterized by the integration of ideas into newly constructed knowledge (which in turn often elicits a follow-up question). The new knowledge constructed during such peer-mediated learning is said to be socially constructed (Bearison, 1982; Damon, 1983; Perret-Clermont, 1980; Vygotsky, 1978).

To illustrate, at the beginning of the Janelle-Katie dialogue segment, Janelle asked Katie to speculate about what it would be like if there were no zonal distinctions in a tide pool. This was a high-level integrative question that asked Katie to go beyond what they had learned in class about the different zones. In posing this question, Janelle was asking Katie to analyze what they already knew about the features of the tide pool zones and the characteristics of the animals that inhabit specific zones and to help Janelle construct new knowledge about the *relationships* between the characteristics of zones and the characteristics of their inhabitants. Clearly, Janelle had already begun on her own to think about those relationships. In fact, she could not have generated the question without having begun to consider how a particular zone in a tide pool affects the animal life living in it. However, in verbalizing her question, she drew Katie, too, into thinking about possible connections. According to Katie's analysis, the animals' characteristics would remain the same, but with the zone distinctions removed, inhabitants would be more vulnerable to predators; they would all eat each other, and the food chain would collapse. Not only was Katie building new understandings about the importance of the distinctions among the zones in a tide pool, she was also gaining experience in the skills of reasoning through a new situation and communicating to others the product of her reasoning. Katie's response was clearly a thoughtful, elaborated one. Thus, in asking her initial question, Janelle was mediating Katie's learning (as well as her own). It is unlikely that either girl alone would have speculated about such a situation, and if she had, it is unlikely she would have actually analyzed the hypothetical situation to arrive at a plausible scenario.

Janelle's follow-up question, "But what about the ones that had camouflage to hide them?" raised a conceptual discrepancy between the two girls' views of what would happen. Her question implied that camouflaged animals may pose an exception to Katie's claim that "there would be no place for the bottom ones to hide." During social construction of knowledge, challenging each other's perspectives on an issue or offering another point of view induces sociocognitive conflict (Mugny & Doise, 1978), which presumably leads to subsequent resolution through discussion. Thus, Janelle's question furthered the mediational process by challenging Katie (and herself) to think about a possible exception within their scenario. This conceptual discrepancy begs to be resolved through further peer discussion. In negotiating understanding and co-constructing meaning through this sort of high-level interaction, Janelle and Katie were mediating each other's learning (Cobb, 1988; Noddings, 1989; Tudge, 1990).

Extended Knowledge-Construction Discourse Pattern

Moreover, in a significant number of instances of knowledge construction interaction in the two studies (King, 1994b; King & Rosenshine, 1993), after the initial question had elicited a response, that response in turn prompted further elaboration from other group members, including the questioner. Those multiple responses built on each other to propel the discussion forward. Such extended discourse patterns often consisted of the following sequence: a thought-provoking "integration" question → a statement connecting two or more ideas or an elaborated explanation → the addition of other newly constructed knowledge (often multiple contributions) to extend the discussion (occasionally including a statement, such as an inference or a generalization, that served to "conclude" the issue or point raised by the question) → a new question (usually prompted by and extending the discussion just generated). This extended discourse pattern was also classified as a knowledge-construction discourse pattern. Figure 7–2 contains a comparison of this extended knowledge-construction discourse pattern and the typical knowledge-construction discourse pattern, discussed previously.

KNOWLEDGE-CONSTRUCTION DISCOURSE PATTERNS

Typical Knowledge-Construction Discourse Pattern

(prompted and guided by the content-free integration questions student pairs were trained in)

Integration question → Statement showing construction of new knowledge → New (usually related) integration question

Extended Knowledge Construction Discourse Pattern

Integration question → Statement showing construction of new knowledge → Supplemental knowledge construction statement → Supplemental knowledge construction statement → Supplemental knowledge construction statement → New (usually related) integration question

COMPREHENSION DISCOURSE PATTERN

(prompted and guided by the content-free comprehension questions student pairs were trained in)

Comprehension question → Paraphrased definition or description showing comprehension → Corrections and addition of detail (when necessary) → New question

Figure 7–2

Trained discourse patterns for knowledge construction and comprehension.

Following, in a representative discussion from an earlier part of the same transcript, is an example of the extended knowledge-construction discourse pattern:

Katie: How are the upper tide zone and the lower tide zone different?

Janelle: They have different animals in them. Animals in the upper tide zone and splash zone can handle being exposed—have to be able to use the rain and sand and wind and sun—and they don't need that much water, and the lower tide zone animals do.

Katie: And they can be softer 'cause they don't have to get hit on the rocks.

Janelle: Also predators. In the spray zone is because there's predators like us people and all different kinds of stuff that can kill the animals and they won't survive, but the lower tide zone has not as many predators.

Katie: But wait!—Why do the animals in the splash zone have to survive?

Here Katie's initial question asked Janelle to compare two specific tide zones. Katie's question is considered an integration question (rather than a simple recall question) because, although the features of the different zones had been covered during the lesson, the differences between them had not been explicitly pointed out. Thus, Katie's question asked the girls to integrate what they already knew (the characteristics of two specific zones) and compare those characteristics to identify differences, that is, to develop new knowledge on their own by extension beyond their existing knowledge. Again, as with Janelle in the earlier discussion, Katie must have already begun to think about this issue of how the zones differ, just to have been able to pose the question. In asking Janelle to think about this issue, she was mediating Janelle's learning about tide pools. In her response, Janelle thought her way through a comparison of the animals in the two zones, thus extending her own (and probably Katie's) understanding of tide pools. Janelle's initial response focused on how the animals inhabiting the zones differ, and she only implied that the water levels differ too. The girls' responses played off of each other as they each contributed material to elaborate the comparison. They continued to mediate each other's learning with Katie's follow-up question on the issue of survival (which Janelle had just brought up). Katie's question "But wait! Why do the animals in the splash zone have to survive?" challenged Janelle's (apparent) assumption that survival is desirable. According to theories of the social construction of knowledge (e.g., Cobb, 1988; Mugny & Doise, 1978, Perret-Clermont, 1980; Vygotsky, 1978), such challenges to one's perspective on an issue serve to mediate learning by inducing sociocognitive conflict and its subsequent resolution through discussion. As before, it is unlikely that either girl alone would have considered these matters and developed on her own the extended understandings that resulted from peer mediation.

Comprehension Discourse Pattern

A few of the content-free open-ended questions (e.g., "Describe _____ in your own words," and "What does _____ mean?") were designed to prompt children to generate *comprehension* questions (King, 1994b; King & Rosenshine, 1993). This type of question was intended to be used by learners to monitor their comprehension of terms, processes, and the like covered in the material being studied. Although the content-specific comprehension questions (e.g., "In your own words, describe an echinoderm," and "What does zonation mean?") were memory-based in the sense that they asked for recall of material presented, they called for students to restate definitions, descriptions, and procedures in their own words. By requiring paraphrasing (as opposed to verbatim repetition of the definitions presented by the teacher), these comprehension questions were intended to induce some reconceptualization by the responder and, at the same time, elicit evidence of real understanding, that is, indications that knowledge had been assimilated into the responder's cognitive structures.

The typical discourse pattern that emerged with this type of question consisted of the following sequence: comprehension question → paraphrase of definition or description → corrections and addition of detail (if necessary) → new question (often an integration question building on the preceding definition or description). The following example of a typical comprehension discourse pattern is taken from the same transcript of Katie and Janelle's discussion.

Janelle: In your own words, describe what the word *camouflage* means.

Katie: Camouflage means that an animal makes its skin or fur the same color as its surroundings.

Janelle: So predators can't see it so easy.

Katie: Yeah! Why is an animal that has camouflage better off than an animal without camouflage?

Analysis of this discourse sequence suggests that Janelle's question prompted Katie to remember the definition of camouflage presented in class and then to paraphrase it to demonstrate her understanding of the term. Katie's response appears to be in her own words and appears to be accurate. However, Janelle apparently feels that it is incomplete or needs some clarification, so she adds a rationale for camouflage. Thus, the two girls are collaboratively reconstructing (co-reconstructing?) the definition of the term as presented in class. Mediating each other's understanding of camouflage in this way results in a more complete definition than either girl is likely to have arrived at on her own.

Figure 7–2 is an illustration of the typical discourse patterns initiated by integration questions and comprehension questions. These trained discourse patterns were classified as knowledge-construction discourse patterns and comprehension discourse patterns, respectively. Results of two studies (King, 1994b; King & Rosenshine, 1993) showed that these discourse patterns mediated science learning for fourth and fifth graders.

In contrast to the discourse patterns elicited by integration and comprehension questions, the response to a factual question (e.g., "What are the three colors of marine algae?") consisted of a simple restatement of factual information recalled from memory (e.g., "Green, brown, and red"), generally with no further response from the group (King, 1994b; King & Rosenshine, 1993). Although these factual-recall questions were not taught to students, they were occasionally posed by students trained in thought-provoking questioning, and they were almost always the kind of question asked by the untrained control-group students, who were not taught questioning skills but were told to ask and answer each other's questions (King, 1994b; King & Rosenshine, 1993).

In general, then, in both of these guided peer-questioning studies (King 1994b; King & Rosenshine, 1993), when a factual question was asked, it was followed by a simple restatement of factual material; when a comprehension question was asked, it was followed by a paraphrase of recalled material; when an integration question was asked, it elicited a thoughtful, elaborated response (often several responses) that evidenced that new knowledge had been constructed, either by integrating several previously encoded ideas or by extending knowledge in some other way beyond what had originally been presented. These discourse patterns were dictated by the format of the questions posed; those questions elicited responses that corresponded in form to the questions asked. In the comprehension and integration discourse patterns, the *student* questions were themselves controlled by the format of the generic content-free questions. Those questions were used to prompt the generation of content-specific questions, which in turn elicited responses that corresponded in form to the questions asked, in terms of the type of thinking required and in the indications of either comprehension of knowledge or construction of new knowledge.

It should be noted that this guided peer-questioning-responding procedure for promoting high-level discourse is not the same as scripting the interaction. Significant differences exist between guided questioning-responding on the one hand and scripted cooperation and reciprocal teaching on the other. First, unlike the other two procedures, guided questioning-responding promotes learning that goes far beyond fact learning and encoding of material explicitly presented. It provides a context and skills for mediating the social construction of new knowledge.

Second, the guided questioning-responding process itself has a great deal of flexibility built into it, and the procedure almost guarantees flexible use. Although the group interaction is structured at a fundamental level, through the forms of the generic questions, guided questioning was designed to provide freedom within structure. For example, students are not required to ask particular questions; rather, they choose the generic question form to use. The freedom to choose the generic questions to use in generating questions is a significant factor in the effectiveness of guided questioning (King, 1994a). Furthermore, although students learn and practice the questioning skills and responding skills in a structured way at first, they soon become very flexible in generating questions as needed, rather than in a formulaic way.

Students' freedom to decide which questions will guide their generation of specific questions is only one aspect of the procedure's flexibility. Once students, even those as young as fourth grade, understand how thought-provoking integration questions and comprehension questions differ from fact questions, and once they have learned the structure for generating their own questions, they need practically no encouragement to adapt the process to flexible use. They frequently adapt the given form of a question to fit the context without losing the question's thought-provoking quality. Students are also urged, when they are about to pose a question to the group, to either (a) select, from several questions they have already generated, one that builds on or relates to the previous discussion sequence, whenever it seems appropriate, or (b) generate a new question on the spot. In this way, they are more likely to extend the line of constructive cognitive activity as far as the group can take it.

Implications for Practice

In her review of productive small-group learning, Cohen (1994) showed that for generative learning to occur in group contexts, the interaction among group members must be at a high cognitive level. As noted previously, most students do not engage in such high-level discourse spontaneously. Indeed, students generally do not even ask thoughtful questions during classroom discussion without being explicitly trained to do so (Dillon, 1988; Graesser, 1992; King, 1990). Furthermore, simply telling students to ask and answer each other's questions is not sufficient to induce thoughtful questioning, elicit explanations, or facilitate knowledge construction (King, 1990, 1992, 1994b). These findings suggest that not only is some kind of guidance or training in high-level discourse needed, but students may actually *require* the sort of guidance these questioning-answering discourse patterns provide. On a practical level, we could say that if we want students to engage in high-level discourse, we need to teach them how to ask thought-provoking questions and how to provide elaborated, thoughtful responses.

Teaching the particular knowledge-construction discourse patterns presented in this chapter to children as young as fourth grade is both feasible and effective. The training can be readily implemented in any real classroom context, as it was in the studies presented (King, 1994b; King & Rosenshine, 1993). Furthermore, those discourse patterns were found to be effective in promoting peer mediated learning, at least at the upper elementary level (King, 1994b; King & Rosenshine, 1993). The role of questioning in these discourse patterns is to stimulate high-level thinking about the material, and the role of elaboration is to clarify understanding, reorganize knowledge, integrate it into conceptual structures, and construct new knowledge. Essentially, translating these effects to any classroom means teaching students how to ask each other questions and how to explain things to each other as a means of mediating each other's learning.

Pilot work on training students in the guided questioning procedure (King, 1989a) revealed that in the absence of additional training, most students tended to follow a routine in their question asking and answering. One member of a group asked a thought-provoking question, another responded, and one of them went on to ask another question without concern for assessing the accuracy or sufficiency of the previous response. Nor did this mechanical question-answer routine lend itself to continuity with any previous or subsequent question-answer sequence. The students seemed more concerned with taking their turns asking the questions. This early pilot work showed the importance of encouraging each student to (a) think about the previous response to evaluate its accuracy and adequacy, (b) elaborate on that response if necessary, and (c) build a follow-up response or question on the previous response in some manner so that connections between responses are evident to all members of the group. These three kinds of activities are both cognitive and metacognitive. Not only do students have to listen carefully to all questions and responses to engage in these activities effectively, but their doing so has additional metacognitive benefits in that it promotes group monitoring of the accuracy and adequacy of the knowledge being constructed. Moreover, building their responses on each other's responses propels the discussion forward to extend knowledge construction. These kinds of cognitive and metacognitive activity, used in concert with thought-provoking questioning, were found to promote intentional skilled mediation of peer learning.

Modeling plays an important part in peer-mediated learning. The components of the knowledge-construction discourse patterns are presented initially through teacher cognitive modeling of question generation, explanation, reasoning, justifying, and the like. Cross-modeling of the discourse patterns within the small groups or dyads further promotes high-level interaction. In some instances, this sort of incidental peer modeling might be relied on in lieu of extended training. For example, even though students did not receive extensive practice in providing feedback and building their follow-up responses or questions on the previous response, students' abilities in these areas were undoubtedly enhanced by observation and imitation of each other's use of these skills.

Research Directions in Group Interaction and Learning

Findings from the studies presented in this chapter suggest that peers may not need to be "more knowledgeable others" in order to scaffold each other's learning. Perhaps, with skill in asking and answering thoughtful questions, they can "bring out the best" in each other with respect to understanding and knowledge building. A possible direction for future research is to examine the effects of training in various discourse patterns for peer learning contexts in which learners are *true* peers, neither of which is more knowledgeable in content and skills.

More sophisticated mediational strategies for use in peer learning contexts need to be developed, and their effectiveness assessed in research settings. For example, I am currently conducting research on the effects of a model of peer tutoring that extends my questioning-explaining model to include guidance in checking for understanding, providing feedback, expanding on responses, probing, and hinting (King, 1998). This transactive peer-tutoring model more closely reflects a Vygotskian (1978) approach to students' scaffolding each other's knowledge construction.

As more sophisticated peer-interaction procedures are developed, it will be important for researchers to keep in mind the need for a delicate balance between freedom and structure. As Cohen (1994) and others have pointed out, there are adverse effects on the level of interaction when too much structure is provided in peer learning. In some instances, it may be more effective to model and encourage certain kinds of interaction rather than to build them firmly into a procedure. For example, although the three kinds of peer mediation (evaluating peer responses for accuracy and adequacy, elaborating on a peer's response if necessary, and building one's follow-up response or question on the previous response) were encouraged in conjunction with questioning and explaining in one of the treatment groups in both the King (1994b) study and the King and Rosenshine (1993) study, no actual devices (prompt cards, charts, etc.) were provided to guide students in such mediation of learning. Nevertheless, those kinds of interaction occurred consistently. Perhaps simply suggesting, modeling, or encouraging can be effective when students feel more flexibility and freedom to apply skills in a spontaneous manner.

Individual differences regarding peer-mediated learning are beginning to be examined. For example, learners differ in their need for structure to guide peer interaction. King (1994a) found that having the freedom to choose which generic questions to use in generating specific questions for peer discussion was more important for students with an internal locus of control than it was for external-locus-of-control students, who were able to tolerate more structure and less freedom.

Finally, an important direction for research in the use of discourse patterns for peer-mediated learning lies in examining how classroom teachers implement various approaches to peer-mediated learning. Another area where attention is needed is teaching classroom teachers how to teach these interactive discourse patterns to their students and examining how they personalize these approaches and adapt them to their own process, as well as how their students do so. In addition, research needs to begin to look at long-term effects of the use of peer-mediated learning on individual learners and on the entire learning environment.

References

Allen, V. L. (1976). *Children as tutors: Theory and research on tutoring.* New York: Academic Press.

Bargh, J. A. & Schul, Y. (1980). On the cognitive benefits of teaching. *Journal of Educational Psychology, 72,* 593–604.

Bearison, D. J. (1982). New directions in studies of social interactions and cognitive growth. In F. C. Serafica (Ed.), *Social-cognitive development in context* (pp. 199–221). New York: Guilford.

Britton, B. K., Van Dusen, L., Glynn, S. M., & Hemphill, D. (1990). The impact of inferences on instructional text. In A. C. Graesser & G. H. Bower (Eds.), *Inferences and text comprehension* (pp. 53–87). San Diego: Academic Press.

Brown, A. L., & Campione, J. C. (1986). Psychological theory and the study of learning disabilities. *American Psychologist, 41,* 1059–1068.

Cazden, C. (1988). *Classroom discourse: The language of teaching and learning.* Portsmouth, NH: Heinemann.

Chan, C. K. K., Burtis, P. J., Scardamalia, M., & Bereiter, C. (1992). Constructive activity in learning from text. *American Educational Research Journal, 29,* 97–118.

Chi, M. T. H., & VanLehn, K. A. (1991). The content of physics self-explanations. *Journal of the Learning Sciences, 1,* 69–105.

Cobb, P. (1988). The tensions between theories of learning and instruction in mathematics education. *Educational Psychologist, 23,* 78–103.

Cohen, E. (1994). Restructuring the classroom: Conditions for productive small groups. *Review of Educational Research, 64*(1), 1–35.

Damon, W. (1983). The nature of social-cognitive change in the developing child. In W. F. Overton (Ed.), *The relationship between social and cognitive development* (pp. 103–142). Hillsdale, NJ: Erlbaum.

Dansereau, D. F. (1988). Cooperative learning strategies. In C. E. Weinstein, E. T. Goetz, and P. A. Alexander (Eds.), *Learning and study strategies: Issues in assessment, instruction, and evaluation.* New York: Academic Press.

Dillon, J. T. (1988). *Questioning and teaching: A manual of practice.* New York: Teachers College Press.

Graesser, A. C. (1992). *Questioning mechanisms during complex learning* (Technical Report). Arlington, VA: Office of Naval Research, Cognitive Science Program.

Johnson, D., & Johnson, R. (1990). Cooperative learning and achievement. In S. Sharan (Ed.), *Cooperative learning: Theory and research* (pp. 33–37). New York: Praeger.

King, A. (1989a). Effects of self-questioning training on college students' comprehension of lectures. *Contemporary Educational Psychology, 14,* 1–16.

King, A. (1989b). Verbal interaction and problem-solving within computer-assisted cooperative learning groups. *Journal of Educational Computing Research, 5,* 1–15.

King, A. (1990). Enhancing peer interaction and learning in the classroom through reciprocal questioning. *American Educational Research Journal, 27,* 664–687.

King, A. (1991). Effects of training in strategic questioning on children's problem-solving performance. *Journal of Educational Psychology, 83,* 307–317.

King, A. (1992). Facilitating elaborative learning through guided student-generated questioning. *Educational Psychologist, 27,* 111–126.

King, A. (1994a). Autonomy and question asking: The role of personal control in guided student-generated questioning. *Learning and Individual Differences, 6*(2), 162–185.

King, A. (1994b). Guiding knowledge construction in the classroom: Effects of teaching children how to question and how to explain. *American Educational Research Journal, 30,* 338–368.

King, A. (1994c). *A model of peer tutoring.* Unpublished manuscript. California State University at San Marcos.

King, A. (1998). Transactive peer tutoring: Distributing cognition and metacognition. *Educational Psychology Review, 10,* 57–74.

King, A., & Rosenshine, B. (1993). Effects of guided cooperative questioning on children's knowledge construction. *Journal of Experimental Education, 61,* 127–148.

Mehan, H. (1979). *Learning lessons.* Cambridge, MA: Harvard University Press.

Mugny, G., & Doise, W. (1978). Socio-cognitive conflict and the structure of individual and collective performances. *European Journal of Social Psychology, 8,* 181–192.

Noddings, N. (1989). Theoretical and practical concerns about small groups in mathematics. *Elementary School Journal, 89,* 607–623.

Palincsar, A. S., & Brown, A. L. (1984). Reciprocal teaching of comprehension-fostering and monitoring activities. *Cognition and Instruction, 1,* 117–175.

Perret-Clermont, A. (1980). *Social interaction and cognitive development in children.* New York: Academic Press.

Pressley, M., McDaniel, M. A., Turnure, J. E., Wood, E., & Ahmad, M. (1987). Generation and precision of elaboration: Effects on intentional and incidental learning. *Journal of Experimental Psychology: Learning, Memory, and Cognition, 13,* 291–300.

Pressley, M., Symons, S., McDaniel, M. A., Snyder, B. L., & Turnure, J. E. (1988). Elaborative interrogation facilitates acquisition of confusing facts. *Journal of Educational Psychology, 80*(3), 268–278.

Rosenshine, B., & Meister, C. (1994). Reciprocal teaching: A review of the research. *Review of Educational Research, 64,* 479–530.

Salomon, G., & Globerson, T. (1989). When teams do not function the way they ought to. *International Journal of Educational Research, 13,* 89–99.

Sharan, S. (1980). Cooperative learning in small groups: Recent methods and effects on achievement, attitudes, and ethnic relations. *Review of Educational Research, 50,* 241–271.

Slavin, R. (1990). Cooperative learning. *Review of Educational Research, 50,* 315–342.

Slavin, R. (1992). When and why does cooperative learning increase achievement: Theoretical and empirical perspectives. In R. Hertz-Lazarowitz and N. Miller (Eds.), *Interaction in cooperative groups: The theoretical anatomy of group learning* (pp. 145–173). New York: Cambridge University Press.

Spires, H. A., Donley, J., & Penrose, A. M. (1990, April). *Prior knowledge activation: Inducing text engagement in reading to learn.* Paper presented at the annual meeting of the American Educational Research Association, Boston, MA.

Swing, S., & Petersen, P. (1982). The relationship of student ability and small group interaction to student achievement. *American Educational Research Journal, 19,* 259–274.

Tudge, J. (1990). Vygotsky: The zone of proximal development and peer collaboration: Implications for classroom practice. In L. Moll (Ed.), *Vygotsky and education: Instructional implications and applications of sociohistorical psychology.* New York: Columbia University Press.

Vedder, P. (1985). *Cooperative learning: A study on processes and effects of cooperation between primary school children.* Groningen, Netherlands: University of Groningen.

Vygotsky, L. S. (1978). *Mind in society: The development of higher psychological processes.* Cambridge, MA: Harvard University Press.

Webb, N. M. (1989). Peer interaction and learning in small groups. *International Journal of Educational Research,* 21–39.

Webb, N. M., Ender, P., & Lewis, S. (1986). Problem solving strategies and group processes in small groups learning computer programming. *American Educational Research Journal, 23,* 243–251.

Wittrock, M. C. (1974). Learning as a generative process. *Educational Psychologist, 11,* 87–95.

Wittrock, M. C. (1990). Generative processes of comprehension. *Educational Psychologist, 24,* 345–376.

Teaching Peer Relationship Competence in Schools

Wendy P. Troop

University of Illinois at Urbana-Champaign

Steven R. Asher

University of Illinois at Urbana-Champaign

If children's school days were spent entirely at their desks, educators and parents might concern themselves exclusively with teaching reading, writing, and arithmetic. Children's school days, however, include numerous occasions during which children interact with each other. Group projects, lunch periods, field trips, recesses, physical education classes, and bus rides are just some of the contexts in which children spend time with their peers. For most children, these times can be very rewarding experiences. They have others to talk to, play with, and confide in and to get help from when they have school and personal problems. These children are well accepted by the peer group and have close dyadic relationships with friends. For other children, however, the social environment of school is more problematic because they have difficulties getting along with their classmates. Some are rejected by peers because they inflict harm on other children. Other rejected children are withdrawn and submissive and are the victims of other children's neglect or ridicule. Still other children are not particularly aggressive or withdrawn but are disliked simply because they have poor social relationship skills. Regardless of the reason for rejection, for children having peer relationship problems, school can become a dreaded place with no escape. Although all children may have days or

141

even weeks in which they feel disliked, some children experience low levels of peer acceptance for years. Available evidence suggests that about 30–50 percent of elementary school children who are highly disliked by peers in their classroom are found to be rejected by their classmates five years later (Coie & Dodge, 1983; Newcomb & Bukowski, 1984). Many children, then, have school careers that are negatively affected by their social relationships with peers.

Extensive research over the past two decades indicates that children with peer relationship problems often lack the types of skills they need to perform effectively such critical social tasks as entering groups, maintaining cooperative play, or resolving interpersonal conflicts (for reviews, see Asher & Coie, 1990). Related research also indicates that providing children with direct instruction in social relationship skills can help children with peer relationship difficulties become better accepted by peers (see Asher, Parker, & Walker, 1996, for a recent review). Our three major objectives in writing this chapter are to document the importance of children's peer relationships to their development, to describe ways of identifying children who are having peer relationship problems, and to provide information that will help educators instruct students in social relationship skills. Accordingly, the first part of the chapter will describe the associations between children's peer relationships and their social, emotional, and intellectual development. Particular emphasis will be placed on how children's peer relationships influence their ability to function in school settings. The second part of the chapter will focus on ways of identifying children who are having peer relationship problems. The focus of the third section will be on helping children develop social relationship skills. As will be seen, direct instruction in social relationship skills is frequently effective, and school professionals can therefore make a difference in the social lives of children.

The Contribution of Peer Relationships to Social Development and School Adjustment

Children's peer relationships can be thought of in two distinct dimensions. One dimension is the extent to which children are accepted by peers. This refers to how well children are liked by the peers with whom they interact on a daily basis. Being accepted or well liked by the peer group means that a child is included in group activities, can readily find a play partner, and is unlikely to be the object of exclusion or harassment. A second, and equally important, dimension of peer relationships is having friends. Friendship is a close relationship between two people that is typically characterized by a shared history, mutual attachment, and special concern for each other's welfare. Recent research supports the idea that acceptance and friendship are distinct dimensions. For example, being accepted by peers does not necessarily equate with having friends, nor does rejection necessarily equate with lacking friends (Parker & Asher, 1993a).

There is reason to believe that being accepted by peers and having friends contribute independently to a child's development (Asher & Parker, 1989; Furman & Robbins, 1985; Sullivan, 1953). On one hand, acceptance by classmates probably contributes to a child's feelings of inclusion, opportunities to participate in activities, and learning of leadership skills. On the other hand, close friends can serve as confidants and as reliable allies. Friends are also more likely than nonfriends to be available for companionship, help, and emotional support. These benefits of peer relationships are vital for healthy social and emotional development. Accordingly, it is plausible that chronic peer rejection and lack of friendships would lead to both concurrent and future difficulties for children, including problems adjusting to school.

Peer Relationships and Healthy School Adjustment

One of the earliest challenges children encounter is adjusting to new school settings. Signs that a child is not adapting well to school include anxiety, school avoidance, negative perceptions of school and peer support, and poor performance. As early as preschool, the nature of children's participation in peer relationships influences their school adjustment. Ladd (1990), for example, found that young children's peer acceptance was related to various indexes of academic adjustment during kindergarten. Rejected kindergartners reported less favorable attitudes toward school, performed poorly, and avoided school more than their average accepted peers.

Friendships also seem to be closely linked to attitudes toward school. Ladd (1990) studied three indexes related to having friends: (a) how many friends a child had when entering kindergarten, (b) how well the child maintained those friendships during the school year, and (c) how many new friends the child made. All three indexes were related to children's adjustment during their first year of school. Children who entered kindergarten with close friends had more positive perceptions of school than children who began kindergarten without any friends. Children who then maintained those friendships were more likely to have positive attitudes toward school at the end of the year than children whose friendships had dissolved. Finally, making new friends in school was related to children's school performance in kindergarten.

The quality of best friendships may also influence children's adjustment to new school settings. Some friendships are characterized by such positive qualities as high levels of trust, emotional support, helpfulness, and ease of conflict resolution. Other friendships have more problems in these areas. In one study, boys who reported frequent conflicts in their friendships had more difficulty adjusting to kindergarten (Ladd, Kochenderfer, & Coleman, 1996). Those boys avoided school more and felt more lonely in school than boys whose friendships were less conflictual. For both boys and girls, certain benefits provided by friendships, such as helping each other and giving validation, were related to positive perceptions of school and classmates.

Later school transitions, such as moving from elementary school to middle school or junior high school, may be just as difficult as or more difficult than beginning grade school. There are new teachers, many unfamiliar classmates, and new responsibilities. Adolescents have reported that they receive less support from school officials during their first year in middle school or junior high school than they did during elementary school (Seidman, Allen, Aber, Mitchell, & Feinman, 1994). If adult support decreases, relationships with peers may play an especially critical role in children's adjustment to a new school. During a stressful period of transition, children may especially benefit from having already developed healthy peer relationships during grade school and from having the capacity for forming and maintaining good peer relations in a new school. Indeed, children who report that they are comfortable in their new school environment often indicate that their easy transition was due to maintaining old friendships and forming new ones (Mitman & Packer, 1982). In another study, children's feelings of comfort and support from peers during grade school predicted whether they showed symptoms of various psychological problems during their first year of junior high school (Hirsch & DuBois, 1992). Children's peer relations may also influence more overt indices of school adjustment, such as misbehaving and skipping school. For example, Berndt and Keefe (1995) found that children who reported negative features in their friendships also reported participating in disruptive behavior at school, and Kupersmidt and Coie (1990) found that rejected adolescents were truant significantly more often than nonrejected adolescents.

Peer Relationships and Loneliness

One reason school may be difficult for children with peer relationship problems is that school becomes a lonely place for them. Children as young as kindergarten understand the concept of loneliness and can reliably identify their own feelings of loneliness (Cassidy & Asher, 1992). Furthermore, for many children, loneliness is not simply a fleeting state. For example, in a study of children in grades 3 through 6, children's reports of loneliness at the beginning of the school year had a .56 correlation with their reports of loneliness at the end of the school year (Renshaw & Brown, 1993). Boivin, Hymel, and Bukowski (1995) found a similar correlation (.53) between children's feelings of loneliness at the end of one school year and their feelings at the end of the next.

Children who are rejected by other children report higher levels of loneliness than children who are better accepted by peers. This association between loneliness and rejection by the peer group has been found for children of various ages, including children in kindergarten and first grade (Cassidy & Asher, 1992), the middle years of elementary school (Asher, Hymel, & Renshaw, 1984; Boivin et al., 1995; Crick & Ladd, 1993; Renshaw & Brown, 1993), and middle school (Parkhurst & Asher, 1992). Rejected children's heightened feelings of loneliness occur in various school contexts, including the lunchroom, recess, and physical education, as well as the classroom (Asher, Hopmeyer, & Gabriel, 1998).

Not all rejected children are equally susceptible to feelings of loneliness. Rejected children who are withdrawn or submissive and easy targets for others' abusive behavior are especially likely to report elevated levels of loneliness (Boivin et al., 1995; Parkhurst & Asher, 1992). Children who are disliked by their classmates because they are highly aggressive show a more complex picture. In elementary school, they are more lonely than better-accepted children, but less lonely than rejected children who are withdrawn or submissive (Williams & Asher, 1987). In middle school, however, their level of loneliness has not been found to differ significantly from that of better-accepted children (Parkhurst & Asher, 1992).

Researchers have proposed alternative explanations for aggressive-rejected children's reporting lower levels of loneliness than rejected children who are withdrawn or submissive. There is evidence that aggressive-rejected children have more companions in school (often other aggressive children) than withdrawn-rejected children (see Cairns, Cairns, Neckerman, Gest, Gariepy, 1987; Williams & Asher, 1991). Other possibilities are that as aggressive children grow older, they increasingly mask feelings of loneliness to maintain a tough persona, or that they even fail to recognize cues that they are having problems getting along with other people (Zakriski & Coie, 1996).

Having friends, and the quality of those friendships, can also influence the degree to which children feel lonely. Even children with only one friend report less loneliness than those who have no friends at all (Renshaw & Brown, 1993). Furthermore, Parker and Asher (1993b) found that children whose friendships were characterized by high levels of validation, companionship, guidance, and intimate disclosure were less lonely than children whose friendships did not have high levels of these qualities. In addition, children who experienced less conflict in their friendships and were able to successfully resolve arguments when they did occur were less lonely than children who had more conflicts with friends and had more difficulty resolving disputes.

Unfortunately, rejected children have fewer friends than do better-accepted children, and even when they have friends, their friendships are of lower quality (Parker & Asher, 1993b). These children are also less likely to have positive relationships with their teachers (Birch & Ladd, 1997; Taylor, 1989), and so their relationships with adults at school may not help much to buffer them from feelings of loneliness.

Peer Relationship Problems and Academic Achievement

Children's peer relationships in school are also related to their academic achievement. The association between low peer acceptance and academic difficulties is well established (e.g., Ide, Parkerson, Haertel, & Walberg, 1981; Kupersmidt & Coie, 1990; Li, 1985; Muma, 1965). For example, in a study of high school students, Kupersmidt and Coie (1990) found that of adolescents failing or close to failing their academic subjects, 42 percent were rejected by classmates. Rejected aggressive children have also been shown to be less motivated than other children to do schoolwork (Wentzel & Asher, 1995). One possible explanation for rejected children's lower academic performance is that the behaviors they display are detrimental to their academic success as well as their social success. For example, rejected middle school children are less helpful and cooperative with classmates and are more likely to fight with others and break rules (Wentzel, 1991). Poor academic performance may also be a cause of low peer acceptance, since children may not want to be friends with classmates they view as less competent academically.

Peer rejection has also been linked to increased rates of dropping out of school (see Kupersmidt, Coie, & Dodge, 1990, and Parker & Asher, 1987, for reviews). To illustrate, Gronlund and Holmlund (1958) reported that 54 percent of poorly accepted boys and 35 percent of poorly accepted girls in their sample dropped out of high school. These rates were quite high compared with the 19 percent of well-accepted boys and 4 percent of well-accepted girls who left school early. Furthermore, peer acceptance predicts later withdrawal from school even when behavioral reputation and early academic competence are taken into account (Kupersmidt, 1983).

Rejected children might drop out of school for various reasons. Wentzel and Asher (1995) found that aggressive-rejected students were lower achieving than average students. Perhaps children who are highly aggressive find acceptance in a subgroup of peers who share and reinforce delinquent involvements and an antipathy to school (Dishion, Andrews, & Crosby, 1995; Dishion, Patterson, & Griesler, 1994). As for withdrawn-rejected children, evidence suggests that they are not lower achieving than average students (Wentzel & Asher, 1995). However, as mentioned earlier, withdrawn-rejected children feel more lonely than aggressive-rejected children and better-accepted children. School might therefore be a very trying place for them, and as a consequence, withdrawn-rejected children might begin to stay home from school as they get older. Such increases in truancy may lead the child to believe that leaving school might be a permanent solution to a seemingly unsolvable problem. We need to know more about the developmental trajectory for both subgroups of rejected children.

To summarize, children's concurrent and future adjustment are influenced by how well they are accepted by the peer group, by whether or not they have friends, and by the quality of those friendships. Children who are rejected by their classmates, who have few friends, and who have friendships of lower quality miss out on the important benefits that positive relationships can provide. Children who have such difficulties often find school a less enjoyable environment. When entering a new school, they develop negative perceptions of school, perform poorly, and attempt to avoid school. Many of these children are unsuccessful academically. Others do better academically, but nonetheless feel lonely and unhappy at school. Eventually, children with peer relationship problems are more likely to drop out of school.

Identifying Children with Peer Relationship Problems

In most classrooms, there are at least two or three children who are poorly accepted by peers or who lack friends. How might educators identify such children? On the one hand, it is tempting to rely on teacher judgment. After all, teachers spend a large amount of time with the children in their classes and therefore get to know the children fairly well. They can also compare a child with the large number of other children they have taught and observed. It turns out, however, that teachers are not as accurate as one might expect in estimating children's peer acceptance, partly because many of children's social interactions occur outside the teacher's view—for example, on the playground, in the lunchroom, or on a bus. Teachers' assessments may also be skewed by a possible tendency to notice rejected students who are aggressive more than children whose social problems are due to submissive or withdrawn behaviors, or to a lack of positive relationship skills.

For these reasons, educators and researchers have long relied on children's reports to provide information about which children are accepted and have friends, and which children are rejected or lack friends in school. Children have the benefit of interacting with each other in multiple contexts, not only in the classroom. Furthermore, since peer acceptance and friendship involve children's feelings toward each other, it seems reasonable to learn about such matters by asking the children directly. Sociometric measures are used to assess children's feelings of attraction to (liking) or rejection of (disliking) their peers. Sociometric measures have a long history in education (Gronlund, 1959; Moreno, 1934) and for good reason. They are reliable and valid indicators of how well children are liked by their peers and whether they have friends. In this section, we will describe the sociometric measures that are most often used to learn about children's level of acceptance and the number of friends they have in their school.

Measuring Acceptance

Children's peer acceptance is most often measured by using either nomination or rating-scale sociometric measures. Nomination methods typically involve asking children to list the three children they like most and the three children they like least. These lists can be obtained by giving children rosters with the names of everyone in their class or grade level. Children then circle on one roster the names of the three people they like most and on a separate roster the names of the three people they like least. Rosters are given to the children, rather then having them write names on a piece of paper, to eliminate spelling and memory errors.

Children's "like most" and "like least" nominations can be used to classify children into five sociometric categories (see Coie & Dodge, 1983; Coie, Dodge, & Coppotelli, 1982; Newcomb & Bukowski, 1984). *Popular* children are those who receive many positive nominations and few negative ones. *Rejected* children are those who receive many negative nominations and few positive ones. *Neglected* children are those who receive few nominations, positive or negative. Children who are *average* in sociometric status receive moderate numbers of both "like most" and "like least" nominations. The last group, labeled *controversial*, receive high numbers of both positive and negative nominations. These children seem to polarize group opinion.

Rating-scale measures of acceptance by peers have also been frequently used. In this method, too, children are given a roster of all of their classmates. The children then rate each classmate according to how much they like to play with or be in activities with that classmate (Asher & Hymel, 1981; Ladd, 1983; Putallaz, 1983; Singleton & Asher, 1977). For example, children in middle to late elementary school can be asked to circle a number from 1 to 5 to show how much they like to play with each classmate. The average rating each child receives from classmates can be used to classify children into three groups: low-accepted, average-accepted, and high-accepted. An advantage of rating-scale measures is that one learns how each child is viewed by every other member of the class. Furthermore, rating-scale sociometric measures do not ask children to indicate their least favorite classmates and, for this reason, are sometimes preferred by teachers and parents.

Measuring Friendship

Using sociometric measures to determine whether children have friends in their classroom is a straightforward matter. Children are typically asked to identify the classmates they consider friends. This can be accomplished by giving children a class roster and having them circle the names of children they consider to be their friends. Educators or researchers usually identify a child as a friend of another if the children nominate each other, that is, if the nominations are reciprocated.

One subtle but important issue concerns the number of friendship nominations that should be requested from children. Educators and researchers sometimes use an unlimited-nomination measure (e.g., "Circle all the names of your best friends in this class"). In other cases, children are asked to name their five best friends or three best friends. Children can even be asked to identify their one "very best friend." The fewer names children are asked to indicate, the higher the proportion of children who will be identified as having no friends. For example, on an unlimited-nomination measure, about 10 percent of children in classrooms of 22–28 students have no reciprocated friendships. On a measure in which children are limited to three friendship nominations, the figure increases to about 20 percent. Temporal criteria can also be used to identify close friends. Because children's friendships are sometimes fleeting, some researchers have restricted their identification of friendships to those in which children nominate each other at two different times (Newcomb & Bagwell, 1996).

Sociometric Measures and Younger Children

Modifications have been made to both nomination and rating-scale sociometric measures to adapt them successfully to use with younger children, such as preschoolers or kindergartners. Invariably, researchers conduct individual interviews, rather than collect sociometric information in a group context. In addition, rather than being given rosters with their classmates' names, children are shown pictures of their classmates (Marshall & McCandless, 1957). This practice allows children to rely on facial recognition rather than on reading skills, which may not be well developed. To assess friendship, children are shown photographs of their classmates and are asked to point to pictures of their best friends. For nomination measures of acceptance versus rejection, children are asked to point to photographs of the children they like the most and like the least. Rating-scale measures of acceptance and rejection have also been used reliably with younger children (Asher, Singleton, Tinsley, & Hymel, 1979) by showing the children photographs of classmates and using a three-point rating scale rather than a five-point scale (e.g., "like to play with a lot" = 3; "like to play with a little" = 2; "like to play with not at all" = 1). Also, drawings of frowning, neutral, and smiling faces can be used to represent each point on the scale. Research using this measure with four-year-olds (Asher et al., 1979) has produced peer acceptance scores that are highly reliable over time.

Ethical Considerations in Sociometric Measures

When children are given a sociometric measure to complete, it is important to ask the children to keep their answers confidential and not to discuss them with classmates afterward. One way to further safeguard confidentiality is to administer sociometric instruments immediately before children engage in an academic subject, rather than right before recess, lunch, or physical education. This reduces the likelihood that children will "compare notes." Still, researchers, parents, teachers, and school officials have sometimes expressed concern that children might change their behavior toward peers or discuss their answers with classmates after completing sociometric assessments. Adults also worry that some children might feel bad about themselves or their peer relationships after completing these measures. Fortunately, research to date suggests that these measures do not produce harmful effects. Observations of preschool and elementary school children's behavior toward their peers before and after completing sociometric instruments indicates that children's interactions do not change as a result of participating in sociometric assessments (Bell-Dolan, Foster, & Sikora, 1989; Hayvren & Hymel, 1984). Teachers and parents also report noticing no changes in children's behavior after the children have completed sociometric assessments (Bell-Dolan, Foster, & Christopher, 1992). As for the concern that children might disclose to peers their responses on sociometric instruments, research suggests that when children do talk to their classmates, almost all of their discussions are about positive evaluations that were given (Bell-Dolan et al., 1992; Iverson, Barton, & Iverson, 1997). As for any emotional impact of sociometric assessment, measures of children's moods and feelings of loneliness indicate that children's emotional states are not adversely affected by sociometric measurement (Bell-Dolan et al., 1989), and children consistently report having enjoyed participating in studies that included sociometric measures (Bell-Dolan et al., 1989; Bell-Dolan et al., 1992; Iverson et al., 1997; Ratiner, Weissberg, & Caplan, 1986).

In sum, children are often the best source of information about who in a class is rejected or lacks friends. Peer nomination or rating-scale measures of acceptance can be used to identify children who are rejected by their peers, and limited or unlimited friendship nominations can be used to identify children who have no friends. All of these measures can be easily created and administered by teachers and other professionals, and their administration does not appear to have negative effects on children's social behavior or attitudes. These measures, used wisely, provide a valuable means of selecting children who need help learning how to relate more successfully with their peers.

Helping Children with Peer Relationship Problems

Imagine that you are a teacher or another school professional who has identified children who are poorly accepted by peers or who lack friends. There are a variety of approaches you might take to improving the children's social experiences at school. One widely used strategy is to pair a poorly accepted child with a better-accepted child and have them do a special activity together, such as working on a project or putting on a presentation for the class. Research on this approach reveals some short-term benefits, but there does not seem to be lasting change in children's acceptance by peers (Lilly, 1971; Rucker & Vincenzo, 1970). Once these special efforts end, advances children have made in their social relationships tend to be lost.

We also know that removing children from their everyday peer context and placing them in a new peer group will not be sufficient for many children. The idea behind this approach is to give children a fresh start with a new group of peers. Unfortunately, research suggests that children who are rejected by peers tend to recreate their problems in a new context. In a remarkable study by Coie and Kupersmidt (1983), children who did not previously know each other were brought together for weekly play groups. The play groups consisted of four boys. After every session, each child was individually interviewed by an adult who drove the child home. The adult asked who the child most liked to play with in the group, who the child liked next best, and so on. Coie and Kupersmidt found that after just three of these play sessions the boys' level of acceptance in the newly formed groups correlated substantially (.54) with their level of acceptance in their regular classrooms. Further analyses indicated that the children who were poorly accepted by peers tended to be those who engaged in aggressive or disruptive behavior rather than more prosocial forms of behavior. These findings suggest that putting rejected children in new groups is an inadequate solution to their problems. The findings also suggest that helping children requires that the children learn ways of behaving more effectively with peers.

The remainder of this chapter, then, is predicated on the assumption that children with peer relationship problems lack social relationship skills and that they can be helped by being provided with direct instruction in these skills. In the subsection that follows, we will describe the types of behavioral competencies displayed by children who are accepted by peers and who make friends. After that, we will discuss several issues that need attention in the designing of school-based instruction in social relationship skills.

The Behavioral Basis of Acceptance and Friendship

What types of behavioral skills do children need in order to form and maintain good relationships with their peers? It is not a simple matter to specify the skills that children need in order to be accepted by peers or to have friends. Part of the complexity is that children (and adults) face a wide range of social tasks in everyday life. For example, children need to learn how to enter groups, handle conflicts or disagreements, maintain conversation, help others, assert their ideas, cope with rejection, apologize for wrongdoing, and respond to ambiguous provocation (situations in which the child is harmed by a peer but it is unclear whether the harm was intended). Certain situations can be quite challenging, even for children who are generally competent in their relationships with others. People differ in what they find difficult, and almost everyone finds some of these tasks challenging. The skills children are taught need to be useful for the particular social tasks they find most difficult.

Another part of the complexity is that what is considered social competence changes as children grow older. It may also differ somewhat by gender, ethnicity, culture, or social class. For example, Chen, Rubin, and Sun (1992) have recently reported that among children in China, shyness is associated with being liked, even though it is not usually considered a social asset among Western children.

Nonetheless, several decades of research on children's peer relations makes it possible to draw certain general conclusions about the behavioral characteristics that lead a child to become liked or disliked by peers and to make or fail to make friends. Various research methods have been used to understand the behavioral dynamics associated with acceptance versus rejection. One method is to observe children who are brought together for the first time (e.g., Coie & Kupersmidt, 1983; Dodge, 1983; Guralnick & Groom, 1987). The children are observed as their sociometric status emerges in a newly formed play group, and the observer has a chance to learn about the behavioral characteristics that lead certain children to be accepted and other children to be rejected by their peers. Another approach is to observe children in their everyday school environment—for example, in the classroom or on the playground (e.g., Ladd, 1983). Still another methodology involves setting up analog situations. The researcher creates a realistic situation between a child being observed and one or more peers. This method has been used to study children's behavior in contexts such as entering a group (e.g., Putallaz & Gottman, 1981) or responding to an ambiguous provocation from a peer (e.g., Dodge, 1980). Another widely used procedure is to present children with various vignettes, usually by reading to them a short paragraph depicting a hypothetical situation, such as an interpersonal conflict over some kind of desired object, activity, or location (Chung & Asher, 1996; Slaby & Guerra, 1988). Children are then asked to indicate how they would respond if confronted with the circumstances being described. Reports from children's peers (e.g., Coie et al., 1982) and teachers (e.g., Cassidy & Asher, 1992) about the children's everyday behavioral style are also informative, because teachers and, especially, peers get to observe children in a wider variety of contexts and over a longer period of time than might be possible for a researcher, whose time with each child may be limited. Also extremely informative are interviews in which children are asked about the characteristics they look for in a friend (e.g., Bigelow & LaGaipa, 1975). Children can be quite articulate about the qualities that make someone a good friend and about the characteristics of their best friends.

These various sources of information have provided a rich and detailed picture of the behavioral characteristics associated with forming and maintaining good relationships with peers. To organize these characteristics into a conceptually mean-ingful framework, Asher and Williams (1987) proposed a *core-questions* frame-work. They suggested that children's reactions to their peers are based on the responses they get to certain core questions they implicitly ask themselves about their relationships with others. These fundamental questions are (a) Is this child trustworthy? (b) Is this child fun to be with? (c) Do we influence each other in ways I like? (d) Does this child make me feel good about myself? (e) Does this child facilitate, and not undermine, my goals? and (f) Is this child similar to me? We will use this framework to describe the various behavioral characteristics associated with being accepted and having friends.

Is this child trustworthy?   People want to have others in their lives whom they can trust and who trust them. Gaining someone's trust involves being honest and loyal to others, keeping others' secrets, and feeling comfortable telling others per-sonal information. Trust is an essential part of developing a close, emotional bond with another person. As children get older, they turn increasingly to their peers to fulfill these needs (for a review, see Berndt & Hanna, 1995). It is not surprising, then, that children report liking peers who are trustworthy (Parkhurst & Asher, 1987) and disliking those who are dishonest (Carlson, Lahey, & Neeper, 1984). Chil-dren also choose to associate with classmates who are loyal to them and won't try to hurt them. For example, they want their friends to stick up for them and to seek out their company rather than the company of others (Berndt, Hawkins, & Hoyle, 1986; Berndt & Perry, 1990; Bigelow & LaGaipa, 1975; Newcomb & Bagwell, 1995). Children who spread rumors about others or try to damage others' social relationships are often disliked (Crick, 1996; Crick, Casas, & Mosher, 1997; Crick & Grotpeter, 1995; Grotpeter & Crick, 1996).

An important part of developing trust with another person is sharing intimate information and feelings. Although adults might expect self-disclosure to become an integral part of children's peer relationships only as the children approach ado-lescence, self-disclosure has been found to be important in the formation of even young children's friendships (Gottman, 1983). Being willing to engage in self-disclo-sure is also related to being well liked by peers (Franzoi, Davis, & Vasquez-Suson, 1994). This is not to say that simply sharing personal information at high rates will lead to peer acceptance and friendships. Often disclosing too much can be prob-lematic. Older children are responsive to peers who share information at a level of intimacy similar to that of the person with whom they are talking. For example, when watching two children interact, older children are not accepting of a child who discloses very personal information to a person who has not done the same (Rotenberg & Mann, 1986). Therefore, self-disclosure, including knowing when and how much to share, is an important skill for children to master.

Is this child fun to be with?   A major reason children form relationships with each other is to have people with whom to share enjoyable activities and experi-ences. Indeed, research supports the notion that sharing activities is the primary reason young children make friends (Bigelow & LaGaipa, 1980; Selman, 1980;

Smollar & Youniss, 1982), and remains an integral part of friendships through child-hood and adolescence (Foster, DeLawyer, & Guevremont, 1986; Parker & Asher, 1993a). As a result, children who have positive peer relationships are typically those who are adept at activities valued by the peer group. For example, for both boys and girls, being good at playing sports is an important skill for gaining peer acceptance (Coie et al., 1982; Gross & Johnson, 1984; McCraw & Tolbert, 1953; Rockhill & Asher, 1992). Well-accepted children are also able to generate ideas for enjoyable activities and games. While playing with peers, children who have posi-tive social relationships display behaviors that enhance others' enjoyment. They have a good sense of humor (Masten, 1986; Rockhill & Asher, 1992; Sherman, 1985; Sletta, Valas, Skaalvik, & Sobstad, 1996), play fairly (Feinberg, Smith, & Schmidt, 1958), are better at waiting their turn (Carlson et al., 1984), show good sportsmanship (Goertzen, 1959), and are not apt to quit games (Rockhill & Asher, 1992). Perhaps partly because of their more skillful play, well-accepted children maintain social interactions for a longer period of time than poorly accepted chil-dren (Dodge, 1983).

Do we influence each other in ways I like?   Although persuasion and influ-ence are inevitable parts of a relationship, people generally do not like to feel that they have been coerced. A number of studies have shown that children who are well liked tend to be cooperative (see Coie, Dodge, & Kupersmidt, 1990, for a review), and that children with close friends are less domineering than those with-out close friends (Clark & Ayers, 1988). Children who have problems with their peer relationships often exert influence in inappropriate ways, such as being bossy (Goertzen, 1959; Rockhill & Asher, 1992) or manipulative (Crick et al., 1997; Crick & Grotpeter, 1995) or using threats (Dodge, 1983). For example, from observations of preschool children's negotiations during social play, Black (1992) found that less well-liked children made more demands, as well as more suggestions, than other children, and they more often rejected the ideas of their peers. Better-liked chil-dren, in contrast, were more likely to incorporate the ideas of their peers when negotiating social play.

Children's success at friendships is also related to how they handle conflicts (see Laursen, 1993). Well-accepted children do not start fights as readily as those who are poorly accepted (Coie & Kupersmidt, 1983). When conflicts do arise, their arguments are relatively brief, and they offer their peers constructive suggestions for resolving the matter. When asked how they would handle hypothetical conflicts, these children endorse prosocial strategies for ending disputes. Children who are not well liked, however, more often respond to conflict with strategies that give them control or even enable them to obtain revenge (Chung & Asher, 1995).

Does this child make me feel good about myself?   Participating in successful social relationships also involves validating others and providing others with emo-tional support. In childhood and adolescence, being nurturing and supportive is important for gaining peer acceptance (Elkins, 1958; Moore & Updegraff, 1964). Chil-dren who have friends are more emotionally supportive and more sensitive to others' feelings (Cauce, 1986). Children with positive peer relationships are also better at perceiving and understanding others' emotions (Denham, McKinley, Couchoud, & Holt, 1990; Putallaz, 1983). These skills may give them the knowledge they need to know when and how to give peers support.

One way children validate their peers' self-worth is by complimenting their achievements and skills. For example, children want their friends to admire their physical abilities when playing sports or games (Zarbatany, Ghesquiere, & Mohr, 1992). Children also like others who are receptive to offers of assistance (Carlson et al., 1984). By being willing to let others help them, children may make their peers feel good about their own abilities. In contrast, children who are not well liked often make their peers feel bad about themselves by being insulting (Coie et al., 1990; Dodge, 1983), conceited (Feinberg et al., 1958), and snobbish (Coie et al., 1982). As children get older, being a bully is also related to being disliked (Coie, Dodge, Terry, & Wright, 1991; Dodge, Coie, Pettit, & Price, 1990). Being bullied may make children feel weak or small, hence bad about themselves and negative toward the person responsible.

Another way that children can make their peers feel good about themselves is by making them feel desired as playmates and friends. Children feel good when others seem genuinely interested in their company. Children who are well liked are receptive to peers' social overtures (Dodge, 1983; Gottman, Gonso, & Rasmussen, 1975) and are better at initiating interactions and including others in activities (Asher & Renshaw, 1981; Gottman et al., 1975). Children who are poorly accepted often try to exclude others from their activities (Dodge, 1983).

Does this child facilitate, and not undermine, my goals?   In the course of a day, children try to accomplish a variety of social, academic, and personal goals. It is not surprising, therefore, that they value peers who help them accomplish their goals. Research indicates that being helpful is important for gaining peer acceptance (Cantrell & Prinz, 1985; Ladd & Oden, 1979; see Coie et al., 1990, for a review) and for making friends (Bigelow & LaGaipa, 1980). Being helpful in academic contexts seems particularly important for developing positive social relationships with classmates. Children report wanting their friends to help them with academic pursuits (Zarbatany et al., 1992), and children who are accepted by their peers do indeed help others with academic tasks (Wentzel, 1994).

In addition to actively helping their peers, children who have successful peer relationships refrain from behaving in ways that indirectly interfere with their peers' goals. Being disruptive is one way that children may impede others' activities and has been found to be negatively related to sociometric status at all ages (for a review, see Coie et al, 1990). Interestingly, being overly dependent on the teacher can also be annoying to classmates. For example, children who are poorly accepted by peers request more help from the teacher than well-liked children (Coie & Kupersmidt, 1983). This might be because well-accepted children do better in school and, therefore, require less help from their teachers. Frequent demands on the teacher's time might undermine the goals of the other children, who may wish to continue a lesson or move to a new activity. Therefore, excessive help seeking might also contribute to low peer acceptance by hindering others' progress.

Children are often faced with conflict situations in which they must negotiate with a peer. In such circumstances, rejected children tend to behave in ways that are inconsiderate of others' needs. For example, in a recent study, pairs of low-status and pairs of high-status first-grade children were placed alone in a room with one toy with which to play. Low-status children were more likely than high-status children to use strategies that benefited themselves but not their partners. High-status children were more likely than low-status children to use cooperative or collaborative strategies that met the needs of both members of the dyad (Putallaz & Sheppard, 1990).

Is this child similar to me? Research suggests that children are more likely to be friends with others who are similar to themselves (e.g., Kupersmidt, DeRosier, & Patterson, 1995). Although the similarities between friends may be attributed to a tendency for people to become increasingly alike as their relationship develops, people also seem to seek out those with whom they share characteristics. Much of the research on children's similarity with friends has concentrated on demographic variables (e.g., sex, race, age). However, children also prefer the company of peers with whom they are alike in attitudes, preferred activities, and personality characteristics. At younger ages, children base friendships on enjoying the same games. Young children's relationships are friendlier if they establish mutually enjoyable activities (Gottman, 1983), and children prefer the company of peers who participate in the same types of play as they do (e.g., constructive play versus dramatic play versus games with rules) (Rubin, Lynch, Coplan, Rose-Krasnor, & Booth, 1994). As children get older, they base their selection of friends increasingly on similarities in attitudes, behavior, and goals (see Epstein, 1989, for a review). Perhaps children feel that similarities with peers validate their own beliefs and values.

To summarize, children who are accepted by peers and who maintain friendships are those who behave in ways that lead them to be perceived as trustworthy, fun to be with, democratic in style of influence, validating of others, facilitative of goals, and similar to peers. Children who have peer relationship problems need help changing their behavior so that their peers will respond affirmatively to the core relationship questions described in this section. In the next section, we will address the topic of teaching children relationship skills.

Teaching Children Relationship Skills

For most children, social skills are learned as a by-product of ongoing interactions with parents, siblings, friends, classmates, teachers, and other children and adults. For some children, however, everyday interactions do not lead to socially skilled behavior, perhaps because they are exposed to poor models or because they fail to learn from the positive models they do have the opportunity to observe. Therefore, many children may need explicit instruction in social skills. This is not to say that social-skills training needs to be carried out in a didactic or highly formal manner. Children do not even need to be aware that they have been identified as needing help. Interventions can be proposed to children as opportunities for adults to learn children's ideas about what makes playing together fun (see Oden & Asher, 1977, for an example), or they can be carried out in the classroom so that all children benefit and no children are put at risk of being stigmatized by being removed for special lessons.

Because social skills play such a large role in children's peer relationships, a great number of programs have been designed to help students gain the knowledge and abilities necessary for getting along with classmates and making friends. Many of these programs have been shown to improve children's social behavior and peer acceptance (for reviews, see Asher et al., 1996; Coie & Koeppl, 1990; Ladd & Asher, 1985). In addition, when improvements in children's social lives occur, they are often maintained over time (Bierman & Furman, 1984; Csapo, 1983; Gottman, Gonso, & Schuler, 1976; Gresham & Nagle, 1980; Ladd, 1981; Oden & Asher, 1977). These successful interventions nonetheless vary in age group, duration of program, use of individual or small-group instruction, specific skills taught, and methods used to teach the skills. Indeed, it is likely that no program will work best in all situations or for all types of children. Accordingly, interventions should be tailored to meet the needs of the children being taught, as well as the needs of the teachers or counselors working with the children. However, certain features are shared by many of the successful social-skill interventions. Therefore, rather than discuss specific programs for improving children's social skills, our goal here is to highlight certain intervention principles and components that appear likely to enhance the efficacy of interventions.

Organizing lessons around social tasks.   One potentially useful way to organize social-skill programs is to focus lessons on specific social tasks. As mentioned earlier, a variety of social tasks can be problematic for children. Children with poor peer relationships often have problems with such tasks as joining others at play (Putallaz & Wasserman, 1990), handling conflicts (e.g., Chung & Asher, 1996), and dealing with ambiguous provocation (Dodge & Feldman, 1990).

Teaching students how to cope with a variety of social tasks provides a framework for organizing social-skill instruction. Each social task requires a number of specific social skills. For example, trying to join classmates at play requires knowing how to initiate conversation, how to demonstrate an interest in the other children's goals and activities, and how to be supportive of others. Social tasks also give children recognizable contexts for discussing and practicing specific social skills. Most children are familiar with the challenge of trying to join other children who are playing a game, or the challenge of helping a friend in need. It is much easier to discuss a skill, such as being supportive of peers, when the children can relate the skill to particular contexts in which it would be useful.

A number of important social-cognitive processes that have been linked to socially competent behavior can also be taught in the context of social tasks. These processes include taking others' perspectives (e.g., Flavell, Botkin, Fry, Wright, &

Jarvis, 1968; Putallaz & Wasserman, 1990), correctly encoding and interpreting social cues (Dodge, 1980), formulating adaptive social goals (Crick & Dodge, 1994; Dodge, Asher, & Parkhurst, 1989; Erdley & Asher, 1996; Parkhurst & Asher, 1992; Taylor & Asher, 1984), controlling impulses (Meichenbaum & Goodman, 1971), controlling anger (Lochman & Dunn, 1993), and making adaptive attributions concerning the causes of personal social successes and failures (Earn & Sobol, 1990; Goetz & Dweck, 1980). It may be most productive to teach these various processes in the context of specific social tasks. Creating intervention lessons around specific social tasks makes it possible to address both the behavioral problems and the social-cognitive problems children may have in particular contexts.

Interventions should be designed to address tasks that tend to cause problems for the children being helped. Teachers and practitioners may rely on a number of useful sources in creating an effective intervention. Formal curricula such as Second Step (Grossman et al., 1997) and Skillstreaming (McGinnis & Goldstein, 1997) have been created to help children perform a variety of social tasks more effectively. Educators can also create their own lessons to meet the specific needs of the children they are coaching. Children differ in the tasks that cause them problems (Dodge, McClaskey, & Feldman, 1985). Thus, teachers may want to use the parts of existing programs that would be helpful for their students and create their own lessons for tasks that are not addressed in those programs. Social-skills instruction can also take place informally as the adults who work with children take advantage of "teachable moments" that occur throughout the school day. Naturally occurring events between children provide a context for discussing and practicing how to handle a difficult social task.

Instructional processes for social-skill intervention.   At the heart of effective social-skills training is good conversation between a knowledgeable and caring adult and an interested and engaged child. Social-skills intervention sessions often begin by discussing a situation that children find relevant and the skills children need to respond effectively. Adults use these discussions to introduce the ideas or concepts to be taught and to give examples of skillful and nonskillful behavior. Children are encouraged and given opportunities to actively contribute to these discussions. Because the ability to generate strategies for handling social tasks is an important skill for children to master, conversations elicit children's own thoughts about how to handle the task, as well as provide an opportunity for the adult to share some ideas. The pros and cons of each suggestion are examined, and the adult and participating children come to an agreement about which ideas might be worth trying and which ones might not. To replace maladaptive patterns of behavior, it is important to stress, not only why some ideas are beneficial, but also why some tactics might be ill conceived. In addition to having opportunities to develop their ability to generate and evaluate strategies, children are often asked to explain how they would enact a particular strategy. This gives them an opportunity to verbally rehearse the skill, and it gives the instructor the opportunity to identify and clarify any misunderstandings the children may have about handling the task (Ladd & Mize, 1983a).

Discussions can also be used to change maladaptive social goals children might have. Children are more likely to adopt prosocial strategies if the strategies are in line with their goals for the task (Ladd & Mize, 1983a). Research has shown that children with peer relationship problems often have goals that hamper their peer relationships. Children who are aggressive, for example, often have the goals of seeking revenge or maintaining a high degree of control when faced with conflicts with peers (Chung & Asher, 1995, 1996) or when responding to ambiguous provocation (Erdley & Asher, 1996). Withdrawn children, on the other hand, may focus too frequently on the goal of avoiding negative interactions with peers (Chung & Asher, 1996; Erdley & Asher, 1996). Therefore, changing children's social goals can be as important as teaching specific skills. Discussions can include reference to the goals that children could pursue when facing a particular task, and adults should encourage children to focus on goals that will help them maintain positive relationships with peers. For example, Oden and Asher (1977) asked children if the social interaction concepts they were learning were helping make games more fun. Such questions implicitly direct children's attention toward certain game-playing goals (e.g., having a good time with a peer) rather than other game-playing goals a child might otherwise single-mindedly pursue (see Taylor & Asher, 1984).

Conversation alone does not always give children everything they need to master a new skill. Modeling is often effective in helping children develop a fuller understanding of how a skill should look in social situations. For this reason, teachers and skillful peers are often called on to demonstrate how to adeptly handle a particular social task. Videotapes or films of children displaying skilled behavior can often be as useful as "live" demonstrations. However, the addition of modeling alone may not be sufficient. Accompanying narratives can help children focus on the appropriate behavior being displayed and its positive outcomes. For example, in O'Connor's (1969, 1972) modeling studies, children were shown a film of young children attempting to join others. Throughout the film, the narrator highlighted what the child in the film was doing to be successful in gaining entry. Social-learning theorists such as Bandura, Zimmerman, and their colleagues (e.g., Bandura & Jeffery, 1973; Bandura, Jeffery, & Bachica, 1974; Carroll & Bandura, 1990; see Zimmerman & Rosenthal, 1974, for a review) have demonstrated the importance of commentaries during modeling sessions in order for children and adults to cognitively represent and imitate desired behavior accurately. Narratives accompanying the modeling of a skill draw children's attention to the relevant behavior demonstrated and to the positive responses that the skillful behavior elicits from others.

Once children understand the concepts and skills taught, they need opportunities to practice translating the newly acquired knowledge into actual behavior (Ladd & Mize, 1983a). This practice can take two forms. One type of practice involves using role playing with classmates. Role plays are easy to create, give children a chance to practice in a relatively low-risk context, and also allow adults to guide children's practice and to provide immediate feedback. However, when children are aware that the situation is contrived by an adult, they may not behave as they would naturally. A second way children can practice various social tasks is by participating in more "real-life" situations created by an adult. For example, to have children practice negotiation skills, an adult can ask a group of children to create a club and then negotiate who is going to be the president. It has been suggested that children benefit by beginning practice sessions in contrived role-play settings with adult support and then moving into more realistic contexts in which adults provide less instruction (Ladd, 1981; Ladd & Mize, 1983a).

Regardless of whether practice is carried out in an imaginary situation or a real one, successive attempts at mastering tasks allow children to refine their skills. With practice, the learned behavior becomes increasingly automatic, and children become more adept at using the skills. Increased proficiency at a social task may also influence children's confidence in their ability to use the newly attained skills. Children are more likely to use a skill if they feel confident in their ability to use it (Bandura, 1977; Erdley & Asher, 1996). Improvement in skill, gained through practice, should increase children's confidence in using the skills in naturally occurring settings.

To help ensure that practice leads to mastery of the task, adults can help children evaluate their performance as they rehearse the skills (Ladd & Mize, 1983a, 1983b). To boost children's confidence, the evaluation should be primarily supportive, focusing on the positive improvements the children make. In addition to evaluative comments, adults can make constructive suggestions (e.g., "You could try facing the other children when you talk to them") to give children specific ideas for improving their social behavior. When making such suggestions, adults need to be careful not to put children down in front of their peers, since children's opinions of their peers are affected by witnessing negative or positive interactions with a teacher or other adult (Flanders & Havumaki, 1963; White & Kistner, 1992).

Children should also be taught to monitor their own social behavior by noticing how other children are responding (Ladd & Mize, 1983b). For example, after a child practices joining others in a game, an adult might say, "Paul and Jill seemed to really like it when you offered to be the scorekeeper in their game. Did you notice that?" Such feedback draws children's attention to the connection between their behavior and their peers' responses. Children can then maintain their current behavior or change their behavior in accordance with the types of responses they are eliciting. Children also need to be able to make such connections during their everyday social interactions. To encourage children's spontaneous peer monitoring, they can be asked to pay attention to how others are responding.

An example of the importance of feedback and self-monitoring is given by Mize and Ladd (1990). While conducting an intervention, they were confronted with the difficult case of a boy, "Biff," who was swinging toys around and was generally out of control. Not surprisingly, Biff's behavior did not make him well accepted by his play partner, a child who repeatedly asked him to stop his annoying behavior. However, Biff believed that his partner was having fun, so he kept going. To help remedy the situation, the researchers showed Biff a videotape of his behavior that day. They explicitly told Biff to concentrate on the reactions of his playmate during a particular episode. Biff commented on the other child's noticeable displeasure, and he subsequently decreased his disruptive actions during the intervention sessions.

After children have observed their peers' responses, there is a natural tendency for them to try to determine why such reactions occurred. Adults can encourage children to make attributions for their peers' responses that will maintain, rather than undermine, their self-confidence. Children who have peer relationship problems are more likely than well-accepted peers to believe that social successes are due to luck, not to more controllable factors (Earn & Sobol, 1990). Feedback linking skillful behavior to positive peer responses may help children see that they have control over how others respond to them. In addition, children's social behavior can be influenced by their interpretations of previous social failures. For example, children who attribute rejected social overtures to their own internal, stable characteristics are less likely to make improvements in their subsequent communication (Goetz & Dweck, 1980). When helping children monitor their peers' negative reactions, adults should encourage them to attribute those reactions to their efforts (e.g., "I should have tried to be more cooperative"), rather than to stable personal characteristics (e.g., "People never want to play with me") (Ladd & Mize, 1983b).

If children are to benefit from social-skills instruction, it seems important to teach these processes in a context that will be enjoyable, inherently rewarding, and nonpunitive. Children are unlikely to learn a new skill if they are being scolded at the same time for misbehavior. A better approach is to construct enjoyable situations in which skills can be taught without an undertone of blame. One way to accomplish this is to teach skills in the context of games with other peers. Board games, card games, and similar games are popular with children of all ages and provide a familiar context for them. Games are also valuable contexts for social learning because children have the chance to engage in a wide variety of social tasks. In game situations, children face such tasks as entering or initiating play, negotiating rules, maintaining friendly competition, managing disagreement, coping with losing, and being a graceful winner. Another reason game playing is a useful training context is that there are many types of goals children can pursue (see Taylor & Asher, 1984); children need to learn how to coordinate game goals, such as winning or getting better at the game, with the goal of maintaining a positive relationship with other children. Thus, the game context provides an enjoyable atmosphere for teaching a variety of task-relevant skills and for helping children focus on more adaptive goals.

Oden and Asher (1977) successfully coached third- and fourth-grade children in social skills by using game playing as a context for teaching various social interaction concepts: participation, cooperation, communication, and validation-support. Instruction in these concepts was embedded in conversations about ideas that might make game playing enjoyable for the child and his or her playmates. During each of the six training sessions, the child got to play a different game with a different classmate. The games provided the child with a chance to try out the ideas from the conversation and to practice them in real-life game-playing situations with peers.

The game-playing context also served another function in this study. Pairing the child with six different classmates for six different game-playing sessions gave classmates the opportunity to interact with the child in an enjoyable atmosphere and to discover that playing with the child could be an enjoyable experience. This experience is important because often a child who has poor peer relationships has developed a negative reputation (see Hymel, Wagner, & Butler, 1990) that results in few invitations to interact socially with peers and therefore few opportunities to demonstrate newly acquired social skills. Positive interactions with peers during training sessions may help a child overcome such a reputation and may thus lead to other enjoyable social experiences during the school day. Evidence from Bierman and Furman (1984) indicates that providing social-skill training with structured peer-interaction opportunities is more effective than social-skill training alone.

Conclusion

In recent decades, researchers, educators, and parents have become increasingly concerned about children's peer relationships. This concern is warranted, given the association between children's functioning with peers and their current and future social and academic adjustment. Children's ability to adapt to school environments, their feelings of loneliness, and their school performance have all been linked to how well the children are accepted by peers and whether they are successful at making and keeping friends.

In this chapter, we have highlighted several issues central to helping students with poor peer relationships. An important consideration is the accurate identification of children needing adult assistance. Sociometric measures provide direct and reliable sources of information regarding children's peer relationships. Rating-scale and nomination measures have been widely used to learn about children's levels of acceptance and their friendships. These sociometric measures can be used successfully at various ages to identify children who are having serious peer relationship problems.

A second major issue involves understanding the behavioral factors that lead certain children to be poorly accepted by peers or lack friends. Here we have suggested that children implicitly respond to their peer relationships in ways described by a set of core questions: (a) Is this child trustworthy? (b) Is this child fun to be with? (c) Do we influence each other in ways I like? (d) Does this child make me feel good about myself? (e) Does this child facilitate, and not undermine, my goals? and (f) Is this child similar to me? These questions act as a set of criteria that children use to appraise their relationships and the behavioral characteristics of their social interaction partners. These core questions also provide us with a framework for describing the various behavioral characteristics associated with being accepted and having friends.

A third major issue discussed in this chapter concerns intervention to assist children with peer relationship problems. Children face a wide range of challenging social tasks in their day-to-day lives, and even the most socially competent child has difficulty with certain social tasks. Our contention is that organizing instruction around specific social tasks can provide children with a meaningful context for discussing social relationship issues and for helping children engage in relationship-promoting processes, such as taking others' perspectives, correctly encoding and interpreting social cues, formulating adaptive social goals, controlling impulses, controlling anger, and making adaptive attributions concerning the causes of personal social successes and failures.

Instruction in social relationship skills can use formal curricula or can occur informally as teachable moments arise throughout the day. Although various social-skill programs have been created, many of the successful ones encompass similar principles and components. For example, they include the use of interactive discussions to teach important relationship concepts, opportunities for children to practice translating this knowledge into action, and feedback to children about their performance, as well as encouragement to monitor their own social interactions. We have suggested the importance of making instruction fun for children, and we have highlighted the game context as one in which social skills can be enjoyably taught. Games also provide a context for overcoming reputation problems, as a child's peers learn that it can be fun to play with someone toward whom they previously had negative attitudes or feelings.

We hope the ideas and research evidence described in this chapter will provide a foundation for helping children who have peer relationship problems. The success of intervention efforts indicates that directly instructing children in social relationship skills can have lasting effects. We conclude, therefore, by emphasizing that educators are in a position to help children whose peer relationship history puts them at risk for serious school adjustment problems.

References

Asher, S. R., & Coie, J. D. (1990). *Peer rejection in childhood.* New York: Cambridge University Press.

Asher, S. R., Hopmeyer, A., & Gabriel, S. W. (1997). *Children's loneliness in different school contexts.* Manuscript submitted for publication.

Asher, S. R., & Hymel, S. (1981). Children's social competence in peer relations: Sociometric and behavioral assessment. In J. D. Wine & M. D. Smye (Eds.), *Social competence* (pp. 125–157). New York: Guilford.

Asher, S. R., Hymel, S., & Renshaw, P. D. (1984). Loneliness in children. *Child Development, 55,* 1456–1464.

Asher, S. R., & Parker, J. G. (1989). The significance of peer relationship problems in childhood. In B. H. Schneider, G. Attili, J. Nadel, & R. P. Weissberg (Eds.), *Social competence in developmental perspective* (pp. 5–23). Amsterdam: Kluwer Academic Publishing.

Asher, S. R., Parker, J. G., & Walker, D. (1996). Distinguishing friendship from acceptance: Implications for intervention and assessment. In W. M. Bukowski, A. F. Newcomb, & W. W. Hartup (Eds.), *The company they keep: Friendship in childhood and adolescence* (366–405). New York: Cambridge University Press.

Asher, S. R., & Renshaw, P. D. (1981). Children without friends: Social knowledge and social skill training. In S. R. Asher & J. M. Gottman (Eds.), *The development of children's friendships* (pp. 273–296). New York: Cambridge University Press.

Asher, S. R., Singleton, L. C., Tinsley, B. R., & Hymel, S. (1979). A reliable sociometric measure for preschool children. *Developmental Psychology, 15*, 443–444.

Asher, S. R., & Williams, G. A. (1987). Helping children without friends in home and school contexts. In *Children's social development: Information for teachers and parents* (pp. 1–26). Champaign: University of Illinois at Urbana-Champaign. (ERIC Document Reproduction Service No. ED 283–625)

Bandura, A. (1977). Self-efficacy: Toward a unifying theory of behavior change. *Psychological Review, 84*, 191–215.

Bandura, A., & Jeffery, R. W. (1973). Role of symbolic coding and rehearsal processes in observational learning. *Journal of Personality and Social Psychology, 26*, 122–130.

Bandura, A., Jeffery, R., & Bachica, D. L. (1974). Analysis of memory codes and cumulative rehearsal in observational learning. *Journal of Research in Personality, 7*, 295–305.

Bell-Dolan, D. J., Foster, S. L., & Christopher, J. S. (1992). Children's reactions to participating in a peer relations study: An example of cost-effective assessment. *Child Study Journal, 22*, 137–156.

Bell-Dolan, D. J., Foster, S. L., & Sikora, D. M. (1989). Effects of sociometric testing on children's behavior and loneliness in school. *Developmental Psychology, 25*, 306–311.

Berndt, T. J., & Hanna, N. A. (1995). Intimacy and self-disclosure in friendships. In K. J. Rotenberg (Ed.), *Disclosure processes in children and adolescents* (pp. 57–77). New York: Cambridge University Press.

Berndt, T. J., Hawkins, J. A., & Hoyle, S. G. (1986). Changes in children's friendship during a school year: Effects on children's and adolescents' impressions of friendship and sharing with friends. *Child Development, 57*, 1284–1297.

Berndt, T. J., & Keefe, K. (1995). Friends' influence on adolescents' adjustment to school. *Child Development, 66*, 1312–1329.

Berndt, T. J., & Perry, T. B. (1990). Distinctive features and effects of early adolescent friendships. In R. Montemayor, G. R. Adams, & T. P. Gullotta (Eds.), *From childhood to adolescence: A transitional period?* (pp. 269–287). Newbury Park, CA: Sage.

Bierman, K. L., & Furman, W. (1984). The effects of social skills training and peer involvement on the social adjustment of preadolescents. *Child Development, 55*, 151–162.

Bigelow, B. J., & LaGaipa, J. J. (1975). Children's written descriptions of friendship: A multidimensional analysis. *Developmental Psychology, 11*, 857–858.

Bigelow, B. J., & LaGaipa, J. J. (1980). The development of friendship values and choice. In H. C. Foot, A. J. Chapman, & J. R. Smith (Eds.), *Friendship and social relations in children* (pp. 15–44). New York: Wiley.

Birch, S. H., & Ladd, G. W. (1997). The teacher-child relationship and children's early school adjustment. *Journal of School Psychology, 35,* 61–79.

Black, B. (1992). Negotiating social pretend play: Communication differences related to social status and sex. *Merrill-Palmer Quarterly, 38,* 212–232.

Boivin, M., Hymel, S., & Bukowski, W. M. (1995). The roles of social withdrawal, peer rejection, and victimization by peers in predicting loneliness and depressed mood in childhood. *Development and Psychopathology, 7,* 765–785.

Cairns, R. B., Cairns, B. D., Neckerman, H. J., Gest, S., & Gariepy, J. L. (1987). *Peer networks and aggressive behavior: Social support or social rejection?* Report from the Carolina Longitudinal Study. Chapel Hill, NC: University of North Carolina at Chapel Hill.

Cantrell, V. L., & Prinz, R. J. (1985). Multiple perspectives of rejected, neglected, and accepted children: Relation between sociometric status and behavioral characteristics. *Journal of Consulting and Clinical Psychology, 53,* 884–889.

Carlson, C. L., Lahey, B. B., & Neeper, R. (1984). Peer assessment of the social behavior of accepted, rejected, and neglected children. *Journal of Abnormal Child Psychology, 12,* 189–198.

Carroll, W. R., & Bandura, A. (1990). Representational guidance of action production in observational learning: A causal analysis. *Journal of Motor Behavior, 22,* 85–97.

Cassidy, J., & Asher, S. R. (1992). Loneliness and peer relations in young children. *Child Development, 63,* 350–365.

Cauce, A. M. (1986). Social networks and social competence: Exploring the effects of early adolescent friendships. *American Journal of Community Psychology, 14,* 607–628.

Chen, X., Rubin, K. H., & Sun, Y. (1992). Social reputation and peer relationships in Chinese and Canadian children: A cross-cultural study. *Child Development, 63,* 1336–1343.

Chung, T. Y., & Asher, S. R. (1995, July). *Children's goals are related to their strategies for responding to peer conflict.* Poster session presented at the annual meeting of the American Psychological Society, New York.

Chung, T. Y., & Asher, S. R. (1996). Children's goals and strategies in peer conflict situations. *Merrill-Palmer Quarterly, 42,* 125–147.

Clark, M. L., & Ayers, M. (1988). The role of reciprocity and proximity in junior high school friendships. *Journal of Youth and Adolescence, 17,* 403–411.

Coie, J. D., & Dodge, K. A. (1983). Continuities and changes in children's social status: A five-year longitudinal study. *Merrill-Palmer Quarterly, 29,* 261–281.

Coie, J. D., Dodge, K. A., & Coppotelli, H. (1982). Dimensions and types of social status: A cross-age perspective. *Developmental Psychology, 18,* 557–570.

Coie, J. D., Dodge, K. A., & Kupersmidt, J. B. (1990). Peer group behavior and social status. In S. R. Asher & J. D. Coie (Eds.), *Peer rejection in childhood* (pp. 17–59). Cambridge, UK: Cambridge University Press.

Coie, J. D., Dodge, K. A., Terry, R., & Wright, V. (1991). The role of aggression in peer relations: An analysis of aggression episodes in boys' play groups. *Child Development, 62,* 812–826.

Coie, J. D., & Koeppl, G. K. (1990). Adapting intervention to the problems of aggressive and disruptive children. In S. R. Asher & J. D. Coie (Eds.), *Peer rejection in childhood* (pp. 309–337). New York: Cambridge University Press.

Coie, J. D., & Kupersmidt, J. B. (1983). A behavioral analysis of emerging social status in boys' groups. *Child Development, 54*, 1400–1416.

Crick, N. R. (1996). The role of relational aggression, overt aggression, and prosocial behavior in the prediction of children's future social adjustment. *Child Development, 67*, 2317–2327.

Crick, N. R., Casas, J. F., & Mosher, M. (1997). Relational and overt aggression in preschool. *Developmental Psychology, 33*, 579–588.

Crick, N. R., & Dodge, K. A. (1994). A review and reformulation of social information-processing mechanisms in children's social adjustment. *Psychological Bulletin, 115*, 74–101.

Crick, N. R., & Grotpeter, J. K. (1995). Relational aggression, gender, and social-psychological adjustment. *Child Development, 66*, 710–722.

Crick, N. R., & Ladd, G. W. (1993). Children's perceptions of their peer experiences: Attributions, loneliness, social anxiety, and school avoidance. *Developmental Psychology, 29*, 244–254.

Csapo, M. (1983). Effectiveness of coaching socially withdrawn/isolated children in specific social skills. *Educational Psychology, 3*, 31–42.

Denham, S. A., McKinley, M., Couchoud, E. A., & Holt, R. (1990). Emotional and behavioral predictors of preschool peer ratings. *Child Development, 61*, 1145–1152.

Dishion, T. J., Andrews, D. W., & Crosby, L. (1995). Antisocial boys and their friends in early adolescence: Relationship characteristics, quality, and interactional processes. *Child Development, 66*, 139–151.

Dishion, T. J., Patterson, G. R., & Griesler, P. C. (1994). Peer adaptations in the development of antisocial behavior: A confluence model. In L. R. Huesmann (Ed.), *Aggressive behavior: Current perspectives* (pp. 61–95). New York: Plenum Press.

Dodge, K. A. (1980). Social cognition and children's aggressive behavior. *Child Development, 51*, 162–170.

Dodge, K. A. (1983). Behavioral antecedents of peer social status. *Child Development, 54*, 1386–1399.

Dodge, K. A., Asher, S. R., & Parkhurst, J. T. (1989). Social life as a goal coordination task. In C. Ames & R. Ames (Eds.), *Research on motivation in education: Goals and cognitions* (pp. 107–135). New York: Academic Press.

Dodge, K. A., Coie, J. D., Pettit, G. S., & Price, J. M. (1990). Peer status and aggression in boys' groups: Developmental and contextual analyses. *Child Development, 61*, 1289–1309.

Dodge, K. A., & Feldman, E. (1990). Issues in social cognition and sociometric status. In S. R. Asher & J. D. Coie (Eds.), *Peer rejection in childhood* (pp. 119–155). New York: Cambridge University Press.

Dodge, K. A., McClaskey, C. L., & Feldman, E. (1985). A situational approach to the assessment of social competence in children. *Journal of Consulting and Clinical Psychology, 53*, 344–353.

Earn, B. M., & Sobol, M. P. (1990). A categorical analysis of children's attributions for social success and failure. *Psychological Record, 40,* 173–185.

Elkins, D. (1958). Some factors related to the choice status of ninety eighth-grade children in a school society. *Genetic Psychology Monographs, 58,* 207–272.

Epstein, J. L. (1989). The selection of children's friends: Changes across the grades and in different school environments. In T. J. Berndt & G. W. Ladd (Eds.), *Peer relationships in child development* (pp. 158–187). New York: Wiley.

Erdley, C. A., & Asher, S. R. (1996). Children's social goals and self-efficacy perceptions as influences on their responses to ambiguous provocation. *Child Development, 67,* 1329–1344.

Feinberg, M. R., Smith, M., & Schmidt, R. (1958). An analysis of expressions used by adolescents at varying economic levels to describe accepted and rejected peers. *Journal of Genetic Psychology, 93,* 133–148.

Flanders, T. Z., & Havumaki, S. (1963). The effect of teacher-pupil contacts involving praise on the sociometric choices of students. In J. M. Seidman (Ed.), *Education for mental health* (pp. 410–414). New York: Thomas Y. Crowell.

Flavell, J. H., Botkin, P. T., Fry, C. L., Wright, J. W., & Jarvis, P. E. (1968). *The development of role-taking and communication skills in children.* New York: Wiley.

Foster, S. L., DeLawyer, D., & Guevremont, D. C. (1986). A critical incidents analysis of liked and disliked peer behavior and their situational parameters in childhood and adolescence. *Behavioral Assessment, 8,* 115–133.

Franzoi, S. L., Davis, M. H., & Vasquez-Suson, K. A. (1994). Two social worlds: Social correlates and stability of adolescent status groups. *Journal of Personality and Social Psychology, 67,* 462–473.

Furman, W., & Robbins, P. (1985). What's the point? Issues in the selection of treatment objectives. In B. H. Schneider, K. H. Rubin, & J. E. Ledingham (Eds.), *Children's peer relations: Issues in assessment and intervention* (pp. 41–54). New York: Springer-Verlag.

Goertzen, S. M. (1959). Factors relating to the opinions of seventh grade children regarding the acceptability of certain behaviors in the peer group. *Journal of Genetic Psychology, 94,* 29–34.

Goetz, T. E., & Dweck, C. S. (1980). Learned helplessness in social situations. *Journal of Personality & Social Psychology, 39,* 246–255.

Gottman, J. M. (1983). How children become friends. *Monographs of the Society for Research in Child Development, 48*(3, Serial No. 201).

Gottman, J., Gonso, J., & Rasmussen, B. (1975). Social interaction, social competence, and friendship in children. *Child Development, 46,* 709–718.

Gottman, J. M., Gonso, J., & Schuler, P. (1976). Teaching social skills to isolated children. *Journal of Abnormal Child Psychology, 4,* 179–197.

Gresham, F. M., & Nagle, R. J. (1980). Social skills training with children: Responsiveness to modeling and coaching as a function of peer orientation. *Journal of Consulting and Clinical Psychology, 18,* 718–729.

Gronlund, N. E. (1959). *Sociometry in the classroom.* New York: Harper.

Gronlund, N., & Holmlund, W. (1958). The value of elementary school sociometric status scores for predicting pupils' adjustment in high school. *Education Journal of Educational Psychology, 44,* 225–260.

Gross, A. M., & Johnson, T. C. (1984). Athletic skill and social status in children. *Journal of Social and Clinical Psychology, 2,* 89–96.

Grossman, D. C., Neckerman, H. J., Koepsell, T. D., Liu, P. Y., Asher, K. N., Beland, K., Frey K., & Rivara, F. P. (1997). The effectiveness of a violence prevention curriculum among children in elementary school. *Journal of the American Medical Association, 227,* 1605–1611.

Grotpeter, J. K., & Crick, N. R. (1996). Relational aggression, overt aggression, and friendship. *Child Development, 67,* 2328–2338.

Guralnick, M. J., & Groom, J. M. (1987). The peer relations of mildly delayed and nonhandicapped preschool children in mainstreamed playgroups. *Developmental Psychology, 24,* 1556–1572.

Hayvren, M., & Hymel, S. (1984). Ethical issues in sociometric testing: The impact of sociometric measures on interactive behavior. *Developmental Psychology, 20,* 844–849.

Hirsch, B. J., & DuBois, D. L. (1992). The relation of peer social support and psychological symptomatology during the transition to junior high school: A two-year longitudinal analysis. *American Journal of Community Psychology, 20,* 333–347.

Hymel, S., Wagner, E., & Butler, L. J. (1990). Reputational bias: View from the peer group. In S. R. Asher & J. D. Coie (Eds.), *Peer rejection in children* (pp. 156–186). New York: Cambridge University Press.

Ide, J. K., Parkerson, J., Haertel, G. D., & Walberg, H. J. (1981). Peer group influence on educational outcomes: A quantitative synthesis. *Journal of Educational Psychology, 73,* 472–484.

Iverson, A. M., Barton, E. A., & Iverson, G. L. (1997). Analysis of risk to children participating in a sociometric task. *Developmental Psychology, 33,* 104–112.

Kupersmidt, J. B. (1983, April). Predicting delinquency and academic problems from childhood peer status. In J. D. Coie (Chair), *Strategies for identifying children at social risk: Longitudinal correlates and consequences.* Symposium conducted at the biennial meeting of the Society for Research in Child Development, Detroit, MI.

Kupersmidt, J. B., & Coie, J. D. (1990). Preadolescent peer status, aggression, and school adjustment as predictors of externalizing problems in adolescence. *Child Development, 61,* 1350–1362.

Kupersmidt, J. B., Coie, J. D., & Dodge, K. A. (1990). The role of poor peer relationships in the development of disorder. In S. R. Asher & J. D. Coie (Eds.), *Peer rejection in childhood* (pp. 274–305). New York: Cambridge University Press.

Kupersmidt, J. B., DeRosier, M. E., & Patterson, C. P. (1995). Similarity as the basis for children's friendships: The roles of sociometric status, aggressive and withdrawn behavior, academic achievement and demographic characteristics. *Journal of Social and Personal Relationships, 12,* 439–452.

Ladd, G. W. (1981). Effectiveness of a social learning method for enhancing children's social interaction and peer acceptance. *Child Development, 52,* 171–178.

Ladd, G. W. (1983). Social networks of popular, average, and rejected children in school settings. *Merrill-Palmer Quarterly, 29,* 283–307.

Ladd, G. W. (1990). Having friends, keeping friends, making friends, and being liked by peers in the classroom: Predictors of children's early school adjustment? *Child Development, 61,* 1081–1100.

Ladd, G. W., & Asher, S. R. (1985). Social skill training and children's peer relations. In L. L'Abate & M. Milan (Eds.), *Handbook of social skills training and research* (pp. 219–244). New York: Wiley.

Ladd, G. W., Kochenderfer, B. J., & Coleman, C. C. (1996). Friendship quality as a predictor of young children's early school adjustment. *Child Development, 67,* 1103–1118.

Ladd, G. W., & Mize, J. (1983a). A cognitive-social learning model of social-skill training. *Psychological Review, 90,* 127–157.

Ladd, G. W., & Mize, J. (1983b). Social skills training and assessment with children: A cognitive-social learning approach. *Child and Youth Services, 5,* 61–74.

Ladd, G. W., & Oden, S. (1979). The relationship between peer acceptance and children's ideas about helpfulness. *Child Development, 50,* 402–408.

Laursen, B. (1993). Conflict management among close peers. In W. Damon (Series Ed.) & B. Laursen (Vol. Ed.), *New directions for child development: Vol. 60. Close friendships in adolescence* (pp. 39–54). San Francisco: Jossey-Bass.

Li, A. K. F. (1985). Early rejected status and later social adjustment: A 3-year follow-up. *Journal of Abnormal Psychology, 13,* 567–577.

Lilly, M. S. (1971). Improving social acceptance of low sociometric status, low-achieving students. *Exceptional Children, 37,* 341–347.

Lochman, J. E., & Dunn, S. E. (1993). An intervention and consultation model from a social cognitive perspective: A description of the Anger Coping Program. *School Psychology Review, 22,* 458–471.

Marshall, H. R., & McCandless, B. R. (1957). A study in prediction of social behavior of preschool children. *Child Development, 28,* 149–159.

Masten, A. S. (1986). Humor and competence in school-aged children. *Child Development, 57,* 461–473.

McCraw, L. W., & Tolbert, J. W. (1953). Sociometric status and athletic ability of junior high school boys. *The Research Quarterly, 24,* 72–80.

McGinnis, E., & Goldstein, A. P. (1997). *Skillstreaming the elementary school child: A guide for teaching prosocial skills.* Champaign, IL: Research Press.

Meichenbaum, D. H., & Goodman, J. (1971). Training impulsive children to talk to themselves: A means of developing self-control. *Journal of Abnormal Psychology, 77,* 115–126.

Mitman, A. L., & Packer, M. J. (1982). Concerns of seventh-graders about their transition to junior high school. *Journal of Early Adolescence, 2,* 319–338.

Mize, J., & Ladd, G. W. (1990). Toward the development of successful social skills training for preschool children. In S. R. Asher & J. D. Coie (Eds.), *Peer rejection in childhood* (338–361). New York: Cambridge University Press.

Moore, S., & Updegraff, R. (1964). Sociometric status of preschool children related to age, sex, nurturance-giving, and dependency. *Child Development, 35,* 519–524.

Moreno, J. L. (1934). *Who shall survive? A new approach to the problem of human interrelations.* Washington, DC: Nervous and Mental Disease Publishing.

Muma, J. R. (1965). Peer evaluation and academic achievement in performance classes. *Personnel and Guidance Journal, 46,* 580–585.

Newcomb, A. F., & Bagwell, C. L. (1995). Children's friendship relations: A meta-analytic review. *Psychological Bulletin, 117,* 306–347.

Newcomb, A. F., & Bagwell, C. L. (1996). The developmental significance of children's friendship relations. In W. M. Bukowski, A. F. Newcomb, & W. W. Hartup (Eds.), *The company they keep: Friendship in childhood and adolescence* (pp. 289–321). New York: Cambridge University Press.

Newcomb, A. F., & Bukowski, W. M. (1984). A longitudinal study of the utility of social preference and social impact sociometric classification schemes. *Child Development, 55,* 1434–1447.

O'Connor, R. D. (1969). Modification of social withdrawal through symbolic modeling. *Journal of Applied Behavior Analysis, 2,* 15–22.

O'Connor, R. D. (1972). Relative efficacy of modeling, shaping, and the combined procedures for modification of social withdrawal. *Journal of Abnormal Psychology, 79,* 327–344.

Oden, S., & Asher, S. R. (1977). Coaching children in skills for friendship making. *Child Development, 48,* 495–506.

Parker, J. G., & Asher, S. R. (1987). Peer relations and later personal adjustment: Are low-accepted children at risk? *Psychological Bulletin, 102,* 357–389.

Parker, J. G., & Asher, S. R. (1993a). Beyond group acceptance: Friendship adjustment and friendship quality as distinct dimensions of children's peer adjustment. In D. Perlman & W. H. Jones (Eds.), *Advances in personal relationships* (Vol. 4, pp. 261–294). London: Kingsley.

Parker, J. G., & Asher, S. R. (1993b). Friends and friendship quality in middle childhood: Links with peer group acceptance and feelings of loneliness and social dissatisfaction. *Developmental Psychology, 29,* 611–621.

Parkhurst, J. T., & Asher, S. R. (1987, April). *The social concerns of aggressive-rejected children.* Paper presented at the meeting of the Society for Research in Child Development, Baltimore, MD.

Parkhurst, J. T., & Asher, S. R. (1992). Peer rejection in middle school: Subgroup differences in behavior, loneliness, and interpersonal concerns. *Developmental Psychology, 28,* 231–241.

Putallaz, M. (1983). Predicting children's sociometric status from their behavior. *Child Development, 54,* 1417–1426.

Putallaz, M., & Gottman, J. M. (1981). Social skills and group acceptance. In S. R. Asher & J. M. Gottman (Eds.), *The development of children's friendships.* (pp. 116–149). New York: Cambridge University Press.

Putallaz, M., & Sheppard, B. H. (1990). Social status and children's orientations to limited resources. *Child Development, 61,* 2022–2027.

Putallaz, M., & Wasserman, A. (1990). Children's entry behavior. In S. R. Asher & J. D. Coie (Eds.), *Peer rejection in childhood* (pp. 60–89). New York: Cambridge University Press.

Ratiner, C., Weissberg, R., & Caplan, M. (1986, August). *Ethical considerations in sociometric testing: The reaction of preadolescent subjects.* Paper presented at the 94th annual meeting of the American Psychological Association, Washington, DC.

Renshaw, P. D., & Brown, P. J. (1993). Loneliness in middle childhood: Concurrent and longitudinal predictors. *Child Development, 64,* 1271–1284.

Rockhill, C. M., & Asher, S. R. (1992, April). *Peer assessment of the behavioral characteristic of poorly-accepted boys and girls.* Paper presented at the annual meeting of the American Educational Research Association, San Francisco.

Rotenberg, K. J., & Mann, L. (1986). The development of the norm of the reciprocity of self-disclosure and its function in children's attraction to peers. *Child Development, 57,* 1349–1357.

Rubin, K. H., Lynch, D., Coplan, R., Rose-Krasnor, L., & Booth, C. L. (1994). "Birds of a feather . . . ": Behavioral concordances and preferential attraction in children. *Child Development, 65,* 1778–1785.

Rucker, C. N., & Vincenzo, F. M. (1970). Maintaining social acceptance gains made by mentally retarded children. *Exceptional Children, 36,* 679–680.

Seidman, E., Allen, L., Aber, J. L., Mitchell, C., & Feinman, J. (1994). The impact of school transitions in early adolescence on the self-system and perceived social context of poor urban youth. *Child Development, 65,* 507–522.

Selman, R. L. (1980). *The growth of interpersonal understanding.* New York: Academic Press.

Sherman, L. W. (1985). Humor and social distance. *Perceptual and Motor Skills, 61,* 1274.

Singleton, L. C., & Asher, S. R. (1977). Peer preferences and social interaction among third-grade children in an integrated school district. *Journal of Educational Psychology, 69,* 330–336.

Slaby, R. G., & Guerra, N. G. (1988). Cognitive mediators of aggression in adolescent offenders: 1. Assessment. *Developmental Psychology, 24,* 580–588.

Sletta, O., Valas, H., Skaalvik, E., & Sobstad, F. (1996). Peer relations, loneliness, and self-perceptions in school-age children. *British Journal of Educational Psychology, 66,* 431–445.

Smollar, J., & Youniss, J. (1982). Social development through friendship. In K. H. Rubin & H. S. Ross (Eds.), *Peer relationships and social skills in childhood* (pp. 279–298). New York: Springer-Verlag.

Sullivan, H. S. (1953). *The interpersonal theory of psychiatry.* New York: W. W. Norton.

Taylor, A. R. (1989). Predictors of peer rejection in early elementary grades: Roles of problem behavior, academic achievement, and teacher preference. *Journal of Clinical Child Psychology, 18,* 360–365.

Taylor, A. R., & Asher, S. R. (1984). Children's goals and social competence: Individual differences in a game-playing context. In T. Field, J. L. Roopnarine, & M.

Segal (Eds.), *Friendship in normal and handicapped children* (pp. 53–78). Norwood: Ablex.

Wentzel, K. R. (1991). Relations between social competence and academic achievement in early adolescence. *Child Development, 62,* 1066–1078.

Wentzel, K. R. (1994). Relations of social goal pursuit to social acceptance, classroom behavior, and perceived social support. *Journal of Educational Psychology, 86,* 173–182.

Wentzel, K. R., & Asher, S. R. (1995). The academic lives of neglected, rejected, popular, and controversial children. *Child Development, 66,* 754–763.

White, K. J., & Kistner, J. (1992). The influence of teacher feedback on young children's peer preferences and perceptions. *Developmental Psychology, 28,* 933–940.

Williams, G. A., & Asher, S. R. (1987, April). *Peer- and self-perceptions of peer rejected children: Issues in classification and subgrouping.* Paper presented at the biennial meeting of the Society for Research in Child Development, Baltimore, MD.

Williams, G. A., & Asher, S. R. (1991). *Behavioral subgroups and extremity of rejection among peer-rejected children in elementary school.* Unpublished manuscript, University at Illinois at Urbana-Champaign.

Zakriski, A. L., & Coie, J. D. (1996). A comparison of aggressive-rejected and nonaggressive-rejected children's interpretations of self-directed and other-directed rejection. *Child Development, 67,* 1048–1070.

Zarbatany, L., Ghesquiere, K., & Mohr, K. (1992). A context perspective on early adolescents' friendship expectations. *Journal of Early Adolescence, 12,* 111–126.

Zimmerman, B. J., & Rosenthal, T. L. (1974). Observational learning of rule-governed behavior by children. *Psychological Bulletin, 81,* 29–42.

Reading Instruction in American Classrooms: Practice and Research

Bonnie Armbruster

University of Illinois at Urbana-Champaign

Jean Osborn

University of Illinois at Urbana-Champaign

The relationship between practice and research is problematic in many fields of education, but it is particularly so in the field of reading. The field is known for unresolved disagreements about reading instruction that persist even in the face of national concern about the reading achievement of many children in American schools.

Many aspects of reading have been the focus of research interest, not only among reading educators, but also among researchers in a number of related disciplines, including cognitive psychology, linguistics, early childhood education, and special education. The United States Department of Education has supported research about reading for almost 20 years in two consecutively funded research centers. In addition, much independent research about reading is supported by grants from government agencies and private foundations.

A great deal has been learned from research about reading. But how much does this research affect practice? How much *should* research affect practice? We know of no conclusive answers to either question, but we believe an examination of some of the major influences on classroom reading instruction will provide a foundation for uniting well-tested practice with rigorous research in order to improve reading instruction in American classrooms.

In the first section of this chapter, we describe some of the ways reading instruction has been practiced in American classrooms over the past several decades. In the second section, we describe some of the research of the past two decades that centers on classroom observations of reading instruction, cognition and reading comprehension instruction, and beginning reading. In the conclusion, we examine classroom practices in the light of research in order to provide research-based recommendations for classroom reading instruction.

Reading Instruction: Practice

We begin this section on reading instruction practices in American classrooms by giving a brief history of some of the trends in beginning-reading instruction. A number of these trends have been enthusiastically promoted at one time or another, and some of them have been peremptorily abandoned. We then discuss some of the problems associated with this cycle of enthusiasm and abandonment, which is sometimes referred to as the swinging of the reading pendulum. Next, we describe in greater detail what was for many decades the predominant approach to reading instruction in American schools: the commercially developed comprehensive basal reading program. Finally, we discuss a highly popular movement—whole language—that emerged in the late 1970s and is still used in a large number of American elementary school classrooms.

Swings of the Reading Pendulum

A swinging pendulum, moving from one enthusiastically promoted approach to reading instruction to another, is often used by critics of American education to describe the state of reading instruction in American elementary schools. The concern is that one approach to instruction is advocated for a period of time and is then abandoned as the pendulum swings to yet another approach. During the past fifty years, a rather amazing number and variety of approaches to reading instruction have been implemented in the elementary classrooms of American schools. The differences among them are most marked in their views of beginning-reading instruction. To give our readers a sense of this variety, we list a sampling of these approaches and describe a few of their most salient features.

Phonics first. Children are required to memorize the alphabet and learn a number of phonics rules before they are given books to read. Some of the widely advertised, commercially developed phonics programs can be described as phonics-first programs.

Sight word. Children learn to read words by "sight." They practice reading in controlled-vocabulary textbooks that provide many opportunities to read the same words over and over again. The language of these rather stilted stories is quite unlike most of the language children hear or speak.

Linguistic readers. Children focus on the identification of the regular spelling patterns of letters within the words; a more current version of this approach includes letter patterns called onsets and rimes. The language of linguistic readers, like that of sight word texts, is stilted and not very natural.

Read by color. Children learn color names as cues to the sounds of letters. They read from books in which the letters of the words appear in different colors.

Read by shape. Children read words that have lines drawn around them to outline their shapes. They are told to remember the shapes of the words as they read.

Language experience. Children learn to read by telling the teacher their experiences. The teacher writes these experiences on the board or on lined chart paper, and all of the children read these stories. The language is that of the students; the vocabulary is not controlled.

Modality preferences. The teacher attempts to determine each child's modality preference; the children are then taught according to their diagnosed strengths as visual, auditory, or kinesthetic learners. The idea is to focus on each child's strengths.

Basal program. Children are taught from the many components of a highly organized, grade-calibrated reading program: they read from student textbooks that are graded for difficulty. ("Readability formulas" are often used to determine text difficulty.) Students work in the many pages of the accompanying workbooks, and they respond to the teacher as she presents lessons from the program's teacher's manual. The teacher may use wall charts, flash cards, and sentence cards provided by the program.

Direct instruction. Children learn the sounds that the letters represent, together with some blending techniques; they practice sounding words out as they read student texts that feature a controlled vocabulary. Later in the program, the students read without first sounding the words out. Attention is given to developing fluency and accuracy.

Whole language. Instruction focuses on reading and writing used for relevant purposes. Teachers read "big books" (oversized versions of trade books), which children are to read collectively. Many of these books feature predictable text; they all feature natural language. The classroom also contains many trade books that the students read independently. Thus, the vocabulary of what the students read is not controlled. A variation of this approach is called **literature-based** instruction.

This list is by no means comprehensive, nor do we imply that each approach has been used at one time or another in every American classroom. Nor should the approaches on the list be considered as necessarily mutually exclusive. Many teachers combine two or more of them into their classroom reading programs. For example, some recent basal programs claim to follow the whole-language approach. Some teachers, however, insist upon the integrity of a single approach.

Sometimes teachers become totally dedicated to the approach they are following and severely critical of those using different approaches. The contentiousness of arguments about beginning reading is well known. We believe that the emotions so often attached to the swings of the pendulum have contributed to the decades of controversy about reading instruction among educators.

The controversy is not confined to educators. Many people—for example, parents, business people, and religious groups—make their beliefs and concerns about beginning-reading instruction known to teachers, school administrators, school board members, members of the press, and legislators.

The swinging pendulum has done little to resolve the vexing educational question: How can teachers best ensure that all of their students become readers? The developers and practitioners of particular approaches often are not particularly adept at dispassionately evaluating the effect of their approach on student learning. For example, are all the children in whole-language classrooms reading wonderful books with understanding and pleasure? The data are inconclusive. What about the phonics programs advertised so heavily in the media? Do the children who go through them learn to read wonderful books with understanding and pleasure? These data are also inconclusive.

Although a number of approaches to reading instruction have moved in and out of American classrooms during the past fifty years, the most pervasive influence on how reading has been taught in American classrooms during this period has been the commercially developed comprehensive basal reading programs. In the next section, we discuss how these comprehensive programs have changed over time, and how their influence has been challenged by political considerations, research, and practice.

Basal Reading Programs

Most of the readers of this chapter probably had experience as students with one of the many basal reading programs that were published in the United States during the past several decades. Those over 50 years old probably learned to read with the famous Dick and Jane, the main characters in the student textbooks of the basal reading program that was used extensively in elementary schools in the 1930s, 1940s, and 1950s. The program's publisher, Scott Foresman, claims that during the 1950s approximately 80 percent of American first graders were in classrooms that used their program (Kismaric & Heiferman, 1996).

Dick and Jane helped young children learn to read with a sight word approach. Stories were written so that selected words appeared repeatedly. The intent was that, in reading these words over and over again, the students would memorize them, and thus know them by sight. Children learned to read by practicing a set of words that gradually increased in number. Instructions to the teacher appeared in a separate teacher's manual, but very little attention was given to teaching individual letters and the sounds these letters represented.

Children in elementary school in the 1960s and 1970s may not have experienced Dick and Jane. Rather, they are likely to have encountered programs developed by several other publishers, for example, Ginn, Houghton Mifflin, Economy, or Harcourt Brace. Although instruction in these programs still centered on sight word learning, some activities were introduced to help students understand phonics—the relationship between letters and sounds.

In the mid-1950s, an event caused a marked change in the approach to beginning-reading instruction in all of the basal reading programs. The event was the publication of a best selling book about reading, Rudolf Flesch's (1955) *Why Johnny Can't Read*. The compelling message of this book was that phonics instruction was important and that schools and programs were deliberately neglecting it.

The strong public response to this message was heeded by the publishers of basal reading programs. So, during the 1960s, basal reading programs began to include more phonics instruction. The approach to phonics instruction used by most publishers is termed *implicit* or *analytic* phonics: the sounds associated with letters are not pronounced in isolation; rather, the teacher focuses on similarities among words, with the goal of having the students identify these similarities. In addition to phonics instruction, most basal reading programs began to include structural analysis, or the identification of root words, prefixes, and suffixes.

These programs did not ignore comprehension instruction. Comprehension, or studying skills, included finding the main idea, discriminating details from main ideas, determining cause and effect, and identifying sequences of events. However, the predominant procedure for determining if children understood what they were reading was for the teacher to ask the comprehension questions provided in the teacher's manual.

Starting in the late 1960s, other major changes occurred in basal reading programs. The programs were becoming bigger and more inclusive as more and more components were added. Student textbooks, teachers' manuals, and accompanying workbooks and ditto masters had served for years as the major components of basal reading programs. Now, in response to marketplace demands, many other products were developed, including more workbooks and ditto masters, sets of supplementary reading books, separate instructional programs for children achieving below grade level, posters, pocket charts, drill cards, and record-keeping and assessment systems. Later, audiovisual components and computer software were added.

The teachers' manuals also changed. They began to go beyond reading to encompass other aspects of the language arts, including instruction in listening, speaking, vocabulary, spelling, grammar, and creative writing, and they extended beyond the language arts to other content areas. Of course, the teachers' manuals got bigger as the topics increased and as the activities and instruction became more elaborate.

In the mid-1970s, some concerns with basal reading programs were based on newly emerging political considerations. The country was in the midst of a powerful Civil Rights movement that drew national attention to the education of all children. Concerns about reading programs focused not only on their instructional effectiveness with students of inner-city schools and rural areas, but also on the cultural suitability of the content. One aspect of the content that aroused a great deal of controversy was the predominance of white, middle-class American culture in the stories and illustrations of the student textbooks. Over time, these books were changed to include a number of multicultural and multiethnic selections. Some attention was also given to the instructional content of the programs, with some companies publishing a second version of their program for students with special needs.

Another concern about the content of basal reading programs was the small amount of written text in the student textbooks. For families and teachers who supplemented the basal student textbooks with lots of other reading, the limited amount of reading provided by these books was not a problem. However, for students whose only source of reading was these books, there simply wasn't enough text available to provide the amount of practice they needed to become fluent and competent readers. (It must be noted that the publishers of basal reading programs did not claim that their student textbooks should be the only source of reading, but the very comprehensiveness of these programs often gave the impression that their student texts would provide a sufficient, if minimum, amount of practice.)

Beginning in the early 1980s, basal reading programs became the subject of research by scholars in many fields. For example, in a follow-up to her well-known study that demonstrated a dearth of reading comprehension instruction in elementary school classrooms (Durkin, 1978–79), Durkin (1984) examined a likely source of that problem: the suggestions for instruction offered in the teachers' manuals of basal reading programs. Among her conclusions about these manuals was that they offered little direct or explicit comprehension instruction. She also noted that they tended to assess comprehension rather than offer suggestions for how to teach it. Beck (1984) identified other problems with instruction in basal reading programs, including inadequate treatment of new vocabulary, activities and directions that did not facilitate reading comprehension, and post-reading questions that failed to build story comprehensibility.

Osborn (1984) examined the workbooks and ditto masters that accompanied basal reading programs and found many ways in which they failed to support instruction. For example, she found that workbook pages were often not relevant to the instruction going on in the rest of the lesson, that they often failed to provide for systematic and cumulative review of previous teaching, and that instructions to the students were sometimes unclear.

The selections in the student textbooks also drew criticisms. Beck (1984) identified numerous problems with basal selections, including limited vocabulary; accompanying pictures that did not highlight, clarify, or complement the text; and mismatches between the assumed and actual prior knowledge of the readers. Other educators and linguists identified one cause of the poor quality of the selections in the student textbooks: the use of readability formulas to write and revise the texts used. For example, Davison (1984) concluded that readability formulas had a "generally negative and harmful effect on the writing and revision of texts to be used as reading materials." (p.137)

The interest of these scholars also focused on how basal programs were developed. Their analyses pointed up the inadequacy of some of the instructional activities in the teachers' guides. The conjecture was that many of the instructional activities in the teachers' guides were neither research- nor practice-based; it appeared, rather, that the activities were created during meetings of authors and editors, without significant tryout in classrooms.

We suspect that by the late 1980s, the publishers of basal reading programs must have felt quite beleaguered by the research community. This was not the end of their troubles, however; they were also confronted by advocates of the emerging whole-language movement. (We describe this movement below.) The whole-language movement did not sanction the use of basal reading programs. Even if a program were to be developed that contained impeccably effective instructional activities for teachers and students, a marvelous variety of multicultural selections, and many more stories for the students to read in the student textbooks, its use would still be a problem for the followers of the whole-language movement. This problem had to do with the very nature of the programs: By definition, all basal reading programs contain organized instructional plans in the teachers' manuals, which teachers are to follow (closely or loosely) while using the teaching aids provided by the program. They also contain textbooks the students are to read and related workbooks they are to work in. Because of this structure, proponents of whole language determined that basal reading programs offered no room for creativity by either teachers or students. In the educational climate promulgated by advocates of whole language, classroom situations that allowed no choice or creativity were considered inflexible and undesirable, and were deemed unproductive and disempowering for students and teachers alike. Grade-calibrated and controlled-vocabulary student textbooks could not offer the natural use of language found in literary works that the students should encounter as they learn to read. We now turn to a discussion of the whole-language approach to reading and writing instruction.

Whole Language

Since the late 1970s, an increasingly popular movement in reading instruction in the United States has been whole language. Whole language has dominated journals, conferences, workshops, university course offerings, and materials development, as well as classroom practice. Whole language has its roots in the open schools movement and progressive education, but it has also been influenced by theory and research, including schema theory, discourse analysis, literary criticism, and reading-writing connections. Although it originated in New Zealand and Australia, the whole-language movement has been greatly influenced by the work of Americans, including Kenneth and Yetta Goodman, Frank Smith, and Donald Graves.

As its name implies, whole language focuses on the relationships between reading, writing, listening, and speaking. It is an approach that views teachers as supporters of student learning—there to help students construct knowledge—rather than as providers of information and presenters of prepared curricula. Some whole-language advocates believe it is neither necessary nor desirable, and may even be harmful, to teach explicitly or provide direct explanation.

For reading, whole language discards traditional comprehension skills, systematic decoding instruction, and rate and accuracy practice. It also eschews organized and grade-calibrated basal reading programs and their associated student textbooks and workbooks.

One persistent problem with whole language is that it is very difficult to define. In response to this problem, Bergeron (1990) undertook the task of constructing a consensual definition from the literature. In her analysis of 64 articles from professional journals from the decade 1979–1989, Bergeron found that over half of the journal articles referred to whole language as a philosophy or an approach (although it was also described as a belief, a method, an orientation, a theory, a program, a curriculum, a perspective on education, and an attitude of mind).

Whole language concepts that were evident in the majority of articles included the following attributes:

- An emphasis on comprehension, or the construction of meaning.
- A focus on functional language, i.e., language used for relevant purposes.
- The use of a wide variety of literature as reading material.
- The use of the writing process, which includes writing, revising, and editing.
- An emphasis on cooperative student work.
- A focus on the affective aspects of learning, such as motivation, enthusiasm, and interest.

From these attributes, Bergeron constructed the following definition of whole language:

> Whole language is a concept that embodies both a philosophy of language development as well as the instructional approaches embedded within, and supportive of, that philosophy. This concept includes the use of real literature and writing in the context of meaningful, functional, and cooperative experiences in order to develop in students motivation and interest in the process of learning. (p. 319)

This definition, though consensually derived, nonetheless seems to us to be too thin to capture what whole language is really about. It omits aspects of whole language that have been very influential—as well as controversial—in reading instruction, particularly beginning-reading instruction. The controversy centers around two closely related whole-language concepts: (a) the acquisition of written language, given the appropriate conditions, is as natural as the acquisition of spoken language; and (b) trade books, written in natural language, should replace the specially written grade-calibrated and controlled-vocabulary texts of traditional basal reading programs.

Advocates of whole language, such as Smith (1973) and Goodman (1986), claim that children learn to read and write as a natural outcome of opportunities to read and write for genuine purposes. Immersing children in opportunities to learn is considered sufficient for children to acquire the alphabetic code. In her book on whole-language instruction, Newman writes: "The children's participation in reading should be invited, but not demanded. The focus of a reading program should be to help children figure out for themselves how written language works." (Newman, 1985, p. 61)

In the whole-language classroom, part of the opportunity to learn is provided by the large number of trade books available. Trade books are used because of the natural language that their writers use, because their vocabularies are not controlled, and because their syntactic structures are not simplified. The claim is that these books "have something relevant to say about children's lives . . . these materials allow children to assume control over their own learning" (Newman, 1985, p. 64).

The empowering of children so that they will be able to control their own learning is a fundamental tenet of whole language.

> They determine what books to read and when to read them. They can choose if, and when, to join in on the group reading, when to read on their own, when to read to someone else, when to ask someone to read to them. When reading is so pervasive, everyone gets into the action. (Newman, 1985, p. 63)

The role of the teacher in a whole-language classroom is that of a guide rather than a purveyor of knowledge and strategies. Whole language advocates claim that because learning to read must be natural, any kind of direct instruction in reading, or in any aspect of language, is at best superfluous, and at worst potentially harmful to literacy development. "To some whole-language advocates, *teaching* is a dirty word. They believe it is neither necessary nor desirable (and even harmful) to teach explicitly, provide direct explanation, or require practice" (Harris & Graham, 1996, p. 27).

This view is not without its critics. In the past few years, a number of researchers have argued that the acquisition of literacy is not a natural process and that many children do not learn what they are not taught explicitly or directly. The past decade has seen a burgeoning interest in research on many aspects of beginning reading. One researcher, Stanovich (1993–94), claims that Goodman's and Smith's views have been refuted by 20 years of research, and that sound and systematic instruction in decoding skills is crucial to the acquisition of written language. He writes:

> That direct instruction in alphabetic coding facilitates early reading instruction is one of the most well-established conclusions in all of behavioral science. . . . Conversely, the idea that learning to read is just like learning to speak is accepted by no responsible linguist, psychologist, or cognitive scientist in the research community. (Stanovich, pp. 285–286)

Special educators, such as Harris and Graham, have also expressed concern that a lack of direct instruction "has serious ramifications for learners with special needs" (1996, p. 27). They assert the need for extensive, structured, explicit, and focused instruction on specific skills, especially for students who face challenges in learning.

Our discussion of the whole-language movement, which concludes with an important concern about this view of reading instruction, brings our review of approaches to reading instruction up to the present. It also completes our discussion of several decades of trends in reading instruction. We now turn to research about several facets of reading instruction.

Reading Instruction: Research

We have selected three domains of research to examine in this section: (1) classroom observations, (2) cognition and reading comprehension instruction, and (3) beginning reading. Efforts in these lines of research began in the mid-1970s and continue to the present. We believe they have many implications for practice.

Classroom Observations

In the 1970s, many researchers spent time in their offices analyzing various aspects of basal reading programs. Another group of researchers spent time in classrooms observing instruction in an attempt to identify the instructional materials, teacher behaviors, management techniques, and verbal interaction patterns characteristic of "successful" instruction, as defined by significant gains in student achievement. The idea was that the behaviors of the best teachers could serve as models for classroom practice. In their important reviews of this observational research, Rosenshine (1983) and Rosenshine and Berliner (1978) brought to the attention of the research community important constructs related to achievement, such as "academic engaged time" and "content covered."

In this section, we discuss a subsequent review (Rosenshine & Stevens, 1984) that focused on classroom instruction in reading. In this comprehensive review of research, Rosenshine and Stevens found three general instructional procedures that were frequently correlated with successful reading instruction: teacher-directed instruction, instruction in groups, and academic emphasis. They described teacher-directed instruction as that which occurs when teachers select materials and tasks, and direct classroom activities. Rosenshine and Stevens found that "students who receive instruction from a teacher consistently do better in reading achievement than those who are expected to learn on their own" (p. 758). In addition, they found that students were more engaged in learning and achieved more when working in teacher-directed groups than when working individually. They also found that an academic emphasis characterized classrooms in which children made greater gains in reading. Examples of academic emphasis include systematic, goal-related activities; lessons and content related to the attainment of specific academic goals; rapidly paced lessons with directly relevant comments, questions, and discussion from the teacher; efficient use of time; involvement of all the students in responding to questions; assignment of regular homework; and holding students accountable for work done in class and at home.

After establishing these three general instructional procedures related to gains in reading, Rosenshine and Stevens proposed a specific instructional model. Based on their analysis of the classroom research, the authors proposed a three-step approach to instruction: (1) a short demonstration, (2) guided practice with feedback and corrections, and (3) independent practice. They observed demonstration to be most effective when the teacher proceeded in small steps, provided many examples, and interspersed demonstrations with questions to check student understanding. Guided practice was most effective when teachers asked frequent, content-relevant questions and when students were successful in answering them at least 80 percent of the time.

The type of feedback and corrections that were most effective depended on the nature of the student's response. Correct responses were best followed by very brief feedback or by another question. The best follow-up to incorrect responses was "sustaining" feedback, or some kind of assistance to help students arrive at a correct answer. Examples of sustaining feedback include asking a simpler question, providing a hint, and reminding students of the process used to arrive at the answer ("process feedback"). Finally, the authors found that independent practice was most effective when teachers monitored it carefully and provided feedback as needed.

We believe the Rosenshine and Stevens review to be a landmark event. Generally, it demonstrated that sufficient research had been conducted on classroom reading instruction to warrant generalizations about classroom practices conducive to growth in reading. Specifically, the review highlighted the central role of the teacher in promoting reading achievement, and pointed up specific teacher behaviors that correlated with reading achievement. The instructional model of demonstration, guided practice, and independent practice is particularly notable because it foreshadowed instructional research on the importance of teacher modeling, scaffolding, and coaching. (We discuss this research in the next section.) Their model also connects with other work on models of instruction published at about the same time, for example, Pearson and Gallagher's (1983) "gradual release of responsibility" model, and the systematic instructional design of the direct-instruction Follow-Through model (Becker, 1977). The direct-instruction model of teaching features teacher modeling, a helping step, and the monitoring of students' independent responses.

The research reviewed by Rosenshine and Stevens, based as it was on classroom observation, was obviously limited to observable teacher and student behaviors. Yet at the same time that classroom observation research was being conducted in the behaviorist tradition, a cognitive revolution was under way, in which the interest of a number of researchers focused on human learning and cognition and on how information is processed and transformed. In the next section, we discuss cognitive theory and research that centered on the reading process, and some studies of how this research has been applied to reading instruction.

Cognition and Reading Comprehension Instruction

During the cognitive revolution, cognitive theory was readily and extensively applied to the field of reading, especially comprehension. Cognitive research in reading burgeoned during the 1970s and 1980s. The research disclosed that reading is a complex, interactive, constructive process involving, at the very least, the reader's prior knowledge, purpose, and motivation, as well as aspects of the text, such as its discourse type and complexity.

One rigorous line of cognitive research studied experts and novices in many domains of expertise. In reading, the goal was to discover cognitive strategies that differentiated successful, "expert" readers from less successful, "novice" readers, and then to teach these strategies directly and explicitly to novice readers. Just as the behaviorally oriented classroom observation research was based on the premise that expert teacher practices could be translated into general use, so the cognitively oriented expert/novice studies were based on the premise that the strategies of expert readers could be taught to novice readers through a method called *direct explanation.*

Direct explanation involves "making explicit the implicit principles and algorithms which govern successful comprehension, rather than merely providing practice opportunities and corrective feedback to errors" (Roehler & Duffy, 1984, p. 265). Roehler and Duffy go on to suggest five principles of direct explanation:

1. The focus is on comprehension processes.
2. Teacher explanations of the processes are metacognitive rather than mechanistic. That is, students are informed about the purpose and utility of a strategy rather than simply exhorted to use it as a system.
3. Teaching should be proactive rather than indirect. In other words, teachers are aware of the function and utility of the strategies they are teaching, they analyze a strategy to identify the features of the required cognitive processing, and they take an active role in teaching students how to do the cognitive processing.
4. What teachers say during instruction is important, not just what students do.
5. In addition to verbal statements, teachers use "assistance devices," such as advance organizers, attention cues, and think alouds. "The teacher acts as the student's ally by making the learning of the skill as clear as possible" (p. 267).

Research on the direct explanation of cognitive strategies reigned during the late 1970s and 1980s. Among the strategies that were taught explicitly or through direct explanation were summarizing (for example, Brown & Day, 1983), question generation (Raphael & Pearson, 1985), and identification and use of text structure (e.g., Taylor & Beach, 1984; Armbruster, Anderson, & Ostertag, 1987).

Some researchers packaged several promising cognitive and metacognitive strategies together into instructional programs. For example, Paris, Cross, and Lipson (1984) developed and implemented "Informed Strategies for Learning," a program designed to improve children's reading comprehension through several comprehension-fostering strategies. Another instructional program consisting of multiple strategies was *reciprocal teaching*, probably the best known and most extensively researched cognitive strategies program of the 1980s.

Reciprocal teaching was first developed and described by Palincsar (1982) and Palincsar and Brown (1984). In reciprocal teaching, students are taught four specific comprehension-fostering activities: question generation, summarization, prediction, and clarification. The strategy instruction takes place in the form of a dialogue between the teacher and the students. The teacher first explains and models the strategies. Then students practice the strategies while the teacher provides coaching and *scaffolding*—instructional support that is adjusted through feedback, explanations, hints, and prompts. Students are also encouraged to provide scaffolding for each other. The original research, published by Palincsar and Brown in 1984, gave rise to many replication studies in the decade that followed.

Rosenshine and Meister (1994) published an extensive review of 16 of these studies. The authors concluded that reciprocal teaching is a generally effective method for fostering comprehension. In addition, Rosenshine and Meister derived many ideas about the teaching of reading comprehension, specifically "five excellent instructional ideas":

1. an emphasis on teaching comprehension-fostering strategies rather than practicing them through answering questions
2. the provision of four specific strategies rather than the scores of distinct skills frequently targeted in basal reading programs of the 1980s
3. the provision for practicing the strategies while reading actual texts, rather than texts contrived for basal readers or standardized tests
4. the popularization of the idea of scaffolding instruction, including procedures for doing so
5. the idea that students can provide support for each other as they work together in reading groups to construct meaning from text

Cognitive research in the 1990s has gone a step beyond the direct explanation of specific cognitive strategies in relatively prescribed, shorter-term programs to more flexible, comprehensive, and longer-term approaches to fostering reading comprehension. An outstanding example is the "Questioning the Author" (QtA) approach of Isabel Beck and her colleagues (Beck, McKeown, Hamilton, & Kucan, 1997). The QtA approach has been implemented for several years in fourth- and fifth-grade reading and social studies classes in two school districts.

The QtA approach is based on two premises. The first premise is that children often do not understand what they read, because authors frequently fail to present ideas clearly and coherently. The second premise is constructivism—the notion that readers need to actively put together, or construct, ideas, rather than to receive them passively. The single goal of QtA is to have students engage with actual classroom texts in order to understand what the author is trying to say.

Engagement with text occurs primarily through discussions in which students respond to the text, the teacher, and each other. In QtA, students and teacher collaborate to make sense of text.

The teacher's main tool in QtA is *queries*, which are designed to prompt discussion and support the construction of meaning as students read. Queries are different from traditional questions: Questions typically evaluate post-reading comprehension and thus focus on product; queries, on the other hand, focus more on process by helping students build meaning during reading.

Two general types of queries are used in QtA. *Initiating queries*, or open-ended questions to get the discussion started, include "What's the author trying to say here?" "What is the author's message?" and "What is the author talking about?" *Follow-up queries*, which focus the discussion and guide the construction of meaning, include "What does the author mean right here?" and "Did the author explain that clearly?"

In addition to queries, the developers of QtA have identified ways in which teachers can keep discussions productive. Specifically, the researchers identified six *discussion moves* to use in responding to student comments. Three of these moves focus attention on what students have brought to the discussion: drawing attention to a student's idea in order to emphasize its importance, encouraging students to return to the text in order to clarify their ideas, and interpreting or rephrasing a student's ideas in order to make them more accessible to others. The other three moves focus on what the teacher brings to discussion: making public some of the processes he or she used in processing text, providing information to clarify the text, and reviewing and highlighting major ideas and understandings.

Research has revealed some remarkable changes in classroom discourse as a result of implementing QtA (see Beck et al., in press; McKeown et al.). According to Beck et al. (1997, p. 103), the changes include

- teachers asking questions that focus on considering and extending meaning rather than simply retrieving information;
- teachers responding to students in ways that extend the discussion rather than evaluating or repeating the responses;
- students talking about twice as much during QtA discussions as they did in traditional lessons;
- students frequently initiating their own questions and comments;
- students talking about the meaning of what they read and about relationships among ideas; and
- students interacting with other students commonly during discussions.

Questioning the Author is an admirable example of a substantial, large-scale development in reading instruction that is based on theory and research in cognitive science.

In sum, cognitive science engendered a major shift in reading instruction. According to cognitive scientists, reading is a constructive process involving the complex interaction of many variables. This research has revealed a great deal about the processes skilled readers use to construct meaning from text. This knowledge about the cognitive aspects of reading has given rise to new ideas about how to help students comprehend what they read. At the same time, research about many aspects of beginning reading has provided information about how to help students learn to read the words. We next examine some of this research.

Beginning Reading

Recall that one of the major tenets of the whole-language movement is that the acquisition of literacy is a natural process that does not require direct or explicit instruction (Goodman, 1986; Smith, 1973), but that a number of researchers investigating beginning reading have not lent support to this view. A compilation and synthesis of this large body of work is available in Adams's important books on beginning reading (Adams, 1990a, 1990b). Adams has gathered information from studies conducted by researchers in a number of disciplines, including neurophysiology, cognitive psychology, eye-movement research, early childhood education, and reading education.

From studies of the word-reading processes of adult readers, Adams concludes that good readers deal with essentially all of the print they see on the pages they are reading, they do it very quickly, and they make decisions about meaning at the same time. In particular, skilled adult readers

- process every letter of every word
- process every word of every sentence
- automatically sound words out
- go directly and automatically from spelling to meaning
- perceive familiar words and spelling patterns holistically
- automatically syllabify words
- automatically analyze the syntactic structure of sentences as they read
- automatically register the syntactic function of words as they are read

Adams's review reveals that skilled readers continuously engage in the fairly complete processing of essentially all of the letters in the words they read, and that—to permit comprehension—they must do so quickly and effortlessly. This view of reading makes it evident that the accurate reading of words is important, and that reading is a complex activity. It thus also seems evident that reading instruction must acknowledge the complexity of the word-reading process.

In her consideration of how children learn to read, Adams cites a number of studies that have implications for beginning-reading instruction. She points to the importance of knowledge of the alphabet, phonemic awareness, and the understanding of letter/sound relationships in reading acquisition. She also acknowledges the importance of home literacy activities, such as story reading, rhyming games, and play with letters and words. Her particular concern is the instructional needs of children who do not bring five years of experiences with books and other forms of written language to their kindergarten and first grade classrooms. It is for these children especially that she strongly recommends systematic and careful instruction in the components of the decoding process, as well as experiences with books being read aloud and other written language activities.

Adams draws particular attention to the role of phonemic awareness in learning to read an alphabetic language. Adams cites a number of studies indicating that a strong predictor of success in learning to read is children's ability to discriminate and identify the phonemes in spoken words. She describes phonemes as the "smaller than syllable sounds that correspond roughly to individual letters" (1990b, p. 40) and points out that it is the *sounds* in spoken words that map onto the letters of printed words.

Adams also points to the even more obvious role of knowledge of the alphabet in learning to read. But she cautions that it is not merely children's knowledge of the letters that predicts their success in reading; it is the speed with which they can recognize letters. She writes, "The speed with which they can name individual letters both strongly predicts success for pre-readers and is strongly related to reading achievement among beginning readers" (1990b, p. 41).

Adams's model of word reading includes the mental processing of both print and speech. She describes orthographic and phonemic processors, as well as meaning and context processors. In her discussion of this model, she points to the importance of reading instruction in establishing paths to spelling, speech, and meaning; providing ample practice in reading and writing; and offering students real reading situations with a great deal of connected text.

In her review of research into the processes of reading and reading instruction, Adams makes some recommendations about reading instruction that are grounded in the research and practices she examined. These recommendations imply a carefully constructed and systematic program of decoding instruction. The design and organization of beginning-reading programs should reflect the complexity of the reading process; the complexity of word recognition should be recognized as well as the complexity of the comprehension process. Such a program is not a random assortment of occasional exercises, nor is it premised on waiting for children to reveal their needs, nor does it assume that learning to read is a natural process that will happen by simply surrounding children with books.

Conclusion

As described in the beginning of this chapter, the practice of reading instruction in American classrooms over the past several decades has been dictated more by trend than by theory, and has been subject to fashion more than to fact. When considered in light of theory and research, some of these practices are sound, while some are questionable. In this conclusion, we consider recent practice in reading instruction, particularly whole language, in light of research about observations of classroom reading instruction, cognition and reading comprehension, and beginning reading. What are some implications for reading instruction that can be derived from the practice and research so briefly reviewed in this chapter? We focus on three topics: the role of the teacher, comprehension instruction, and beginning-reading instruction.

First, the research on reading instruction in the classroom, reviewed by Rosenshine and Stevens (1984), highlighted the central role of the teacher in reading instruction. The teacher is critical in selecting materials, tasks, and activities, and in achieving an "academic emphasis." The instructional model of Rosenshine and Stevens, which foreshadowed several similar models, emphasizes the importance of teacher demonstration (i.e., modeling), guided practice (i.e., scaffolding and coaching), and independent practice. This research-based conclusion about the centrality of the teacher is not supported by whole-language advocates. Rather, whole language is pupil-centered; teachers assume more of a "guiding" role than a direct teaching role.

Second, the cognitively based research on reading comprehension suggests the following implications for comprehension instruction:

- Reading is a constructive process in which readers actively build, rather than passively receive, meaning. Therefore, the goal of reading should be for readers to engage actively with text in order to construct meaning.
- Because reading is a constructive process, it involves an interaction of reader variables and text variables. Instruction must take into consideration the background knowledge of the reader and the nature of the text.
- Reading instruction should focus on teaching the processes of meaning construction.
- Students should receive instruction and practice in constructing the meaning of text continuously, over an extended period of time, rather than in short, infrequent lessons.
- Because the mental processes involved in reading comprehension are covert, teachers should model and explain the processes.
- Teachers should provide scaffolding and coaching in order to support students in their attempts to construct meaning. They should do so until students are able to function independently.
- Students and teachers can collaborate to understand text. In addition, students can work with other students to construct meaning.

Note that some of these implications are very similar to some of the tenets of whole language. For example, most whole-language advocates would agree that the goal of reading is the construction of meaning, and that learning is a social activity in which meaning is constructed by collaborating teachers and students. Whole language advocates believe that language arts should not be taught as a separate subject, but should be taught over an extended period of time by integrating language arts with other subject areas. A point of probable disagreement is that whole-language advocates believe that teachers should take a "guiding" role in reading instruction rather than the more direct role supported by the cognitively oriented research on reading comprehension. (This point was also noted with regard to the behaviorally oriented research on classroom practices.)

A third area of research with implications for reading instruction is the research on beginning reading. Some of the implications of this body of research follow:

- Reading comprehension depends on the ability to decode words relatively quickly and effortlessly.

- The single most important activity for building the knowledge and skills eventually required for reading appears to be reading aloud to children regularly and interactively.

- Because children have special difficulty analyzing the phonemic structure of words, reading programs should include explicit instruction in blending.

- Activities designed to develop young children's awareness of spoken words, syllables, and phonemes significantly increase their later success in learning to read and write.

- Systematic phonics instruction is a means not only of teaching children to sound words out, but also of directing their attention to the spellings of words.

- To maximize word recognition growth, the wording of children's early texts should be carefully coordinated with the content and schedule of phonics lessons.

- Repeated readings of text are found to produce marked improvement in children's word recognition, fluency, and comprehension.

- Programs for all children, good and poor readers alike, should strive to maintain an appropriate balance between phonics activities and the reading and appreciation of informative and engaging texts.

- Children should be given as much opportunity and encouragement as possible to practice their reading. Beyond the basics, children's reading facility, as well as their vocabulary and conceptual growth, depends strongly on the amount of text they read.

Again, these research implications are both similar to and different from the tenets of whole language. On the one hand, the whole-language approach and the research-based recommendations of Adams agree that opportunity and encouragement to read are important for reading development. On the other hand, strict adherents of whole language argue that children are naturally predisposed toward the acquisition of written language. They disavow the value of systematically teaching any reading skills, including phonics, and of providing texts that reflect the content of phonics instruction. Research findings do not support this view. Rather, research supports the systematic teaching of decoding skills, including phonemic awareness, knowledge of the alphabet, and sound-symbol relationships.

As we write this chapter, a great deal of interest from the research community, as well from educators and other groups, is focusing on beginning reading. What is needed, these groups propose, is a well-balanced program that draws the best from both approaches to beginning-reading instruction.

We opened this chapter with a discussion of reading instruction practices that educators have enthusiastically embraced, then sometimes abandoned. We worry that these varying and often opposing practices are too easily labeled as swings of the pendulum and then dismissed. We believe that knowledge about what children need to understand as they learn to read *is* available to educators. The challenge to the field is to combine the best of what is known from rigorous basic research and evaluation of practice into powerful programs of reading instruction, and then to work toward a more consensual view of reading instruction. We believe such efforts will lead to classroom programs of reading instruction that will make reading success a reality for all children in American schools.

References

Adams, M. J. (1990a). *Beginning to read: Thinking and learning about print.* Cambridge, MA: MIT Press.

Adams, M. J. (1990b). *Beginning to read: Thinking and learning about print— A Summary.* Urbana-Champaign: University of Illinois, Center for the Study of Reading.

Armbruster, B. B., Anderson, T. H., & Ostertag, J. (1987). Does text structure/summarization instruction facilitate learning from expository text? *Reading Research Quarterly, 22,* 331–346.

Beck, I. L. (1984). Developing comprehension: The impact of the directed reading lesson. In R. C. Anderson, J. Osborn, and R. J. Tierney (Eds.), *Learning to read in American schools: Basal readers and content texts* (pp. 3–20). Hillsdale, NJ: Lawrence Erlbaum

Beck, I. L., McKeown, M. G., Hamilton, R., & Kucan, L. (1997). *Questioning the Author: An approach for enhancing student engagement with text.* Newark, DE: International Reading Association.

Becker, W. (1977). Teaching reading and language to the disadvantaged—what we have learned from field research. *Harvard Educational Review, 47,* 518–543.

Bergeron, B. (1990). What does the term *whole language* mean? Constructing a definition from the literature. *Journal of Reading Behavior, 22,* 301–329.

Brown, A. L., & Day, J. D. (1983). Macrorules for summarizing texts: The development of expertise. *Child Development, 54,* 968–979.

Davison, A. (1984). Readability—appraising text difficulty. In R. C. Anderson, J. Osborn, and R. J. Tierney (Eds.), *Learning to read in American schools:*

Basal readers and content texts (pp. 121–139). Hillsdale, NJ: Lawrence Erlbaum.

Durkin, D. (1978–79). What classroom observations reveal about reading comprehension instruction. *Reading Research Quarterly, 14,* 481–533.

Durkin, D. (1984). Do basal manuals teach reading comprehension? In R. C. Anderson, J. Osborn, and R. J. Tierney (Eds.), *Learning to read in American schools: Basal readers and content texts* (pp. 29–38). Hillsdale, NJ: Lawrence Erlbaum.

Flesch, R. (1955). *Why Johnny can't read.* New York: Harper & Row.

Goodman, K. S. (1986). *What's whole in whole language?* Portsmouth, NH: Heinemann.

Harris, K. R., & Graham, S. (1996). Memo to constructivists: Skills count, too. *Educational Leadership, 53*(5), 26–29.

Kismaric, C., & Heiferman, M. (1996). *Growing up with Dick and Jane: Learning and living the American Dream.* New York: Scott Foresman.

McKeown, M. G., Beck, I. L., & Sandora, C. A. (1996). Questioning the Author: An approach to developing meaningful classroom discourse. In M. G. Graves, B. M. Taylor, & P. van den Broek (Eds.), *The first R: Every child's right to read* (pp. 97–119). New York: Teachers College Press; Newark, DE: International Reading Association (published simultaneously).

Newman, J. M. (1985). Using children's books to teach reading. In J. M. Newman (Ed.), *Whole language: Theory in use* (pp. 55–64). Portsmouth, NH: Heinemann.

Osborn, J. (1984). The purposes, uses, and contents of workbooks and some guidelines for publishers. In R. C. Anderson, J. Osborn, and R. J. Tierney (Eds.). *Learning to read in American schools: Basal readers and content texts* (pp. 45–111). Hillsdale, NJ: Lawrence Erlbaum

Palincsar, A. S. (1982). *Improving the reading comprehension of junior high students through the reciprocal teaching of comprehension-monitoring strategies.* Unpublished doctoral dissertation, University of Illinois at Urbana-Champaign.

Palincsar, A. S., & Brown, A. L. (1984). Reciprocal teaching of comprehension-fostering and comprehension monitoring activities. *Cognition and Instruction, 2,* 117–175.

Paris, S. G., Cross, D. R., & Lipson, M. Y. (1984). Informed strategies for learning: A program to improve children's awareness and comprehension. *Journal of Educational Psychology, 76,* 1239–1252.

Pearson, P. D., & Gallagher, M. C. (1983). The instruction of reading comprehension. *Contemporary Educational Psychology, 8,* 317–344.

Raphael, T. E., & Pearson, P. D. (1985). Increasing students' awareness of sources of information for answering questions. *American Educational Research Journal, 22,* 217–236.

Roehler, L. R., & Duffy, G. G. (1984). Direct explanation of comprehension processes. In G. G. Duffy, L. R. Roehler, & J. Mason (Eds.), *Comprehension instruction: Perspectives and suggestion* (pp. 265–280). New York: Longman.

Rosenshine, B. (1983). Teaching functions in instructional programs. *Elementary School Journal, 83,* 335–351.

Rosenshine, B., & Berliner, D. (1978). Academic engaged time. *British Journal of Teacher Education, 4,* 3–16.

Rosenshine, B., & Meister, C. (1994). Reciprocal teaching: A review of the research. *Review of Educational Research, 64*(4), 479–530.

Rosenshine, B., & Stevens, R. (1984). Classroom instruction in reading. In P. D. Pearson, R. Barr, M. L. Kamil, & P. Mosenthal (Eds.), *Handbook of reading research* (Vol. 1, pp. 745–798). New York: Longman.

Smith, E. (1973). *Psycholinguistics and reading.* New York: Holt, Rinehart & Winston.

Stanovich, K. (1993–94). Romance and reality. *The Reading Teacher, 47*(4), 280–291.

Taylor, B. M., & Beach, R. W. (1984). The effects of text structure instruction on middle-grade students' comprehension and production of expository texts. *Reading Research Quarterly, 19,* 134–146.

The Architecture of Literacy Activities

Patterns in Classrooms and Potentials for Learning

Charles Fisher
University of Michigan

Elfrieda H. Hiebert
University of Michigan

For more than a century, promoting literacy has been a primary goal of American schools. Compared with most areas of the school curriculum, literacy has been burdened (or blessed) with a variety of alternative visions and practices for accomplishing its goals. Hardly a decade has passed without a major debate about which literacy activities are appropriate and why they should be universally implemented. On several occasions, the same, or at least very similar, positions have been championed and abandoned in one decade only to arise anew a little later. Given the amplitude and frequency of swings in both theory and practice in the field, there would appear to be little gain from either predicting the future or analyzing the past. This caution notwithstanding, there do appear to be some changes in the field that are more than mere fashion.

At the beginning of the 20th century, reading and "'riting,"—two of the three R's—were viewed as essentially separate entities (Kaestle, Damon-Moore, Stedman, Tinsley & Trollinger, 1991). As the century comes to a close, the processes of

195

reading, writing, speaking, and listening are acknowledged as not-so-separate components of literacy. This shift from separate notions of reading and writing to a more inclusive domain called literacy is indicative of a substantial change in how the field is conceptualized. What were once relatively independent domains are now viewed as a single, though complex, domain with overlapping and interdependent parts.

Not only has the content of literacy become more inclusive, but the processes of literacy are also in the throes of radical revision. The reading and writing components of the old triumvirate were typically viewed as processes that were carried out by individuals in isolation and developed by accretion of specific identifiable skills. The learning processes of individual students, and especially the relationships between learner and teacher on one hand and learner and text on another, filled center stage. In contrast, current notions of literacy are increasingly influenced by interactional factors and a view of knowledge as socially constructed (Berger & Luckmann, 1966; Graubard, 1991). Contemporary notions of literacy suggest an active role for learners, more interaction among learners, more integration of reading, writing, speaking and listening, and use of literacy processes for meaningful communication. While this list in far from complete, it indicates some fairly obvious ways in which contemporary notions of literacy might be applied to instructional design.

In the past few decades, large numbers of literacy teachers have explored these ideas through adoption and adaptation of writing process models, whole language, and literature-based literacy programs. Though far from attaining universal acceptance, this view of literacy has made major inroads in both mainstream literacy organizations and numerous state curriculum guidelines (e.g., California Language Arts/English Framework Committee, 1987; Texas Education Agency, 1990).

In this chapter, we explore selected aspects of how these major shifts—to a more integrated notion of literacy and to a revaluing of the social dimensions of literacy learning—are playing out in elementary school classrooms. Casting our work as exploration is intentional on at least two counts. First, the shifts in question are large-scale, long-term processes that are by no means complete. Second, there is little or no tightly coupled relationship between theory and practice in education that supports causal connections between theoretical designs for instruction and what actually happens in classrooms. Since classroom instruction is implemented mainly by individual teachers, each of whom interprets theory in a local context, there is usually more variation observed in classroom instruction than could be conveniently accounted for by any existing theory. Since most teachers are influenced by several theories at any given time, mapping practice onto theory (or vice versa) is, at best, a very complex undertaking.

We begin with a social constructivist notion that learning is, in part, a process of structuring and restructuring knowledge (Edwards & Mercer, 1987). Opportunities for structuring and restructuring knowledge are increased, or limited, by the kinds and amounts of literacy activities in which students participate during instruction. In this sense, the activities, that is, what students do and the products they produce, are central to their learning.

The kinds and amounts of literacy activities that students experience in schools are highly influenced by individual teachers, since it is teachers who, within certain constraints, interpret local policies. One would expect the literacy activities implemented by teachers with a holistic view of literacy to differ from those implemented by teachers who view literacy as composed of relatively separate skills. Similarly, one would expect the activities to vary depending upon teachers' views of individual versus social learning factors. Can these hypothesized differences be observed, and if so, what implications might they have for student opportunities to structure and restructure knowledge?

We pursue this general question by presenting a field study of literacy activities in classrooms with contrasting approaches to instruction. After identifying patterns in student literacy activities, we attempt to describe the potential of specific patterns for creating, or diminishing, opportunities for students to structure and restructure knowledge. We conclude the chapter by suggesting implications of various task and talk structures for teachers, teacher educators, and researchers.

Before presenting empirical data, we would like to suggest that architecture may be a useful metaphor for thinking about literacy instruction. From a student's point of view, literacy learning can be thought of as participation in an extended series of literacy tasks and activities.[1] Metaphorically speaking, each activity is like a small space or room that the learner inhabits for a relatively short period of time. While individual literacy activities or rooms are important, the architecture metaphor reminds us that we must pay attention to the kind of building or structure that is being built. In this sense, we can look at the overall shape of the edifice by examining the *distribution* of tasks and activities. Presumably we want a variety of useful building blocks (i.e., tasks and activities) that are placed and connected to construct an appropriate "building." By implication, this metaphor suggests teacher as architect, both at the level of designing the elemental building blocks and at the level of creating a stable, attractive, productive building.

A Field Study of Classroom Literacy Activities

We observed literacy learning activities in a school district that offered an interesting contrast in instructional philosophies. The district had a flexible curriculum for literacy learning and no requirements regarding commercial textbook programs. Some teachers had moved to a literature-based approach which made heavy use of a writer's workshop or writing process model. This approach, taken by a minority of teachers, was referred to locally as literature-based (L-B) integrated learning. The majority of teachers in the district used a skills-oriented (S-O) approach to lit-

---

[1] For all practical purposes, this series of literacy activities can be thought of as beginning at birth and continuing throughout life. By focusing on the tasks and activities that occur in school, we are looking at only a portion, albeit a very important portion, of the activities that affect literacy learning.

eracy, in which children's participation in higher-order comprehension and composition was predicated on prior mastery of lower-level skills. Both approaches were acknowledged by district leaders and taught by experienced, competent teachers. We often found both approaches being implemented in the same school.

The field study involved one full week of observations in each of eight classrooms in a two-by-two, crossed design: Instructional approach (literature-based or skills-oriented) and grade level (second or sixth) constituted the factors. The eight teachers, six females and two males, were highly experienced and well-regarded teachers in this suburban district. From individual interviews and classroom observations, all of the participants appeared to have strong, long-standing commitments to teaching and education. Observations occurred during the last half of the second semester, which meant that instructional patterns were well in place. Videotapes, field notes, interview data, curriculum materials and student work products were gathered for the entire school day, although only data on literacy learning are used for this chapter. The data gathering and analysis procedures have been described in detail elsewhere (see Fisher & Hiebert, 1990; Hiebert & Fisher, 1991, 1992).

Tasks and Activities

Literacy learning events were analyzed from a task perspective. Influenced by the work of Doyle (1983) and other researchers (Blumenfeld, Mergendoller & Swartout, 1987; Mergendoller, 1988), this perspective views schoolwork as a series of tasks that are defined primarily by student products and the operations and resources used to produce them.

In the current data set, tasks were identified by the goals and objectives toward which students were working. These goals and objectives were inferred by the researchers after observing the instruction, and, in many cases, after several reviews of a videotape of the instruction. For example, students in the L-B classes regularly spent time writing stories on topics of their choice. The beginnings and ends of these writing tasks were clearly signaled by the teacher. Most of what students did within the time boundaries of a writing task contributed to a task product (i.e., a story on whatever topic the student chose). Within a task, students' actions were usually not homogeneous but rather unfolded as a sequence of relatively discrete activities or subtasks. Activity boundaries within tasks were identified by major shifts in what students actually did to carry out their work. During a particular writing task students spent a period of time drafting text. Later in the same task, students talked in pairs or triads about what they had already drafted. During these discussions, students often read to each other and asked and answered questions about each other's text. The time spent drafting text was considered one activity and the time spent in small group discussion was considered a second activity; both nested within a single writing task.

We identified each of the tasks that students engaged in during one week of school. Some tasks extended over more than one day. All tasks were categorized according to their primary association with a subject area. In this chapter, we are examining only those tasks that were directly related to literacy learning, regardless of when they occurred during the school day or week. Literacy tasks were further broken down into separate activities to describe shifts in how students were organized and to typify how classroom conversation was structured.

Two aspects of literacy activities are central to our analysis, and both are everyday elements of instructional planning in practically every classroom. The first is organizational format, that is, the arrangements of individuals and groups that are set up to allow learning to occur. While classroom learning phenomena are highly complex, there is only a handful of generic patterns of social organization and teacher-student interaction that occur over and over again. These activity formats characterize the overt behaviors of teachers and students during instruction. We observed 17 activity formats[2] during literacy activities (see Table 10–1 for categories and brief definitions).

A second aspect of activities that influences students' opportunities for structuring and restructuring knowledge is the function of the activity in the learning task. We made distinctions among three functions. In the field study, some activities prepared students to participate in or anticipate the learning processes of the task. These activities functioned to set the task itself. That is, instruction during these activities either described the task, provided students with various specifications regarding both the task product and the processes to be followed in developing the product, or related the task to other ideas and experiences that were familiar to students.

A second category of activity function pertained to the "work" of the task. During these activities, students carried out actions required to produce the task product. For example, students might draft a composition or they might read a chapter in a book.

Finally, there were activities that allowed students to reflect in some manner on the experiences, implications, or learning that occurred while producing the task product(s). During such activities, students and teachers interacted about the content, products, and processes that were encountered during previous activities. These interactions offered students structured opportunities to reflect on what they and their peers had done. These activities usually, but by no means always, took the form of a discussion during which the climate was like that of a debriefing session (as opposed to an evaluation). These three functions are somewhat analogous to the before, during, and after phases of a reading episode (Betts, 1946).

In addition to these three activity functions—labeled set, work, and debriefing—there were two additional activity functions that occurred. There were a number of relatively short periods of time spent on various kinds of school- or classroom-level management. A fifth category included explicit public grading of completed work.

Each activity was coded in terms of its primary literacy domain (either reading, writing, spelling, or language arts), format (one of the format categories in Table

---

[2] The last four categories in Table 10–1 (book selection, dictation, art, and miscellaneous) occurred infrequently and are combined in a category labeled miscellaneous in the remainder of the chapter.

Table 10–1
Categories of organizational format observed during literacy activities.

Activity Format	Description
Silent reading	Students read silently.
Student reads story	Students listen as another student reads from a "chapter" book.
Teacher reads story	Students listen as teacher reads aloud.
Listening station	Students use earphones to listen to tape recording of book.
Small-group instruction	Instruction is given to students grouped by ability, with different materials for each group.
Student-led discussion	One or more students are in charge of the conversation, with students talking at least half of the time.
Teacher-led discussion	Teacher is in charge of conversation but talks less than 75 percent of the time.
Teacher-led instruction	Teacher is in charge, directing the minute-to-minute action and talking more than 75 percent of time.
Verbal directions	Teacher gives explicit direction on what, when, where, and how to do task.
Seatwork (worksheet)	Students work independently on worksheets.
Seatwork (other)	Students work independently on highly specified short-answer questions.
Testing	Students complete short-answer and workbook activities labeled by teachers as tests.
Generating text (writing)	Students work on drafting or revising text.
Book selection	Students browse through available materials to pick a book to read.
Dictation	Students copy from chalkboard or from teacher's verbal statements.
Art	Students construct physical objects related to reading activity (not "book" illustrations).
Miscellaneous	Unusual events occur, like listening and talking to a visiting children's-book author.

10–1), function (either set, work, debriefing, grading, or management), and duration. On many occasions, several different activities were operating simultaneously. In calculating the duration of activities per class, times for each activity were weighted by the number of participating students.

Observations of Classroom Literacy Activities

From classroom observations and later review of videotapes, we describe a vignette from each of the four cells of the design. We begin with these vignettes as a way of introducing some tasks and activities that were common for their literacy approach and grade level. We have chosen to describe reading vignettes from classrooms at the sixth-grade level (we observed relatively little writing in the sixth-grade S-O classrooms) and writing vignettes at the second-grade level. Following the vignettes, we present quantitative descriptions summarizing all observed literacy tasks and activities.

Vignette 1: Reading activities in a sixth-grade, S-O classroom.

8:29–8:30   *Following the day's opening exercises, students are sitting in their assigned seats. The teacher announces beginning of reading period, reminding students to complete assignments. Assignments are made for week-long periods; students' assignments are similar in nature but specific passages differ as a function of membership in one of three groups.*

8:30–8:45   *Teacher asks one of the three groups—Celebrations I (the name designates the textbook in which students are reading, and the number designates one of the two groups in the class working in this textbook)—to meet at the front of the room. The six members of the Celebrations I group join the teacher while the 20 students in the other two groups work on assignments at their seats. In the group meeting, the teacher begins by reading the next week's assignment from a sheet (a photocopy has been distributed to group members). The assignment includes: completing page 52 in the workbook accompanying the Celebrations textbook, reading pages 138–153 (a narrative passage), writing responses to comprehension questions in the textbook that accompany the narrative passage, and reading page 154 (a poem). Students ask a few questions, mostly about the mechanics of the written responses.*

8:45–9:06   *The teacher's meeting with the Celebrations I group continues, but at this point the format of the meeting changes as the teacher asks students questions about the setting and plot of the story that they read for the previous week's assignment. The remaining class members continue to work on their assignments.*

9:06–9:41   *The Celebrations I group returns to their desks to begin working individually on their group-designated weekly assignments. The teacher marks papers of individual students during this period. Students can choose to have their entire week's reading assignment verified for accuracy and completion by the teacher at one point in time, or they can have each of the separate components checked as it is completed. Most students choose the component-by-component option. Most students took about 10–15 minutes for the longest component and have completed it during the previous independent work period. As a result, several students wait in line to have their work checked.*

Vignette 2: Reading activities in a sixth-grade, L-B classroom.

8:12–8:27   *Students are sitting at their desks, following the day's opening announcements. The teacher states that for the next several days, work in both reading and writing will focus on moods generated by texts and the elements authors use to elicit mood in their writing. The teacher points out that a given setting (such as being in the mountains) can elicit many moods. Students give personal examples of moods during trips to the mountains. The teacher then asks students to identify the mood—and how the author created it—in a passage that the teacher is about to read. Teacher reads from* Tuck Everlasting *(Babbitt, 1975). Students then describe their feelings while listening to the passage and identify words and emphases of the author that led to the creation of these moods. The teacher summarizes the techniques and strategies that students have identified and ends the discussion with a request that students identify passages in the books they are currently reading that elicit particular moods.*

8:27–8:58   *Students and the teacher read silently in books of their choice.*

8:58–9:07   *The teacher ends the silent reading period by asking students to share, in groups of four to five, portions of their books that create mood. Students read selections to one another and comment when the reading is over. The teacher moves from group to group, listening and asking questions about the content.*

9:07–9:18   *The teacher tells students that it is time to begin writing responses to what they have read. Their assignment during this particular week is to write two letters, one to a peer and one to the teacher, about what they have read. The teacher adds that students should keep in mind the techniques used by their authors to create mood, and they should use these techniques during the writers' workshop which will follow recess. Students then begin work on their letters, which are due at week's end.*

Vignette 3: Writing activities in a second grade, S-O classroom.

2:05–2:12   *Children are sitting at their desks, clustered in groups of six. Teacher passes out a sheet with the statement "If I were the pig who caught the wolf, I would make wolf stew." Students are directed to copy the final versions of their recipes for wolf stew (which they wrote on a previous day) onto this sheet. The teacher also returns students' original drafts, on which she has marked errors. Most are spelling errors, since the wolf recipes consist primarily of lists of ingredients without connecting text. In cases where students have written procedures for the recipe, errors in usage and punctuation have also been marked. The teacher reminds children that they are making a class book for a district book fair; she emphasizes that neatness counts. Children begin to copy their wolf recipes.*

[Break for recess]

2:29–3:05   *Children continue to copy their recipes for wolf stew. The teacher calls on individual students to bring their products to her desk, and she comments on legibility of handwriting and accuracy of spelling.*

[End of school]

[Next school day]

8:59–9:01   *Children listen as teacher gives directions for their activities during the first period of the day: (a) finish copying their wolf recipes, (b) complete a worksheet on the workings of the eye, and (c) complete a worksheet on parts of speech.*

9:01–9:21   *Students complete worksheets while individuals are called to the teacher's desk, where progress is marked and recorded.*

Vignette 4: Writing activities in a second-grade, L-B classroom.

9:11–9:25   *Students are sitting on the carpet in front of the teacher. The teacher introduces* My Five Senses *(Aliki, 1989) by reminding students that they are studying how writers use human senses in their writing. The teacher reads aloud from* Charlotte's Web *(White, 1952). The teacher asks, "What senses does E. B. White make us use?" After several responses, the teacher states that today's focus will be on using the sense of sight. Children are to use their sense of sight when observing a butterfly (in a small cage) in the classroom. The butterfly has emerged from its cocoon over the weekend.*

9:25–9:35   *Pairs of students (one pair at a time) use paper and pencil to record observations of the butterfly for about five minutes. Each member of a pair observes for half of the time and writes during the remainder of the time. At the end of the observation period, partners share with one another what they have written.*

9:35–9:50   *Children return to their individual tables, which are clustered in groups of four. In these groups, children now have a "shared writing" time: they talk about their current writing project and how they might bring in the sense of sight. The teacher circulates from group to group during this period.*

9:50–10:05   *All members of the class, including the teacher, work on their compositions. Several children work in pairs.*

Patterns in Literacy Tasks and Activities

These vignettes provide an introduction to the instructional activities that students experienced in the two approaches to literacy. While observation data were collected in only one school district, the tasks and activities in the vignettes appear to be typical of literacy activities being implemented in several parts of the country.

The vignettes provide information on individual tasks and activities or, in the architecture metaphor, on the building blocks of instruction. However, the vignettes do not provide a clear look at the whole "building", or literacy space, that is created by concatenating long series of activities. To render this latter view we can examine profiles or distributions of tasks and activities. To this end, summary information on literacy tasks and activities is presented in Table 10–2.

To understand what the figures in Table 10–2 mean in relation to the particular dimensions of literacy activities of concern here—organizational formats and functions—information on the overall context of the tasks and activities in these classrooms would be helpful. While the style and quality of the architecture of literacy activities are of paramount concern (i.e., what students are doing), the amount of time (i.e., the size or "bulk" of the building, to extend the architecture metaphor) is a starting point for understanding students' experiences in different contexts. For this information, we turn to an earlier report on this project (Fisher & Hiebert, 1990), which examined influences of literacy tasks and activities on cognitive complexity and opportunities for student autonomy. The report also described the amounts of time spent within content areas, and here we briefly summarize the primary patterns for literacy tasks and activities.

In forty days of observation (five full days in each class), a total of 180 literacy tasks[3] were identified. Tasks were coded by their primary emphasis within the domain of literacy, yielding 110 reading tasks, 31 writing tasks, 27 spelling tasks, 6 language arts tasks, and 6 miscellaneous tasks. The language arts tasks all occurred in the S-O sixth-grade classes and consisted of teacher-led worksheet activities on grammar and punctuation. For the current analysis we have focused on the 168 reading, writing, and spelling tasks and dropped the language arts and miscellaneous tasks (representing 7 percent of the tasks and 5 percent of the instructional time).

There were substantial differences in the amounts of time students spent in literacy activities by approach and grade level. Students in the L-B classes spent 3.0 (grade 2) and 2.7 (grade 6) hours per day on literacy activities compared with 2.2 and 1.6[4] hours per day in the S-O classes. The difference between grade levels was

---

[3] The 180 literacy tasks represented 41 percent of the 441 tasks identified during the eight weeks of instruction.

[4] When the language arts and miscellaneous tasks are included in the sixth-grade S-O classes, 2.0 hours per day were spent in literacy tasks.

Table 10–2

Time spent in literacy activities by approach, grade level, and organizational format.

| | Literature-Based Approach | | | | | | Skills-Oriented Approach | | | | | |
| | Grade 2 | | | Grade 6 | | | Grade 2 | | | Grade 6 | | |
	Reading	Writing	Spelling	Reading	Writing	Spelling	Reading	Writing	Spelling	Reading	Writing	Spelling
Silent reading	138	*	*	152			63		15	155		
Student reads story	32			*			20					
Teacher reads story	51	*		67	*		*			*		
Listening station	19			*			26					
Small-group instruction	10											
Student-led discussion	22	85	*	14	76			11	*			
Teacher-led discussion	32	*	*	98	47		*			33		*
Teacher-led instruction	42	66	*	75	41		91		*	54	14	*
Verbal directions	*	*	10	*	*		14	10		12		*
Seatwork (worksheet)							200					
Seatwork (other)	28	73		*		*	61	13	28	121		20
Testing			12			*	11		*	*		*
Generating text	50	110		31	153		*	59		*		37
Miscellaneous	44	*	14	*			*		*			
Column totals	489	273	128	463	337	5	521	93	47	385	14	88
Total literacy	890			805			661			487		

Notes: Cell entries are average duration in minutes per class per week. Column totals include times represented by asterisks.
*Indicates that cell entry is less than 10 minutes per class per week.

relatively consistent across approaches, with second graders spending approximately 15 minutes more per day in literacy activities than sixth graders.[5]

When literacy tasks and activities were categorized by primary emphasis—reading, writing, or spelling—additional patterns were identified. Time spent on reading tasks was fairly consistent for three of the four groups, ranging from 93 to 104 minutes per day. Time spent on reading tasks in the sixth-grade S-O classes was considerably lower at 77 minutes per day.

When writing tasks were examined, even larger differences were found. Students in the two L-B groups spent 55 (grade 2) and 67 (grade 6) minutes per day on writing while students in the S-O classes spent 19 and 3 minutes per day. Students in the sixth-grade S-O classes spent very little time generating text. (Inclusion of the language arts tasks does not raise this figure, because the language arts tasks included no opportunities for generation or revision of text.)

For spelling activities, no clear pattern emerged for time spent by grade level or approach. The second-grade L-B group and both the second- and sixth-grade S-O groups devoted 26, 9, and 18 minutes per day, respectively, to explicit spelling activities, while the sixth-grade L-B classes averaged 5 minutes per week on spelling.

These patterns from the earlier analyses were convincing in their portrayal of differing student experiences in terms of time allocated to particular areas of literacy. Quantity of time spent on literacy areas, however, is only an index of the potential importance of particular literacy experiences; it is the quality and substance of the activities that are important. However, differences in duration can reflect differences in opportunities to structure and restructure knowledge, and it is to this issue that we now turn.

Organizational formats of reading and writing activities.   Table 10–2 reveals that some organizational formats were used frequently while others were rarely used. Four of the fourteen formats—silent reading, generating text, teacher-led instruction, and seatwork (other)—accounted for 63 percent of the time students spent in reading, writing and spelling activities. Four more formats—seatwork (worksheet), teacher-led discussion, student-led discussion, and teacher-read story—accounted for an additional 29 percent of instructional time. Table 10–2 also indicates that, within the L-B and S-O approaches, there were large differences in the ways that formats were used.

Since time allocations for spelling were inconsistent across approaches and grade levels, and because spelling activities are unlikely to directly influence learners' opportunities to structure and restructure knowledge, we do not explore them further in the current analysis. With attention focused on reading and writing, we continue to unpack tasks and activities by examining patterns in social organization.

Organizational formats are described for reading and writing in turn.

---

[5] This comparison includes the language arts and miscellaneous tasks for the sixth-grade S-O classes.

Reading. As noted earlier, the amount of time devoted to reading activities was fairly similar across the four groups, with the exception of the sixth-grade, S-O classes. For this latter group, reading activities occupied about 20 minutes less time per day than for the other three groups. The amount of time spent in reading activities is important only insofar as students are engaged in meaningful literacy work. Time devoted to reading activities may be lengthy while the activities in which students participate as readers may not support their growth as readers. To capture some of the qualitative differences in how students spent their time, reading and writing formats were rank-ordered by the amount of time spent in each activity. The resulting configurations appear in Table 10–3.[6]

For reading activities, two formats—silent reading and teacher-led instruction—were common in all four groups, but the ranks associated with these common formats differed from group to group. While silent reading was the most prominent format for three of the groups, this format was preempted by seatwork with worksheets in the grade 2 S-O group. Seatwork with worksheets was highly ranked in both S-O groups but in neither of the L-B groups.

In contrast, opportunities to write about one's interpretations and responses to reading were prominent in both L-B groups, but absent from both of the S-O groups. In the S-O groups, students' opportunities for sharing interpretations of their reading were confined to seatwork and, at grade 6, participating in teacher-led discussions. In the L-B groups, second graders did engage in seatwork, but rather than worksheets, their seatwork generally involved the construction of story maps or other frameworks for representing what they had read. These framework-building activities, at least in theory, provided younger students in the L-B group with scaffolds for generating text about their reading. Second graders were not left to discover ways of responding to text for themselves, but were introduced to frameworks or structures to support increasingly complex interpretations of text. Seatwork with these framework-building properties was not observed in the older L-B group. These explicit supports were apparently no longer used by the time students reached the middle grades.

The L-B and S-O groups also differed in terms of opportunities for talk about text. In the S-O groups, talk about text was primarily in the form of teacher-led instruction and, in grade 6, teacher-led discussion. While teacher-led instruction occurred in the L-B groups, it was less highly ranked (grade 2) or ranked behind teacher-led discussion (grade 6) and constituted only one of several formats for verbal interaction.

For students in the L-B groups, there were more opportunities—and more diversity in formats—for listening to and talking about text as well as for sharing interpretations of text through writing. In the S-O classrooms, as prescribed by the general approach, students were more solitary. They were provided fewer opportunities to talk about what they were reading and fewer strategies for interpreting and representing text. These patterns in the S-O groups departed radically from

---

[6] Any format that accounted for less than five minutes per day was dropped from Table 10–3.

Table 10–3
Organizational formats in rank order for reading and writing activities.

L-B Grade 2	L-B Grade 6	S-O Grade 2	S-O Grade 6
Reading Activities			
Silent reading	Silent reading	Seatwork (worksheets)	Silent reading
Teacher reads story	Teacher-led discussion	Teacher-led instruction	Seatwork (worksheets)
Writing (about reading)	Teacher-led instruction	Silent reading	Teacher-led instruction
Miscellaneous (Resource presentations)	Teacher reads story	Seatwork (other than worksheets)	Teacher-led discussion
Teacher-led instruction	Writing (about reading)		
Student reads story			
Seatwork (other than worksheets)			
Writing Activities			
Writing	Writing	Writing	
Student-led discussion	Student-led discussion		
Teacher-led instruction	Teacher-led discussion		
	Teacher-led instruction		

the typical expectations of textbook-based instruction. Instruction had moved away from the usual guidance in teachers' manuals. The skills themselves had become the focus of teaching.

Writing.   Students in the L-B classes, compared with those in S-O classes, spent approximately three times as much time on writing tasks. The L-B classes averaged about an hour per day in writing while the S-O classes averaged about 20 minutes (grade 2) and less than 5 minutes (grade 6) per day. Writing tasks, defined as generating and revising text, were not a significant component of instruction in the S-O classes, although they did average about 20 minutes per day on grammar usage exercises similar to those found in the language arts subtests of major norm-referenced tests.

What was remarkable about the profile of formats used during writing activities (see Table 10–3) was the role of talk. In the L-B classrooms, students spent more time in formats where they had opportunities to listen to peers talk about their writing, brainstorm ideas, and understand the structures and strategies of writing (151 and 184 minutes per week in grades 2 and 6 respectively) than they did in actual writing (110 and 153 minutes per week in grades 2 and 6 respectively). Talk, both between students and teacher and among students, was regarded as an integral part of composition.

Writing was occurring in the second-grade S-O classrooms, but students spent less time and the tasks were more highly constrained than in L-B classes. Interviews with second-grade S-O teachers indicated that they were being influenced by the excitement expressed by some of their colleagues who were implementing the L-B approach. They were "trying new things," as one of the teachers put it. To the second-grade S-O teachers, "writers' workshop" apparently meant that students needed to write. As a result, second graders in S-O classes were not doing worksheets in the same way that they were doing worksheets in reading. There was some room for expression in composing, as evidenced by the wolf stew recipes. For the L-B teachers, "writers' workshop" meant talking and listening as much as it meant writing.

The choice of the sixth-grade S-O teachers to emphasize grammar exercises rather than composition is an important one, particularly in light of the teachers' beliefs that they were preparing their students for middle school. It is uncertain whether their notions of the academic demands of the middle and high schools of the district were accurate.

Functions of reading and writing activities.   Literacy activities were also categorized by function. In this section we examine the profiles of set, work, and debriefing functions[7] for reading and writing activities in the four groups of classrooms defined by approach and grade level. Amounts of time spent by students in the three activity functions are displayed in Table 10–4.[8]

Reading.   An examination of the distributions of time spent in set, work, and debriefing activities during reading revealed three trends. First, the amount of time spent on work activities was consistently high across approaches and grade levels. All four groups spent more than an hour per day on work activities in reading (grade 2 S-O classes were highest with more than an hour and a half per day).

---

[7] Five functions were coded but two (grading and management) have been dropped from this analysis in order to underscore the role of set, work, and debriefing functions in structuring and restructuring knowledge.

[8] For consistency with Table 10–2, Table 10–4 includes activity function data for spelling. No analysis for activity functions during spelling was undertaken.

Table 10–4
Time spent in literacy activities by approach, grade level and function.

	Content Area	Set min./wk. (%)	Work min./wk. (%)	Debrief min./wk. (%)	Row Total min./wk.
	Reading	72 (15)	381 (78)	36 (7)	489
L-B (gr. 2)	Writing	29 (11)	150 (55)	94 (34)	273
	Spelling	11 (9)	111 (87)	*	128
L-B (gr. 2) subtotal		112 (13)	642 (72)	136 (15)	890
	Reading	83 (18)	345 (75)	35 (8)	463
L-B (gr. 6)	Writing	67 (20)	165 (49)	105 (31)	337
	Spelling	*	0 (0)	0 (0)	5
L-B (gr. 6) subtotal		155 (19)	510 (63)	140 (17)	805
	Reading	38 (7)	477 (92)	6 (1)	521
S-O (gr. 2)	Writing	10 (11)	72 (77)	11 (12)	93
	Spelling	*	44 (94)	0 (0)	47
S-O (gr. 2) subtotal		51 (8)	593 (90)	17 (3)	661
	Reading	16 (4)	357 (93)	12 (3)	385
S-O (gr. 6)	Writing	0 (0)	14 (100)	0 (0)	14
	Spelling	*	84 (95)	0 (0)	88
S-O (gr. 6) subtotal		20 (4)	455 (93)	12 (2)	487
L-B Subtotal		267 (16)	1152 (68)	276 (16)	1695
S-O Subtotal		71(6)	1048 (91)	29 (3)	1148
Column Total		338 (12)	2200 (77)	305 (11)	2843

Notes: Cell entries are in minutes per week with row percentages in parentheses. Column totals include times represented by asterisks.

* Indicates that cell entry is less than 10 minutes per week.

The second and third trends differentiated the L-B and S-O approaches. The L-B classes spent more time than the S-O classes in both set and debriefing activities. Students in L-B classes, compared to students in S-O classes, spent about twice as much time in set activities and more than three times as much time in debriefing activities. Within the L-B approach, durations of set and debriefing activities were similar across grades, with approximately twice as much time spent on set activities. Within the S-O groups, debriefing activities were relatively rare during reading.

In the L-B classes, there was a tendency, but not without considerable variation, to begin a task with a set activity and then progress to a work activity and finally to a debriefing activity. In the S-O classes, this triad of functions was truncated so that a set activity was followed by a work activity and then the set activity for the next task and so on. Typically, when students in S-O classes finished a worksheet or silent reading, they moved on to the next activity without an explicit debriefing activity. Rarely was there sharing of what they had read or recognition that the task was complete.

To further illustrate the role of activity functions in mediating student opportunities to learn, we return to the vignettes presented earlier in the chapter. The first two vignettes illustrate differences in opportunities in the two sixth-grade groups for students to orient to the task during set activities as well as to share responses and interpretations after reading of text.

In Vignette 1, the set activity emphasized details of the assignment but did not create a context for the task (for example, by identifying prior knowledge). Even though students read the same passages (some groups slightly later than others), the task ended in a grading activity rather than with opportunities to discuss what had been done during the work activity. The teacher's intentions for students were apparently to grasp task directions and then to complete the tasks accurately. When interviewed, the teacher stated that students needed to be prepared for middle school, where they would be expected to understand teachers' oral descriptions of assignments. Grading consumed a substantial part of periods designated as literacy instruction. When there were debriefing activities, the sessions were fairly short and partially focused on the requirements of the assignment, as opposed to the content of the passage or the students' interpretations of it.

In Vignette 2, the set activity emphasized understanding of the underlying strategies prior to reading text. For this teacher, discussions both before and after reading text constituted an important part of literacy. From her interview it was clear that she expected students to read extensively outside of class and that reading during class was a time to gain new insights and strategies for understanding text.

Writing. The difference between the two approaches (in the amount of time spent on the three activity functions) was even greater for writing tasks than for reading tasks (see Table 10–4). In the L-B classes, students at both grade levels spent more than two hours per week in set and debriefing activities. In the S-O classes, second-grade students spent about 20 minutes per week in set and debriefing activities while sixth graders did not engage in these functions at all. In the L-B classes, relatively more time was spent on debriefing activities than set activities— the reverse of the pattern for reading tasks. In the second-grade S-O classes, about 20 percent of writing time was distributed evenly over set and debriefing activities, with each function averaging less than 3 minutes per day.

In Vignette 3, students in the S-O group were working on recipes for wolf stew. Note that there was no debriefing activity for this task. Even within the constraints of the task, some students came up with inventive lists of ingredients.

In this S-O classroom, the wolf recipe task came to a close with a seatwork activity: copying the recipe for later publication. When the next task was signaled, the wolf recipe task was at an end. The teacher bound the book and relayed it to a central school district location, where parents or school visitors had access to the children's contributions. The children themselves, however, did not review or otherwise reflect on their products—at least not as a structured part of instruction.

During observations of S-O classes, all writing tasks began with verbal directions. Any questions that students asked during set activities pertained to procedures and time constraints. As a result, students in S-O classes moved into work activities relatively quickly with only minimal orientation to the task at hand. As Vignette 4 illustrates, this was not the case in the second-grade L-B classes. Considerable time was spent discussing strategies that might be used during the succeeding work activity. Further, students had time to share what they had written after the work activity. Even on days when "author's chair" did not take place, students were encouraged to talk to one another about problems or solutions that arose as they composed and revised text. All of the L-B second graders had experimented with "pair writing," where authors collaborated on writing a story together or in writing sequels to one another's stories.

Literacy Activities and Potential for Learning

Several decades ago, the kinds and amounts of tasks in which students spent their school days were shown to be relatively powerful indicators of students' learning in classrooms (Fisher & Berliner, 1985; Rosenshine & Stevens, 1986). In classrooms where little time was devoted to reading, students read poorly, while in classrooms with comparable populations of students—even the classroom next door—longer periods of reading were associated with higher levels of performance. While these indices predicted students' learning, the classroom observations that accompanied these quantitative analyses made it clear that there were vast differences in what constituted literacy activities across classrooms. By examining the formats and functions of these activities, we can get a glimpse of the mechanisms of learning.

In the field study, distributions of literacy activities differed markedly, implying distinct learning experiences for students in the two instructional approaches. L-B classes provided more opportunities for activation of prior knowledge; refining, elaborating, and chunking knowledge; and relating what had been learned to other knowledge. In S-O classes, these processes were implicit or unconscious, which effectively placed responsibility for their practice on individual students. In the S-O classes, generative and reflective contexts that support such processes (such as writing or speaking) occurred infrequently. In the L-B classes, writing and speaking were valued as accomplishments in their own right. To use Wells's (1986) term, they were used as "meaning makers." In the S-O classes, the task itself, or at least completion of the task, frequently seemed to drive what happened. In L-B classes, meaning-making was in the foreground and tasks seemed to be a background support for facilitating that process.

The most striking difference between the two approaches occurred in opportunities for writing. In the L-B classes, not only was more time devoted to writing as a subject area, but students spent more time generating and revising text as part of reading periods. The social constructivist perspective on learning emphasizes the role of talk in constructing meaning. Writing also is a potent occasion for constructing meaning. Like talk, writing provides a means for students to express interpretations of what they have learned through reading and listening and, thereby, a means for students to structure and restructure knowledge. They can give ideas a new spin. They can make their mark on the world. In interpreting our observational findings within the social constructivist perspective, we argue that the prominence of writing in the L-B classrooms and the nature of the writing tasks opened avenues for expressing, interpreting, and generating knowledge that were not available to students in the S-O classrooms. Even when opportunities were available, the S-O instruction provided little or no scaffolding for making meaning.

The qualitative differences in the formats and functions of activities were apparent in reading as well as writing. Students in the L-B classrooms engaged in different profiles of activities with different roles and expectations for participants. The times when they read and wrote on their own were preceded more frequently by explicit opportunities for gaining insights into the processes and content of literacy—information that they were expected to use in their subsequent reading and writing. There were also occasions in L-B classrooms when students could share what they had learned during their independent reading and writing activities. On these occasions, they were able to talk with one another and the teacher to articulate ideas and intentions. These opportunities to discuss what one is learning or has learned are at the heart of learning, whether from a developmental (Piaget, 1964), cognitive science (Anderson & Pearson, 1984), or sociohistorical perspective (Wertsch, 1985).

The L-B and S-O approaches to literacy resulted in students having substantially different amounts and kinds of tasks during literacy instruction. As a result, some students had more opportunities than others to benefit from specific principles of learning. We will consider these principles and then illustrate how extended opportunities for writing and talking led to increased opportunity for structuring and restructuring knowledge.

Structuring and Restructuring Knowledge

Meaning, as numerous scholars have argued, is made by relating new knowledge to one's previous experiences through existing schemata (Bruner, 1990). Since humans are highly social animals, this individual construction of knowledge does not take place in a vacuum. To a great extent, the distinctive properties of human knowledge and thought derive from the nature of social activity. Vygotsky (1978) for example, saw social interaction as a primary means whereby the practices and symbol systems of culture are acquired. The delicate balance between thought and language mirrors the complex relationship between individual and social factors in learning. Thought is not equivalent to language, but children's thought processes are influenced by their social interactions.

What characteristics of schoolwork encourage students to relate new information to existing knowledge structures? During interviews, teachers in both instructional approaches asserted that schoolwork tasks should have explicit connections with students' prior knowledge and that instruction should include active exploration of these connections. In actual practice, opportunities to relate prior knowledge to schoolwork tasks varied considerably from class to class, particularly as a function of the teacher's philosophical orientation.

Vignettes 1 and 2, from sixth-grade classrooms, exemplify task structures that differ in opportunities for students to activate prior knowledge. Generally speaking, students in L-B classes, compared with S-O classes, spent much more time setting the tasks and thereby activating prior knowledge about the task. It is presumably not just the amount of time in the set function, but rather the distribution of time over functions, that may be critical for student learning.

Opportunities to reorganize or restructure knowledge after a learning activity have also been advocated as a potent feature of learning environments (Tharp & Gallimore, 1988). Patterns in student opportunities for reorganizing knowledge were analogous to those for activating prior knowledge. These differences were particularly marked in debriefing activities, that is, activities in which students reflected on the meaning of their previous actions and explored possible relationships with other knowledge. During literacy instruction, students in L-B classes spent 16 percent of their time in debriefing activities, compared with 3 percent in S-O classes (see Table 10–4).

The contrast was equally striking in the vignettes described earlier. For example, in the vignette from the sixth-grade L-B classes, students talked with one another about mood in their books, and explored their understandings of compositions during writing periods (which, in turn, were discussed). In contrast, students in S-O classes typically ended a task by closing their books and beginning the next task.

In the S-O classes, there was more emphasis on evaluation. In Vignette 1, students in S-O classes recorded in their notebooks the title and summary (among other things) of what they had read. However, even this activity appeared to be driven more by desire to complete the task than by the desire to construct meaning from the previous reading activity. In L-B classes, debriefing activities were characterized by questions like "What do you think?" while in S-O classes they were characterized by "Did you do it?" or "Did you get it right?"

Writing and speaking as media for structuring and restructuring knowledge.   Language, whether it is read, written or spoken, is the primary medium through which knowledge is structured and restructured (Barnes, 1995; Wells, 1986). Typically in schools, reading and listening are the means whereby children are thought to acquire knowledge. While new ideas obviously are gained through these language processes, it is through writing and speaking that one communicates what it is that has been constructed through reading and listening. In fact, important portions of the construction itself may occur in the acts of writing and speaking. To some extent, the broad shifts in conceptualization of knowledge, teaching, and learning that serve as the backdrop for this paper can be thought of as a rebalancing of the roles of reading and listening on the one hand and of writing and speaking on the other. We now consider some differences in the role of, and opportunities to practice, writing and speaking in different task structures.

Learning to write and writing to learn. There were conspicuous differences between the L-B and S-O approaches in the amounts and kinds of writing done by students. The term writing has been used in two ways in the current work: as a subject or content area and as an activity format. As a subject area, writing is an area of the school curriculum in which students engage in learning to write. The purpose of writing, in this sense, is to acquire knowledge about, and skilled performance in, the general process of writing. Used in this way, the writing process is in the foreground, so to speak, and the content or substance being written about is of secondary importance. Students in the L-B classes spent much more time on writing as a subject than those in S-O classes (about 20 percent of all classroom instruction in the former; about 4 percent in the latter). This distribution represents not only a substantial difference in opportunity to learn but also makes a strong statement about the relative value placed on writing compared to other subject areas.

As an activity format, writing identified time during which students were actually generating, editing, or revising extended text. In the L-B classrooms, much of this writing occurred during time set aside for writing as a subject, but there was also much writing as an activity format in other subject areas. In S-O classes, writing as an activity format in other subject areas was much less frequent (approximately one hour per week compared to three hours per week in the L-B classes). Thus, students in S-O classes were afforded little opportunity to organize and reorganize their thoughts in the explicit manner required by writing.

By leaving a concrete trace or product, thinking is, to some extent, objectified through writing. Writing, by its very nature, requires meaning-making and, at least potentially, communicating that meaning to another. Writing, from this point of view, is one of the activities that one can engage in while struggling to make sense of a topic. It is the meaning-making that is in the foreground, with writing functioning as a process that supports meaning-making. Writing as an activity format is writing to learn.

Classroom Tasks and Classroom Talk

The L-B and S-O classes differed not only in amounts and distributions of time and activity functions but also in how classroom talk unfolded within activity functions. Students in L-B classes participated in more verbal interactions (32 and 45 percent of literacy instruction for grades 2 and 6 respectively) than students in S-O classrooms (25 percent at both grades 2 and 6). Furthermore, the content of classroom talk in L-B classes was influenced more by student participation.

In one instance in an L-B class, we observed the teacher beginning a discussion with a question. However, rather than waiting for the "right" answer, the teacher spent most of her time listening as children spoke, and writing their responses on a pad of paper for future reference. In this case, the discussion took the form of a brainstorming session. Some of the student suggestions that were generated during the brainstorming session appeared as choices that students could elect in another task later in the day. Although this kind of classroom talk did not dominate discourse patterns in the L-B classes, examples like this occurred often enough to provide students with a sense of ownership and community concerning classroom tasks.

In contrast, teachers' talk was dominant in S-O classes. Students talked infrequently, and their utterances were usually embedded in the teacher-initiation/student-response/teacher-evaluation recitation triad (Cazden, 1988). Communication between students was more likely to be clandestine than part of the instructional plan.

These very different patterns of participation in classroom talk were accompanied by equally divergent content. In the S-O classrooms, teachers' talk often pertained to procedural directions or the "telling" of information. For example, in a unit on Japan, a sixth-grade S-O teacher presented a lecture on Japanese customs. In contrast, a second-grade L-B teacher had children generate the distinction between moths and butterflies by comparing and contrasting live examples, rather than "telling" the children the information. In L-B classes, student talk was used as an opportunity to organize and reorganize information with an emphasis on meaning-making as well as on acquisition of particular meanings.

While the two approaches to literacy instruction differed in duration of literacy activities, students in both approaches spent about the same amount of time in work activities. However, students in L-B classes, as compared to S-O classes, spent much more time in set and debriefing activities. These differences in the use of set and debriefing functions represent differences between the instructional approaches in the kinds and amounts of opportunities for activating background knowledge and reorganizing knowledge structures.

Set activities in reading and writing were dominated by teacher-led discussion and teacher-led instruction in the L-B classes and by teacher verbal directions (procedural information on the who, what, where, and when of the task itself) in the S-O classes. This meant that students in the L-B classes spent from 90 to 150 minutes per week actively contributing to discussions about upcoming reading and writing or listening to the teacher speak about reading and writing content issues. With the exception of second-grade classes in reading (about 15 minutes per week), students in the S-O classes spent no time in discussion or teacher-led instruction during set activities, but regularly received verbal directions specifying what they were to do in procedural terms. These differences represented more opportunities for students in L-B classes to activate background knowledge and to interact with other students and teachers about the substance of reading and writing during the set function.

Debriefing activities in reading and writing showed even more marked differences between approaches. After work activities in both silent reading and generating text, students in L-B classes regularly met in small or large groups to summarize what they had read or written and to share interpretations of the material. These debriefing sessions usually took the form of student-led discussions where students summarized their own work and students posed and answered questions as part of the discussion. This allowed both speakers and listeners to review what they had done during the work function, try out alternative representations of their knowledge, and establish linkages with other knowledge.

In S-O classes, these opportunities for reflection did not occur regularly and were very limited in duration. This does not mean that activation of background knowledge and reorganization of knowledge structures did not take place in S-O classes, but rather that the structure of the reading and writing tasks and activities did not provide time or structural support for these processes. Nor is it necessarily the case that students in L-B classes actually activated or reorganized knowledge, but these processes were encouraged by the task characteristics in these classes.

The predominant pattern of activities within tasks in S-O classes (that is, teacher presents what to do and how to do it, students do it, and then the teacher presents what to do next and how to do it, and so on), subtly, and not so subtly, focuses both the students' and teacher's attention on task completion for its own sake. This focus can lead to the types of questions that students often ask their classmates during instruction: "How many have you got done?" "Which page are you on now?" The focus on task completion as a primary, if unannounced, goal in schooling has been suggested by Doyle (1983) and observed in science classes (Mergendoller, Marchman, Mitman, & Packer, 1988). In contrast, time spent in the L-B classes on activating background knowledge and on interpreting text after it had been read or written tended to encourage connections among school activities, other knowledge, and experiences of students, thereby shifting the focus of school literacy learning toward meaning.

Next Steps for Teachers, Teacher Educators, and Researchers

Long before American educators had heard of Vygotsky, teachers were advised to engage their students in talk before, during, and after reading (Betts, 1946). In the directed reading activity used with basal textbooks for generations, teachers were guided in asking students questions that would orient them to text before they read and that would encourage interpretations after reading. It may be that practice never met the ideal, or that the hierarchical skill model that dominated instruction in the 1970s moved teachers increasingly further away from discussion. Whatever the cause, by the time Durkin (1978–79) observed comprehension instruction in the early 1970s, reading was not embedded in rich discussion. Opportunities for student talk were limited to cursory responses to test questions, which assessed whether students had gotten the right answer.

Durkin's portrayal came at a time when the theoretical and empirical bases for the beneficial influence of social interaction on comprehension and composition were beginning to emerge. While constructs like scaffolding or zone of proximal development still may not be common in the vocabularies of practitioners, the message that talk promotes comprehension and composition has been widespread in American education for decades. By the 1990s, the notions underlying literary response and process writing have come to dominate the literature on literacy instruction.

Future Research

The field study suggested several next steps for research on the architecture of literacy activities. Our comments are limited to the format and function variables, which we believe warrant closer examination.

The format categories are a collection of standard patterns (e.g., seatwork, silent reading, reading groups, writing) and some ad hoc categories to distinguish among verbal interactions, i.e., student-led discussion, teacher-led discussion, teacher-led instruction, and verbal direction (task related). The categories are grounded in observations of classroom practice, but they lack an underlying conceptual framework. Although the categories are recognizable to anyone familiar with schools, and they represent, in most cases, core activities that teachers use in planning instruction, it would be useful to develop one or more conceptual frameworks within which to order the categories.

The function variable has potential for useful description of classroom processes. On the one hand, these categories relate, more or less directly, to a variety of frameworks for instructional analysis, but classroom activities themselves do not fit neatly into these three categories. This lack of correspondence between category descriptions and activities themselves is presumably one reason for the lower inter-rater agreement on coding of activity functions. Part of the difficulty with this variable is that literacy tasks are not accomplished in the linear sequence (set, work, and debriefing) that the three functions tend to suggest. To some extent, the functions are an analog (although a simplistic one) of reading and writing process models. Although we tend to think of steps in the reading or writing process, these steps are not as linear as some process models might lead us to believe. The phenomena being described (reading and writing) can be conceptualized at a gross level in terms of a sequence of steps but, as we look more closely, there is a limit to the applicability of this way of thinking. The activity function variable then is useful at the level of characterizing gross opportunities for activating background knowledge and reorganizing knowledge structures, but for finer description, these three categories lose their usefulness.

In our fieldwork, literacy tasks and activities have been described primarily by a nonparticipant observer. Although most teachers and students will readily recognize the task characteristics that we used, our analysis does not account well for the perceptions of the participants themselves. Representation and understanding of these segments of literacy instruction would benefit from more interaction between researchers, teachers, and students.

Some Implications for Practice

The large-scale shifts in conceptualization of literacy instruction are replete with implications for teachers and teacher educators. To the extent that these shifts represent a rebalancing—of reading and listening on one hand and writing and speaking on the other—the task for teachers is to explore what these shifts might look like in their own classrooms. One way, but presumably not the only way, is to intentionally design tasks and activities to bring about noticeable shifts. Taking action could involve new configurations of activity formats and functions or new patterns of classroom talk. It may be especially useful to attend to the distribution of literacy activities and their characteristics. In the architecture metaphor, the teacher's task is to design and build spaces in which students can make meaning.

The task for teacher educators is to create experiences for teachers that reveal their roles as architects. This task is particularly challenging since the very shifts that teacher educators should aim for in schools must also be initiated in their own programs. For example, it may be as, or even more, difficult to shift patterns of talk in teacher training programs than in classrooms and schools. In any case, the general direction of change is clearly indicated and a set of tools, though incomplete and relatively crude, is available.

References

Aliki (1989). *My five senses*. New York: Crowell.

Anderson, R. C., & Pearson, P. D. (1984). A schema-theoretic view of basic processes in reading comprehension. In P. D. Pearson, R. Barr, M. L. Kamil, & P. Mosenthal (Eds.), *Handbook of reading research* (pp. 255–292). New York: Longman.

Babbitt, N. (1975). *Tuck everlasting*. New York: Farrar, Straus & Giroux.

Barnes, D. (1995). Talking and learning in classrooms. *Primary Voices K-6, 3*(1), 2–7.

Berger, P. L., & Luckmann, T. (1966). *The social construction of reality*. New York: Doubleday.

Betts, E. A. (1946). *Foundations of reading instruction*. New York: American Book.

Blumenfeld, P., Mergendoller, J., & Swarthout, D. (1987). Task as a heuristic for understanding student learning and motivation. *Journal of Curriculum Studies, 19*(2), 135–148.

Bruner, J. (1990). *Acts of meaning*. Cambridge, MA: Harvard University Press.

California Language Arts/English Framework Committee. (1987). *English–language arts framework for California public schools: Kindergarten through grade 12*. Sacramento, CA: California Department of Education.

Cazden, C. B. (1988). *Classroom discourse: The language of teaching and learning*. Portsmouth, NH: Heinemann.

Doyle, W. (1983). Academic work. *Review of Educational Research, 53*(2), 159–199.

Durkin, D. (1978–79). What classroom observations reveal about reading comprehension instruction. *Reading Research Quarterly, 15,* 481–533.

Edwards, D., & Mercer, N. (1987). *Common knowledge: The development of understanding in the classroom.* New York: Methuen.

Fisher, C. W., & Berliner, D. C. (Eds.) (1985). *Perspectives on instructional time.* New York: Longman.

Fisher, C. W., & Hiebert, E. H. (1990). Characteristics of tasks in two literacy programs. *Elementary School Journal, 91,* 6–13.

Graubard, S. R. (Ed.) (1991). *Literacy: An overview by fourteen experts.* New York: The Noonday Press.

Hiebert, E. H., & Fisher, C. W. (1992). The tasks of school literacy instruction: Trends and tensions. In J. Brophy (Ed.), *Advances in research on teaching* (Vol. 3, pp. 191–223). Greenwich, CT: JAI Press.

Hiebert, E. H., & Fisher, C. W. (1991). Task and talk structures that promote literacy. In E. H. Hiebert (Ed.), *Literacy for a diverse society: Perspectives, practices, and policies* (pp. 141–156). New York: Teachers College Press.

Kaestle, C. F., Damon-Moore, H., Stedman, L. C., Tinsley, K., & Trollinger, W. V., Jr. (1991). *Literacy in the United States: Readers and reading since 1880.* New Haven: Yale University Press.

Mergendoller, J. R. (Ed.). (1988). Schoolwork and academic tasks [Special issue]. *Elementary School Journal, 88*(1).

Mergendoller, J. R., Marchman, V. A., Mitman, A. L., & Packer, M. J. (1988). Task demands and accountability in middle-grade science classes. *Elementary School Journal, 88*(1), 251–265.

Piaget, J. (1964). Development and learning. In R. Ripple & V. Rockcastle (Eds.), *Piaget rediscovered* (pp. 7–19). Ithaca, NY: Cornell University Press.

Rosenshine, B. V., & Stevens, R. (1986). Teaching functions. In M. C. Wittrock (Ed.), *Handbook of research on teaching* (3rd ed., pp. 376–391). New York: Macmillan.

Texas Education Agency (1990). *Proclamation of the State Board of Education advertising for bids on textbooks* [Proclamation 68]. Austin: Texas Education Agency.

Tharp, R., & Gallimore, R. (1988). *Rousing minds to life: Teaching, learning and schooling in social context.* New York: Cambridge University Press.

Vygotsky, L. S. (1978). *Mind in society.* Cambridge, MA: Harvard University Press.

Wells, G. (1986). *The meaning makers: Children learning language and using language to learn.* Portsmouth, NH: Heinemann.

Wertsch, J. V. (Ed.) (1985). *Culture, communication, and cognition: Vygotskian perspectives.* Cambridge: Cambridge University Press.

White, E. B. (1952). *Charlotte's web.* New York: HarperCollins.

Middle School Literacy Instruction

Robert J. Stevens
Pennsylvania State University

Lynne A. Hammann
Pennsylvania State University

Timothy R. Balliett
Pennsylvania State University

Historical Roots of Middle School

Since the turn of the twentieth century, there has been a great deal of discussion about the best way to educate adolescents. With the passage of child labor laws and compulsory-education laws, schools for children 12 to 18 years old became a significant change on public education's landscape. Education for adolescents became the norm.

Initially, elementary schools accommodated students through eighth grade, and high schools spanned ninth through twelfth grades. However, many educators and psychologists became concerned about the results of this configuration. Many felt that the elementary school model did not adequately challenge early adolescents with higher-level content in mathematics, science, and the humanities (Clark & Clark, 1993). They felt that students would be better educated by teachers who were content specialists, rather than generalists, as the teachers in elementary schools typically are.

At the same time, G. Stanley Hall developed the notion of adolescence as a separate developmental stage in which students had qualitatively different abilities. He proposed that adolescence was an important transition period between childhood and adulthood, a period when the individual developed reasoning abilities and a sense of independence (Davidson & Benjamin, 1987). Hall argued that adolescence was therefore a critical developmental stage and one that schools should nurture. The National Education Association (NEA) and the child study movement collaborated in advocating for schools that were responsive to the unique needs of adolescents, and as a result, the first junior high schools were built in the early 1900s (Clark & Clark, 1993).

The junior high schools were aptly named, for in structure and operation they were much like little high schools (Clark & Clark, 1993). They were not as large as high schools but were typically much larger than neighborhood elementary schools. Junior high schools spanned seventh through ninth grades to provide instruction geared to the needs of early adolescents. The teachers were primarily content-area experts giving students departmentalized instruction. The students traveled from room to room and from teacher to teacher during the school day to get instruction in six to eight different subjects. Although the new structure of schools for adolescents did reduce dropout rates and grade retention, questions remained as to whether junior high schools were truly responsive to the needs of early adolescents (Eichhorn, 1966; Lounsbury, 1990).

As early as the 1960s, there were criticisms of the large, departmentalized junior high schools, and by the 1970s and 1980s schools seemed to embrace the middle school movement. The goal was to create a school structure that would facilitate the transition of students from the smaller neighborhood elementary school to the large, departmentalized high school (Eichhorn, 1966; Lounsbury, 1990). It was thought that the ninth grade should move to the high school so that all the college preparatory courses would be offered in one location (George & Alexander, 1993), and the middle school should comprise sixth through eighth grades—or all the students who were in early adolescence. The role of the middle school was to nurture the growing independence and problem-solving skills of early-adolescent students in a strongly academic environment. Essentially the objective was to create a school that had the adult support and guidance typically found in elementary schools, with the academic rigor and cognitive challenge of high school curricula. Eventually this age or grade configuration was widely adopted throughout the country, but essentially for the wrong reasons. Often the switch to the middle school was a matter of administrative convenience, to handle declining enrollments in high school and an overabundance of secondary-certified teachers, rather than a change of curricula and instruction to respond to the needs of the students (Oakes, Quartz, Gong, Guiton, & Lipton, 1993).

Same Problems, Different Grades

The structural changes to the schools for early adolescents, going from junior high schools to middle schools, did little to change the process of instruction and its products. The transition from elementary school to middle school is still marked by problems in students' achievement, attitudes, and attendance. Students in middle school perceive the schools as less supportive (Seidman, Allen, Aber, Mitchell, and Feinman, 1994), and they become less attached to school (Gottfredson, 1987). As students make the transition to middle school, their grades and attendance rates go down, and their truancy rates increase (Carnegie Task Force on Education of Young Adolescents, 1989; Gottfredson, 1987). All of these measures are good predictors of a student's potential for dropping out of school (Ekstrom, Goertz, Pollack, & Rock, 1987; McDill, Natriello, & Pallas, 1985). As a result of these disturbing findings, the Carnegie Task Force on Education of Young Adolescents proposed significant changes in middle-level education to better meet the educational needs of early adolescents. These changes were broad, including changes in curricula, instructional practices, teacher preparation, school governance, and parent and community involvement.

Instruction in Middle Schools

Descriptive research in middle schools has indicated that although many middle schools have adopted the language of the middle school philosophy, their implementation of that philosophy has been slow (Jackson, 1990; Lounsbury, 1991). Structurally, middle schools continue to be departmentalized, with little or no interdisciplinary planning between subject-matter teachers (Clark & Clark, 1993; Epstein & Mac Iver, 1990; Oakes et al., 1993). For example, in seventh grade only 10 percent of students have teachers who are on interdisciplinary teams that plan instruction together (Epstein & Mac Iver, 1990).

Instructional and curricular practices that directly affect classroom instruction have also been slow to change. The instruction in the middle grades is predominantly didactic, and learners are most frequently passive (Clark & Clark, 1993; Epstein & Mac Iver, 1990; Mac Iver & Epstein, 1993). Teachers also put a strong emphasis on controlling student behavior and discipline (Brophy & Evertson, 1978). There is very little use, especially in urban middle schools, of instructional activities that require students to interact with one another during learning (Mac Iver & Epstein, 1993). The curricula focus primarily on teaching students facts and having the students memorize them. Students infrequently engage in solving problems, discussing answers, or debating alternatives (DiCintio & Stevens, 1997; Mergendoller, Marchman, Mitman, & Packer, 1988; Oakes et al., 1993).

Given this instructional environment, it should be no surprise that students in middle schools are less attentive in class and find schoolwork meaningless and often irrelevant. In middle schools where teachers use more passive instruction and require factual learning, there are lower rates of homework completion, more student boredom, and lower perceptions of school's usefulness (Mac Iver & Epstein, 1993). Similarly, it should be no surprise that in such learning environments, there are poorer attitudes toward school, lower motivation for learning, and declines in attendance (Carnegie Task Force on Education of Young Adolescents, 1989).

Middle School Mismatch

It has been suggested that typical middle school instruction is diametrically opposed to the cognitive and social development of students in early adolescence (Eccles & Midgley, 1989). The difficult transition documented in declining motivation, attendance, and achievement may be due to structural and instructional characteristics of middle schools that are unresponsive to the development and needs of the students.

Cognitive Mismatch

By the time students reach sixth grade, they have developed a broad knowledge of academic subjects. They have a foundation of skills in reading, math, and writing, and during the upper elementary years, they have begun to apply those skills to solving problems and completing more complex tasks in content areas. Their knowledge and their cognitive development enable early adolescents to think better about options, hypotheses, and alternative explanations. Students at this age are more capable of learning abstract concepts and engaging in the metacognitive activities of planning, monitoring, controlling, and evaluating their cognitive processes (Steinberg, 1993). Yet, as noted above, most instruction takes little advantage of the ability and knowledge of students during middle school. Studies have shown that after the transition to middle school, there are even fewer problem-solving and application activities and an even greater emphasis on factual learning than in the elementary grade just before middle school (DiCintio & Stevens, 1997; Feldlaufer, Midgley, & Eccles, 1988).

Social Mismatch

Not only is early adolescence a time of important cognitive changes, but it is also marked by significant social development. Students in early adolescence have more desire for control and decision making, skills that are typically promoted during the elementary years (Eccles et al, 1993). Early adolescent development is also typically marked by an increased push for independence, greater peer orientation, and self-consciousness. Yet middle school instruction typically offers students little engaging or interactive instruction and places a heavy emphasis on following directions. In spite of the increasing maturity and independence of adolescents, there is evidence middle school instruction offers less autonomy than the students typically had in elementary school the year before the transition (Midgley & Feldlaufer, 1987). There is also an increase in normative evaluation, emphasizing social comparison and competition for grades during middle school (Gullickson, 1985). All these characteristics of middle school instruction seem to run counter to the students' abilities and needs.

Middle School Literacy Instruction

Literacy instruction in middle school is typically departmentalized into two classes, reading and English. For the most part, these two classes are taught separately, with little connection between the reading instruction in reading class and the literature, language arts, and writing instruction in English class (Irvin, 1990). What is taught in reading is integrated even less with other content-area classes, in spite of the wide recognition in the reading research community that upper-elementary and middle-level reading instruction is more a matter of reading to learn than of learning to read (cf. Anderson, Hiebert, Scott, & Wilkinson, 1985; Davidson & Koppenhaver, 1988; Irvin, 1990). Investigations of instruction in both developmental reading classes and remedial reading classes found little use of reading strategy instruction, no integration of reading and writing, and few if any applications to expository reading (Irvin & Connors, 1989). These findings led the researchers to conclude that reading instruction in middle school lags severely behind reading research and best practice (Irvin, 1990).

The same criticism may be true for the "other half" of literacy instruction, taking place in English classes. Typically in middle school, writing instruction is the exclusive domain of English teachers (Irvin, 1990). However, there seems to be only a minor emphasis on writing in English classes. Fewer than half of the middle schools that responded to a survey used writing process instruction at least weekly in English class (Becker, 1990).

A Conceptual Basis for Change

The literature about middle school offers a plethora of ideas for restructuring the school and the classroom to best utilize students' skills and abilities and accommodate their needs. Yet, most are very general—for example, suggesting that instruction should be developmentally appropriate (or serve the needs of the age group), curricula should prepare students for society, and teachers should use a variety of instructional tasks. Advocating such changes is much like telling adolescents they should be good and thoughtful. What does it mean?

A more specific conception that more directly addresses classroom instruction and the nature of learning tasks is offered by Maehr and Anderman (1993) in the TARRGET model for school environment change. The name TARRGET is an acronym for the elements of the model, which describe the nature of the learning tasks that would promote learning and motivation in a more effective middle school: tasks, autonomy, resources, recognition, grouping, evaluation, and time. The TARRGET conception of instruction suggests the following:

Tasks. The tasks should be challenging, interesting, and meaningful.

Autonomy. Students should develop more autonomy and control of their learning.

Resources. School districts should invest resources in improving schools.

Recognition. Students need recognition of their academic success and improvement.

Grouping. Various kinds of instructional grouping and student learning groups should be used to promote learning.

Evaluation. Student evaluation should be based on mastery of the content, on improvement, and on effort.

Time. Larger blocks of time should be allocated to each class to permit more extended and meaningful learning activities.

The TARRGET model focuses on alterable variables in the classroom and school that can help implement many of the concepts of the middle school movement.

Changing Middle School Literacy Instruction

The issues raised here concerning instruction in middle schools and specifically in literacy have motivated an effort to reorganize the curricula, instruction, and organization of English and reading classes. The goal was to initiate elements of the middle school reform at the classroom level rather than as rhetoric at the school or district level.

Integration of Reading and English Classes

Typically, middle schools departmentalize students' instruction, causing students to get reading instruction from one teacher and English from another. However, reading and English clearly have a great deal of overlap and a continuity of skills. To take advantage of the natural connection, it is important to have the same teacher teach both reading and English in an integrative fashion. This practice will promote the interconnections between the content areas and increase the potential for students to transfer knowledge and skills they've learned. By having the same teacher teach both reading and English, it is also possible to give a double period of instruction in literacy (90 minutes rather than two 45-minute periods). A longer period provides the teachers with more flexibility to change their instruction and, most important, allows students to engage in extended instructional activities, like writing, that require more time. Finally, teaching reading and English in an interdisciplinary fashion can reduce the overall student-teacher ratio, one of the primary goals of the middle school movement. Since teachers teach two courses to each group of students, they end up teaching half as many students.

Literature as the Basis for Reading Instruction

A major change in curriculum was to give students meaningful and interesting experiences in literacy by providing reading instruction in the context of the literature students typically read in English class. Literature-based reading instruction was seen to motivate students more, through the intrinsic quality and interest of the reading material (e.g., Paris, Wasik, & Turner, 1991). The instruction also involved thematic units of two kinds: units about specific authors (e.g., O. Henry, Langston Hughes, William Saroyan) and units based on genres of writing (e.g., short stories, legends, science fiction). Thematic units seemed to increase students' interest, as well as providing a more organized approach to teaching literature, one that promoted students' transfer of what they learned in reading one work to the reading of another work in the same style.

Studying literature also makes writing a central issue in literacy instruction. The overarching theme is to have students read, understand, and interpret selections by famous authors. That work should then provide part of the foundation for writing activities focused on expressing their own experiences, ideas, and feelings. The writing of the famous authors becomes both the model and the motivation for students in the writing process.

Meaningful Follow-up Activities for Students

One of the most significant problems of traditional reading instruction is that the follow-up activities have little or no relationship to what the students have read. As a result, students often do not see them as important or meaningful (Beck, McKeown, McCaslin, & Burkes, 1979; Osborn, 1984). However, meaningful follow-up activities can further students' understanding of what they have read and challenge them to deeper understanding of literature. In this way students will improve their comprehension and will learn skills that they can apply to reading and comprehending other selections. The use of such activities will also increase the perceived relevance of follow-up activities, which may in turn increase the likelihood that students will be motivated to complete them.

Instruction on Text Comprehension Strategies

In the past 20 years, there has been a significant amount of research in reading comprehension instruction, resulting in the identification of specific comprehension strategies that are effective in improving students reading performance (Dole, Duffy, Roehler, & Pearson, 1991; Palincsar & Brown, 1984; Paris et al., 1991). Yet, it is surprising how little explicit instruction middle school students receive on comprehension strategies (Irvin, 1990). Strategy instruction gives the students the skills to better comprehend what they've read and interpret what the author intended. At the same time, strategies for identifying main ideas, summarizing, and clarifying are generalizable skills that students can use in other content areas.

During early adolescence students are making the transition from learning to read to reading to learn (Anderson & Armbruster, 1984; Anderson et al., 1985), and it is important for reading instruction to address this change by teaching students strategies for identifying, organizing, and learning information presented in text (Paris et al., 1991). To do this, it is necessary to give students instruction on study strategies in the context of reading instruction. It is also important for students to practice this process by reading factual material and using the strategies in context.

Focus Instruction in Language Arts on Writing

In the past fifteen years, the development of a writing-process approach to instruction in writing and language arts has changed the way we think about language arts instruction. However, most language arts teachers still spend little time on writing activities, instead spending most of their language arts time on language mechanics instruction and using grammar textbooks (Bridge & Hiebert, 1985). Language arts instruction should focus on writing as the primary goal and should integrate instruction in language mechanics and usage into improving students' writing. With this focus, the students' language arts instruction would become more meaningful and useful. Also, since the mechanics and usage instruction would be embedded in the context of writing, students would be more likely to remember and use the skills than they are when the skills are taught as an abstraction outside the context of students' own writing performance (Flowers & Hayes, 1980; Graves, 1978). At the same time, the writing emphasis is more intrinsically motivating to students because they can see the usefulness of the instruction to improving their expression of ideas. Also, students are motivated by enjoyment of the subject if they are encouraged to write about things that are meaningful to them and that they can share with their peers through writing (Flowers & Hayes, 1980; Graves, 1978).

Using Instructional Activities to Promote Learning and More Positive Peer Relations

Peer relationships take on critical importance to students during adolescence, and research suggests that a student's relations with his or her peers play an important role in the student's attachment to school (Parker & Asher, 1987). Furthermore, students who do not develop good peer relations are much more likely to drop out of school. Yet, during the middle grades, students often perceive less support at school and more negative peer relations, leading to less attachment to school (Seidman et al., 1994).

The TARRGET model suggests that changes in the classroom structure can promote both learning and peer relations in the classroom. Cooperative learning is an alternative classroom structure that has been shown to facilitate students' academic growth and promote positive peer relations and positive attitudes toward school (Johnson & Johnson, 1989; Slavin, 1990). In particular, the group goals used in cooperative learning give the students a reason to collaborate and share their ideas. As a result, the students develop a sense of interdependence, which promotes more positive relationships between the students. For one to succeed, all of the students in the group must succeed.

Cooperative classroom processes also cause a change in at least some of the evaluation structures in the classroom. Because in cooperative learning student recognition depends in part on the whole group's success at accomplishing a learning task, students develop task goals rather than performance goals (Nichols, 1994). Task goals are those in which the student focuses primarily on mastering the content and learning from the instructional task. The focus is thus on the intrinsic utility of learning. When students have performance goals, their main focus is on doing well in comparison with others, or looking good. They have a more competitive or extrinsic motivation for engaging in and completing instructional tasks. There are many benefits for students who adopt task goals. Typically, students with task goals pursue deeper understanding of the content (Meece, Blumenfeld, & Hoyle, 1988; Nolen, 1988) and are more likely to focus on effort as a means of attaining success (Pintrich & Schunk, 1996). Students with this kind of motivation are more likely to persevere at learning tasks, and they have a more positive attitude toward school (Maehr & Anderman, 1993).

The application of the theoretical notions in the TARRGET model is obviously no simple task. The model approaches school restructuring for middle-level students in a multifaceted fashion. To some degree, the model's developers suggest that the only way to really achieve any of the goals of the model is to implement all of the components (Maehr & Anderman, 1993). In an attempt to create a more appropriate instructional model for middle school literacy instruction, Stevens and a colleague took on the challenge of the multifaceted approach and redesigned reading and English classes for two urban middle schools, calling the program Student Team Reading and Writing (Stevens & Durkin, 1992).

Student Team Reading and Writing

The Student Team Reading and Writing (STRW) program used cooperative learning as the basis for restructuring reading and language arts instruction in middle school. The goal was to take advantage of both the academic and the social benefits of having students engage in meaningful dialogue about instructional tasks (e.g., Slavin, 1990; Stevens, 1994). For cooperative learning to have this kind of impact, it must have a structure that promotes interdependence among the students as well as individual accountability for each student. Well-structured cooperative learning includes both group goals and individual accountability, and these two factors work together to promote both academic and social outcomes. Group goals give students a reason to cooperate or share their ideas. Individual accountability makes all students responsible for learning and reduces the potential for students to rely on others in the group to do the work, a tendency known as the "free-rider effect" (Slavin, 1990). The combination of the two elements creates a structure that fosters positive interdependence, in which students rely on and help one another, which in turn increases achievement and productivity and improves attitudes toward others (Deutsch, 1949; Johnson & Johnson, 1989).

Cooperative learning also makes learning processes more active, as students discuss their learning tasks with one another. In this kind of academic dialogue, students provide one another with models of the complex cognitive processes that are typical of the tasks involved in this curricular realignment. As students interact, they internalize the strategies and processes needed to master the tasks (Vygotsky, 1978). The cooperative dialogue also encourages students to give one another elaborative explanations, which help them generate a deeper understanding of what has been taught (Brown & Palincsar, 1989; Webb, 1985). At the same time, students provide feedback to one another on the processes they are learning or applying in the instructional tasks. This is particularly important in the case of complex cognitive tasks, since much of students' learning occurs when they receive guidance and feedback from either the teacher or peers (Rosenshine & Meister, 1997).

Finally, cooperative learning builds students' responsibility for their own learning and gives them a greater sense of input into or control of their education (Johnson & Johnson, 1989; Johnson, Johnson, & Holubec, 1991). Cooperative learning structures encourage all students to succeed by collaborating to achieve a goal through effort and mastery, rather than by competing. The structure gives all students an opportunity to participate and feel successful, which in turn has a positive effect on students' perceived competence and self-efficacy (Schunk, 1989).

Teams

The STRW students were assigned to teams of mixed abilities. Within the teams, each student was assigned a partner. Partners worked together to complete follow-up activities. Students' scores on the individual-accountability activities (e.g., quizzes) contributed to a team score. Teams were recognized for their success in attaining prespecified levels of performance on the accountability measures, determined by the average score of each team's members. Research on cooperative learning has found that this sort of recognition, based on the individual performance of all of the team members, develops interdependence among team members and is typically related to positive effects on students' academic performance (Slavin, 1983, 1990).

Integration of Reading and English Classes

Literacy instruction in a departmentalized middle school is the domain of two courses: reading and English. To adequately integrate literacy instruction into a meaningful whole and to reduce the replication of instruction across the two subjects, the reading and English classes were combined in a double period taught by one teacher. This created a number of advantages while still meeting the district's required class time in both reading and English. First, the double period created the potential for teachers to use time more flexibly, allowing them to engage in longer, projectlike instructional tasks that required more than the typical 45 minute period. For example, teachers were able to implement integrated reading and writing tasks in which students read and analyzed a writing genre or writer's style and then attempted to write in that genre or style. Second, since one teacher was teaching reading, writing, and language arts, the double period greatly facilitated the meaningful integration of the three areas. As in the example just given, a teacher could easily and seamlessly move from a reading activity to a writing activity. Third, the combining of the classes reduced the duplication of instruction in the two subjects, an effect teachers noticed very quickly. Things like vocabulary development and some reading-for-understanding activities had previously been taught in both courses. When the courses were combined, the lack of duplication immediately permitted more efficient time use.

Reading Instruction

The reading instruction part of the Student Team Reading and Writing program consisted of three principal elements: literature-related activities, direct instruction in reading comprehension and study strategies, and selection-related writing. In all of these activities, students worked in heterogeneous learning teams. All activities followed a regular cycle, which involved teacher presentation, team practice, independent practice, peer checking, additional practice, and individual accountability.

Literature-related activities. The students used an American literature anthology as the source of the reading selections. The selections were introduced and discussed in teacher-led instruction. Teachers set the purpose for reading, introduced new vocabulary, reviewed old vocabulary, discussed the selection after students had read it, and so forth. After the students read the literature selection, they completed a series of follow-up activities that were specifically related to what they had read. The activities included the following:

Partner reading. Students read the selection silently and then read it orally with their partners. During oral reading, the students took turns reading, alternating paragraphs. The listener followed along and corrected any errors the reader made. This method of repeated reading gives students a great deal of practice reading orally and has been found to contribute significantly to students' reading fluency (Samuels, 1979).

Comprehension of the selection. The students were given written activities, called Treasure Hunts, that focused on comprehension of the structure and content of the literature selection. Halfway through the selection, the students stopped reading to do their Treasure Hunts. They discussed and wrote answers to questions. In their answers, they described the characters, setting, and problem in the story and predicted how the problem in the story might be resolved. They might also discuss questions related to the author's purpose or style and the interpretation of figurative language or literary techniques used. Research in reading comprehension has found that understanding story structures is important for students' comprehension (Fitzgerald & Spiegel, 1983; Short & Ryan, 1982; Stein & Glenn, 1979) and that discussing predictions and summaries of stories can increase students' comprehension (Palincsar & Brown, 1984).

Word mastery activities. Students were given a list of new or difficult words that were related to the selection. The word mastery activities focused on the students' ability to decode and understand the meaning of the new words.

Decoding practice involved rapid review of the words with a partner so that each student developed automatic decoding of the new words. Automaticity of vocabulary is important for preventing the comprehension problems that typically occur when students have not mastered the vocabulary relevant to the content they are reading (Perfetti, 1985; Rosenshine & Stevens, 1986). The students learned the meaning of the new words through practice in writing *meaningful sentences* with the vocabulary. A meaningful sentence is one that indicates what the word means in the context of the sentence (i.e., "The octopus wrapped his eight long legs around the undersea diver," not "I saw an octopus").

Summarizing the main points of the selection. After reading and discussing the selection, students summarized the main points of the story to their partners. These summaries were prompted by the partner, who asked specific questions about important elements or episodes in the selection. The partner then checked the summary for completeness and adequacy of detail. In previous research, having students summarize in their own words what they read had been found to be a very effective way to enhance the students' comprehension and retention of the material (Doctorow, Wittrock, & Marks, 1978; Weinstein, 1982).

Selection-related writing. For each selection, the students were given an open-ended writing assignment on a topic related to the selection. For example, the students might be asked to use their predictions from the Treasure Hunt to write a new end to the selection, or they might be asked to compare and contrast characters from the selection or from different selections. In writing their responses to the prompt, students used a modified writing process, in which they discussed their ideas with their partners, drafted a version of the response, made revisions based on their partners' feedback, edited their writing, and created a final copy. Part of the purpose of the writing activity was to further students' comprehension and understanding of the selection by having them write an extended response to the story or a part of the story (Wittrock, 1986). The activity also helped to strengthen the connection between reading literature and writing by having students transfer the skills and strategies that they learned in writing to constructing good responses for the reading activities.

Instruction on reading comprehension and study strategies.   Students regularly received direct instruction on reading comprehension strategies and study strategies. The instruction involved teaching students how to use a given strategy and how to check and monitor strategy use, as well as teaching the motivation for using the strategy (Paris, Cross, & Lipson, 1984). The goal was to use a cognitive-apprenticeship method of instruction to develop students' abilities to perform complex tasks with adequate support and then to gradually reduce the support as the students took on more responsibility for performing the task (Collins, Brown, & Newman, 1989). The instruction began with the teacher's explanation of the importance of the strategy for solving problems students might encounter in comprehending text or learning information presented in text. The teacher described in detail how to use the strategy and modeled its use with a brief passage that was provided. Then the teacher guided the students through a series of practice activities in which they tried to use the strategy. The teacher provided prompts and reminded the students of the steps as they worked through the initial practice. As students improved, teachers would reduce their support, or scaffolds, as students continued their guided practice. When students exhibited some proficiency in the new strategy, the teacher would then give them independent practice, in which they would work individually and discuss their answers with their peers. Thus, the peers provided an additional level of support as students became increasingly independent in their use of the strategy.

The reading comprehension strategies were based on a large body of research that has shown that students' reading comprehension can be significantly improved through instruction and practice in specific reading comprehension strategies, such as strategies for identifying main ideas, drawing conclusions, and interpreting figurative language (e.g., Palincsar & Brown, 1984; Paris, Lipson, & Wixson, 1983; Stevens, 1988). The study strategies helped students locate, organize, and retain important information presented in text. The goal of strategy instruction was to prepare students to make the transition from learning to read to reading to learn. Beginning in middle school, in most of students' reading experiences in school, a primary focus is on retaining specific information presented in text, typically content-area text. Teaching students strategies for locating, organizing, and remembering information from text can greatly increase their ability to learn the content because they become actively engaged in understanding and organizing the information they're reading (Anderson & Armbruster, 1984; Baker & Brown, 1984). Active learning and cognitive organization enhance students' ability to remember the important information they have read.

Writing Instruction

The writing part of the program combined a writing-process approach with language arts instruction. The goal of the writing-process approach was to make writing the focus of language arts instruction and to have instruction in grammar, language expression, and language mechanics relate to students writing. With that approach, grammar, expression, and mechanics become more meaningful to students because the skills can be understood in the context of the concrete activity of writing. Also, because the learning of the skills is contextualized, the skills are more likely to be retained. Students were encouraged to use the new skills actively in their writing, further increasing their processing of the information and improving their understanding of the skills.

The writing process. The students were taught to use a writing-process approach when they wrote. The process involved planning, drafting, revising, editing, and making a final draft. One important characteristic of this approach was that it involved an iterative process of writing, as opposed to the "one-shot" writing that is typical of writing instruction (Bridge & Hiebert, 1985; Graves, 1978). A process approach to writing is more realistic because good writing is typically the result of writing and rewriting a composition. Classroom research has shown that using process writing can lead to great improvement in students' writing performance (Raphael, Englert, & Kirschner, 1986; Stevens, Madden, Slavin, & Farnish, 1987; Stevens & Slavin, 1995).

Initially, the teacher provided instruction on how to complete each step of the process. The steps were modeled, and the students actively engaged in each step. The students were also taught how to work with their peers on each of the steps as a way of integrating cooperative-learning processes with the writing process.

Planning. The student determined what the topic of the writing would be, often within constraints specified by the teacher (e.g., "Write a short story in the style of O. Henry"). Peers discussed their topics and their plans for developing the topics in their writing. Students gave their partners feedback about the aspects they liked and the points they wanted clarified or expanded.

Drafting. After devising a plan, the student wrote a first draft of the composition. The goal of the first draft was to get the ideas on paper. Students were taught to focus on expressing their ideas and presenting them in a logical, cohesive sequence. Also, students were specifically taught to ignore spelling and mechanics at this step in the process, as those concerns were addressed separately.

Revision. Once the first draft of the composition was complete, the student read the writing to a peer to get feedback on the clarity and organization of the ideas in the draft. Again students were taught to give one another meaningful feedback, telling what they liked and what they wanted to know more about. This feedback gave the writer valuable information about how an audience responded to and understood what was written. The student could then use the feedback to revise the writing and make it better or more easily understood.

Editing. After revising the content, the writer gave the composition to a peer for editing. During editing, students focused on giving feedback on mechanics and spelling. They were given an editing checklist to help them focus on specific skills as they edited another student's work. Often they focused on specific mechanics skills that they had recently mastered during their language arts lessons (described in a later subsection). The writer used the feedback to correct errors and improve the quality of the composition. Before the final draft, the teacher also read the paper, in the role of a copy editor, to correct all of the errors so that the student's final draft would be in finished form.

Final draft. The final draft was complete when the author had finished writing the composition in its final form, including all of the corrections. The final step was for the author to share the composition with the audience, the class.

Writing concept lessons.   Once students learned to use all of the steps in the writing process, the teacher provided instruction on and models of styles and techniques of writing. The lessons included such topics as improving descriptions, organizing ideas, and getting the audience's attention. There were also lessons on specific styles of writing—for example, explanatory writing, persuasive writing, and writing personal and business letters. The STRW program provided a set of writing concept lessons, but teachers were also encouraged to develop their own lessons based on students' needs and interests. Often teachers used authors whose work the class was reading in the literature anthology as models for specific types of writing. An advantage of this instructional strategy was that it further strengthened the connections between reading and writing.

Integrated language arts lessons.   Teachers periodically taught lessons on language mechanics and language usage from a set of materials provided by the STRW program. Teachers were told to select language arts lessons that met the needs they identified in their evaluations of their students' writing. The goal of the lessons was to give students skills that would help improve their writing. Each lesson included specific writing-related activities, to increase the likelihood that students would transfer what they learned to their own writing. Students were also taught how to edit for errors relevant to the newly acquired skill. In subsequent writing-process activities, the new language mechanics skills were added to the editing checklist so that students would apply what they had learned to writing and editing their own work and to editing the writing of their classmates.

Research on the Student Team Reading and Writing Model

The STRW model has been successfully used in urban middle schools to restructure literacy instruction (Stevens & Durkin, 1992). Two large urban middle schools, each with nearly 900 students, implemented the STRW model in all of their reading and English classes (encompassing sixth through eighth grades). The school population was predominantly minority students (approximately 80 percent), and about two-thirds of the students were from low-income families.

Teacher training.   The teachers in the STRW schools were trained in the components and processes of the model for a week during the summer. The training consisted of an explanation of the processes and the rationale behind them and a simulation of the components of the program. Teachers were given a detailed manual that described each of the components. Before the beginning of the school year, the teachers were given all of the American literature books and support materials they needed to implement STRW.

During the first three months of implementation, the project staff observed the teachers' use of the program and gave the teachers feedback to help them improve their implementation. The goal of the observations was to coach the teachers to become proficient in these new instructional models. The project staff also met with the teachers during and after school, often attending meetings of the reading and language arts department. At these meetings teachers' questions and problems were discussed to resolve any problems teachers were having and to use their feedback to improve the programs. As the teachers became more proficient with STRW, the coaching and meetings decreased until the project staff were simply monitoring the teachers' implementation periodically. The department heads at both schools also supported the implementation of the program by becoming experts in the model so that they could act as local information resources for teachers.

Contrast schools.   Three middle schools were used as contrasts for the STRW schools in evaluating the model. The schools matched the STRW schools in demographics (socioeconomic status and racial makeup) and had slightly higher initial achievement on standardized tests than did the STRW schools. The literacy instruction in the contrast schools was fairly traditional, much like that described earlier in this chapter. The students were taught by different teachers in reading and English. The reading teachers used a basal reading series and related adjunct materials provided with the basal (e.g., workbooks and worksheets). The English teachers used a literature anthology for the literature component and a grammar book for the language arts portion of their class. The English teachers did use a writing-process approach to writing instruction, but it was not integrated with the literature they were reading. Most of the classes were fairly teacher-centered, with the teachers often using a transmission model of instruction. The comparison teachers did occasionally use group activities or, sometimes, cooperative learning, but not on a daily basis.

Achievement outcomes.   At the end of a year of using STRW, students had significantly higher achievement in reading vocabulary, reading comprehension, and language expression, as measured by the California Achievement Test. There were no significant differences on language mechanics. The fact that these results were found on standardized achievement tests strengthens the case for the effectiveness of the STRW model. Typically, achievement tests are designed to be stable and cover a breadth of content that is not specifically related to the instruction and content in the intervention. Furthermore, the magnitudes of the significant differences were impressive, again given that they were attained on a standardized test. Students in STRW scored one-third of a standard deviation higher in reading vocabulary and language expression, and one-quarter of a standard deviation higher in reading comprehension.

Attitudinal and social outcomes.   The students in the STRW program also showed significantly more positive attitudes toward reading and writing than did their peers in more traditional classes. They indicated that they liked reading and writing more, and that they felt more competent in writing. There was no significant difference in students' feelings of competence in reading, although students in STRW had positive feelings about their reading competence. Finally, students in STRW indicated significantly better peer relations on a sociometric measure that asked them to list their friends in the class. The students listed significantly more friends than did their peers in the contrast schools.

Conclusions

This study suggests that a multifaceted approach to middle school literacy, an approach like the Student Team Reading and Writing program, can produce significant improvement in students' achievement, attitudes toward the subjects, and peer relations. The model was in many ways an embodiment of the TARRGET model for restructuring middle schools. It attempted to take a large-scale approach to restructuring, including altering course schedules, lengths of periods, curricula, classroom organization, instructional processes, and student evaluation.

Reading instruction. The model used state-of-the-art instructional strategies for the teaching of reading and writing, applying much of what has been learned in both reading research and writing research over the past 20 years. At the very least, this model provides an important translation of that research to middle school, a translation that is long overdue (Irvin, 1990). One important component of this application of the research was to make a transition in middle school reading instruction from a learning-to-read focus to more of a reading-to-learn focus. The comprehension-strategy and study-strategy instruction were aimed at helping students understand and analyze the reading material and know how to search the text for information and organize that information for later use. It is our belief that this transition is an important goal for middle school reading instruction, to prepare students for the demands they will face in content area reading, which will begin to predominate in their reading activities in school.

Language arts instruction. Clearly an emphasis on writing in language arts instruction provides many advantages with few or no disadvantages. Getting students actively engaged in writing and providing them with direct instruction and guided practice in writing can result in their becoming better at writing. This approach may sound simplistic, but not so long ago writing was seen as a skill that was not necessarily teachable (Young, 1978). Perhaps more important than students' increased writing performance, this study suggests that students' perceptions about themselves as writers also changed; they felt more competent at writing as a result of the instruction and practice. It is also important to note that in spite of the emphasis on writing, students in STRW did not lose ground on mechanics skills in comparison with their peers. This seems to suggest that learning mechanics in the framework of writing, rather than through skill lessons in a grammar book, provides a better alternative by contextualizing the knowledge.

Integration of reading and writing. There are no data that directly support the integration of the two courses into one, but feedback from some of the teachers seemed to confirm its utility. Although some of the teachers initially remarked on the additional work required to prepare two subjects rather than one, they offered opinions that the effort seemed to be worthwhile and to make sense. By the latter half of the year, the teachers were describing the benefits of the integration for helping students see the connections between reading the literature and writing.

Teachers began to teach in ways that made reading and writing seamless and often took advantage of the authors and genres in the literature book as models for their writing lessons.

Classroom processes.   The use of cooperative-learning processes seemed to provide academic, social, and attitudinal advantages in these middle school classes. By having students interact on academic tasks, the cooperative-learning processes took advantage of the increasing peer orientation of early adolescence and used it as a strength. Students were used to help and encourage one another and, in essence, became an instructional resource. This practice created the positive peer relations found on the sociometric measures, as students became more familiar with and friendlier toward their classmates. Since the students were also working on common goals that required all of the team members to succeed for any of them to succeed, students became interested in and supportive of one another's academic success. This kind of supportive learning environment may have led to the improved attitudes toward school—school is a nicer place when someone cares that you succeed.

The cooperative-learning processes also provide a structured way for students to become actively engaged in learning without creating management problems for the teacher. Teachers most frequently encounter management problems when students are working on activities not directly controlled or managed by the teacher (Rosenshine & Stevens, 1986). For example, when students engage in tasks like reading and answering questions about what they've read, or in extended writing activities, they are more likely to get off task. Yet, these are very important learning activities because they often require learners to become actively engaged and to use what they have learned. Students typically get off task because they do not know what to do, they need feedback on what they've done, or they are not motivated to engage in the task. Cooperative learning reduces these problems because students explain to each other what to do, give each other feedback, and encourage each other to complete the work and do it well. In this way, students can help create and maintain a classroom climate that promotes learning.

Middle school instruction.   Perhaps the most perplexing thing about the middle school literature is that instruction seems to focus on lower-level tasks requiring factual learning and memorization, at the expense of problem solving and discussion of answers. The transition to higher grades (e.g., from fifth to sixth) would be expected to coincide with a similar move to higher-level tasks that require more thinking, analysis, and weighing of alternatives, yet the literature documents the opposite (DiCintio & Stevens, 1997; Feldlaufer et al., 1988; Mergendoller et al., 1988; Oakes et al., 1993). Although some have suggested this is a developmental mismatch (Eccles & Midgley, 1989), to us the problem seems more fundamental. As students become older and gain more knowledge and skills in academic subjects, they should be challenged to use the skills and knowledge in increasingly complex ways. Any shift backward on this continuum seems counterproductive, no matter what the age of the child. Fourth-grade instruction should be more challenging and more complex than third-grade instruction, as eleventh grade should be more challenging than tenth, and sixth more challenging than fifth. Learning is more than accumulating facts, no matter what a child's age, and instruction that is limited to that is necessarily flawed.

Future Research

Middle school instruction is certainly a fertile area for programmatic research. There are survey studies and observational studies indicating that improvements can be made. Similarly, rhetoric abounds about what middle schools should be. Yet the question remains: What is the most effective instruction for early adolescents in middle school?

In the area of literacy instruction, much the same is true. Compared with elementary-level literacy instruction, there is a dearth of systematic classroom research at the middle level. There is a need for more research like that described here, attempting to integrate the literacy instruction that typically occurs in reading and English classes. Similarly, there is a need to apply the principles and practices that have been found effective in elementary reading and writing instruction to teaching middle level students. In applying those principles, we need to remember that problem solving and complex tasks are needed in this content to challenge learners at all age levels.

Finally, there is a need to go beyond the simple integration of reading and English described in this chapter to broader conceptions of both reading and writing. For most students middle school is a critical time in the development of reading for information. Yet there is typically little integration of reading and information-gathering skills in content-laden courses like science and social studies. The research in reading of content-area texts needs to move beyond simply the teaching of study strategies into more systematic integration of reading instruction into the content areas. Furthermore, writing is another domain that transcends content areas, and research should be done to integrate writing across content-area instruction. More research needs to focus on teaching students how to develop the factual or technical writing skills typically used in science and social studies, which are the most commonly used writing skills beyond middle school. The transition to middle school is a critical passage into more content specialization, and research is needed on developing literacy skills specifically to meet those needs.

References

Anderson, T. H., & Armbruster, B. B. (1984). Studying. In P. D. Pearson (Ed.), *Handbook of reading research* (pp. 657–680). New York: Longman.

Anderson, R. C., Hiebert, E. H., Scott, J. A., & Wilkinson, I. (1985). *Becoming a nation of readers*. Washington, DC: National Institute of Education.

Baker, L., & Brown, A. L. (1984). Metacognitive skills in reading. In P. D. Pearson, R. Barr, M. Kamil, & P. Mosenthal (Eds.), *Handbook of reading research* (pp. 353–394). New York: Longman.

Beck, I., McKeown, M., McCaslin, E., & Burkes, A. (1979). *Instructional dimensions that may affect reading comprehension: Examples from two commercial reading programs* (Technical Report No. 1979/20). Pittsburgh, PA: University of Pittsburgh, Learning Research and Development Center.

Becker, H. J. (1990). Curriculum and instruction in middle grade schools. *Phi Delta Kappan, 71,* 450–457.

Bridge, C., & Hiebert, E. (1985). A comparison of classroom writing practices, teachers' perceptions of their writing instruction, and textbook recommendations on writing practices. *Elementary School Journal, 85,* 155–172.

Brophy, J., & Evertson, C. (1978). Context variables in teaching. *Educational Psychologist, 12,* 310–316.

Brown, A. L., & Palincsar, A. S. (1989). Guided, cooperative learning and individual knowledge acquisition. In L. Resnick (Ed.), *Knowing, learning, and instruction: Essays in honor of Robert Glaser* (pp. 393–451). Hillsdale, NJ: Erlbaum.

Carnegie Task Force on Education of Young Adolescents. (1989). *Turning points: Preparing American youth for the 21st century.* New York: Carnegie Corporation.

Clark, S. N., & Clark, D. C. (1993). Middle level school reform: The rhetoric and the reality. *Elementary School Journal, 93,* 447–460.

Collins, A., Brown, J. S., & Newman, S. E. (1989). Cognitive apprenticeship: Teaching the crafts of reading, writing, and mathematics. In L. Resnick (Ed.), *Knowing, learning, and instruction: Essays in honor of Robert Glaser* (pp. 453–494). Hillsdale, NJ: Erlbaum.

Davidson, E. S., & Benjamin, L. T. (1987). A history of the child study movement in America. In J. Glover & R. Ronning (Eds.), *Historical foundations of educational psychology.* New York: Plenum.

Davidson, J., & Koppenhaver, D. (1988). *Adolescent literacy: What works and why.* New York: Garland.

Deutsch, M. (1949). An experimental study of the effects of cooperation and competition upon group processes. *Human Relations, 2,* 199–231.

DiCintio, M. J., & Stevens, R. J. (1997). Student motivation and cognitive complexity of mathematics instruction in six middle grades classrooms. *Research on Middle Level Education Quarterly, 20,* 27–42.

Doctorow, M., Wittrock, M., & Marks, C. (1978). Generative processes in reading comprehension. *Journal of Educational Psychology, 70,* 109–118.

Dole, J. A., Duffy, G. G., Roehler, L. R., & Pearson, P. D. (1991). Moving from the old to the new: Research on reading comprehension instruction. *Review of Educational Research, 61,* 239–264.

Eccles, J. S., & Midgley, C. (1989). Stage-environment fit: Developmentally appropriate classrooms for young adolescents. In C. Ames & R. Ames (Eds.), *Research on motivation in education: Volume 3. Goals and cognitions* (pp. 139–186). New York: Academic Press.

Eccles, J. S., Wigfield, A., Midgley, C., Reuman, D., Mac Iver, D., & Feldlaufer, H. (1993). Negative effects of traditional middle schools on students' motivation. *Elementary School Journal, 93,* 553–574.

Eichhorn, D. H. (1966). *The middle school.* New York: Center for Research in Education. Reprinted jointly by the National Association of Secondary School Principals and the National Middle School Association in 1988.

Ekstrom, R., Goertz, M., Pollack, J., & Rock, D. (1987). Who drops out of high school and why? Findings from a national study. In G. Natriello (Ed.), *School dropouts: Patterns and policies* (pp. 52–69). New York: Teachers College Press.

Epstein, J. L., & Mac Iver, D. J. (1990). *Education in the middle grades: National practices and trends.* Columbus, OH: National Middle School Association.

Feldlaufer, H., Midgley, C., & Eccles, J. S., (1988). Student, teacher, and observer perceptions of the classroom environment before and after the transition to junior high school. *Journal of Early Adolescence, 8,* 133–156.

Fitzgerald, J., & Spiegel, D. (1983). Enhancing children's reading comprehension through instruction in narrative structures. *Journal of Reading Behavior, 14,* 1–18.

Flowers, L., & Hayes, J. (1980). The dynamics of composing: Making plans and juggling constraints. In L. Gregg and E. Steinberg (Eds.), *Cognitive processes in writing* (pp. 31–50). Hillsdale, NJ: Erlbaum.

George P. S., & Alexander, W. M. (1993) *The exemplary middle school.* New York: Harcourt Brace Jovanovich.

Gottfredson, G. (1987). American education: American delinquency. *Today's Delinquent, 6,* 5–70.

Graves, D. (1978). *Balance the basics: Let them write.* New York: Ford Foundation.

Gullickson, A. R. (1985). Student evaluation techniques and their relationship to grade and curriculum. *Journal of Educational Research, 79,* 96–100.

Irvin, J. L. (1990). *Reading and the middle school student: Strategies to enhance literacy.* Needham Heights, MA: Allyn & Bacon.

Irvin, J. L., & Connors, N. A. (1989). Reading instruction in middle level schools: Results from a U.S. survey. *Journal of Reading, 32,* 306–311.

Jackson, A. (1990). From knowledge to practice: Implementation of the recommendations of *Turning points. Middle School Journal, 21,* 1–3.

Johnson, D., & Johnson, R. (1989). *Cooperation and competition: Theory and research.* Edina, MN: Interaction Books.

Johnson, D., Johnson, R., & Holubec, E. (1991). *Cooperation in the classroom.* Edina, MN: Interaction Books.

Lounsbury, J. H. (1990). Middle level education: Perspectives, problems, and prospects. *Educational Horizons, 68,* 63–68.

Lounsbury, J. H. (1991). *As I see it.* Columbus, OH: National Middle School Association.

Mac Iver, D. J., & Epstein, J. L. (1993). Middle grades research: Not yet mature, but no longer a child. *Elementary School Journal, 93,* 519–534.

Maehr, M. L., & Anderman, E. M. (1993). Reinventing the middle schools for early adolescents: Emphasizing task goals. *Elementary School Journal, 93,* 593–610.

McDill, E., Natriello, G., & Pallas, A. (1985). Raising standards and retaining students: The impact of reform recommendations on dropouts. *Review of Educational Research, 55,* 415–433

Meece, J. L., Blumenfeld, P. C., & Hoyle, R. H. (1988). Students' goal orientation and cognitive engagement in classroom activities. *Journal of Educational Psychology, 80,* 514–523.

Mergendoller, J. R., Marchman, V. A., Mitman, A. L., & Packer, M. J. (1988). Task demands and accountability in middle-grade science classes. *Elementary School Journal, 88,* 251–265.

Midgley, C., & Feldlaufer, H. (1987). Students and teachers' decision-making fit before and after the transition to junior high school. *Journal of Early Adolescence, 7,* 225–241

Nichols, J. D. (1994). Cooperative learning and student motivation. *Contemporary Educational Psychology, 19,* 167–178.

Nolen, S. (1988). Reasons for studying: Motivational orientation and study strategies. *Cognition and instruction, 5,* 269–287.

Oakes, J., Quartz, K. H., Gong, J., Guiton, G., & Lipton, M. (1993). Creating middle schools: Technical, normative, and political considerations. *Elementary School Journal, 93,* 461–480.

Osborn, J. (1984). The purposes, uses, and contents of workbooks and some guidelines for publishers. In R. Anderson, J. Osborn, & R. Tierney (Eds.), *Learning to read in American schools* (pp. 45–112). Hillsdale, NJ: Erlbaum.

Palincsar, A. S., & Brown, A. L. (1984). Reciprocal teaching of comprehension-fostering and monitoring activities. *Cognition and Instruction, 1,* 117–175.

Paris, S., Cross D., & Lipson, M. (1984). Informed strategy for learning: A program to improve children's reading awareness and comprehension. *Journal of Educational Psychology, 76,* 1239–1252.

Paris, S. G., Lipson, M. Y., & Wixson, K. K. (1983). Becoming a strategic reader. *Contemporary Educational Psychology, 8,* 293–316.

Paris, S., Wasik, B., & Turner, J. (1991). The development of strategic readers. In R. Barr, M. Kamil, P. Mosenthal, & P. D. Pearson (Eds.), *Handbook of reading research* (Vol. 2, pp. 609–640). New York: Longman.

Parker, J. G., & Asher, S. R. (1987). Peer relations and later personal adjustment: Are low-accepted children at risk? *Psychological Bulletin, 102,* 357–389.

Perfetti, C. (1985). *Reading ability.* New York: Oxford University Press.

Pintrich, P. R., & Schunk, D. H. (1996). *Motivation in education: Theory, research, and applications.* Upper Saddle River, NJ: Prentice Hall.

Raphael, T., Englert, C., & Kirschner, B. (1986, April). *The impact of text structure instruction within a process writing orientation on fifth- and sixth-grade students' comprehension and production of expository text.* Paper presented at the annual meeting of the American Educational Research Association, San Francisco.

Rosenshine, B., & Meister, C. (1997). Cognitive strategy research in reading. In S. A. Stahl & D. A. Hayes (Eds.), *Instructional models in reading* (pp. 85–107). Hillsdale, NJ: Erlbaum.

Rosenshine, B., & Stevens, R. (1986). Teaching functions. In M. Wittrock (Ed.), *Handbook of research on teaching* (pp. 376–391). New York: Macmillan.

Samuels, J. (1979). The method of repeated readings. *The Reading Teacher, 32,* 403–408.

Schunk, D. H. (1989). Social cognitive theory and self-regulated learning. In B. Zimmerman & D. H. Schunk (Eds.), *Self-regulated learning and academic achievement: Theory, research and practice* (pp. 83–110). New York: Springer Verlag.

Seidman, E., Allen, L., Aber, J. L., Mitchell, C., & Feinman, J. (1994). The impact of school transition in early adolescence on the self-system and perceived social context of poor urban youth. *Child Development, 65,* 507–522.

Short, E., & Ryan, E. (1982, April). *Remediating poor readers' comprehension failures with a story grammar strategy.* Paper presented at the annual meeting of the American Educational Research Association, New York.

Slavin, R. (1983). *Cooperative learning.* New York: Longman.

Slavin, R. (1990). *Cooperative learning: Theory, research, and practice.* Upper Saddle River, NJ: Prentice Hall.

Stein, N., & Glenn, C. (1979). An analysis of story comprehension in elementary school children. In R. Freedle (Ed.), *New directions in discourse processing* (Vol. 2, pp. 53–120). Norwood, NJ: Ablex.

Steinberg, L. (1993). *Adolescence.* New York: McGraw-Hill.

Stevens, R. J. (1988). Effects of strategy training on the identification of the main idea of expository passages. *Journal of Educational Psychology, 80,* 21–26.

Stevens, R. J. (1994). Cooperative learning and literacy instruction. In N. Ellsworth, C. Hedley, & A. Baratta (Eds.), *Literacy: A redefinition.* Hillsdale, NJ: Erlbaum.

Stevens, R. J., & Durkin, S. (1992). *Student Team Reading and Writing: A cooperative learning approach to middle school literacy instruction* (technical report). Baltimore: Johns Hopkins University, Center for Research on Effective Schooling for Disadvantaged Students.

Stevens, R. J., Madden, N., Slavin, R. E., & Farnish, A. (1987). Cooperative Integrated Reading and Composition: Two field experiments. *Reading Research Quarterly, 22,* 433–453.

Stevens, R. J., & Slavin, R. E. (1995). The Cooperative Elementary School: Effects on students' achievement, attitudes, and social relations. *American Educational Research Journal, 32,* 321–351.

Vygotsky, L. S. (1978). *Mind in society: The development of higher psychological processes.* Cambridge, MA: Harvard University Press.

Webb, N. (1985). Student interaction and learning in small groups: A research summary. In R. Slavin, S. Sharan, R. Hertz-Lazarowitz, C. Webb, & R. Schmuck (Eds.), *Learning to cooperate, cooperating to learn* (pp. 147–172). New York: Plenum.

Weinstein, C. (1982). Training students to use elaboration learning strategies. *Contemporary Educational Psychology, 7,* 301–311.

Wittrock, M. C. (1986). Students' thought processes. In M. Wittrock (Ed.) *Handbook of research on teaching* (pp. 297–314). New York: Macmillan.

Young, R. (1978). Paradigms and problems: Needed research in rhetorical invention. In C. Cooper & L. Odell (Eds.), *Research in composing*. Urbana, IL: National Council of Teachers of English.

Designing and Delivering Effective Mathematics Instruction

Marcy Stein

University of Washington, Tacoma

Douglas Carnine

University of Oregon

Mathematics instruction in American schools and students' mathematics achievement are often central to discussions about the efficacy of our educational system. The media frequently report that the business community, the government, and the general public have expressed increased concern for the mathematics performance of students in the United States (Corwin, 1997; Toch, 1996). Concern that students are not being prepared to compete in a global economy or are underprepared to join a technological workforce has been fueled by data gathered in both international and national studies of mathematics achievement. For example, the researchers who conducted the first large-scale international comparison of mathematics achievement (Husen, 1967) found that by the end of high school, American students lagged significantly behind their same-age peers from other industrialized nations. More recent international studies examining mathematics achievement have found similar results (U.S. National Research Center, 1996). Stevenson and his colleagues reported that as early as first grade, American students perform behind students from Taiwan, Japan, and mainland China (Stevenson et al., 1990; Stevenson, Chen, & Lee, 1993; Stevenson, Lee, & Stigler, 1986).

Moreover, the gap appears to widen by fifth grade and widen even more by the eleventh grade (Stevenson et al., 1993).

National studies of mathematics achievement paint a similar picture of poor performance by American students. Anrig and LaPointe (1989) noted that

> only 16 percent of them [eighth-grade students] have mastered the content of a typical 8th grade mathematics textbook; that is, they can (65 to 80 percent of the time) "compute with decimals, fractions, and percents; recognize geometric figures; and solve simple equations." The vast majority of them, more than 2,800,000 out of 3,500,000, cannot do these kinds of tasks successfully at least 50 percent of the time. (p. 7)

As a result of the lackluster performance of American students on academic achievement tests in several content areas, including mathematics, educational reform has once again surfaced in discussions of standards, accountability, assessment, and even teacher education. While much is written about how to implement these various aspects of reform, many scientists and educators are calling attention to the need for empirical research to serve as the foundation on which this reform is based (Ellis & Fouts, 1997; Geary, 1994; Grouws, 1991; Slavin, 1989). The research community has long been aware of the need to integrate research findings into instructional practices and provide evidence for the efficacy of those practices *before* their dissemination. However, despite general agreement that providing such evidence is critical to student success, education has been replete with untested, unproven instructional methods, resulting in naive acceptance of the latest educational fads.

For an example of an educational reform movement in mathematics that, surprisingly, has not been solidly grounded in the research literature, educators can examine *Curriculum and Evaluation Standards for School Mathematics* (National Council of Teachers of Mathematics [NCTM], 1989). These standards, touted by many as a model of mathematics reform, prescribe what a "high-quality mathematics education for North American students, K–12, should comprise" (NCTM, 1989, p. 1). The goals of the standards include increasing the value students place on mathematics, students' confidence in doing mathematics, and their ability to reason and communicate mathematically as well as their ability to solve problems. However, despite statements from the NCTM about the importance of evidence of effectiveness, the council has produced little compelling evidence to support the adoption of the standards they claim will boost student achievement. Moreover, despite this dearth of supporting evidence, the standards have been accepted by teachers, textbook publishers, test makers, and business people. This reform effort in mathematics prompted Chester Finn Jr. (1993), former Assistant Secretary of Education, to write a commentary aptly titled, "What If Those Math Standards Are Wrong?" in which he expressed his concern for the lack of a research base for the NCTM recommendations.

In an effort to locate the research upon which the standards were based, one of the authors of this chapter requested and was sent a report from the Research Advisory Committee (1988) of the NCTM, published before the Standards, that stated: "The Standards document contains many recommendations, but in general, it does not provide a research context for the recommendations, even when such a context is available" (p. 339). In this report, the Research Advisory Committee expressed its expectation that the final Standards document would clarify the basis for the recommendations. However, as Bishop (1990) pointed out, the final document failed to provide further clarification:

> It is a little surprising that there is not much reference to the research literature concerning mathematics learning and teaching. There is no impression of the existence of a substantial body of research on which, for example, the proposals in the Standards are based. Recommendations and exhortations appear to be supported only by opinion—authoritative opinion, it is granted—but opinion nonetheless. (p. 366)

That there is a need for reform in mathematics instruction in our classrooms is clearly evidenced by the international and national studies documenting the mathematics achievement of American students. That educational reform should be based on publicly verifiable knowledge, rather than subjective, personal belief systems, is an ideal to which some educators and researchers subscribe, yet one that many ignore.

There is considerable evidence, however, that teachers can make a difference in the mathematics performance of the students in their classrooms and that mathematics achievement in this country can be improved. The purpose of this chapter is to highlight and integrate important and relevant research findings from the recent literature on mathematics learning and teaching. We begin with a discussion of *research-based* mathematics instructional programs that have been field-tested extensively in classrooms throughout the United States, with significant results. We continue with a section on the *design* of effective mathematics instruction and a section on the *delivery* of that instruction, integrating these sections with lessons learned from program evaluation research, as well as research in the areas of instructional design, mathematics learning and teaching, and teacher effectiveness.

Programs That Work

We have identified four instructional models, all of which have been supported by empirical research, to describe briefly in this section: the Missouri Mathematics Effectiveness Project, cooperative learning, ClassWide Peer Tutoring (CWPT), and Direct Instruction. Each was designed as a developmental (not remedial) model to meet the needs of students representing a wide range of abilities, especially those who may be at risk for academic failure. In fact, much of the research on each model was conducted with students from economically disadvantaged communities.

There are several reasons for beginning our discussion of effective mathematics instruction with a description of these models. First, as implied earlier, we take seriously our responsibility to provide experimental evidence of student achievement to support the instructional recommendations we make. Second, by examining the instructional models, first separately and then as a group, we are better able to extrapolate those features of effective instruction that appear to be related to increased student performance. Finally, we illustrate many of the design and delivery features described in the following sections with examples from these models.

The Missouri Mathematics Effectiveness Project

This project (Good & Grouws, 1979) was among the first experimental studies to demonstrate the relationship between specific teaching activities and student achievement in the area of mathematics. Prior to this study, the teacher effectiveness literature consisted largely of process-product studies that yielded correlations between specific teaching behaviors and student performance. In fact, Good and Grouws based their instructional intervention on the results of a naturalistic observation study of mathematics teachers, from which they were able to identify a set of factors that distinguished the highly effective teachers from those who were less effective. After integrating their findings with variables suggested by other teacher effectiveness studies, they derived five key instructional features to include in their model of mathematics instruction: daily review, development, seatwork, homework assignment, and special reviews. (See Good, Grouws, & Ebmeier, 1983, for a more complete description of these variables.)

Good and Grouws (1979) then tested the effectiveness of providing staff development in the form of in-service training on this model, by comparing the mathematics performance of students in the treatment classrooms with that of students in the control classrooms, where teachers were encouraged to maintain their own style of teaching. Good and Grouws determined that the level of implementation of their model was quite high in the treatment classrooms. Only 2 of the 21 treatment teachers scored low on measures of implementation, and the treatment teachers did exhibit more of the treatment teaching behaviors than did the control teachers. More important, the results of this study provided evidence that the Missouri Mathematics Effectiveness Model was effective in increasing mathematics achievement as measured by both standardized and criterion-referenced mathematics tests.

This study is significant for several reasons. First, the researchers demonstrated under experimental conditions that how students are taught mathematics has an impact on what students learn about mathematics. Perhaps even more significantly, the researchers demonstrated that teachers using this instructional system could increase the achievement of low-income, inner-city students and overcome the risk of low expectations. Another relevant finding from this study is that the development component of the instructional system (i.e., the explanation and initial teaching of new concepts) was the most difficult component for teachers to implement. The implications that this finding has for the evaluation, selection, and use of instructional material are discussed in the section on designing effective mathematics instruction.

Cooperative Learning

Cooperative learning is an instructional model characterized by the use of student teams to enhance learning. In his analysis of cooperative learning, Slavin (1983) found that the interdependence of two features, group goals and individual accountability, was critical to student success in any cooperative learning model. The team-assisted instruction (TAI) program for mathematics instruction is an example of the application of cooperative learning to the teaching of mathematics (Slavin, Leavey, & Madden, 1984). In TAI, students work in heterogeneous teams but on mathematics materials designed to meet their individual needs. Members of the team help each other with problems as well as check work and perform other "managerial" duties. In addition to the teamwork, teachers work at specified times with homogeneous groups drawn from all teams, delivering direct instruction on important mathematics concepts and skills. At the end of each week, all team members are assessed by means of criterion-referenced measures, and team points are allocated according to team performance. The TAI program has been described as integrating both individualized instruction and direct instruction with cooperative learning teams and cooperative incentives (Slavin & Karweit, 1984). It should be noted that other generic models of cooperative learning, such as the student teams-achievement division (STAD), have also been applied to the teaching of mathematics (Nattiv, 1994).

Several studies have demonstrated that students taught mathematics through TAI have outperformed students in control conditions (Slavin et al., 1984; Slavin & Karweit, 1984; Stevens & Slavin, 1995). A particularly interesting study (consisting of two experiments) investigated the mathematics achievement effects of three different instructional models commonly used to teach mathematics (Slavin & Karweit, 1985): individualized instruction (exemplified by TAI), whole-class instruction (using the Missouri Mathematics Program [MMP]), and within-class ability grouping (using the principles of the MMP applied to two homogeneous groups of students). In both experiments, TAI and the ability-grouped instruction increased achievement in mathematics computation more than the MMP and traditional whole-class instruction (present in experiment 2 only). No achievement differences between TAI and ability-grouped instruction were found in either experiment.

In experiment 2, students taught by teachers using MMP did significantly outperform those who were taught by teachers using more traditional instruction, thereby replicating earlier research on the MMP. No treatment effects were found on measures of understanding of mathematics concepts and applications in either experiment. Finally, in both experiments, students' attitudes toward math class were more positive for TAI groups, and more teachers reportedly chose TAI when given the opportunity to choose any method (other than the one they had used before) for training and materials.

ClassWide Peer Tutoring

ClassWide Peer Tutoring (CWPT) is an instructional system that employs simultaneous tutoring throughout the entire class. The tutor-tutee pairing is established at the beginning of each week, along with assignments of tutoring pairs to teams. All students are both tutors and tutees, and therefore, all students are taught to provide feedback through appropriate error correction. The CWPT system is similar to TAI in its use of interdependent social reward structures for both individual and team performance. However, CWPT differs from TAI in that mathematics instruction and practice are organized for an entire class and not completely individualized. The CWPT system was designed to maximize students' academic engaged time in the classroom, promote high levels of mastery, and ensure sufficient content coverage.

Although CWPT is not restricted to use with economically disadvantaged students, this instructional model has been effective in producing achievement gains for such students, commensurate with those of their more advantaged peers. In a longitudinal study that followed students from first grade through fourth grade (Greenwood, Delquadri, & Hall, 1989), the experimental low-socioeconomic-status (low-SES) group, using CWPT, achieved greater gains in mathematics (and language and reading) than did the low-SES control group. At the same time, no differences in academic performance were evident between the low-SES experimental group (using CWPT) and a high-SES comparison group (using traditional instruction). Notably, in this study, student satisfaction with tutoring was quite high.

In a follow-up study two years later, at the end of sixth grade, Greenwood, Terry, Utley, Montagna, and Walker (1993) examined the achievement of the low-SES experimental group, the low-SES control group, and the students not at risk for failure. They found that the CWPT students maintained their advantage over their low-SES peers on the mathematics subtest of the standardized achievement test, produced significantly higher scores on tests of science and social studies (areas not previously measured), were referred less often for special education services, and, when referred, were referred for less restrictive services. In the area of mathematics, the CWPT students also performed similarly to the students not at risk.

A substantial amount of research has been conducted on different models of classwide peer tutoring (Fantuzzo, Polite, & Grayson, 1990), the effects of supplemental peer practice (Good, Reys, Grouws, & Mulryan, 1990; Kohler, Ezell, Hoel, & Strain, 1994), and teachers' perceptions of classwide peer tutoring and curriculum-based measurement (Phillips, Fuchs, & Fuchs, 1994). Findings of both short-term and longitudinal studies support the continued use of CWPT and suggest that this model is an exemplary preventive and prereferral intervention strategy for those students most at risk for academic failure.

Direct Instruction

The term *direct instruction* has appeared in the literature in various contexts, often referring to systematic instruction. The Direct Instruction Model, described in this section, is a comprehensive instructional model involving many of the features of the previously discussed models, including organizational structure (in this case, small-group instruction), systematic teacher preparation, and the use of guided and frequent practice with feedback, as well as a system for monitoring student and teacher performance. However, a defining feature of the Direct Instruction Model is the use of a carefully designed curriculum based on *Theory of Instruction* (Engelmann & Carnine, 1991). Such a curriculum explicitly teaches not only algorithms for computation but also generalizable rules and strategies for solving problems. The nature of the curriculum differs from those used in other instructional models primarily in the specificity of the major instructional strategies. The instructional model emphasizes the identification of and instruction in background knowledge, a carefully designed sequence of instruction, and the use of cumulative introduction and review to integrate new and previously introduced skills and concepts (Carnine, Grossen, & Silbert, 1995; Gersten, Woodward, & Darch, 1986).

In 1968 the Direct Instruction Model was selected as one of the nine major instructional models to be evaluated as part of Project Follow Through, a federally funded project designed originally for the development and implementation of innovative teaching practices in schools serving low-income student populations. More than 180 school districts have been involved in Project Follow Through. The major models reflected a range of educational philosophies, including Piagetian approaches, models based on discovery learning, and three models based on behavioral principles. The Direct Instruction Model was implemented in communities throughout the United States, including Flippin, Arkansas; the Rosebud Sioux Reservation in South Dakota; inner-city schools in New York and Washington, D.C.; rural schools in Williamsburg County, North Carolina; and Hispanic communities such as East Las Vegas, New Mexico.

An independent evaluation of Project Follow Through was conducted by ABT Associates for the U.S. Office of Education (Stebbins, St. Pierre, Proper, Anderson, & Cerva, 1977). The measures used to determine mathematics achievement were the math problem-solving and math computation subtests of the Metropolitan Achievement Test and the mathematics subtest of the Wide Range Achievement Test. The data from the evaluation were quite revealing. The results indicated that low-income primary-grade students who received the full three- to four-year Direct Instruction mathematics program outperformed students who were taught by other approaches (either experimental or traditional) in all mathematics subtests of the Metropolitan Achievement test. The Direct Instruction students achieved a level higher than expected for students of similar demographic characteristics, one that was commensurate with their middle-income peers (Gersten & Carnine, 1984).

In a follow-up study of fifth- and sixth-grade students who had been in Direct Instruction mathematics programs in the primary grades but were no longer in the programs, results indicated consistent positive findings in the area of mathematics problem solving, weaker but significant effects in mathematics concepts, and null effects in computation (Becker & Gersten, 1982). The results of the follow-up study seem to suggest that the Direct Instruction students maintained those skills that were most generalizable—for example, problem-solving skills. Once the students left third grade, they were taught multiplication and division computation skills through more traditional instruction and no longer demonstrated significant achievement in the area of computation. Notably, evidence of the effectiveness of Direct Instruction is not limited to data from Project Follow Through but comprises a rich literature that has been summarized recently by Adams and Engelmann (1996).

Summary

The four instructional models described in this section share many features, including teacher-directed instruction, high levels of academic engagement, continuous monitoring of progress, and frequent feedback to students. More important, they have all been evaluated experimentally to determine their relative effectiveness in improving the mathematics performance of students, especially those at risk for academic failure. Notably, most of the features of these instructional models are related to either what is taught or how it is being taught. To further analyze those characteristics of programs that work, and to extrapolate recommendations for practitioners, we devote the remaining sections of this chapter to the *design* of effective mathematics instruction and the *delivery* of that instruction.

Instructional Design

In this section, we discuss issues related to both general curriculum design and the design of specific cognitive strategies that promote conceptual understanding and provide the basis for problem solving. Our recommendations are based on instructional-design theory (Engelmann & Carnine, 1991) and are derived from features of programs that have been demonstrated to be effective. We also provide examples from commercial programs (unidentified) to illustrate the instructional-design features we discuss. Finally, we provide an abbreviated version of an evaluation tool that can be adapted to evaluate and modify commercial instructional programs to make their content more accessible to students, especially those at risk for academic failure.

Although evidence of the reliance of teachers on commercially developed instructional materials has been well documented (Garner, 1992; Goodlad, 1984; Lindquist, 1984), many involved in educational reform have minimized the role that curriculum materials play in daily teaching. In *Professional Standards for Teaching Mathematics* (NCTM, 1991), the NCTM has identified six standards important for the teaching of mathematics, organized into four categories. Only one of those standards addresses the "worthwhile tasks" used in mathematics teaching. In a summary of the recommendations for choosing these tasks, the authors write, "Textbooks can be useful resources for teachers, but teachers must also be free to adapt or depart from texts if students' ideas and conjectures are to help shape teachers' navigation of the content" (p. 32). Although few educators would dispute that teachers must adapt curriculum materials to meet the needs of their students, many would acknowledge that well-designed curriculum materials serve as a useful tool for organizing and developing understanding of important concepts.

Moreover, many teachers who are teaching mathematics in our schools have not had adequate preparation to do so (Ball, 1990). For example, a case study of a fifth-grade teacher attempting to implement the California Mathematics Framework (similar to the NCTM curriculum standards) revealed that the teacher modeled finding the perimeter by multiplying length by width and modeled finding volume by calculating feet times yards (Heaton, 1992).

Ball and Cohen (1996) have recently suggested that educators rethink the role that curriculum materials play in the classroom. They acknowledge that in some educational communities, the use of commercially developed instructional programs has come to be associated with a lack of creative teaching. For example, many teachers have been led to believe that reading instruction should occur only through the use of trade books and literature, rather than through the use of a commercial basal reading program. In mathematics, curriculum materials are often replaced by manipulatives or teacher-made materials.

To make the best use of curriculum materials, teachers need to understand how most materials are developed and how to evaluate the instructional integrity of the materials. Problems with commercial programs have been well documented. Both Trafton (1984) and Lindquist (1984) have commented on the fact that publishers of mathematics curriculum materials rarely field-test their materials with students to determine effectiveness. Carnine, Jitendra, and Silbert (1997), Mayer, Sims, and Tajika (1995), and Kameenui and Griffin (1989) all have conducted curriculum analyses of basal mathematics programs and have consistently found the materials in need of significant modification. The curriculum design features addressed in this chapter include instructional strands, rate of introduction of skills and concepts, and practice and review.

Instructional Strands

Most commercial programs are organized according to a spiral curriculum. That is, most mathematics topics are introduced each year, in units that allegedly become increasingly more complex. For example, each grade level in a commercial program would contain a unit on fractions, and that unit would consist of review of previously introduced fraction skills and the introduction of new skills. However, as Taylor (1989) argues, the spiral curriculum merely reintroduces the same content each year because the previous year's instruction has most likely been forgotten. He characterizes the spiral curriculum as "a spiral with a nearly constant radius and students who end up going around in circles" (p. 635).

According to Porter (1989), a relatively large percentage of the topics taught in commercial programs receive brief coverage. On the average, in one study, teachers devoted less than 30 minutes of instructional time during the entire year to each of 70 percent of the topics in the program (e.g., telling time might receive 25 minutes during the entire first grade). Porter recounts that teachers have begun to refer to the brief content coverage as "teaching for exposure." Most teachers are faced with the dilemma of exposing students to the range of topics expected to be covered at their grade level or teaching fewer topics more thoroughly.

An alternative to the spiral curriculum is the organization of lessons around strands, where each strand represents a sequence of instruction on a certain topic. The sequence begins with instruction on the skills that must be acquired before the target skill is introduced. The sequence then includes teacher-directed instruction for the target skill, systematic opportunities for practice, and finally, integration of the target skill with previously introduced skills or concepts later in the sequence. Once the sequence for several skills is determined, then lessons can be designed around each of the strands, with the teacher spending 5- to 10-minute segments on different topics. See Figure 12–1 for an example of a scope-and-sequence chart for instruction using strands.

Figure 12–1
Curriculum design with
instructional strands.

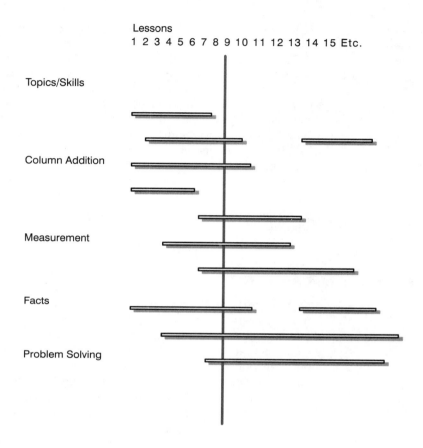

Organizing instruction around strands can be advantageous for several reasons. First, students are more easily engaged with a variety of topics. Spending 30 minutes on a single skill (e.g., subtraction with regrouping) can be very tedious for some students. In contrast, a lesson organized around strands might consist of 8 minutes on column addition with regrouping, followed by 7 minutes on measurement concepts, 5 minutes reviewing math facts, and 15 minutes on problem solving. (See lesson 9 in Figure 12–1.)

Second, strands permit a more reasonable sequence of instruction, making cumulative introduction and review feasible. The cumulative introduction of skills and concepts allows sufficient time for teachers to address component or prerequisite skills before integrating them during instruction. For example, rather than spending 30 minutes once on the place value concepts required in regrouping and then spending the next lesson introducing the regrouping skill, strands permit a teacher to spend approximately 7 minutes each on 3 days ensuring that the prerequisite place value skills have been mastered before introducing the regrouping strategy.

Organizing the instruction on skills and concepts by strands is only one way to improve the instructional curriculum by using principles of instructional design.

Curriculum design principles also address the rate at which new concepts or skills are introduced, and the adequacy and appropriateness of practice and review.

Rate of Introducing New Skills and Concepts

A notable problem with many mathematics programs that are designed according to a spiral curriculum is the rate of introduction of skills and concepts. As mentioned earlier, most mathematics programs teach only one skill or concept per day. Depending on the skill, this practice can result in spending too much time on a less important skill or, conversely, not enough time on important ones. For example, in the second-grade level of one program we examined, all of the addition and subtraction facts to 12 are introduced in 7 lessons in the first chapter. In two later chapters, 7 lessons are devoted to addition facts to 18, and 5 lessons to subtraction facts to 18. A total of 19 lessons in an entire year is an extremely fast rate for many students to learn and remember their addition and subtraction facts. Retention is much more likely with a cumulative introduction and review that is more gradual, yet provides more practice opportunities distributed frequently throughout the entire year.

Another example of a problematic rate of introduction can be seen by examining fraction instruction in a popular third-grade basal mathematics program. The following is a list of the lesson numbers and corresponding objectives in a chapter on fractions and decimals from this program.

Lessons	**Objectives**
Lesson 1	To name parts of a whole
Lesson 2	To name fractional parts of regions
Lesson 3	To find equivalent fractions
Lesson 4	To use objects to develop an understanding of comparing fractions
Lesson 5	To write fractions for parts of sets
Lesson 6	To use division to find a fractional part of a set
Lesson 7	[An objective not related to fractions]
Lesson 8	To use the estimation technique of using a benchmark to estimate fractional parts
Lesson 9	To use mixed numbers
Lesson 10	To add and subtract fractions with like denominators

This example of chapter objectives does not indicate which objectives represent review and which represent new concepts. Objectives 1–4 and 7–9 are identified as "core objectives," presumably to alert the teacher that those objectives represent concepts to be mastered at this grade level. However, the actual lessons for objectives 1 and 2 involve asking students to produce the names for fractional parts—for example, *fifths, thirds, halves.* In examining the second-grade level of this program, we found a variety of activities that require students to use the fractional terms *halves, thirds,* and *fourths.* As a result, students in third grade are being asked to spend an entire math instructional period on activities that, most likely, they already know. Yet, they are given only one lesson to master the concept of equivalent fractions, a very difficult one for many students to grasp, before moving on to another difficult concept: comparing fractions.

To modify instructional programs to meet the needs of their students, teachers must have a good sense of whether the students already have the prerequisite knowledge for mastery of the new concept and must balance the amount of time allocated for instruction with the difficulty of the concept. Both the need to teach (or assess) prerequisite skills and the level of complexity of the new instruction will influence the rate of introduction of new instructional material.

Clarity of Explanations

The instructional strategies to which students are introduced must be evaluated carefully for their integrity and clarity, as well as their generalizability. In many currently published programs, teachers are encouraged to provide opportunities for students to discover mathematics relationships and algorithms on their own or in cooperative groups. This philosophical approach has not been supported by experimental research in mathematics education. On the contrary, as illustrated earlier, evidence from large-scale implementations of instructional models for teaching mathematics, especially with economically disadvantaged students, suggests that teacher-directed instruction is critical to student success (Gersten & Carnine, 1984; Good et al., 1983; Slavin & Karweit, 1985).

An essential component of teacher-directed instruction is what Good et al. (1983) call the *development* portion of the lesson, in which the teacher provides explanations, demonstrations, and illustrations of important concepts or skills. The development component is arguably the most difficult component for teachers to master, for various reasons, not the least of which are poor subject-matter knowledge on the part of the teachers and poorly designed instructional materials containing faulty algorithms and vague strategies for problem solving.

Teachers' need for a sound mathematics curriculum that contains well-designed instructional strategies is underscored by the great number of mathematics teachers who do not know the subject matter. In a study of prospective teachers, Ball (1990) reported that on a questionnaire, only 30 percent ($n = 217$) of the prospective elementary teachers could provide an example of an appropriate representation of division with fractions; approximately 40 percent ($n = 35$) of secondary teachers provided an acceptable representation. When teachers were interviewed, the percentages dropped dramatically; not one elementary teacher provided an acceptable representation, and only 4 percent of secondary teachers were able to do so. In her summary, Ball (1990) articulated three criteria of adequate mathematics knowledge:

1. Teachers' knowledge of concepts and procedures should be accurate.

2. Teachers should understand the underlying principles and meanings of the mathematics they teach.

3. Teachers need to understand the relationships among mathematical ideas and concepts.

These findings suggest that given many teachers' lack of mathematics knowledge, in order for instructional materials to be useful tools, they must contain well-designed, unambiguous, generalizable strategies that will promote conceptual understanding along with critical procedural knowledge. Although the responsibility for preparing teachers to teach mathematics belongs to teacher education programs, inservice teachers can be made aware of simple instructional-design tenets that would assist them in determining whether the strategies included in their teaching materials are worthwhile to teach their students.

Four criteria help teachers determine whether the instructional explanations provided in commercial programs are adequate: generalizability, efficiency, explicitness, and accuracy. First, the strategy that the teacher presents to students must be generalizable. That is, the strategy must be applicable to a wide range of problem types. For example, often students are introduced first to fractions with 1 in the numerator (e.g., ½, ⅓, ¼) by means of the concept of a pie (or a pizza). Limiting the initial fraction instruction to those fractions and using a single object (or figure) divided into sections may cause naive students to think that fractions can only be represented by a single figure and that fractions must have 1 in the numerator. Typically, students are introduced to proper fractions in the next grade and are finally given instruction in improper fractions in later grades. By the time students are introduced to improper fractions, however, many of them have already developed common misconceptions about fractions. One such misconception is that in a fraction the top number must always be smaller than the bottom number. When asked to draw a picture of ⁵⁄₄, students who have learned this misconception about fractions will draw a picture of ⅘ instead.

Generalizability of instructional strategies also contributes to instructional efficiency. With a more generalizable strategy, the teacher spends less time in remediation and reteaching and can spend more time helping students integrate the skills they have learned. For example, a more efficient instructional strategy for introducing students to fraction concepts is one in which students are taught that (a) the bottom number represents the number of parts in each whole and (b) the top number represents the number of parts that are shaded. Students are then given practice in drawing pictures of fractions with an exercise that looks something like Figure 12–2. This explanation of fractions teaches a conceptual understanding of fractions that applies to all problem types (i.e., proper and improper fractions). Combined with practice in drawing pictures of fractions, the strategy helps prevent the confusion that inevitably occurs for some students when improper fractions are introduced in the third, fourth, or fifth grade.

Another criterion for evaluating the integrity of instructional strategies is the degree of explicitness. Teaching explicit strategies does not imply that students must merely memorize content. Explicit teaching ensures that students learn the steps in the cognitive strategies so that they can apply them appropriately to a range of problem types. Many educators confuse explicit instruction with rote instruction. With explicit instructions, students do not memorize the answers to a set of examples; they learn a set of procedures that when successfully applied to the examples, will result in the correct answer and a deeper understanding of the relationships inherent in the mathematics content.

Figure 12-2
Understanding fractions.

Draw the picture that represents each fraction.

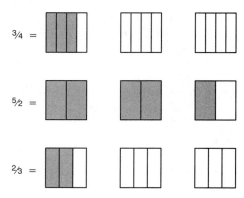

For example, contrast the following explanations, designed to teach students to determine whether they must regroup in subtraction.

First Explanation

Directions to the Teacher: Read aloud the directions [for the worksheet]. For the first exercise, ask students to visualize *using cubes to complete their work and tell them to* reason *their way through the answer. When they determine an answer, they write it in the circle. Then they use cubes to work the exercise, place the answer in the answer space, and compare it to the one in the circle. When all exercises have been done, have students discuss their answers and the strategies they used to try to do the exercises in their heads.* [emphasis in original]

Second Explanation

Directions to the Teacher: Read aloud the following:

1. *Here's a rule about renaming with subtraction problems: When we take away more than we start with we must rename.*
2. *First Problem: What number are starting with in the ones column? We're starting with 5 and taking away 9. Must we rename? Right, we have to rename because we're taking away more than we started with; 9 is more than 5.*
3. *Next Problem: What number are we starting with in the ones column? What number are we taking away? Must we rename if we take away 3? We don't rename. We're not taking away more than we start with.*

Because of space limitations, we have included in neither example all of the related instructional activities. However, the text quoted does contain the core strategies that students are encouraged to use when determining whether they must regroup for subtraction. In the first explanation, the students are to use their previous experiences with cubes to help them mentally determine the answer (and if they need to rename). That activity is followed by one in which the teacher encourages pairs of students to generate their own rules for finding the answer without using cubes. The next activity listed is the completion of a worksheet on which students use cubes to solve the subtraction problems. To summarize, the program encourages the use of mental computation, manipulatives, and rule generation in determining the need to regroup in subtraction.

In the second explanation, the students are given a rule, the teacher models the application of the rule, and then the teacher leads students in applying the rule themselves. It should be noted that before introducing the rule, the teacher demonstrated with manipulatives the concept of regrouping.

The examples clearly illustrate the differences between a more student-directed approach and teacher-directed strategy instruction. The teacher-directed instruction in the second explanation gives students explicit information so that they can determine whether they must regroup. However, the use of the rule does not constitute rote instruction. Rather, the teacher using the rule will be able to assess student understanding by evaluating students' ability to apply the rule consistently, both to examples that require renaming and to those that do not.

A final criterion to use in evaluating the instructional integrity of a mathematics strategy is whether the strategy is accurate or inadvertently encourages student misconceptions. A faulty strategy may teach what we call a *misrule,* a strategy that is likely to be misapplied or overgeneralized. For example, in the fractions chapter of one third-grade program, a word problem similar to the following is presented: *Mrs. Slate picked 12 tomatoes. She will cook ⅓ of them. How many tomatoes will she cook?* The students are taught that they can find ⅓ of 12 by mentally dividing 12 by 3. The students are then given practice on five additional fraction problems that can be solved by division.

Although the division strategy will work for the given problem and all similar problems that involve fractions with a numerator of 1 (e.g., 1/2 of 8, ¼ of 36), the strategy cannot be applied to problems that do not contain fractions with a numerator of 1. Yet, the instruction fails to alert students to exactly *when* the strategy will work and when they must choose another. The misrule that some students will learn from that instruction is simple: when you see a similar problem, divide the whole number by the denominator of the fraction. It is quite predictable that many students solving the problem, *What is ⅘ of 200?* will divide 200 by 5.

Practice and Review

Although few people argue about the amount of practice required to learn a foreign language, read music, or master a tennis serve, many educators underestimate the amount of practice necessary for acquiring mathematics knowledge and skills. The phrase *drill and practice* (sometimes, pejoratively, "drill and kill") is frequently used to criticize programs that subscribe to a more teacher-directed, systematic approach to mathematics instruction. Critics who speak of drill and practice often imply that mathematics instruction that contains frequent written practice activities fails to promote the type of conceptual understanding considered a more authentic goal of mathematics instruction. However, as mentioned earlier, evidence from research reviews and program evaluation studies suggests that explicit teaching accompanied by sufficient practice provides students with opportunities to acquire important skills and concepts more easily (Dempster, 1991). Learning procedures to a level of automaticity allows students to understand how the procedures work and how to better integrate strategies to solve more sophisticated problems.

A related criticism leveled by progressive educators is that providing too much practice will have a negative impact on student motivation. However, our experience is that nothing diminishes student motivation more than failure. When students are well prepared for their independent work and when students see their own improvement, motivation only increases.

Summary

As a means of summarizing the information on instructional design presented in this section, we have included an outline for evaluating mathematics instructional materials, divided into three categories: instructional organization (including rate of introduction), clarity of explanations and problem-solving strategies, and practice and review (see Figure 12–3). The outline is intended to serve as an example of topics and questions that can guide educators in their evaluation of the instructional integrity of the commercial materials they examine. Note that the outline does not constitute a complete system for curriculum evaluation and adoption but may be adapted for use in that process. We recommend that educators identify a set of target skills and concepts to analyze for each grade level. Once the target skills have been identified, educators should examine only the core teaching materials represented in most teacher's manuals, using the topics in Figure 12–3. Notice that we do not recommend the use of checklists in this process. Evaluating materials requires the careful identification and analysis of specific teaching recommendations in each program.

Instructional Delivery

In their well-cited review of research on teacher effectiveness, Rosenshine and Stevens (1986) identified several teaching functions that were related to student achievement:

1. Daily review, checking previous day's work and reteaching if necessary;
2. Presentation of new content/skills through demonstrations, modeling and high frequency questions;
3. Guided Practice;

I. Instructional organization

    A. Identify the organizational structure of the program. Is it a spiral curriculum? Does it use instructional strands?

    B. Identify the sequence of instruction for target skills and concepts.

    C. Identify the rate of introduction of target skills and concepts.

II. Clarity of explanations and problem-solving strategies

    A. Identify the steps in the instructional strategies recommended for target skills and concepts.

    B. Evaluate each strategy:

        1. Is it generalizable? Is it useful for a range of problem types?

        2. Is the strategy efficient?

        3. Is it accurate? Does it lead students to generate a possible misrule?

        4. Does the program provide recommended correction procedures for errors?

    C. Are component skills or prerequisite background knowledge identified and taught before the strategy is introduced?

    D. Is the strategy taught in an explicit manner? Are there provisions for teacher modeling? Is the amount of teacher assistance gradually reduced?

III. Practice and review

    A. Are a sufficient number of practice examples provided to ensure initial mastery?

    B. Does the program provide opportunities for discrimination practice?

    C. Identify provisions for continuing practice and review.

Figure 12–3
Evaluating mathematics instructional materials.

    4. Correctives and Feedback;

    5. Independent practice to promote automaticity, and

    6. Weekly and monthly cumulative review. (p. 379)

These teaching functions were derived from both correlational and experimental studies that examined the relationships between specific teaching behaviors and student academic achievement. In this chapter, *instructional delivery* refers to those specific teaching behaviors that exist independent of instructional materials or curriculum. We have organized our discussion of instructional delivery around two major topics: (1) the opportunity to learn mathematics, as evidenced by allocation of instructional time, the amount of guided and independent classroom practice, and the amount of outside activity related to mathematics (i.e., homework), and (2) instructional grouping. These features of instructional delivery are by no means exhaustive, but each is derived from the research literature and has been shown to be related to student success.

The Opportunity to Learn Mathematics

The opportunity to learn mathematics is perhaps the most salient of instructional delivery features. The teaching-effectiveness literature reviewed by Rosenshine and Stevens (1986) and exemplified by studies such as the Beginning Teacher Evaluation Study (Denham & Lieberman, 1980) called attention to the importance of both sufficient *allocation* of instructional time and sufficient *academic engaged time*. That is, successful teachers not only scheduled adequate time in their daily schedules for the teaching of mathematics but also ensured that students were highly engaged in learning during that time. In the Beginning Teacher Evaluation Study (BTES), researchers found that students performed at a higher achievement level when more time was allocated to instruction and that the engagement rates of students in both reading and mathematics were significantly higher during teacher-directed instructional time than during independent practice. As a result, teachers were more likely to increase student achievement by not only allocating ample time for mathematics instruction but also spending a higher percentage of that time directly interacting with students (Rosenshine, 1980).

In addition to directly instructing students, successful teachers in the study also encouraged high levels of engagement through the use of *guided practice*. Many students need a transition between the explanation given in the introduction and the problems provided for independent practice. Good et al. (1983) found that guided practice is an effective way for teachers to monitor student performance and increase the likelihood that students will be successful during independent work. In guided practice, the teacher asks questions that prompt students in the application of the strategy previously introduced. The teacher monitors students carefully and provides only the assistance necessary for students to successfully solve the problem. The teacher gradually removes the additional help and merely monitors as students complete their work, intervening only when necessary. In essence, the use of guided practice helps set the stage for successful independent student performance. A major finding of the BTES was that engagement in academic tasks at a *high success rate* correlated highly with student academic success (Denham & Lieberman, 1980). The researchers referred to this as *academic learning time* (ALT). Guided practice is an instructional delivery strategy that facilitates an increase in ALT.

The data from international studies of mathematics achievement also support the role that opportunity to learn plays in student achievement. The results of several international studies confirm significant differences among nations in the amounts of both *engaged* and *allocated* time spent on mathematics instruction. Stevenson et al. (1986) reported that in the fifth grade, American students spent approximately 65 percent of allocated instructional time engaged in the mathematics lesson, while the engagement rate for students from Japan was approximately 87 percent and that of

Chinese students was about 92 percent. In a later study, Stevenson et al. (1990) reported that American first-grade teachers spent an average of 1 1/2 to 2 hours less time per week on mathematics instruction than teachers in Japan and Taiwan. American fifth-grade teachers spent about 4 1/2 hours less time per week on mathematics instruction than teachers in Japan and about 8 hours less than teachers in Taiwan. From these data, it appears that same-age students in Japan and Taiwan have a greater opportunity to learn mathematics than their American peers.

The international studies have provided additional evidence that suggests *homework* is related to student achievement. Lapointe, Mead, and Askew (1992) found a relationship between the amount of homework adolescent students received and their mathematics achievement. Stevenson et al. (1990) found similar results when studying the mathematics performance of children in the United States, China, and Japan. Interestingly, they found not only that students in China and Japan spent significantly more time than their American peers working on mathematics at home, but also that the Chinese and Japanese students reported more positive attitudes toward the homework than did students in the United States.

While it is simplistic to assume that increased opportunity to learn will guarantee success for all students, this instructional-delivery feature is one that is within the purview of all teachers and their administrators. Allocating sufficient instructional time *and* ensuring that the time is spent wisely can have a positive impact on student performance. Teacher-directed instruction, guided practice, and well-designed homework assignments are inexpensive means of increasing student opportunity to learn and possibly increasing student achievement in mathematics.

Instructional Grouping

Instructional delivery also takes into account the instructional arrangement in the classroom, that is, instructional grouping. Educators faced with increasingly disparate groups of students in any given classroom have historically looked upon instructional grouping as a means of meeting diverse student needs. Several reviews of research on instructional grouping have found that homogeneous grouping can be beneficial to students, provided that the grouping doesn't become tracking, in which students are relegated to a particular group for all of their academic instruction, with little or no flexibility to move among groups according to their academic performance (Lou et al., 1996; Slavin, 1987).

Instructional-grouping issues are analogous to issues of academic engagement in a very important way. That is, the issue in instructional grouping is less one of *where* a student is taught than of *how* and *what* students are being taught. Similarly, issues of engagement, as mentioned earlier, involve not only the number of minutes spent in mathematics, but also the level of success students have when they are engaged in mathematics tasks.

Three of the instructional models outlined in the first section of this chapter integrate some aspect of instructional grouping into their models. Cooperative learning and ClassWide Peer Tutoring utilize instructional grouping as a means of providing sufficient practice to students. Note that both models incorporate a combination of teacher-directed instruction and peer support, provided in pairs or small groups. The Direct Instruction Model of Project Follow Through utilized homogeneous grouping in kindergarten through third grade. It is important to note that data from that model showed that students in the lowest-performing groups made approximately the same rate of progress as students in the higher-performing groups (Gersten, Becker, Heiry, & White, 1984). Since Project Follow Through, additional studies involving the use of Direct Instruction in the area of mathematics have demonstrated results for both small- and large-group arrangements.

Finally, although the initial research on the Missouri Mathematics Program (MMP) was implemented in large groups, the model can easily be adapted for use with small groups as well. In fact, in their study comparing the effects of whole-class, ability-grouped, and individual instruction on student performance in mathematics, Slavin and Karweit (1985) argued that ability grouping and individual instruction may, in fact, "be more faithful operationalizations of the principles on which the MMP is based than the MMP (whole class instruction) itself, and the more positive achievement effects observed for these methods might validate rather than repudiate these principles" (p. 364).

The need for more research on the use of small-group instruction, especially in the area of mathematics, has been expressed by several researchers (Good, Grouws, Mason, Slavings, & Cramer, 1990; Ross, Smith, Lohr, & McNelis, 1994; Taylor, 1989). Many in the research community are less interested in questions of whether to group for instruction than in substantive questions regarding efficient, effective uses of instructional grouping that will result in clear improvement of student learning. Under what conditions does instructional grouping benefit students? What types of instructional activities are best suited to small-group instruction? What type of teacher education is essential to preparing teachers to utilize grouping strategies more effectively? Can schools afford to provide small-group instruction in mathematics?

Summary

Although opportunity to learn and instructional grouping are by no means the only components of instructional delivery, the research literature suggests that they are necessary, though not sufficient, conditions for effective mathematics instruction. Interestingly, other instructional delivery features include some of those mentioned in the section on instructional design. For example, rate of introduction of new skills and concepts, clarity of explanations, and adequate practice and review are all features that can be addressed by the curriculum used in the classroom, by the teacher, or, preferably, by both. Ideally, these features are considered by program designers during the development of instructional materials. However, the features must also be addressed by classroom teachers as they reflect on their daily teaching.

Integrated throughout Rosenshine and Stevens's teaching functions is the need for constant monitoring of student performance. Teachers monitor students to determine what content must be reviewed or retaught and what has been mastered. Once teachers determine student needs through careful monitoring, they can use some of the instructional-design recommendations to adjust their instruction. Teachers can determine (a) whether they are introducing too many concepts too fast (rate of introduction), (b) whether the instruction was clear or confusing (clarity of explanations), or even (c) whether their students need more practice examples to retain previously taught strategies and concepts (practice and review).

Conclusion

From the preceding descriptions of programs that work, and the discussion of instructional-design and delivery features that are related to student success, it should be obvious that some answers to the difficult questions of how to improve mathematics teaching and learning in this country lie in the integration of findings from several different lines of research. From instructional models that have demonstrated positive effects on student performance in mathematics and from the teacher effectiveness literature, we can learn the characteristics of implementation that seem necessary for classroom change. We can also extrapolate from that research literature the features of effective instruction that are related to curriculum (instructional design) and those that are related to implementation (instructional delivery). It is the coordination of classroom organization, curriculum materials, and teaching expertise that will benefit our students. The most efficient classroom organization will not have a sufficient influence on student learning without sound curriculum materials and a skilled teacher to implement that curriculum. The most carefully designed curriculum will not have an adequate effect on student performance without a skilled teacher who can monitor student performance and adjust the curriculum accordingly, utilizing a classroom schedule that provides maximum learning opportunities for students.

Clearly, improving the mathematics performance of students in the United States requires that educators make responsible instructional decisions based on available research; that the research community investigate questions of importance to practitioners, using appropriate research methodologies; that the media make relevant research findings available to the general public; and that parents of school-aged children support school-based efforts at home. One means of achieving our educational goals lies in a commitment by educators to pursue rigorous scientific inquiry designed to answer important questions of what works. Without this commitment, education will be cursed with the proverbial swinging pendulum, and many children will be precluded from achieving their academic potential.

References

Adams, G. L., & Engelmann, S. (1996). *Research on Direct Instruction: Twenty-five years beyond Distar.* Seattle, WA: Educational Achievement Systems.

Anrig, G. R., & LaPointe, A. E. (1989). What we know about what students don't know. *Educational Leadership, 47*(3), 4–9.

Ball, D. L. (1990). Prospective elementary and secondary teachers' understanding of division. *Journal for Research in Mathematics Education, 21,* 132–144.

Ball, D. L., & Cohen, D. K. (1996). Reform by the book: What is—or might be—the role of curriculum materials in teacher learning and instructional reform? Educational *Researcher, 25*(9), 6–8.

Becker, W. C., & Gersten, R. (1982). A follow-up of Follow Through: The later effects of the Direct Instruction Model on children in fifth and sixth grades. *American Education Research Journal, 19*(1), 75–92.

Bishop, A. J. (1990). Mathematical power to the people. *Harvard Educational Review, 60*(3), 357–369.

Carnine, D., Grossen, B., & Silbert, J. (1995). Direct instruction to accelerate cognitive growth. In J. Block, S. Everson, & T. Guskey (Eds.), *Choosing research-based school improvement programs.* New York: Scholastic.

Carnine, D., Jitendra, A. K., & Silbert, J. (1997). A descriptive analysis of mathematics curricular materials from a pedagogical perspective. *Remedial and Special Education, 18*(2), 66–81.

Corwin, R. L. (1997, January 5). Math-teaching fads failing U.S. students. *The Los Angeles Times,* pp. A1–A2.

Dempster, F. N. (1991). Synthesis of research on reviews and tests. *Educational Leadership, 48,* 71–76.

Denham, C., & Lieberman, A. (Eds.). (1980). *Time to learn.* Washington, DC: U.S. Department of Education, National Institute of Education.

Ellis, A. K., & Fouts, J. T. (1997). *Research on educational innovations* (Rev. ed.). Larchmont, NY: Eye on Education.

Engelmann, S., & Carnine, D. W. (1991). *Theory of instruction: Principles and applications* (2nd ed.). New York: Irvington Press.

Fantuzzo, J. W., Polite, K., & Grayson, N. (1990). An evaluation of reciprocal peer tutoring across elementary school settings. *Journal of School Psychology, 28,* 309–323.

Finn, C. E., Jr. (1993, January 20). What if those math standards are wrong? *Education Week,* p. 36.

Garner, R. (1992). Learning from school texts. *Educational Psychologist, 27,* 53–63.

Geary, D. C. (1994). *Children's mathematical development.* Washington, DC: American Psychological Association.

Gersten, G. M., Becker, W. C., Heiry, T. J., & White, W. A. T. (1984). Entry IQ and yearly academic growth of children in Direct Instruction programs: A longitudinal study of low SES children. *Educational Evaluation and Policy Analysis, 6*(2), 109–121.

Gersten, R., & Carnine, D. (1984). Direct Instruction mathematics: A longitudinal evaluation of low SES elementary students. *Elementary School Journal, 84*(4), 395–407.

Gersten, R., Woodward, J., & Darch, C. (1986). Direct Instruction: A research-based approach to curriculum design and teaching. *Exceptional Children, 53*(1), 17–31.

Good, T. L., & Grouws, D. A. (1979). The Missouri Mathematics Effectiveness Project: An experimental study in fourth-grade classrooms. *Journal of Educational Psychology, 71,* 355–362.

Good, T. L., Grouws, D. A., & Ebmeier, H. (1983). *Active mathematics teaching.* New York: Longman.

Good, T. L., Grouws, D. A., Mason, D. A., Slavings, R. L., & Cramer, K. (1990). An observation study of small-group mathematics instruction in elementary schools. *American Education Research Journal, 27*(4), 755–782.

Good, T. L., Reys, B. J., Grouws, D. A., & Mulryan, C. M. (1990). Using work-groups in mathematics instruction. *Educational Leadership, 47*(4), 56–62.

Goodlad, J. (1984). *A place called school: Prospects for the future.* New York: McGraw-Hill.

Greenwood, C. R., Delquadri, J. C., & Hall, R. V. (1989). Longitudinal effects of class-wide peer tutoring. *Journal of Educational Psychology, 81*(3), 371–383.

Greenwood, C. R., Terry, B., Utley, C. A., Montagna, D., & Walker, D. (1993). Achievement, placement, and services: Middle school benefits of classwide peer tutoring used at the elementary school. *School Psychology Review, 22*(3), 497–516.

Grouws, D. A. (1991). Improving research in mathematics classroom instruction. In E. Fennema, T. P. Carpenter, & S. J. Lamon (Eds.), *Integrating research in teaching and learning mathematics* (pp. 199–215). Albany: State University of New York Press.

Heaton, R. M. (1992). Who is minding the mathematics content? A case study of a fifth grade teacher. *Elementary School Journal, 93* (2), 153–162.

Husen, T. (1967). *International study of achievement in mathematics: A comparison of twelve countries* (Vols. 1 & 2). New York: Wiley.

Kameenui, E. J., & Griffin, C. C. (1989). The national crisis in verbal problem solving in mathematics: A proposal for examining the role of basal mathematics programs. *The Elementary School Journal, 89*(5), 575–593.

Kohler, F. W., Ezell, H., Hoel, K., & Strain, P. S. (1994). Supplemental peer practice in a first grade math class: Effects on teacher behavior and five low achievers' responding and acquisition of content. *The Elementary School Journal, 94*(4), 389–403.

Lapointe, A. E., Mead, N. A., & Askew, J. M. (1992). *Learning mathematics.* Princeton, NJ: Educational Testing Service.

Lindquist, M. M. (1984). The elementary school mathematics curriculum: Issues for today. *The Elementary School Journal, 84*(5), 595–608

Lou, Y., Abrami, P. C., Spence, J. C., Poulsen, C., Chambers, B., & D'Apollonia, S. (1996). Within-class grouping: A meta-analysis. *Review of Educational Research, 66*(4), 423–458.

Mayer, R. E., Sims, V., & Tajika, H. (1995). A comparison of how textbooks teach mathematical problem solving in Japan and the United States. *American Education Research Journal, 32*(2), 443–460.

National Council of Teachers of Mathematics (1989). *Curriculum and evaluation standards for school mathematics.* Reston, VA: Author.

National Council of Teachers of Mathematics. (1991). *Professional standards for teaching mathematics.* Reston, VA: Author.

Nattiv, A. (1994). Helping behaviors and math achievement gain of students using cooperative learning. *The Elementary School Journal, 94*(3), 285–297.

Phillips, N. B., Fuchs, L. S., & Fuchs, D. (1994). Effects of classwide curriculum-based measurement and peer tutoring: A collaborative researcher-practitioner interview study. *Journal of Learning Disabilities, 27*(7), 420–434.

Porter, A. (1989). A curriculum out of balance: The case of elementary school mathematics. *Educational Researcher, 18*(5), 9–15.

Research Advisory Committee. (1988). NCTM curriculum and evaluation standards for school mathematics: Responses from the research community. *Journal for Research in Mathematics Education, 19*(4), 338–344.

Rosenshine, B. V. (1980). How time is spent in elementary classrooms. In C. Denham & A. Lieberman (Eds.), *Time to learn* (pp. 107–123). Washington, DC: U.S. Department of Education, National Institute of Education.

Rosenshine, B., & Stevens, R. (1986). Teaching functions. In M. Wittrock (Ed.), *Handbook of research on teaching* (3rd ed., pp. 376–391). New York: Macmillan.

Ross, S. M., Smith, L. J., Lohr, L., & McNelis, M. (1994). Math and reading instruction in tracked first-grade classes. *The Elementary School Journal, 95*(2), 105–119.

Slavin, R. E. (1983). *Cooperative learning.* New York: Longman.

Slavin, R. E. (1987). Ability grouping and student achievement in elementary schools: A best evidence synthesis. *Review of Educational Research, 57*(3), 293–336.

Slavin, R. (1989). PET and the pendulum: Faddism in education and how to stop it. *Phi Delta Kappan, 70*(10), 752–758.

Slavin, R., & Karweit, N. (1984). Mastery learning and student teams: A factorial experiment in urban general mathematics classes. *American Education Research Journal, 21*, 725–736.

Slavin, R., & Karweit, N. (1985). Effects of whole-class, ability grouped, and individualized instruction on mathematics achievement. *American Education Research Journal, 22*, 351–367.

Slavin, R., Leavey, M., & Madden, N. (1984). Combining cooperative learning and individualized instruction: Effects on student mathematics achievement, attitudes, and behaviors. *Elementary School Journal, 84*, 409–422.

Stebbins, L. B., St. Pierre, R. G., Proper, E. C., Anderson, R. B., & Cerva, T. R. (1977). *Education as experimentation: A planned variation model* (Vols. IV A–D). Cambridge, MA: ABT Associates.

Stevens, R. J., & Slavin, R. E. (1995). The cooperative elementary school: Effects on students' achievement, attitudes, and social relations. *American Education Research Journal, 32*(2), 321–351.

Stevenson, H. W., Chen, C., & Lee, S. Y. (1993). Mathematics achievement of Chinese, Japanese, and American children: Ten years later. *Science, 259*, 53–58.

Stevenson, H. W., Lee, S. Y., Chen, C., Lummis, M., Stigler, J., Fan, L., & Ge, F. (1990). Mathematics achievement of children in China and the United States. *Child Development, 61*, 1053–1066.

Stevenson, H. W., Lee, S. Y., & Stigler, J. W. (1986) Mathematics achievement of Chinese, Japanese, and American children. *Science, 231*, 693–699.

Taylor, R. (1989). The potential of small-group mathematics instruction in grades four through six. *The Elementary School Journal, 89*(5), 633–642.

Toch, T. (1996, April 1). The case for tough standards. *U.S. News & World Report, 120,* 52–56.

Trafton, P. R. (1984). Toward more effective, efficient instruction in mathematics. *The Elementary School Journal, 84*(5), 514–528.

U.S. National Research Center. (1996, December). *Third international mathematics and science study* (Report No. 7). East Lansing: Michigan State University.

Teaching Social Studies for Understanding, Appreciation, and Life Application

Jere Brophy
Michigan State University

Janet Alleman
Michigan State University

Wₑ are especially pleased to contribute to this volume honoring Barak Rosenshine because our work focuses on social studies, and Barak started out as a social studies teacher. In recent years, we have engaged in several forms of research on the teaching and learning of social studies in the elementary grades. The work has been designed to help teachers become more goal oriented in their social studies teaching and, in particular, to help them teach the subject for understanding, appreciation, and life application of its content. It complements and builds on two previously established lines of work: process-outcome research and research on teaching school subjects for understanding and use of knowledge.

We begin this chapter by describing the nature and summarizing the major findings of these two lines of research that cut across the school subjects. Then, as a bridge to our work in social studies, we explain how research on process-outcome relationships and on teaching for understanding has produced considerable consensus concerning the value of certain teaching methods, but also has reopened some basic curricular issues. As a result, research on teaching has recently begun to focus on what is taught as well as on how it is taught. In our work, this has meant conducting detailed critical examinations of social studies textbook series and other instructional materials, developing principles for goal-oriented unit planning and for selecting and implementing powerful learning activities, studying patterns of growth and change in children's knowledge about topics addressed in elementary social studies, and developing and testing units of instruction on the basic human needs and experiences (cultural universals) that are the focus of social studies in the primary grades.

Process-Outcome Research

Process-outcome research was designed to identify relationships between classroom processes (what the teacher and students do in the classroom) and student outcomes (changes in students' knowledge, skills, values, or dispositions that represent progress toward instructional goals). Two forms of process-outcome research that became prominent in the 1970s were school effects research and teacher effects research. *School effects research* (Creemers & Scheerens, 1989; Good & Brophy, 1986; Teddlie & Stringfield, 1993) identified several characteristics that are observed consistently in schools that elicit good achievement gains from their students:

1. Strong academic leadership that produces consensus on goal priorities and commitment to instructional excellence
2. A safe, orderly school climate
3. Positive teacher attitudes toward students and positive expectations of students' abilities to master the curriculum
4. An emphasis, in allocating classroom time and assigning tasks to students, on instruction in the curriculum (not just on filling time or on nonacademic activities)
5. Careful monitoring of progress toward goals through student testing and staff evaluation programs
6. Strong parent involvement programs
7. Consistent emphasis on the importance of academic achievement, including praise and public recognition of students' accomplishments

Teacher effects research (Brophy & Good, 1986; Reynolds, 1992; Waxman & Walberg, 1991) has identified teacher behaviors and patterns of teacher-student interaction associated with student achievement gains. Teacher effects research was initially limited to correlational studies and focused mostly on basic skills instruction in the early grades. However, it eventually broadened to include a wider range of grade levels and subject-matter areas and to include experimental verification of some of the causal hypotheses suggested by its correlational findings. Important conclusions established through this research include the following:

1. The difference teachers make. Some teachers reliably elicit greater gains than others, because of differences in how they teach.

2. Teachers' expectations, role definitions, and sense of efficacy. Teachers who elicit strong achievement gains accept responsibility for doing so. They believe that their students are capable of learning and that they (the teachers) are capable of teaching them successfully. If students do not learn something the first time, such teachers teach it again, and if the regular curriculum materials do not do the job, such teachers find or develop others that will.

3. Exposure to academic content and opportunity to learn. Teachers who elicit greater achievement gains allocate most of the available time to activities designed to accomplish instructional goals. They do not schedule many activities that serve little or no curricular purpose.

4. Classroom management and organization. These teachers are also effective organizers and managers who establish their classrooms as effective learning environments and gain the cooperation of their students. They minimize the time spent getting organized, making transitions, or dealing with behavior problems, and maximize the degree to which students are engaged in ongoing academic activities.

5. Active teaching. Teachers who elicit greater achievement gains do not merely maximize "time on task"; they also spend a great deal of time actively instructing their students. In their classrooms, more time is spent on interactive lessons featuring teacher-student discourse, and less time on independent seatwork. Rather than depend solely on curriculum materials as content sources, these teachers interpret and elaborate the content for students, stimulate them to react to it through questions asked in recitation and discussion activities, and circulate during seatwork times to monitor progress and provide assistance when needed. They are active instructors, not just materials managers and evaluators. It is important to note, however, that most of their instruction occurs during brief presentations or subsequent interactive discourse with students; it rarely if ever takes the form of extended lectures. Characterizing them in terms introduced more recently, we might say that teachers who elicit greater achievement gains are typically eclectics who use a combination of transmission-oriented and constructivist approaches to teaching.

6. A supportive learning environment. Despite their strong academic focus, these teachers maintain pleasant, friendly classrooms and are perceived by their students as enthusiastic, supportive instructors.

In addition to these more generic findings, teacher effects research has contributed knowledge about qualitative aspects of instructional methods and classroom processes. For example, research on teachers' presentations and demonstrations (including work by Barak Rosenshine) has verified the importance of delivering these presentations with enthusiasm and organizing and sequencing their content so as to maximize their clarity and "learner friendliness." Various studies have shown the value of

1. pacing, gestures, and other oral communication skills;
2. avoiding vagueness, ambiguity, and discontinuity;
3. beginning with advance organizers or previews that include general principles, outlines, or questions that establish a learning set;
4. briefly describing the objectives and alerting students to new or key concepts;
5. presenting new information with reference to what students already know about the topic;
6. proceeding in small steps sequenced in ways that are easy to follow;
7. eliciting student responses regularly to stimulate active learning and ensure that each step is mastered before moving to the next;
8. finishing with a review of main points, stressing general integrative concepts; and
9. following up with questions or assignments that require students to encode the material in their own words and apply or extend it to new contexts.

Concerning teacher-student interaction processes, teacher effects research has indicated the value of

1. adjusting the difficulty level of questions to the students' levels of ability and prior knowledge;
2. addressing questions to the class as a whole rather than designating an individual respondent in advance (to encourage all of the students, not just the one who is eventually called on, to listen carefully and respond thoughtfully to each question);
3. allowing sufficient wait time to enable students to process the question and at least begin to formulate responses to it, especially if the question is complicated or demands a high cognitive level of response; and
4. incorporating and building on students' contributions.

Concerning learning activities and assignments, the research suggests that they should be varied and interesting enough to motivate student engagement, new or challenging enough to constitute meaningful learning experiences rather than pointless busywork, and yet easy enough to allow students to achieve high rates of success if they invest reasonable effort. The effectiveness of assignments is enhanced when teachers explain the work and go over practice examples with students before releasing them to work independently, and then circulate to monitor progress and provide help when needed.

Research on Teaching for Understanding and Use of Knowledge

The process-outcome research of the 1970s was important, not only because it contributed the findings summarized in the preceding section, but also because it began to provide education with a knowledge base capable of moving the field beyond testimonials and unsupported claims toward scientific statements based on credible data. However, this research was limited in several respects. First, it focused on important but very basic aspects of teaching. These aspects differentiate the least effective teachers from other teachers, but they do not include the more subtle fine points that distinguish the most outstanding teachers. Second, because most of this research relied on standardized tests to measure outcome, it assessed mastery of relatively isolated knowledge items and skill components without assessing the degree to which students had developed understanding of networks of subject-matter content or the ability to use this information in authentic application situations.

During the 1980s a newer kind of research emerged that emphasized the teaching of subject matter for understanding and use of knowledge (Bereiter & Scardamalia, 1987; Brophy, 1989, 1995; Bruer, 1993; Resnick & Klopfer, 1989). This research focused on particular curriculum units or even individual lessons, taking into account the teacher's instructional goals and assessing student learning accordingly. The researchers determined what the teacher was trying to accomplish, recorded detailed information about classroom processes as they unfolded during the lesson or unit, and then assessed learning by using evaluation measures keyed to the instructional goals. Often these included detailed interviews or portfolio assessments, not just conventional short-answer tests.

Research on teaching for understanding focuses on attempts to teach both the individual elements in a network of related content and the connections between them, to the point that students can explain the information in their own words and can access and apply it in appropriate situations in and out of school. Teachers accomplish this by explaining concepts and principles with clarity and precision and by modeling the strategic application of skills by means of think-aloud demonstrations that make overt for students the usually covert strategic thinking that guides the use of the skills for problem solving.

Although it reinforces and builds on findings indicating that teachers play a vital role in stimulating student learning, current research also focuses on the role of the student. It recognizes that students do not merely passively receive or copy input from teachers, but instead actively mediate it by trying to make sense of it and to relate it to what they already know (or think they know) about the topic. Thus, students develop new knowledge through a process of *active construction of meaning*. To get beyond rote memorization and achieve true understanding, they need to develop and integrate a network of associations linking new input to preexisting knowledge and beliefs anchored in concrete experience. Thus, teaching involves inducing *conceptual change* in students, not infusing knowledge into a vacuum. When students' preexisting beliefs about a topic are accurate, these beliefs facilitate learning and provide a natural starting place for teaching. When students harbor misconceptions, however, the misconceptions need to be corrected so that they do not persist and distort the new learning.

To the extent that new learning is complex, the construction of meaning required to develop a clear understanding of it takes time and is facilitated by the interactive *discourse* that occurs during lessons and activities. Clear explanations and modeling by the teacher are important, but so are opportunities to answer questions about the content, discuss or debate its meanings and implications, or apply it in authentic problem-solving or decision-making contexts. These activities allow students to process the content actively and "make it their own" by putting it in their own words, exploring its relationships to other knowledge and to past experience, appreciating the insights it provides, or identifying its implications for personal decision making or action. Increasingly, research is pointing to thoughtful discussion, and not just teacher lecturing or student recitation, as characteristic of the classroom discourse involved in teaching for understanding.

Researchers have also begun to stress the complementary changes in teacher and student roles that should occur as learning progresses. Early in the process, the teacher assumes most of the responsibility for structuring and managing learning activities and provides students with a great deal of information, explanation, modeling, and cueing. As students develop expertise, however, they can begin regulating their own learning by asking questions and by working on increasingly complex applications with increasing degrees of autonomy. The teacher still provides task simplification, coaching, and other scaffolding needed to assist students with challenges that they are not yet ready to handle on their own, but this assistance is gradually reduced in response to gradual increases in student readiness to engage in independent and self-regulated learning. (For more information and subject-specific examples, see Good & Brophy, 1995, 1997.)

Research on teaching school subjects for understanding and use of knowledge is still in its infancy, but it has already produced successful experimental programs in most subjects. Even more encouraging, analyses of these programs have identified a set of principles and practices that are common to most if not all of them (Anderson, 1989; Brophy, 1989, 1992b; Prawat, 1989). These common elements, which might be considered components of a model or theory describing good subject-matter teaching, include the following:

1. The curriculum is designed to equip students with knowledge, skills, values, and dispositions that they will find useful both in and out of school.

2. Instructional goals emphasize developing student expertise within an application context and emphasize conceptual understanding of knowledge and self-regulated use of skills.

3. The curriculum balances breadth with depth by addressing limited content but developing this content sufficiently to foster conceptual understanding.

4. The content is organized around a limited set of powerful ideas (key understandings and principles).

5. The teacher's role is not just to present information, but also to scaffold, guide, and respond to students' learning efforts.

6. The students' role is not just to absorb or copy input, but also to actively make sense and construct meaning.

7. Students' prior knowledge about the topic is elicited and used as a starting place for instruction, which builds on accurate prior knowledge and stimulates conceptual change if necessary.

8. Activities and assignments feature authentic tasks that call for problem solving or critical thinking, not just memory or reproduction.

9. Higher-order thinking skills are not taught as a separate skills curriculum. Instead, they are developed in the process of teaching subject-matter knowledge within application contexts. Those contexts call for students to relate what they are learning to their lives outside school by thinking critically or creatively about the subject matter or by using it to solve problems or make decisions.

10. The teacher creates a social environment in the classroom that could be described as a learning community, featuring discourse or dialogue designed to promote understanding.

Shifting Attention to Curricular Issues

These consensus ideas about teaching for understanding have been emphasized in position statements about good teaching that have been released in recent years by leading organizations concerned with instruction in the major school subjects (including the National Council for the Social Studies, 1993). With their emphasis on depth of development of powerful ideas over breadth of content coverage, however, these ideas about instructional methods have reopened basic curricular issues: Which topics should be retained in the curriculum, and which should be excluded? For each retained topic, what key ideas should be developed in depth? More generally, what is worth teaching to students in grades K–12, and why?

Like the process-outcome research that preceded it, research on teaching for understanding has finessed such curricular issues rather than addressed them. Process-outcome research did it by using standardized tests as the criteria for learning. More recent research has done it by equating the teaching of K–12 school subjects with enculturation into the academic disciplines. This leads to problematic curricular decisions because the academic disciplines and the K–12 school subjects are different entities with different purposes and goals.

An academic discipline is a community of inquiry that is organized to generate increasingly differentiated and elaborated knowledge about a particular content domain. The discipline focuses primarily on expanding this specialized knowledge base, not on exploring its applications to everyday life or its connections with other forms of knowledge. In contrast, school subjects are collections of knowledge organized for instruction to K–12 students as preparation for everyday living and performance of adult roles in society. Although informed by the academic disciplines, school subjects are mechanisms for providing students with a basic general education, not for preparing them to be disciplinary specialists. Therefore, decisions about what to include in the school curriculum should be shaped by deliberations about what constitutes the basic knowledge that all citizens need. This knowledge base must be informed by the disciplines, but selected, organized, and taught as general education rather than as induction into an academic discipline.

Knowledge taught in schools should be consistent with disciplinary knowledge as it is currently understood and represented, but curricular issues cannot be resolved by looking solely to the disciplines for definitive answers. Nor can they be resolved through purely empirical methods, because they involve value questions. However, curricular arguments always contain implied assumptions that can be tested empirically, such as readiness assumptions (that students at a given grade level are ready to learn particular content) or transfer assumptions (that mastery of such content will enable them to handle certain life situations effectively). By clarifying and testing these embedded claims, researchers on teaching can contribute important empirical input to curricular debates. We have attempted to make such contributions through our work on elementary social studies. To prepare to do so, however, we have found it necessary to analyze social education purposes and goals, to critique instructional materials, to articulate principles for developing topical units and selecting learning activities, to elicit information about students' prior knowledge and misconceptions, and to engage in other forms of scholarly work in addition to research on teaching (as this term has been understood conventionally). We summarize this work in the remainder of the chapter.

Critiques of Elementary Social Studies Textbooks

Serious concerns have been expressed about elementary social studies curriculum and instruction. Some of these concerns are rooted in fundamental disagreements about what the primary goals and content emphases should be in the subject, especially in the primary grades. However, much dissatisfaction is focused on the elementary social studies series offered by the major publishers. These series constitute the core, and in some cases, the entirety, of the social studies curriculum taught to most elementary students. Complaints focus on the parade-of-facts content in the textbooks and on the reading-recitation-seatwork-test curriculum that results when teachers depend heavily on textbook series not only for content but for suggested questions, learning activities and assignments, and assessment methods. To understand these problems better and begin to develop ideas about how to address them, we began our work with detailed examinations of popular elementary social studies textbook series.

Critiques of textbooks in these series have pointed to contrasting problems in the primary and intermediate grades. The primary-grade textbooks do not include enough content, and much of what is included does not need to be taught. Ravitch (1987) complained of "tot sociology," content that students have no interest in and do not need to study anyway because they learn it through everyday experiences. Larkins, Hawkins, and Gilmore (1987) characterized textbook series for grades K–3 as "hopelessly noninformative" because children already know that families contain parents and children, that people live in houses, wear clothes, and eat food, and so on. They identified much of the content of K–3 textbooks as redundant because children already possess the knowledge; superfluous because they will acquire it without instruction; text-inappropriate because it should be learned more directly than through reading; sanitized; biased; or not related to important social-education goals.

Both Ravitch (1987) and Larkins et al. (1987) blamed the problem on the expanding-communities organizational structure, which focuses on the self in kindergarten, family and school in first grade, neighborhood in second grade, community in third grade, the state and region in fourth grade, the United States in fifth grade, and the world in sixth grade. These authors called for more emphasis on history and geography in grades K–3, using content drawn from storybooks, biographies, and other alternatives to traditional textbooks.

Critiques of social studies textbooks in the middle grades have pointed out their emphasis on breadth of coverage at the expense of depth of development of key ideas. This leads to problems in coherence—the extent to which sequences of ideas or events make sense and the relationships among them are made apparent. Beck and McKeown (1988) identified three problems common in recent fifth-grade history textbooks: (1) a lack of evidence that clear content goals were used to guide the writing with an eye toward what students were supposed to learn, so that the texts read as chronicles of miscellaneous facts rather than as narratives built around key themes; (2) unrealistic assumptions about students' prior knowledge, so that key elements needed to understand a sequence were merely alluded to rather than explained sufficiently; and (3) inadequate explanations that failed to clarify causal connections between actions and events. Beck, McKeown, and Gromoll (1989) noted similar coherence problems in geography texts.

Woodward (1987) identified three problems in the way skills are handled in elementary social studies series. First, more is promised than is delivered. Lessons listed in scope-and-sequence charts as developing a particular skill often merely mention it. Second, skills that are easily measured, such as map and globe skills, get repeated unnecessarily, whereas inadequate attention is given to information gathering, report writing, critical thinking, decision making, and value analysis. Third, skills content is typically separated from knowledge content rather than integrated with it in natural ways.

Our own critiques have focused not just on the content in the student textbooks, but on the questions, activities, and assessment methods provided or suggested in the manuals (Brophy, 1992a; Brophy & Alleman, 1992/1993). They reaffirm the criticisms reviewed here and point to several additional problems:

1. Stated goals frequently did not appear to have been the primary considerations driving curriculum development.

2. Few of the activities labeled "critical thinking" or "application" actually involved these cognitive processes.

3. There was little attention to students' preexisting knowledge or misconceptions.

4. Many captions and questions focused on irrelevant details of photos or illustrations instead of connecting them to key ideas.

5. Suggested questions focused on recitation of miscellaneous facts rather than on structuring reflective discussion of the content.

6. There was little use of data retrieval charts and other mechanisms for analyzing and synthesizing content in ways that promote understanding.

7. Many of the suggested activities focused on trivial aspects of content, did not promote progress toward significant social-education goals, or were unnecessarily time-consuming or complicated.

8. Many of the skills exercises and most of the activities ostensibly intended to promote integration across subjects lacked significant social-education value.

9. Test questions were mostly limited to factual recognition and retrieval items that required little if any critical thinking, development of an argument, sustained writing, or authentic applications.

Many activities were mostly busywork: word searches, cutting and pasting, coloring, connecting dots, learning to recognize states from their outlines, memorizing state capitals and state symbols. Many others were built around peripheral definitions or facts that have little application potential (e.g., identifying clothes that would be worn to a birthday party). Others distorted content representation because they were built around exotic rather than prototypical examples (igloos, stilt houses, or camping tents instead of more typical houses) or around forced categorizations (distinguishing things done at home from things done at school; classifying foods as breakfast, lunch, or dinner foods). Some activities called for knowledge that had not been taught in the curriculum and was not likely to have been acquired elsewhere (have first graders role-play scenes from Mexico when all they have learned about Mexico is its location on a map).

Skills curricula often were intrusively imposed on knowledge curricula in ways that used isolated bits of knowledge as bases for skills exercises. Thus, students were asked to chart or graph unimportant information that was never used, to count how many states' names begin with the letter *C*, or to classify American-made products according to whether they were described as made in the United States, the U.S., or the U.S.A.

Some integration activities addressed multiple goals effectively (write advertisements that might have been used to lure Europeans to immigrate to colonial Pennsylvania; compare historical accounts of Paul Revere's ride with the romanticized version in Longfellow's poem, and discuss differences between historians and poets). Others, however, were forced or pointless (alphabetize the state capitals; find geographical coordinates for Revolutionary War battle sites).

Some 1986–1988 social studies series seemed more like language arts extension curricula than social studies curricula. These problems continue in more recent curriculum series, which feature inserted literature selections and more emphasis on extended writing assignments and cooperative learning activities. These newer series are less likely to call for practice of molecular language arts skills, such as alphabetizing, but they still reveal a lack of goal-oriented integration of knowledge and skill components. Many of the inserted literature selections and the questions and activities associated with them have little connection to major social-education goals, and cooperative learning is often suggested for activities that do not lend themselves well to the cooperative format. Thus, the publishers are still making piecemeal responses to miscellaneous coverage and inclusion pressures, rather than offering coherent social-education curricula.

The Need for Goal-Oriented Instructional Planning

Social studies textbook series feature broad but shallow coverage of a great range of topics and skills. Lacking both coherence of flow and structuring around key ideas developed in depth, these textbooks are experienced as parades of disconnected facts and isolated skills exercises. These problems have evolved as unintended consequences of publishers' efforts to satisfy state and district curricular guidelines that feature long lists of topics and skills to be covered rather than succinct statements of major goals to be accomplished.

Other problems result from a lack of fit between the expectations of publishers and those of teachers. The economics of publishing do not allow the companies to customize their textbook series even for states or regions, let alone local districts or schools, so publishers offer broad coverage and avoid controversy. They seek to provide basic resources, but expect teachers to pick and choose what to use and to supplement those resources with additional content sources and activities. Elementary teachers, however, have limited preparation time and often expect the publishers not merely to provide them with good instructional materials, but also to tell them what to teach and how to teach it.

Most elementary teachers and many secondary teachers who are assigned to teach social studies courses have not had enough social studies preparation to allow them to develop a coherent view of what social education is all about. Consequently, they depend on their instructional materials and tend to focus their planning on the procedural mechanics of implementing lessons and activities, without giving much thought to their purposes or how they might fit into the larger social-education program. To the extent that they rely on textbooks and the ancillary materials provided and follow the manual's lesson development instructions, the result will be a reading-recitation-seatwork curriculum focused on memorizing disconnected knowledge and practicing isolated skills.

These problems underscore the need to shift from content coverage lists to statements of major social-education goals as the basis for developing curricula and planning instruction. A curriculum is not an end in itself but a means, a tool for accomplishing educational goals. These goals are learner outcomes—the knowledge, skills, attitudes, values, and dispositions to action that one wishes to develop in students. Ideally, curriculum planning and implementation decisions will be driven by these goals, so that each element—the basic content, the ways this content is represented and explicated to students, the questions asked, the types of teacher-student and student-student discourse that occur, the activities and assignments, and the methods used to assess progress and grade performance—is included because it is believed to be needed as a means of moving students toward accomplishment of the major goals. The goals are the reason for the existence of the curriculum, and beliefs about what is needed to accomplish them guide each step in curriculum planning and implementation.

The National Council for the Social Studies (NCSS, 1993) has identified social understanding and civic efficacy as the goals that underlie powerful social studies teaching. *Social understanding* is integrated knowledge of the social aspects of the human condition: how these aspects have evolved over time, the variations that occur in different physical environments and cultural settings, and emerging trends that appear likely to shape the future. *Civic efficacy* is readiness and willingness to assume citizenship responsibilities. It is rooted in social studies knowledge and skills, along with related values (such as concern for the common good) and dispositions (such as an orientation toward confident participation in civic affairs).

The NCSS position statement goes on to identify five key features that social studies teaching must have if it is to accomplish its goals of social understanding and civic efficacy: Social studies teaching is powerful when it is meaningful, integrative, value-based, challenging, and active. In elaborating, the position statement identifies principles of good social studies teaching that reflect the features described earlier of teaching for understanding and use of knowledge, along with values and dispositions related to civic efficacy.

Topical Units as the Basis for Planning

Most commonly, social studies curricula have been organized around (1) disciplinary concepts, generalizations, or themes; (2) questions or social issues; or (3) interdisciplinary treatment of topics. The first alternative is best suited to courses in the secondary grades that are based on a single academic discipline (although even here, the previously discussed distinctions between the school subjects and the academic disciplines should be kept in mind). The second alternative is difficult to use as a primary basis for organizing courses, especially in the elementary grades, where students do not yet possess sufficient background knowledge to enable them to engage in reflective dialogue in which they are expected to support their opinions about social issues by citing relevant arguments and evidence. We believe that elementary social studies curricula should include opportunities for reflective dialogue and debate whenever they are appropriate, but we do not believe that it is feasible to organize the entire curriculum around social questions and issues.

Instead, we believe that instructional units featuring interdisciplinary treatment of topics provide the best basis for selecting and organizing content for elementary social studies. In comparison with disciplinary structures, topical units offer more flexibility concerning the nature and sources of content. Guided by social-understanding and civic-efficacy goals, teachers can include any sources of content that seem appropriate, drawing not only from the social studies foundational disciplines (history and the social sciences), but from the arts, sciences, and humanities, from current events, and from the students' familial and cultural backgrounds. The point is to develop a basic network of useful knowledge about the topic, not to develop knowledge within a particular discipline. Our most recent work in elementary social studies has focused on developing and testing units on cultural universals for the primary grades.

Selecting and Representing Content

In goal-oriented unit planning, content is selected and represented as a means of accomplishing a goal, not merely as material to be covered. For example, in teaching a history unit on the American Revolution to fifth graders, we would emphasize the goals of developing understanding and appreciation of the origins of American political values and policies. Consequently, our treatment of the revolution and its aftermath would emphasize the historical events and political philosophies that shaped the thinking of the writers of the Declaration of Independence and the Constitution. Content coverage, questions, and activities would focus on the issues that developed between England and the colonies and on the impacts these had on various types of people, as well as on the ideals, principles, and compromises that went into the construction of the Constitution (especially the Bill of Rights). Primary emphasis would be placed on the various forms of oppression that different colonial groups had experienced (and the influence of this on their thinking about government), as well as the ideas of James Madison and other key framers of the Constitution. There would be less emphasis on Paul Revere and other revolutionary figures who are not known primarily for their contributions to American political values and policies. There would be no emphasis at all on content unrelated to these goals, such as the details of particular battles.

This example is not intended to suggest that our preferred goals and content emphases are the only or even necessarily the best ones to adopt in teaching about the American Revolution. It is only intended to illustrate how clarity of primary goals encourages the development of units that are likely to cohere and to function as tools for accomplishing those goals and, in the process, to result in instruction that students find meaningful, relevant, and applicable to their lives outside school. The particular goals to emphasize will vary with one's social-education philosophy, the ages and needs of the students, and the purposes of the course. Teachers of military history in the service academies, for example, would have very different goals and would approach a unit on the American Revolution with very different content emphases.

Planning and Implementing Learning Activities

In examining instructional materials and observing in classrooms, we have addressed certain fundamental questions about the nature and roles of learning activities: What are the intended functions of various types of activities? What is known about the mechanisms through which they perform these functions (if they do)? What is it about the most useful activities that makes them so successful? What faults limit the value of less useful activities? What principles might guide teachers' planning and implementation of activities?

To address these questions, we have reviewed and synthesized scholarly writings on the characteristics of good learning activities, and have built on them in four ways: (1) expanding them to include additional principles, (2) grouping the principles according to priority levels, (3) distinguishing principles that apply to each individual activity from principles that apply only to groups of activities considered as sets, and (4) identifying principles describing how teachers might structure and scaffold activities for their students, in addition to principles describing features of the activities themselves.

To accomplish those tasks, we have alternated between top-down and bottom-up analyses. The top-down analyses involved applying theoretical and logical tests to principles drawn from the scholarly literature. We assessed the validity, breadth of applicability, and level of importance of these principles, both by discussing them as abstract generalities and by applying them to particular social studies activities to see if what they implied about the value of those activities matched the assessments that we or others had developed by considering the activities themselves. For the bottom-up analyses, we identified activities (suggested in manuals or by teachers) that we agreed were particularly useful, as well as others that we agreed were flawed in various ways. Then we analyzed these activities to articulate more clearly what made the good activities good and the other activities undesirable or ineffective. Where possible, we rephrased our insights as more general principles and then subjected these principles to top-down analysis. Eventually, we synthesized our conclusions into a framework for use in planning and implementing learning activities (Brophy & Alleman, 1991) and used it as a basis for analyzing college students' memories and perceptions of the goals and value of activities that they had experienced in social studies classes as elementary students (Alleman & Brophy, 1993–1994).

Our synthesis identified four principles as necessary criteria for each activity considered for inclusion in a unit:

1. Goal relevance.   Activities must be useful as means of accomplishing worthwhile curricular goals (phrased in terms of target capabilities or dispositions to be developed in students). Each activity should have a primary goal that is an important one, worth stressing and spending time on. Its content base should have enduring value and life-application potential, not just cultural-literacy status as a term that students might encounter in general reading or social discourse. There must be at least logical (preferably research-based) reasons for believing that the activity will be effective in accomplishing its primary goal.

2. Appropriate level of difficulty. Each activity must be difficult enough to provide some challenge and extend learning, but not so difficult as to leave many students confused or frustrated. Teachers can adjust difficulty levels either by adjusting the complexity of activities themselves or by adjusting the degree to which they structure and scaffold the activities for their students.

3. Feasibility. Each activity must be feasible for implementation within the constraints under which the teacher must work (space and equipment, time, types of students, etc.).

4. Cost effectiveness. The educational benefits expected to be derived from the activity must justify its anticipated costs (for both teacher and students) in time and trouble.

In selecting from activities that meet these primary criteria, teachers might consider several secondary criteria, which identify features that are desirable in activities but not strictly necessary:

1. Along with its primary goal, the activity allows for simultaneous accomplishment of one or more additional goals (e.g., application of communication skills being learned in language arts).
2. Students are likely to find the activity interesting or enjoyable.
3. The activity provides an opportunity to complete a whole task rather than just isolated practice of part-skills.
4. It provides students with opportunities to engage in higher-order thinking.
5. It can be adapted to accommodate students' individual differences in interests or abilities.

In addition to these criteria for individual activities, curriculum developers and teachers should also consider principles that apply to sets of activities. Each principle might not apply to each separate activity in a unit, but the set as a whole should reflect the principles:

1. The set should contain a variety of activity formats and student response modes (as a way to accommodate individual differences).
2. Activities should progressively increase in level of challenge as student expertise develops.
3. Students should apply what they are learning to current events or other aspects of their lives outside school.
4. As a set, the activities should reflect the full range of goals identified for the unit.
5. Where students lack sufficient experiential knowledge to support understanding, sets of activities should include opportunities for them to view demonstrations, inspect artifacts or photos, visit sites, or in other ways experience concrete examples of the content.

6. Students should learn relevant processes and procedural knowledge, not just declarative or factual knowledge, to the extent that doing so is important to developing basic understanding of the topic.

7. Activities that are "naturals" for developing understanding of a unit's content should be included in the set for the unit (e.g., retrieval charts and other comparison/contrast methods are natural activities when the content has focused on different examples of a concept, such as Indian tribes, geographic regions, or governmental forms; in teaching history, natural activities include activities designed to develop understanding of sequences of causes, effects, and subsequent implications, as well as comparisons of historical events with contemporary events that appear to be following similar patterns).

Along with principles for selecting learning activities, we have developed principles for structuring and scaffolding these activities for students. A complete activity should ordinarily include the following stages:

1. Introduction (The teacher communicates the goals of the activity and cues relevant prior knowledge and response strategies.)

2. Initial scaffolding (The teacher explains and demonstrates procedures if necessary and then asks questions to make sure that students understand what to do, before releasing them to work on their own.)

3. Independent work (Students work mostly on their own, but with teacher monitoring and intervention as needed.)

4. Debriefing/reflection/assessment (Teacher and students revisit the activity's primary goals and assess the degree to which they have been accomplished.)

The key to the effectiveness of an activity is its cognitive engagement potential—the degree to which it gets students thinking actively about and applying content, preferably with conscious awareness of their goals and control of their strategies. If the desired learning experiences are to occur, student involvement must include cognitive engagement with important ideas, not just physical activity or time on task. The success of an activity in producing thoughtful student engagement with important ideas depends not only on the activity itself, but also on the teacher structuring and teacher-student discourse that occur before, during, and after the activity.

Assessing Development and Change in Students' Social Studies Knowledge

The research findings and curriculum and instruction principles summarized so far provided most of the underpinnings for our efforts to develop powerful social studies units. However, an important piece was missing: information about developments in children's knowledge about social studies topics.

Drawing on neo-Vygotskian theories about teaching in the zone of proximal development, on research on novices' acquisition of expertise within particular knowledge domains, and on work on knowledge construction and conceptual change, mathematics and science educators have been developing more powerful methods of teaching these school subjects. These methods include connecting with students' prior knowledge and experience and engaging them in actively constructing new knowledge and correcting existing misconceptions. There is great potential for application of these methods to social studies, but its realization cannot occur until a significant base of information is built concerning children's developing knowledge in domains emphasized in social studies curricula. We have been working to develop such a base of information by interviewing students before and after their social studies units to determine the nature of their prior knowledge, to document changes in response to instruction, and to identify commonly occurring naive conceptions or misconceptions that may need to be addressed. So far, these analyses have been developed most fully with respect to fifth graders' ideas about U.S. history (Brophy & VanSledright, 1996).

We have found that most fifth graders know that history has to do with the past, although many of them think that it is limited to the exploits of famous or important people or to events that occurred long ago, not realizing that history includes the recent past and the lives of everyday people. Many students initially confused history with archaeology because they did not know much about ways to discover information about the distant past except for digging up bones and other material found underground. They did not realize that a variety of written records, extending back thousands of years, is available to historians.

Some of their misconceptions involved overgeneralization of specific examples (all American Indians lived in tepees and hunted buffalo; colonies were small villages surrounded by wooden stockades). Others simply repeated inaccuracies commonly included in stories told to children (everyone but Columbus thought that the earth was flat). Still others included elements generated by the children themselves in an attempt to make sense of these stories and fill in the explanatory gaps in them. For example, instead of saying that the Pilgrims landed *at* Plymouth Rock, several children said that they landed "on" Plymouth Rock. Follow-up questioning indicated that some of them believed that the Pilgrims settled at Plymouth because they literally sailed into Plymouth Rock and had to stop there because their ship was damaged. Similarly, when asked why people came to the New World, several students suggested that Europe was getting too crowded. Other misconceptions were related to the use of children's literature, as in the case of students who listed Johnny Tremain as a signer of the Declaration of Independence and Louisa May Alcott as a female participant in the Revolution.

Some students declined to speculate when they realized that their knowledge was limited, but others concocted imaginative elaborations in their attempts to generate coherent stories based on the limited historical information they possessed. Our favorite informant was interviewed initially as a fourth grader, about American history topics she would study the following year. She told us that although Columbus gets credit for discovering America, when he reached it he found that it was already owned by Amerigo, who was "a pirate or something" who had gotten here two years previously and decided to name the place after himself. She had reconstructed this narrative from information retained after viewing an episode of *The Chipmunks* TV show in which Simon and Alvin were helping Theodore prepare for a history test. This girl also reported that the Pilgrims had settled at Plymouth Rock, which she located somewhere in the Upper Peninsula of Michigan, and that their ship was called the Mayflower, which is how we got the saying "April showers bring May flowers." The Pilgrims had come to the New World because "their own world was getting wrecked by something. Someone was like trashing it. They were ruining their world and they had to find a new one." The first winter was rough because the people did not know how to survive in the New World and "they had just one little loaf of bread and it had to last them all winter. Then the Indians brought them food when the spring came for Thanksgiving and that's how we got Thanksgiving. They had turkey and stuffing."

It's fun to report these more fanciful narratives, and it's interesting to learn about where students get their ideas about social studies topics before studying them in school. The scientific purpose of this line of work, however, is to identify general developmental trends in students' social learning that can be incorporated within powerful approaches to elementary social studies curriculum and instruction. For ideas about how what we have learned from interviews can be used to improve the teaching of American history in fifth grade, see Brophy and Alleman (1996) or Brophy and VanSledright (1996).

In the coming years, our research will trace developments in students' knowledge of universal needs and experiences, such as food, clothing, shelter, families, communities, work, transportation, and communication, and will then follow up by developing and assessing social studies units on these topics. These units will be structured around powerful ideas and will be informed by the disciplines of history, geography, and the social sciences. However, unit content will be selected and organized primarily to accomplish general preparation for life in our society, not induction into these disciplines, and instruction and assessment will be designed accordingly.

Learning and Teaching About Cultural Universals

Research and development of this kind is especially needed with regard to knowledge domains addressed in the primary grades, where social studies courses are interdisciplinary and organized around topics. Critics who complain that the content taught in these grades is trite, redundant, and unlikely to help students achieve significant social-education goals often blame the problem on the expanding-communities framework commonly used to organize the curriculum (Larkins, Hawkins, & Gilmore, 1987; Ravitch, 1987). Within this framework, students begin by studying the familiar in the here and now, and only gradually move backward in time and outward in space.

Our analyses of instructional materials suggest that content problems in elementary social studies are due, not to the choice of topics addressed within the expanding-communities framework, but to the way that these topics have been taught. Many of the topics—families, communities, food, clothing, shelter, government, occupations, transportation, and communication, among others—provide a sound basis for developing fundamental understandings about the human condition. They tend to be cultural universals—basic human needs and social experiences found in all societies, past and present. If these topics are taught with an appropriate focus on powerful ideas, students will develop a basic set of connected understandings about how the social system works, how and why it came to be the way it is, how and why it varies among locations and cultures, and what all of this might mean for personal, social, and civic decision making.

We have been developing and testing experimental units on cultural universals in the primary grades, beginning with shelter and clothing. In doing so, we have emphasized four principles for selecting and developing content. First, using contemporary and familiar examples, the unit should help students understand how and why the social system functions as it does with respect to the cultural universal being studied. In the case of shelter, for example, the unit begins with the forms of shelter commonly found in the contemporary United States, especially in the students' own neighborhoods. Instruction helps students to articulate the tacit knowledge that they already possess, as well as to expand on it and embed it within a knowledge network structured around powerful ideas.

Second, each unit includes a historical dimension illustrating how human responses to the cultural universal have evolved through time by means of inventions and other cultural advances. For example, shelters have evolved from caves and simple huts to sturdier and more permanent homes, such as log cabins, to modern, weather-proofed homes that feature running water, heat, light, and insulation. Technological advances have enabled us to meet our shelter needs and wants more effectively, yet by investing less personal effort and time than in the past.

Third, each unit includes a geographical-cultural dimension that exposes students to current variations in human responses to the cultural universal. Different forms of shelter exist in different geographical locations, in part because of differences in climate and the local availability of construction materials and in part because of cultural differences. Along with the historical dimension, this geographical-cultural dimension of the unit extends students' concepts to include examples different from the ones they view as prototypical. This helps them to place themselves and their familiar social environments into perspective as parts of the larger human condition as it has evolved through time and as it varies across cultures. In the language of anthropologists, such units "make the strange familiar" and "make the familiar strange" to students.

Fourth, each topic is developed with emphasis on its applications to students' current and future lives. This is accomplished through critical-thinking and decision-making activities designed to raise students' consciousness of the fact that they will be making choices (both as individuals and as citizens) about appropriate responses to each of these cultural universals. The emphasis is not on inculcating preferences for particular choices but instead on building knowledge about the trade-offs associated with the major choice options. Shelter, for example, may engender discussions of the trade-offs offered by different housing types and locations (urban, suburban, rural) or the problem of homelessness and what might be done about it.

Units on cultural universals that incorporate these principles address many of the same topics taught traditionally as part of the expanding-communities curriculum. However, they are far more powerful than ostensibly similar units found in contemporary textbooks. They focus on the elementary and familiar in that they address fundamental aspects of the human condition by connecting with experience-based tacit knowledge that students already possess. However, they do not merely reaffirm what students already know. Instead, they raise students' consciousness of and help them to construct articulated knowledge about aspects of the cultural universal that they have only vague and tacit knowledge about now. The units also introduce students to a great deal of new information, develop connections to help them transform scattered items of information into a network of integrated knowledge, and stimulate them to apply the knowledge to their lives outside school and to think critically and engage in value-based decision making about the topic (Brophy & Alleman, 1996).

So far, the experimental shelter unit has been field-tested in a first- grade classroom and a second-grade classroom. Data collected for each study included audiotaped recordings of each classroom session, field notes, work samples, pre- and postunit student interviews, and teacher interviews. The data are being analyzed to assess students' levels of prior knowledge about unit content; their levels of interest in the topics addressed; the questions, comments, and misconceptions they articulated in class and during interviews; and the degree to which the unit's goals were accomplished.

Preliminary findings from the second-grade study indicate that the students displayed interest in key understandings about shelter and the ability to acquire those understandings by participating in the unit. They were especially interested in the historical aspects of shelter and made connections with the stories included in their literacy program (e.g., *Little House on the Prairie*). They were also intrigued by the unusual (e.g., the moving of a house in the community from one location to another).

The students experienced demystification by learning about such things as the "pink stuff" that they came to understand as insulation, the location and function of their furnace, and the steps in building a house—that a plan was needed and that you could "put big things inside" even after the roof was on. Most of the students knew nothing about home loans and believed that you had to possess the full purchase price of a home before you could move into it. Many were initially unclear about the differences between owning and renting, and many confused renting an apartment with staying in a hotel for a short period of time. They learned a great deal about the trade-offs involved in designing a home within a budget.

Few of the students had clear ideas about the kind of housing they might want as adults, except that many noted that they wanted to live near their families and some wanted to move (from Michigan) to warmer climates. Many also mentioned locating the house near something (a wooded area, a lake, a school, etc.) but they did not have much to say about features of the house itself except that it would need to be big enough to accommodate their family.

Most of the students were rather egocentric in their interests and points of view on the topic. Nevertheless, all of them were able to learn about, and most of them developed appreciation for, the ways in which shelters have improved over time and have been adapted to local conditions; the economics and mechanics involved in supplying utilities to modern homes; the role of governmental agencies in regulating the housing industry; the role of financial institutions in enabling families to purchase homes; the steps involved in planning and constructing a home and the workers and jobs involved at each step; the reasons people might become homeless and the mechanisms that society has established for assisting them; and many other aspects of the topic that extended their purviews beyond egocentric or childish concerns. As we continue with these studies, we will learn more about what key ideas children at a given grade level appear ready to learn about each topic and how these ideas may be taught to them successfully.

Implications for Practice

Implications for practice were embedded in much of the chapter, so they will not be repeated in detail here. Most of them are embodied in the notion of goal-oriented curricular planning, with its implication that not only content representation and development, but also questions and classroom discourse, activities and assignments, and assessment methods, are included because they are expected to function as means of promoting progress toward major social-understanding and civic-efficacy goals. Instead of a broad but shallow parade of facts, the content is structured around key ideas developed in depth and with emphasis on their connections and applications. Instead of rapid-fire drill and recitation, classroom discourse features thoughtful discussion and debate. Instead of filling in blanks in silent isolation, most activities and assignments involve authentic applications, and many involve collaboration in pairs or small groups. Instead of being restricted to recall or recognition tests, assessment involves developing portfolios of application work and responding to evaluation questions that call for problem solving, decision making, and other forms of higher-order thinking. These and other implications for practice are elaborated in detail and exemplified in sample unit plans in Brophy and Alleman (1996).

It should be noted that these implications for instruction in K–12 classrooms apply also to the education of preservice teachers in college classrooms. Here, too, a shift is needed from breadth of coverage and lecture-recitation-test teaching to development of key ideas in depth, conceptual change, reflective discussion, authentic activities, and other hallmarks of teaching for understanding, appreciation, and life application.

Considerations for Future Research

At least with regard to issues raised in this chapter, lines of needed research in social studies learning and teaching are unusually easy to identify. This is true because, in contrast to the situation with mathematics and science, social studies has not yet developed much of the knowledge base needed for planning the curricular aspects of attempts to teach the subject for understanding, with emphasis on conceptual change. Two large bodies of work are needed, which we call developmental studies and educational studies.

Developmental studies are designed to trace patterns of growth and change in what children know (or think they know) about topics addressed in the social studies curriculum, especially the cultural universals emphasized in the primary grades. What key ideas in these domains do students ordinarily develop through everyday experiences and cultural exposure? These ideas may not need to be taught in school, and may instead function as a base of prior knowledge that the social studies curriculum can connect with and build on. What important ideas are not ordinarily learned through everyday experience (and thus will need to be taught at school)? What naive ideas or misconceptions about content taught at a given grade level are commonly seen in students in that grade (and thus will need to be addressed through conceptual-change teaching methods)? In general, developmental studies are needed to provide social studies educators with information about students' prior knowledge and misconceptions.

Educational studies involve the development and testing of instructional units based on models of powerful social studies teaching, such as our model for developing units on cultural universals for the primary grades. Unit development is informed by research on children's interests in and knowledge about the topic and by current thinking among disciplinary specialists and social studies educators concerning (1) which content relating to the topic is most important for students at that grade level to know, (2) how this content might be structured around key ideas, and (3) how it might be taught to students at that grade level in ways that enable them to appreciate its significance, develop connections among its key ideas, and apply these ideas to their lives outside school.

Once developed, units are tested at one or more grade levels. Researchers use multiple and varied data collection methods to address questions such as the following: What did the students know (or think they know) about the topic prior to the unit? How did these ideas change in response to the instruction and learning experiences provided during the unit? What aspects of the unit were taught and learned largely as anticipated? What aspects were not? If certain content was omitted or taught differently than anticipated, what was the reason for this (teacher simply forgot, didn't think it was important, didn't think it would go over well with the students, etc.)? If certain content was taught as planned but not learned as anticipated, what was the reason for this (students did not find it meaningful, it appeared to be over their heads, examples were confusing, etc.)? What unanticipated insights or misconceptions were communicated through students' questions or comments, and how did the teacher respond to these "teachable moments?" Did the questions produce animated and thoughtful discourse? Did the activities and assignments engage the students and produce their intended outcomes? In general, what do the findings suggest concerning the suitability of this content for primary-grade students, the grade level or levels at which it might be taught, and the ways in which the unit might be improved?

Conclusion

Process-outcome research developed important knowledge about some of the most basic aspects of teaching, especially about relationships between teacher behaviors and student gains on standardized achievement tests. Subsequent research on teaching school subjects for understanding and use of knowledge complemented these findings by developing information about the more subtle and sophisticated aspects of teaching that distinguish the most successful teachers from those who are less outstanding. Gradually, consensus has developed around instructional principles that emphasize developing key ideas in depth and applying them in authentic activities. However, this consensus about instructional methods has led to a reopening of curricular issues in research and scholarship on subject-matter teaching. Progress in social studies has lagged somewhat behind that in other subjects, especially mathematics and science, where rich literatures have developed concerning growth and change in children's domain knowledge and methods of teaching for understanding and conceptual change. Our work is designed to develop parallel forms of knowledge in social studies, especially knowledge about the learning and teaching of cultural universals in the primary grades. In the process, it has involved analysis of curriculum guides and instructional materials, development of guidelines for selecting content and learning activities, and studies of children's knowledge and misconceptions about key ideas, along with more conventional research on teaching.

References

Alleman, J., & Brophy, J. (1993–1994). Teaching that lasts: College students' reports of learning activities experienced in elementary school social studies. *Social Science Record, 30*(2), 36–48, & *31*(1), 42–46.

Anderson, L. (1989). Implementing instructional programs to promote meaningful, self-regulated learning. In J. Brophy (Ed.), *Advances in research on teaching: Volume 1. Teaching for meaningful understanding and self-regulated learning* (pp. 311–343). Greenwich, CT: JAI.

Beck, I., & McKeown, M. (1988). Toward meaningful accounts in history texts for young learners. *Educational Researcher, 17*(6), 31–39.

Beck, I., McKeown, M., & Gromoll, E. (1989). Learning from social studies texts. *Cognition and Instruction, 6,* 99–158.

Bereiter, C., & Scardamalia, M. (1987). An attainable version of high literacy: Approaches to teaching higher-order skills in reading and writing. *Curriculum Inquiry, 17,* 9–30.

Brophy, J. (Ed.). (1989). *Advances in research on teaching: Volume 1. Teaching for meaningful understanding and self-regulated learning.* Greenwich, CT: JAI.

Brophy, J. (1992a). The de facto national curriculum in U.S. elementary social studies: Critique of a representative example. *Journal of Curriculum Studies, 24,* 401–447.

Brophy, J. (1992b). Probing the subtleties of subject-matter teaching. *Educational Leadership, 49*(7), 4–8.

Brophy, J. (Ed.). (1995). *Advances in research on teaching: Volume 5. Learning and teaching elementary subjects.* Greenwich, CT: JAI.

Brophy, J., & Alleman, J. (1991). Activities as instructional tools: A framework for analysis and evaluation. *Educational Researcher, 20*(4), 9–23.

Brophy, J., & Alleman, J. (1992/93). Elementary social studies textbooks. *Publishing Research Quarterly, 8*(4), 12–22.

Brophy, J., & Alleman, J. (1996). *Powerful social studies for elementary students.* Fort Worth, TX: Harcourt Brace.

Brophy, J., & Good, T. (1986). Teacher behavior and student achievement. In M. C. Wittrock (Ed.), *Handbook of research on teaching* (3rd ed., pp. 328–375). New York: Macmillan.

Brophy, J., & VanSledright, B. (1996). *Teaching and learning history in elementary schools.* New York: Teachers College Press.

Bruer, J. (1993). *Schools for thought: A science of learning in the classroom.* Cambridge, MA: MIT Press.

Creemers, B., & Scheerens, J. (Guest Eds.). (1989). Developments in school effectiveness research [Special issue]. *International Journal of Educational Research, 13,* 685–825.

Good, T., & Brophy, J. (1986). School effects. In M. C. Wittrock (Ed.), *Handbook of research on teaching* (3rd ed., pp. 570–602). New York: Macmillan.

Good, T., & Brophy, J. (1995). *Contemporary educational psychology* (5th ed.). New York: Longman.

Good, T., & Brophy, J. (1997). *Looking in classrooms* (7th ed.). New York: Longman.

Larkins, A., Hawkins, M., & Gilmore, A. (1987). Trivial and noninformative content of elementary social studies: A review of primary texts in four series. *Theory and Research in Social Education, 15,* 299–311.

National Council for the Social Studies. (1993). A vision of powerful teaching and learning in the social studies: Building social understanding and civic efficacy. *Social Education, 57,* 213–223.

Prawat, R. (1989). Promoting access to knowledge, strategy, and disposition in students: A research synthesis. *Review of Educational Research, 59,* 1–41.

Ravitch, D. (1987). Tot sociology, or what happened to history in the grade schools? *American Scholar, 56,* 343–353.

Resnick, L., & Klopfer, L. (Eds.). (1989). *Toward the thinking curriculum: Current cognitive research.* Alexandria, VA: Association for Supervision and Curriculum Development.

Reynolds, A. (1992). What is competent beginning teaching? A review of the literature. *Review of Educational Research, 62,* 1–35.

Teddlie, C., & Stringfield, S. (1993). *Schools make a difference: Lessons learned from a 10-year study of school effects.* New York: Teachers College Press.

Waxman, H., & Walberg, H. (Eds.). (1991). *Effective teaching: Current research.* Berkeley, CA: McCutchan.

Woodward, A. (1987). Textbooks: Less than meets the eye. *Journal of Curriculum Studies, 19,* 511–526.

Name Index

Subject Index